D0502619

75
FSG

ALSO BY SAMUEL MOYN

Origins of the Other: Emmanuel Levinas Between Revelation and Ethics

A Holocaust Controversy: The Treblinka Affair in Postwar France

The Last Utopia: Human Rights and History

Human Rights and the Uses of History

Christian Human Rights

Not Enough: Human Rights in an Unequal World

HUMANE

HOW THE

UNITED STATES

ABANDONED PEACE

AND

REINVENTED WAR

HUMANE

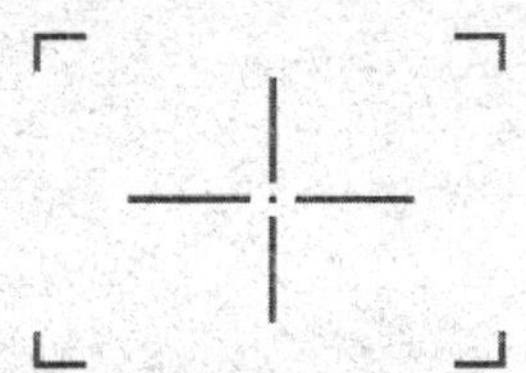

SAMUEL MOYN

FARRAR, STRAUS AND GIROUX
NEW YORK

Farrar, Straus and Giroux
120 Broadway, New York 10271

Printed in the United States of America
First edition, 2021

Portions of chapter 1 originally appeared, in slightly different form, in the spring 2020 issue of *Plough Quarterly*.

Frontispiece photograph and details on title page by Mehmet Recep Ozdemir / Shutterstock.com.

Library of Congress Cataloging-in-Publication Data
Names: Moyn, Samuel, author.
Title: Humane : how the United States abandoned peace and reinvented war / Samuel Moyn.
Description: First edition. | New York : Farrar, Straus and Giroux, 2021. | Includes bibliographical references and index.
Identifiers: LCCN 2021015727 | ISBN 9780374173708 (hardcover)
Subjects: LCSH: War (International law) | International law—United States. | United States—Military policy.
Classification: LCC KZ6385 .M835 2021 | DDC 341.6—dc23
LC record available at https://lccn.loc.gov/2021015727

Designed by Janet Evans-Scanlon

www.fsgbooks.com
www.twitter.com/fsgbooks • www.facebook.com/fsgbooks

10 9 8 7 6 5 4 3 2 1

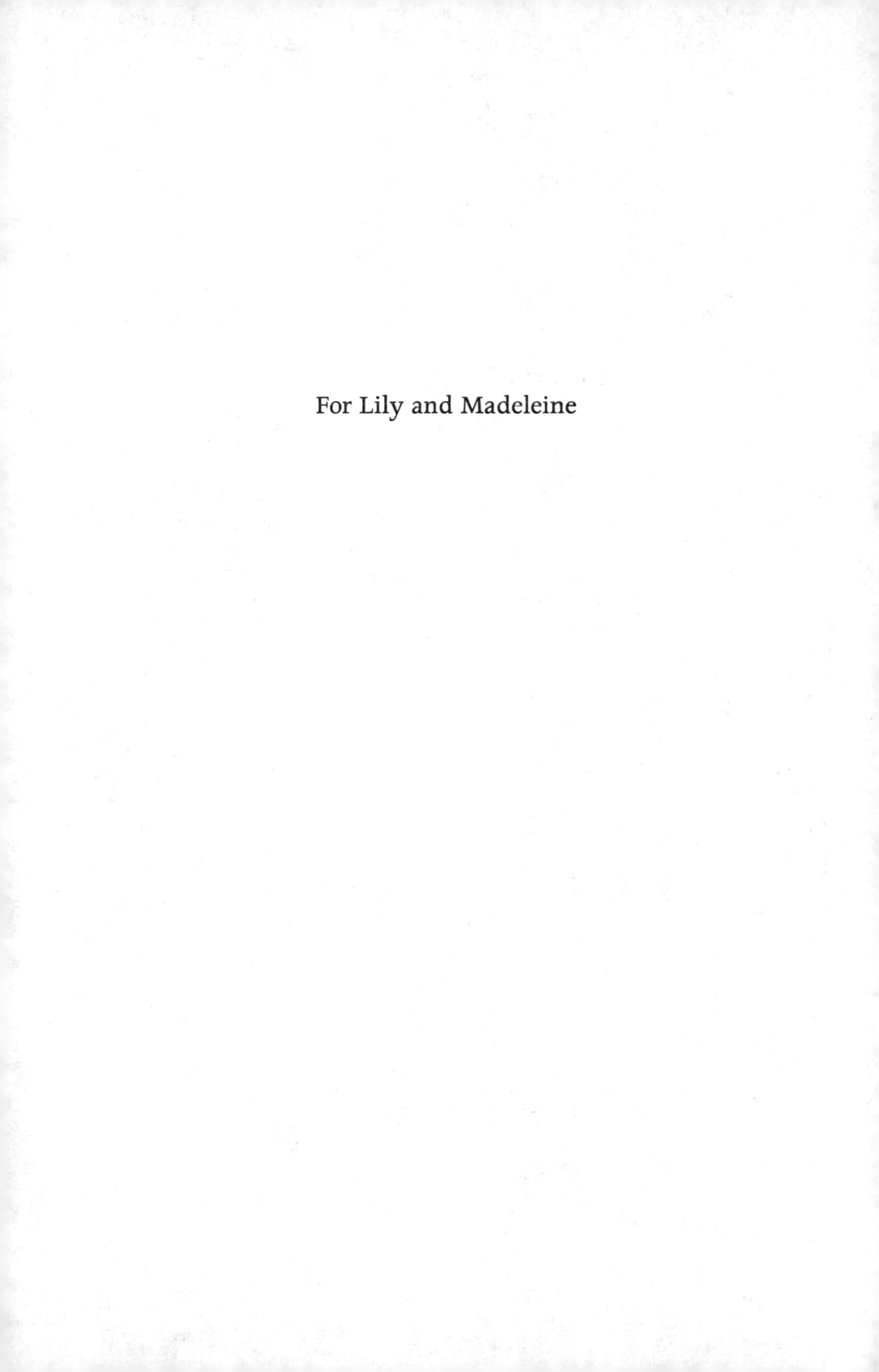

For Lily and Madeleine

I shall say no more about the Americans, for whatever the outcome of the present war, I have lost somewhat the hope of seeing on the earth a nation that is really free and lives without war. This spectacle is reserved for centuries far away . . .

—A.R.J. TURGOT, 1776

The lawyers clean up all details.

—DON HENLEY, 1989

Contents

HUMANE

Prologue

THE SKY IS THE SAME SHADE OF BLUE, EQUALLY FLAWLESS IN TWO towns separated by nine time zones, as the weddings begin at noon. The sun has cleansed the blemishes from the heavens, as if in answer to the prayers of the brides that bad weather not darken their special day. The guests arrive. The couples and their families, after the joyous ceremonies, wander toward the tents set up for the celebration. The festive meals unfold in parallel, until the sky changes.

In New Canaan, Connecticut, fancy waiters in tuxedos serve a menu featuring a high-end caterer's best globally sourced fare: toasted tabouleh salad with crispy chickpeas, oven-roasted rainbow trout with orange reduction, passion fruit panna cotta, with gluten-free and vegan options for those who ask. The colors of the tablecloths perfectly match the wedding party's attire, and the tasteful centerpieces convey just the right amount of creativity without seeming obtrusive. The wedding planner has done her job well.

In Kandahar Province, Afghanistan, the festivities are downmarket in comparison but homey and sweet. The mothers of the betrothed assist in the preparation of local favorites: lamb kebabs, rice, and firni, a milk custard scented with rose water. Despite the differences in culture and in wealth, at both celebrations there is an abundance of family joy in the ritual affirmation of the life cycle and the tender love of the couples.

The father of the bride in Connecticut, a corporate lawyer, has splurged on the latest in wedding videography, which includes fifteen minutes of aerial feed from a drone. The guests at the Afghan wedding have become inured to a far more sophisticated form of the same technology buzzing high above their heads, but none of them sought it out or sent it. Those attending the wedding in Connecticut, almost all Americans with a few foreign friends, had more to do with the intrusion. The reason is that one country, in an unprecedented era of interstate peace, has established a relationship of dominance over the other, reserving the right to kill even when it does not exercise it. War, far from disappearing, is transforming into such a relationship.

Endless war has become part of the way Americans live now, on par with their Evites and online wedding registries. America's conflicts abroad remain brutal and deadly, but what's frightening about them is not only the injury or fatality they inflict. It's true that, for several years, Afghan weddings all too often ended in a funeral. A scandalous number of civilian deaths occurred when American counterterrorist strategy took advantage of the fact that nuptials drew senior terrorists from hiding. One might presume that the Connecticut wedding would make the *New York Times* Vows section. The death by drone of a terrorist at the wedding half a world away would appear on the front page.

But now imagine that nobody dies at the Afghan ceremony, though the nuptials are nevertheless punctuated by the macabre boom of a drone strike bringing justice on impact to a confirmed militant a mile away. The guests in the tent eat their meal not only relieved that the United States has stopped bombing weddings so frequently (which it has), but also painfully aware that they are subject to a new kind of rule. It still matters that their sky is not quite without blemish, and that they still hear booms. In a few years, other machines may inspire a similar disquiet. So-called autonomous weapons systems—robot warriors—may hold quarries for capture. Meanwhile, U.S. Special Forces may operate as a kind of global police, one that kills only when it faces too much resistance after inviting surrender.

In our time, swords have not been beaten into plowshares. They have been melted down for drones. Yet for all their faults, it is also true that drones are increasingly the cleanest mode of war ever conceived. They hover nearby and, when they attack, do so with painstaking real-time targeting in the name of precision and thus civilian care. Indeed, drones are symbolic of the fact that the United States made a clear choice to make war more humane—an imperative shaped by intense, sustained pressure from diverse communities of activists and armed forces, with an eye on the acceptability of violence for different audiences. That imperative also affects emerging forms of cyberwarfare and the Special Forces that operated in more than three-quarters of the countries on the planet in a recent year (even if only to pass through on the way to their ultimate destination). Sometimes the choice to wage humane war is for the sake of ethics, sometimes it is for optics, and often it is both. It is never a matter of technological possibility alone.

Today, there are more and more legal obligations to make war more humane. Countries like the United States of America have agreed to obey those obligations, however permissively they interpret them and inadequately apply them in the field. Absolutely and relatively, fewer captives are mistreated and fewer civilians die—by far—than in the past. In Vietnam, civilians perished by the millions when directly targeted or collaterally killed by U.S. forces. (If one included events indirectly caused by regional Cold War policies a half century ago, the death count would have to include the Cambodian genocide and would probably exceed five million.) In Iraq—easily the most gruesome theater among recent U.S. wars—some 200,000 civilians have lost their lives since 2003, most of them in civil war and disorder rather than because Americans bombed or shot at or near them. The very idea of more humane war may seem a contradiction in terms. The truth is that it has changed the face of one of the oldest practices in history.

The New Canaan bride works for a humanitarian organization that pressured her country to avoid excessive civilian casualties. She hopes to follow in the tradition of an uncle she has always admired, though he has been increasingly cantankerous and tiresome at family gatherings.

An old man now, he preserves the memory of his protest against the Vietnam War as a noble act. She does not share his certainty that her generation's wars are unjust. And she takes some solace in the knowledge that she has made the world a better place. The United States of America may not be the heaven on earth that the Congregationalist founders of her hometown dreamed of when they named it; but its ways in the world are certainly much improved since Vietnam.

As for her wedding guests, they all voted for Barack Obama in part because he promised to wage the ongoing hostilities with greater morality, compared with the war criminal who preceded him. As a hundred Aperol spritzes bob on trays across the grassy landscape, the guests grimace during the obligatory conversation about the coming election. They genuinely fear that their fellow voters could put a madman in power who will return American war to its not-so-distant brutal ways. A few months later, they might glower when he wins, convinced that they are not to blame for the results. Even so, they have not entirely forgotten that at their elite colleges they learned the classical wisdom that endless conflict and far-flung expansion distort the politics of republics, whatever the methods and style of the fighting. Though victims beyond our borders suffer even more, war abroad often leads to tyranny at home.

Of all the peoples in the annals of warfare, Americans are the ones who have invented a form of war righteously pursued as superior precisely for being more humane, and one tolerated by audiences for that very reason. It has also been Americans who are revealing—contrary to literature since Homer—that the most elemental face of war is not death. Instead, it is control by domination and surveillance, with mortality and even violence increasingly edited out. Whatever other blame or credit our civilization earns, Americans are proving that war's evil is less and less a matter of illicit killing or even suffering. Nevertheless, war may be no less sinister for that.

WHEN I WAS A YOUNG AMERICAN, MY COUNTRY WENT TO WAR AGAIN. I was working in the White House, as a lowly intern, when NATO bombed Serbia to prevent mass killings in Kosovo. The intervention looked like the final violence necessary to put right a globe that had been disfigured by the necessities of the Cold War but was now on the brink of peace. I supported it. Only later did it seem the early stages of something altogether unexpected—and for many unintended. It has come to be called America's "endless war," especially as the campaigns against global terror after September 11, 2001, started off and ground on.

Looking back from our vantage point, it can appear that U.S. war was always endless, starting with the Cold War or World War II before it or violence at home and abroad as the country pushed to its current frontiers and explored imperial spaces beyond. But our experience after 1989, moving from the end of history into endless war, is hardly just another stage of violence, or more of the same. For one thing, it was legitimate in 1989 to expect a different path. The United Nations had promised a world of free and equal peoples; with the superpower competition ended, why shouldn't that promise now be fulfilled? For another, as time passed it seemed like the main concerns Americans expressed about their wars were changing. Those concerns were unprecedented and in their way uplifting—but they did nothing to contain the wars themselves.

As my country's war dragged on, I set out to discover where the moral imperative of peace had come from, when my country had honored it, why it had spurned it, and how in my lifetime many became less committed to peace than to making America's global violence less cruel, especially by newly relevant standards of the international laws of war. And I wondered: When and how had those standards become relevant in the first place? To understand these developments struck me as crucial—and not just for reckoning with our past. We had made a moral choice to prioritize humane war, not a peaceful globe. Pondering this choice might help us avoid mistakes in our future.

The result is an antiwar history of the laws of armed conflict in the American experience. Its goal is to trace one of the subtlest developments in warfare since September 11, a development that may leave an enduring mark. America's distant history includes almost unending examples of brutal war, though also a contribution to dreams of organized peace. Our very recent history includes the catastrophic quagmires of Afghanistan and Iraq, with war crimes along the way. But as the presidency of George W. Bush wound down, it also—and in response—allowed an innovative new form of war to emerge instead of peace.

Barack Obama perfected it, and even Donald Trump continued it. The network of bases the United States maintains abroad for "unmanned aerial vehicles," the anodyne name for armed drones, expanded, along with their deployment to surveil and strike. In an escalating wave, each of the three recent U.S. presidents before Joseph Biden took power turned to the Special Forces more and more frequently. And cyberwarfare has become more and more routine. These tools have introduced a novelty in the annals of military violence: they have made belligerency more humane.

The American way of war is more and more defined by a near complete immunity from harm for one side and unprecedented care when it comes to killing people on the other. It is informed by the standards of international law that constrain fighting. Most remarkably, America's military operations have become more expansive in scope and perpetual in time by virtue of these very facts. And it is possible that this is only a stage in a continuing transition toward less and less brutality and death in wartime.

To tell the story of humane American war is not to belittle or brush off its horrendous toll but to appreciate its full horror and future realities. In Afghanistan and Iraq, new scenes of American-perpetrated carnage—including captive abuse and civilian death—led to strong pushback. After the terror attacks of September 11, 2001, the laws constraining how war was fought became touchstones not just to America's activists, and not just to its armed services, but to broad audiences deliberating about the morality of the country's acts—most notably after the revelations of abuses up to and including torture at the Abu Ghraib prison in Iraq and in the initially law-free zone of the Guantánamo Bay site. Suddenly everyone was talking about the Geneva Conventions, giving the laws calling for humanity in war a political and public significance they had never had in any country or era.

As much as any other factor, that pushback drove a profound transformation of how the United States fights. Today, the country takes almost no prisoners and relies on the more regulated violence of missiles from the sky or on the Special Forces, with few boots on the ground. The gore and mortality of America's initial modes of intervention after September 11 have, to a remarkable extent, been removed, like bugs that programmers delete as they learn from experience.

If there is a moral problem with this result, it lies in the residual violence America's new form of war still inflicts—and also in the normalization of humane control itself. We can hold out the occasional possibility that war emancipates and liberates while still worrying that America's recent wars fail to achieve success while leading to less freedom than subjugation, and in a chilling new guise. At some point, today's deterritorialized and endless war may mutate into an unprecedented new system: rule and surveillance by one or several powers across an astonishingly large arc of the world's surface, patrolled by armed drones or paid visits by the Special Forces acting as quasi-permanent military police. Indeed, even if barely foreseeable today, our time has brought into view a possibility that we might greet with relief if it were not so unsettling, too: a future of war beyond killing.

IS IT GOOD ENOUGH—IS IT GOOD AT ALL?—THAT AMERICAN WAR COULD someday become as humane as advocates both within and outside government can make it? Would it be better or worse if global American war became global American policing, with killing not the core of the practice but a regrettable exception?

To pose such questions, it is essential to combine histories usually kept apart. One is about how expectations and rules for peace instead of war developed; the other is about the development of rules for humane conduct within hostilities when they break out. These two histories are mostly separated, on the grounds that rules for more humane war should apply regardless of the moral and legal justification of a war itself. But U.S. history—especially since the end of the Cold War—requires seeing that the erosion of one body of law can work in nefarious tandem with the imposition of the other. Increasingly, we live without antiwar law. We fight war crimes but have forgotten the crime of war.

Americans were once among the most influential propagators of the millennialist Christian idea that war might end on this earth. They led the effort to impose international limits on making war. From the beginning, however, there was lively debate about how that ambition fit together with the noble goal of making war more humane. Those worries were, in fact, more lively in the nineteenth century when it was novel to pursue peace and humanity, and the ragtag advocates of each agenda sometimes worked together even as they wondered if one goal threatened the other. For more than a century, however, suspicions that the pursuit of humane war could postpone peace were entirely abstract. War was too brutal, and early laws to govern it did not aim to make it more humane.

In 1945, the United Nations Charter, which the United States did the most to draft, prohibited force—and therefore most wars—with only narrow exceptions. At the Nuremberg trials, the country took the lead in charging Adolf Hitler's henchmen with "aggression." Yet as the United States crossed the Rubicon in the mid-twentieth century to become the guarantor of global order, it began fighting wars in many more places than before. As it did so, America's worldwide presence became as brutal as the imperial history from which the country itself emerged. For a while after 1945, the whole world became "Indian country" as the United States exported homegrown violence and adapted the no-holds-barred practices such as genocide and torture refined over centuries by European empires fighting counterinsurgent small wars or conventional big ones. The Pax Americana made a difference but not because it was humane—or even peaceful. The United States preserved order in part of the world after 1945—but did so in a way that postponed the coming of humane war.

Yet even as Americans began to fight brutally in more and more places after World War II, their country's ascendancy occurred in a novel time. It was now less and less allowable (or at least feasible) to exclude the bulk of humanity from the protections of a new international humanitarian law or sustain the openly racist cultures that had allowed earlier horrors. By and large, the laws of war had been made by and for the white Europeans who were finally at peace with one another, and no longer ruling the nonwhite world so violently. The United States faced a moral situation European empires never had. Decolonization abroad, and domestic revolt and reform in an America that fought its global wars with racially integrated armies and eventually with an African American president, changed the score.

A grand mutation occurred under America's watch. There had been laws of war before the late twentieth century. But they were always haunted by the allegation that they were laws of inhumanity, licensing untold violence, with little constraint and less compassion. That changed. Rules governing bombardment from the sky were finally invented, and older rules began to be taken seriously. International law did not bring global peace or lessen global hierarchy. But there is no doubt that increased expectations of humanity in warfare began to reign. At the same time, this change came with a cost: the moral improvement of belligerency could risk merely prettifying it.

The revelation of the My Lai massacre, where U.S. soldiers slaughtered women and children during the Vietnam War, helped bring that conflict to a close. The revulsion and outrage added fuel to the fire of America's last major peace movement, uniting liberals and leftists, the religious and the secular, pacifists and veterans. After September 11, there was one extraordinary day in February 2003 when, with the Iraq War looming, Americans joined nearly ten million protestors across the world in the most gargantuan moment of dissent against any war in history. A little more than a year later, the revelation of photographic mementos of torture at Abu Ghraib had a galvanizing effect, but it was a different one: the blemish of inhumanity was removed from a continuing war on terror.

With high dudgeon on both sides, Americans had a torture debate. It diverted them from deliberating on the deeper choice they were making to ignore constraints on starting war in the first place. Some radioactive memos were torn up, others left on the books. Newspapers covered the laws of war like never before, elevating experts on the subject as if they had a privileged relationship to morality and to policy, which are very different things. Reports issued from activists who shamed the United States for violating laws governing the fight, while the government's lawyers and soldiers interpreted the rules more permissively; the remarkable thing was the consensus all the parties shared that these were the rules that mattered. As for rules keeping the United States from embroilment in endless global violence in the first place, to say nothing of broader ethical and strategic frameworks, they became casualties of "counterterror."

Of course, there are many reasons for America's militarization of contemporary geopolitics, including the existence of real threats in a dangerous world, the move from conscripted to volunteer armed forces, and a Beltway expert "blob" and military procurement system that have both become self-perpetuating over the years. But the effort to reform conflict and make it more humane also had a role in this story, and that element requires attention precisely because such reform is always a good thing. It is easy to overlook it or downplay its coexistence with evil outcomes or ignore how it helped those outcomes seem more righteous to more observers. The story of the humanization of war is about how bad things can happen to people who want to be good.

If light- and no-footprint conflict represents the future, it's in part due to the wreckage of the Middle East that heavy-footprint American wars have left behind. But it is also due to the reformist zeal for humane war. Together, both factors afford the United States more legitimation among citizens and spectators who endorse or tolerate war in part because of its contemporary humanization. In this combination, precedents are also being set for future wars, including ones conducted by other powers.

It is precisely because this evolved version of military force is different that activists and audiences should be fully aware of the risks. Unless pursued in tandem with an impassioned commitment to controlling the use of force in the first place, this new form of war is especially apt to endure in time and spread in space. Calling for more humanity in war is hardly a bad thing, while aiming for intolerable cruelty always is. But if we accept that humane war involves unexpected risks, the lesson is to embrace more peace, in order that our future advocates do not ensure humanity in wars they accept too complacently, and that our future leaders are not allowed to brag of their achievement of less brutality, while waging too much war.

WHATEVER THE INTENTIONS OF ITS DESIGNERS, AMERICA'S "FOREVER war" shows for the first time that war—for all its sickening violence—can be transmuted into a system of humane control. It forces the recognition that the peremptory command to minimize suffering is not enough. The ultimate stakes of regulating conflict ought to be a world freer from domination.

If what Americans have done to war is unprecedented, it was never entirely unimaginable. The origins of today's humane war lie in Europe, where the greatest critic of the originally European hope to make warfare "civilized" anticipated our situation and ran in dismay from it. Inspired by American pacifists, he indicted the European reformers who colluded with states to entrench a humane form of violence. And he indicted the publics who thought the resulting improvements morally excused their implication in greater evils. Doubted for good reason at the time, his warnings are applicable to Americans now.

Hailed as the greatest novelist of all time, he started out as a soldier who spent two years in the Caucasus before experiencing war in earnest and developing his earliest anxieties about humanizing conflict. He went on to refine his criticisms over decades, before ending his career with a novella suffused with his youthful memories of the Caucasus—a novella about a declining empire facing Muslim terrorism on its fringes.

His name was Leo Tolstoy.

PART I

BRUTALITY

CHAPTER ONE

The Warning

COUNT LEV NIKOLAYEVICH TOLSTOY WENT TO WAR IN 1851, AT AGE twenty-two. The young aristocrat dropped out of university, entered the army, then spent three years in the Caucasus Mountains. As a junior officer, he was mobilized west with the outbreak of the Crimean War in 1854, nearly dying in a blizzard on the transfer by horse-drawn sleigh. After a stint on the Romanian front, where the strife had broken out after Western powers opposed Tsar Nicholas I's designs over Ottoman lands, Tolstoy was sent to the war-torn peninsula that gave the conflict its name. There Tolstoy, who had been born in 1828, acquired a skepticism of making war humane that matters even today. Especially today.

It would last his whole life long—but it would take a radically different shape in his youth and his old age. Revisiting the origins of the laws of war with Tolstoy, whatever his idiosyncratic and objectionable conclusions, is of enormous value today. He offered the most eloquent and thought-provoking reservations ever leveled against the attempt to "humanize" war, highlighting the moral risk of failing to combine the desire for less brutal war with skepticism toward war itself—since war routinely makes the world worse, no matter how humanely fought, and almost never better.

While a soldier, Tolstoy passed almost a year in and around Sevastopol, where the Crimean War would end in an eleven-month siege of the picturesque Russian town on the Black Sea by a multinational alliance of armies. Arriving in its midst, Tolstoy manned one of Sevastopol's fortified high bastions during the climactic ten-day bombardment of the town. Tolstoy wrote three short stories about the siege, culminating in an account of that final battle for the city. These stories first crystallized his belief that war itself is the moral evil to be concerned about, not the niceties of how it is fought.

The sketches, which established Tolstoy's national fame, begin with his introduction to Sevastopol under siege in December 1854, in a moment of quiet when he is rudely led into the amputation room for wounded soldiers. "You will see ghastly sights that will rend your soul," he writes, "you will see war not with its orderly beautiful and brilliant ranks, its music and beating drums, its waving banners, its generals on prancing horses, but war in its real aspect of blood, suffering, and death." The sketch concludes with nationalist hopes for Russian victory, but its concern for wounded soldiers already led in a different direction: not to aspirations for better treatment but to grim reflections on the propriety of the enterprise of killing.

Then everything changed. In the second sketch, set six months later, in May 1855, brief concern evolved into barbed criticism. After six months of siege, the reports of bullets and the shriek of cannon fire rang in his ears as they were traded from ramparts to trenches daily. And the "angel of death hovered unceasingly," for in a stalemated confrontation "the question the diplomats did not settle still remains unsettled by powder and blood."

But Tolstoy did not conclude his sketch with powder and blood. Rather, he chose a truce that had been established for humane purposes. And he found the morality of caring for soldiers' bodies during a pause in the fracas wanting. Beneath the incongruously resplendent sun, the officers of both sides manage to agree to a truce during which each would take responsibility for its dead and wounded. "Yes, there are white flags on the bastions and the trenches but the flowery valley is covered with dead bodies." The scene was certainly sickening: "Hundreds of men, with curses and prayers on parched lips, tossed and groaned," among "the corpses in the flowering valley," "the bodies of men who two hours earlier had been filled with all manner of hopes and desires." While the officers chat across lines about tobacco, the caregiving takes place before the engagement resumes.

About the ability of warring armies to agree to a moment of humanity during hostilities, the sketch is caustic. The humane treatment of the wounded does not interfere with the greater evil of war, Tolstoy reflects, let alone lead to peace. "Thousands of people crowd together, look at, speak to, and smile at one another. And these people—Christians professing the one great law of love and self-sacrifice—on seeing what they have done do not at once fall repentant on their knees." Instead, they pick up where they left off: "The white flags are lowered, the engines of death and suffering are sounding again, innocent blood is flowing and the air is filled with moans and curses."

The exhibition of humanity was little more than a pause amid death-dealing. Humanity might even make it worse. What Tolstoy could not yet know was that a decade hence another battle would prompt the invention of international law for humane war. Rafts of new treaties covering more topics have since followed, protecting soldiers in more situations along with more kinds of people—civilians, especially—and regulating means and methods of warfare, too. As for Tolstoy, he went a different way, refining and elaborating his suspicion that making war humane only allowed it to break out more often or drag on endlessly.

AMERICANS ONLY RECENTLY HAVE COME TO FACE A BINARY CHOICE between two forms of interminable war: intense or humane, dirty or clean. Some time ago, Americans were at the forefront of another possibility: pacification. The ambitions of those Americans exerted an enormous influence on Tolstoy and on twentieth-century politics before almost disappearing in the twenty-first.

The transatlantic peace movement was one of the most extraordinary novelties of the nineteenth century, the more so since it was genuinely unprecedented. The idea of making war more humane had roots in practices of restraint in warfare deep in the mists of history. The idea that peace was available in human affairs, by contrast, was a genuine novelty. One Quaker complained that because people could not envision a world without war, they acquiesced in it as "in the rising of the sun, without any other idea than that it is part of the ordinary processes of the world." Yet Enlightenment theorists and nineteenth-century movements arose convinced that there was no need to wait for the end of days when, as the biblical prophets had promised, nation would not lift up their swords against nation, nor learn war anymore.

Now modernity afforded a new sense of possibility. Other plagues, such as hierarchy, poverty, and slavery, also came to seem, especially after the French Revolution, eliminable rather than eternal. It was suddenly credible that, even if animal aggression was eternal, human beings could transcend it through self-reform and finally put the scourge of war in the past. The evil that pacifists condemned had to be reimagined as a practice that could be brought to an end. "All history is the decline of war," Ralph Waldo Emerson explained in 1838. The trouble was that "the right of war remains."

To spread the word that war ought not to be tolerated as ordinary, Americans founded the first nongovernmental associations aiming at pacifying international relations in 1815. Soon, their fledgling activism was dwarfed by British movements, thanks especially to the Peace Society, formed in 1816. By the later nineteenth century, Continental Europe was awash in peace mobilization, too.

For a long time, it was Christians, citing the example of Jesus himself, who most frequently dreamed the dream of an end to war. For many proponents of a peace mobilization—Tolstoy not least—pacifism followed simply from taking Christianity seriously. A few transatlantic sects, such as Anabaptists, Mennonites, and Quakers, had for centuries understood refusal to take up arms as part of their faith. They were right to think that Jesus's message had less to do with making war humane than with turning the other cheek.

In the nineteenth century, Christian pacifism boomed. The American seer William Lloyd Garrison, the devout abolitionist who campaigned against slavery, had war in his sights, too. The Massachusetts senator and radical Republican Charles Sumner condemned the "war system of the commonwealth of nations" in 1845, as the country's invasion of Mexico was brewing. It was probably the most influential antiwar speech in U.S. history. Then there was Adin Ballou, whom Tolstoy would come to admire even more. Born in 1803 in Rhode Island, Ballou converted to pacifism in 1838. An austere Christian minister, he founded the utopian community of Hopedale, Massachusetts, and crisscrossed New England to preach peace (as well as abolition, socialism, and temperance). Unlike Garrison—who publicly announced that his antislavery campaign trumped his nonviolent creed when John Brown raided Harper's Ferry in 1857—Ballou refused in the Civil War to give "allegiance to the war god when with his battle-axe he cleft asunder the fetters of the slave." Most onetime American pacifists—like Sumner—followed Garrison's lead in the crisis. But after the destruction of slavery, American peace movements would surge again.

As the nineteenth century passed, secular radicals and later liberals joined the mix, alongside Christian pacifists. One of the leading ideologues of eternal peace in the second half of the nineteenth century was the Englishman William Cobden, who insisted that free trade could someday unify humanity where Christianity had graphically failed to do so. The American Non-Resistance Society never numbered more than two hundred members and was shuttered after a decade. To achieve greater impact, the movement would have to shift away from Christian ethics. It would have to make compromises, especially with those who proposed arbitration schemes and supranational organizations that did not establish a complete ban on armed force in all circumstances.

Fragmented by tenacious debates over the use of force to destroy slavery, the U.S. wing of the peace movement declined through the coming of the Civil War. In Europe, by contrast, it took off after

1850. Lulled by more than three decades of post-Napoleonic peace, the continent's burghers and Christians were shocked by the Crimea events and then the Austro-Sardinian War of 1859.

Across the Atlantic and in the United States, peace circles debated a recurring issue: Was it permissible for a state to undertake "defensive" responses when unbidden attacks occurred? Should pacifists scorn those who left room for some wars? Many were skeptical from the start about any exception for self-defense, which later became almost the sole legal basis for war in the United Nations Charter of 1945, as it remains today. Any exception, purists said, could easily become the pretext for aggression. As one agitator angrily put it, "A peace society which allowed a right of defensive war was one to which a Tamerlane or a Napoleon might consistently belong."

Meanwhile, a new breed of internationalists offered scores of proposals for peace through the second half of the nineteenth century. Often they relied on international law, envisioning new bilateral and multilateral treaties. Sumner, to take only one example, proposed the use of international law to banish war. Tolstoy was to be more skeptical that states could voluntarily agree to get along—and his skepticism only increased when they promised to fight their wars with one another humanely.

IF THE ATTEMPT TO END WAR WAS INSPIRED AT FIRST BY ESCHATOlogical visions, the effort to humanize it had another point of departure—a Christianity of good works, which evolved into a secular enlightenment ethic of identifying with the pain of others. By the Enlightenment, the use of investigative torture to ferret out the truth from suspects and harsh punishment once they were deemed guilty may already have been on the wane. The rise of sentimental ethics singling out bodily violation as among the most offensive evils drove campaigns against both, and made an important contribution to the rise of antislavery ideology, too.

By the mid-nineteenth century, the German philosopher Friedrich Nietzsche could complain that what "civilization" now meant was the treatment of physical cruelty as the worst evil, with pain regarded as ever more hurtful, and torture an especially taboo infraction. ("We tremble even at the very thought of torture being inflicted on a man or an animal and we undergo unspeakable misery when we hear of such acts," Nietzsche commented dismissively.) The effort to abolish or diminish physical pain swept the agenda of social reform, touching practically all areas of life and law, from the criminal process to industrial policy, to medical care. The surprise, perhaps, is how long it took reformers to add making war specifically humane to their agenda. Still, as the post-Napoleonic European peace began to disintegrate in stages after 1850, proposals accumulated with a vengeance.

Overwhelmingly, the leading early cause was the mistreatment of soldiers, especially when they were wounded on the battlefield. The wars of the period had already galvanized women's activism to help wounded soldiers. In fact, it was a set piece of the public morality of the age. Florence Nightingale, eminent Victorian, became one of the most idealized do-gooders of all time for her work ministering to her empire's wounded soldiers in the Crimea. The American Dorothea Dix made a pilgrimage to Constantinople in hopes of meeting Nightingale—who was then enjoying international veneration that outstripped even the patriotic celebration of victorious armies. Dix decried the deplorable preparations of the Union Army's Medical Bureau after the carnage of Bull Run in 1861; the nurse Clara Barton, who would go on to found the American branch of the Red Cross, got her start healing the Northern wounded.

But there was no formal system that would permit philanthropic engagement in wars and make it a regular feature of the conflicts of states in the self-styled "civilized world." To go beyond the ad hoc organization of local remedies, a collection of elites would need to come together and cajole states into conducting their clashes within "civilized" limits, at least on paper. When generals like those at Sevastopol did not do the work on their own, humanitarians were needed. The time was ripe. As high politics increasingly depended on public legitimacy, and the public included not just bloodthirsty zealots but organized peacemongers, states could split the difference between freedom of action and the appearance of virtue through showy agreements on paper to humanize war.

It may have been accidental that Swiss gentlemen captured the cause when they founded the Red Cross in the 1860s, and that as a result Geneva remains to this day the city most associated with making warfare more humane. Still, after their own minor civil war in 1847, the Swiss had fewer other problems to solve and low levels of political conflict by comparison with other countries. A cipher named Henry Dunant was in the right place at the right time to give Swiss gentlemen a high international task. A pious Calvinist, he had restricted his moral engagements as a youth to familiar causes such as relief for the poor and support for orphans, and all on a local scale. He was on a business trip when he wandered onto the stage of history. Though there only briefly, he got a star turn in the drama of humane war.

In the 1850s, Dunant represented Genevan investors in the business of settling the new French colony of Algeria, and he acquired his own land in the territory. Hoping to convince France's Emperor Napoleon III to grant a water concession so that Dunant could irrigate his property, he set off to find him during a French war with Austria in its northern Italian holdings in June 1859. Dunant ran across the site of the Battle of Solferino in Lombardy, where the biggest clashes of forces since the time of the first Napoleon had just occurred—and was horrified by what he saw. Leaving the battlefield, he continued his search for Napoleon III, whose attaché curtly turned down Dunant's business proposition. He then returned to Solferino and tended to the wounded.

Dunant wrote a pamphlet about the carnage. Describing himself as a "tourist," he narrated the battle (which he had not witnessed) before turning to the aftermath, with bodies alive and dead strewn over more than twelve miles of countryside. It took three days to bury the corpses (not including the horses), amid "a fetid stench."

In emotional prose, Dunant described how soldiers lacking water lapped it from bloody puddles, near handsome boys converted to hideous carrion. But Dunant's most influential pages were reserved for how badly organized was the care for the wounded. Stricken fighters were abandoned as gangrene and infection set in, or if they healed in unsanitary conditions guaranteed to lead to the same results. "Their faces black with flies that buzzed around their wounds, they looked every which way for help that no one gave."

The depiction of such harrowing scenes had invited a variety of responses before, from grim acceptance of God's inscrutable justice, to Francisco Goya's mockery of the human folly of Napoleon's counterinsurgency in his country. Dunant's sentimental prose, by contrast, voiced the conscience of a new era in which the body in pain mandated socially organized relief and an episode of legal reform. Indeed, the success of Dunant's call for identification with suffering in war played on the tide of pacifist sentiment. The celebrated French literary critics Edmond and Jules de Goncourt, after overpraising Dunant's writing as "better, a thousand times better, than Homer," concluded that it was an antiwar tract in effect if not in intent. "One finishes this book cursing war."

But in the 1860s, Dunant was not a peacemonger. Dunant's own proposal was to accept war and to form international brigades to help soldiers in circumstances like those he had witnessed. Dunant and some Genevan notables founded what became the International Red Cross (so named in 1876). Their first idea was to call on states to write an international treaty guaranteeing that a humanitarian brigade could assist the medical services of European armies if and when they failed on their own.

Of these notables, the most consequential was Gustave Moynier, who would prove in the long run far more important than Dunant for his long service, his pragmatic sensibility, and his distinctive moral vision. A Swiss lawyer, Moynier gruffly rejected the visionary idealism that annoyed him in Dunant and insisted on bringing militaries themselves on board the humanitarian project. In doing so, he hoped for Christian virtue and humanitarian compassion to be advanced through state connivance in general and military consent in particular. He did not hesitate to affirm that making war humane would "advance God's reign on earth." Apparently, God would have to work in mysterious ways. From the start, General Guillaume Dufour, a Swiss war hero, was recruited to help brand and lead the humane war project.

From the start, too, however, Moynier advertised his realistic movement as one that could fulfill the peace movement. Treating enemies better, he hoped, might prove a stepping-stone to turning the other cheek. "We must leave to war all its horrors, as the only way to open the eyes of those who order it and those who pay the price," a Lyons doctor had complained of the Red Cross project of humanizing unnecessary evil. Moynier responded that such an objection, taken to an extreme, would imply the abolition of all army medical services, not merely the backup the Red Cross hoped to provide. And in any case, humanizing war might work better than the "sterile sentimentalism" of the peace movement in revealing war's cruelties.

True, Moynier later acknowledged grudgingly, the notion of "civilized war" was "nonsense" and there was a hard core of immorality that would always remain even once humanization was done. "War without the spilling of blood would no longer be war," Moynier admitted. Even if states played along, an essentially inhumane activity could be taken only so far in a humane direction. But, he insisted, this hardly implied that the goal was not worth pursuing.

Called to Geneva by Dunant, Moynier, and their colleagues, representatives of twelve European states met twice, in 1863 and 1864, and agreed to a first set of treaty rules for war. The treaty protected brigades of caregivers as neutrals in future conflicts. It would take a long time to be carried out, but the treaty eked out a bit of room for international legal obligation and humane treatment in the brutal activity of war. (It portended things to come long after—not for nothing would the U.S. president Barack Obama offer a shout-out to Dunant in his Nobel Peace Prize address in 2009.)

In the short term, no one would have predicted the canonization of Dunant or the prestige of his project. Within three years of the Geneva treaty, in the midst of a bank failure due in part to Genevan investments in Algeria that a not very competent Dunant had arranged, he was forced out of his outfit. After disappearing, he was presumed dead. Decades later, expelled by Moynier from the organization he helped inspire and living modestly in a senior center in the picturesque resort town of Heiden near Lake Constance, Dunant was rediscovered by a passing journalist. An elderly man recalled to life for a few years of celebrity, he became the poster senior of a project that had accelerated in the prior decades. With earlier life recrafted hagiographically and his 1901 Nobel Prize reported across the world, Dunant now assumed the appearance of a white-bearded guru, much like the greatest critic of the humanizing enterprise he had helped launch.

IT WOULD TAKE TOLSTOY SOME TIME TO SOUND THE ALARM THAT HU-manitarianism could entrench war. On the way to doing so, he had one of his most famous characters embrace the inverse proposition: brutality can make it rare.

"One thing I would do if I had the power," Prince Andrei, the debonair and reflective leading man of *War and Peace*, declares, "I would not take prisoners." It comes to the hero as an epiphany: if in battle an enemy soldier were captured, or if he laid down his arms and surrendered, it should not save him from death. No one today thinks it is permissible to kill enemies in war summarily when they are captured or surrender. In fact, to do so is today a gross war crime. How could Andrei take a position that would have made even the worst counselors of inhumanity in recent American wars—George W. Bush's lawyers, who exempted the country precisely from rules about how to treat captives—blanch?

At the Battle of Austerlitz years earlier, Prince Andrei had been wounded and given medical attention as a prisoner of war by no less an authority than Napoleon himself. Yet the night before the greatest battle of the age, at Borodino, Prince Andrei argued that making war humane not only denatured it but also, even worse, risked the postponement of peace. Tolstoy had sat down in 1863 to begin what became his most famous novel (it appeared in 1869), so Prince Andrei's speech might well have been a direct response to the Geneva Convention. Tolstoy has Prince Andrei refer quite specifically to the fledgling and original attempt by states to make their clashes with one another more humane: "They talk to us of the rules of war," Prince Andrei says, "of mercy to the unfortunate." And adds: "It's all rubbish."

Andrei's position was a direct attack on Dunant's dream. The prince's attack was rooted not in any immediate appeal to the ethics of peace Tolstoy would later embrace but instead in the peculiar belief that intensifying war could advance peace indirectly. And to understand this belief, and Tolstoy's eventual reasons for giving it up, it is critical to detour into another agenda for modernizing war: to make it more intense.

The most celebrated theorist of war of the age and all time, the Prussian nobleman Carl von Clausewitz, clarified that the point of engagement is annihilation, and he asserted "the dominance of the destructive principle," which he feared earlier theorists of war had downplayed. In his four decades in the Prussian Army, the "god of war" had lived through a trio of Napoleonic battles, including Borodino—where, on the bloodiest day of the century, a European army forced Napoleon's epic advance to a draw at the gates of Moscow in 1812. It was a site that, fifty years later, Tolstoy himself would visit in a hunting wagon halfway through his work, consulting peasants and planning his own narrative, including Prince Andrei's mortal wounding there.

In his masterpiece, *On War* (1832), Clausewitz had warned against the "kind-hearted" fiction that a nation could wage a war "without too much bloodshed." Not only was it useless, but morally reforming war could exacerbate its evil. "Mistakes which come from kindness are the very worst." Treating the carnage in war as a sin for which to atone or—worse—a blemish on the most beautiful activity in life was something like a moral error. "It would be futile—even wrong—to try to shut one's eyes to what war really is from sheer distress at its brutality," Clausewitz explained. Concerns about how gory and gruesome the commitments to intensity could become were petty. "The fact that slaughter is a horrifying spectacle must make us take war more seriously," he allowed, "but not provide an excuse for gradually blunting our swords in the name of humanity." As he observed, "Sooner or later someone will come along with a sharp sword and hack off our arms."

Dunant founded the international law of war. But it fell to a disciple of Clausewitz's to offer a brutal answer to the humane aspirations of the Swiss and their descendants—to offer the first national code for fighting. Born in Prussia, too, in 1798 or 1800, Franz Lieber was a young enlistee who saw action near Waterloo, before fleeing to the United States in the repressive years leading up to the abortive 1848 revolution. Francis in America (and Frank to his friends), Lieber refused to pity victims of war. Lieber's code went in a different direction, legalizing shock and awe, with humanity a fringe benefit rather than a true goal.

Opinionated to his core, Lieber said pacifists were the ones who really deserved compassion. "How much are those to be pitied," he explained in a widely used ethics textbook that he published in 1839, "whose hearts remained cold" at "the nobleness of human nature" on display when a "citizen [is] bleeding and dying for his beloved country." Lieber wrote to the American poet Henry Wadsworth Longfellow's wife, Fanny, saying the truth was that "blood" was the "vital juice" of civilization. (As for those lily-livered pacifists in his time who cited Jesus's command to turn the other cheek, Lieber was apoplectic: "Christ taught principles," he acknowledged, but they were "not absolute mathematical formulas [and] if the various passages of the Bible were to be taken literally, no book would contain greater contradictions.")

When he was given the chance as a Columbia University law

professor and government consultant to write rules for the Union Army in 1862, Lieber made them most consistent with the Clausewitzian agenda of intensifying war. Erected as one of its founding fathers later, Lieber was not really part of the tradition of making war humane. He condoned horrendous acts such as punishing civilians and denying quarter—which meant that, when enemies surrendered in hopes of avoiding death, you could kill them anyway. Instead, Lieber was an excellent example—like Clausewitz—of how those actually committed to intense war sometimes pretended to be friends of peace. For Lieber, anything necessary in war, more or less, ought to be legal; if there was such a thing as excess violence and suffering, it was because it was necessary to achieve victory, which hastened peace.

Clausewitz already got into the act. "Battle exists for its own sake alone," he had insisted. But it also had an extra advantage. It "led directly to peace." Lieber told a similar story as his master. "If destruction of the enemy is my object, it is not only my right, but my duty, to resort to the most destructive means." But thankfully, he added, "the more actively this rule is followed out, the better for humanity." Intensity bred pacification, albeit as a fringe benefit of an already great thing.

Just before he gives his speech, Prince Andrei is passed on horseback by none other than Clausewitz himself. Tolstoy probably never read him. He gave the Prussian theoretician a cameo in *War and Peace* all the same, to doubt the value of "theory" in the face of the chaos and confusion that defined the clash of military forces. Famously, in *War and Peace* Tolstoy wanted to smash the Clausewitzian mythology of Napoleon and with it the whole idea that war was amenable to intentional control. As for theorizing about battle at windy altitudes, Tolstoy found it ridiculous, and Clausewitz trots through his scene to imply as much. Yet Tolstoy also has Clausewitz, in addition to delivering a disastrous plan for the next day's battle, defend brutality, too: "The only aim is to weaken the enemy," Clausewitz remarks from his saddle (in German in the Russian novel), "so one cannot, of course, take into account the losses of private persons."

In his dream of not taking prisoners, Tolstoy's character ironically sounded a Clausewitzian note. What Prince Andrei was suggesting in his speech was that intensification would lead to more humanity and less suffering over time—for all its brutality in the short run—precisely because it would lead to more peace. Not taking prisoners "by itself would change the whole war and make it less cruel," Andrei says. If Clausewitz was right that intensity led indirectly to pacification, intensification also turned out to be more humane than humanization! On its own, paradoxically, humanization could foment more war, and less humane outcomes. Furthermore, Andrei insisted, making war more humane could lead war to be an easier matter to start: a less fateful and momentous choice, because the stakes were lower. "If there was none of this magnanimity in war," he continued in his impassioned homily, "we should go to war only when it was worthwhile going to certain death."

When audiences shrank from the argument that intense wars were good in themselves, advocates of intensification offered blind guesses about the future. It wasn't just that bloody wars would become less routine. They also suggested that shock and awe would end more quickly once it started. As Lieber forecast, "intense wars are of short duration."

Yet advocates of making war humane offered an exactly parallel guess on behalf of their own cause. Already in 1864, Gustave Moynier called the Geneva Convention the path down "a slope where there is no stopping; the end of the road cannot be less than the condemnation of war in absolute terms." The laws of war would become "secret agents of pacification," Moynier foresaw in one of his rare moments of visionary enthusiasm. "The humanization of war could end only in its abolition," he promised his funders. "The [Geneva] Convention has furnished an argument in favor of the brotherhood of men. Recognizing that after all they all belong to the same family, men have concluded that they ought to begin by showing some regard for another's suffering, up to a certain point . . . pending the time when a still stronger conviction of their common humanity shall lead them to understand that the very idea of their killing one another is monstrous." In short, it was not intensification that would indirectly abet pacification, but humanization.

In fact, the argument that Tolstoy the novelist puts in Prince Andrei's mouth depends for its success on complete speculation. Could it really work to make war more brutal in the short run so that it became less common and more humane in the long run? Was there evidence for that proposition in the history of Tolstoy's own time, let alone the brutal and long wars of the twentieth century he did not live to see? Equally hypothetical and unproven, however, was the occasional suggestion of advocates of humanization like Moynier that *they* were the ones bringing about peace indirectly.

After a conversion experience, Tolstoy gave up Prince Andrei's shortsighted view. But Aylmer Maude, his biographer and friend, was absolutely right that the speech anticipated Tolstoy's mature attack on "humanity" in warfare on pacifist grounds, "like the lightning of a coming storm." For Andrei's main commitment is not to prediction but to truth and the risks of suppressing it. Prettification of evil is quite simply prevarication, and it could lead people to compromise with it. "Get rid of falsehood," Andrei counsels, "and let war be war," "the most horrible thing in life." Soon Tolstoy devoted most of his energy to the different proposition that making war humane could court the risk of endless war, and above all cover up its horrors. It is the way he did so that applies to our own situation, as we endure the forever if occasionally more humane war of our time.

WHILING AWAY HIS TIME IN BETWEEN THE BLOODY EPISODES OF Sevastopol in 1855, Tolstoy had "a great idea, a stupendous idea," "to the realization of which I feel capable of devoting my entire life." He explained: "This idea is the founding of a new religion appropriate to the stage of development of mankind—the religion of

Christ, but purged of beliefs and mysticism, a practical religion, not promising future bliss but giving bliss on earth." But for the moment, there was still gambling and whoring to get done.

After Tolstoy completed *Anna Karenina* in 1877, he became increasingly moody. In a midlife crisis, Tolstoy began surreptitiously frequenting a Russian Orthodox monastery. But his thinking slowly drove him beyond organized religion to an austere and idiosyncratic Christianity. Disgusted more and more by the family life he had chosen in the meantime, with two of his children in early graves, the novelist largely put fiction behind him. From his deathbed in 1883, Ivan Turgenev begged Tolstoy to return to his better talent. Even Tolstoy's earlier novels, however, were only to become world-famous in tandem with his self-transformation into a railing moralist with global appeal. A cantankerous attitude toward his once-beloved wife, Sonya, overtook him, and his ten children increasingly found him overbearing and unbearable, before his family decamped to Moscow and left him in the countryside, where he increasingly adopted peasant ways.

One of the many over the centuries who chose Christ over Christianity, Tolstoy adopted a vision of nonresistance so personal and totalistic that it bears little relationship to the faith most Christians have taken as their own. Tolstoy translated the Gospels himself, elevating the message of the Sermon on the Mount into a personal religion that transcended existing sects (and certainly Russian Orthodoxy, which returned the favor by excommunicating him). Thunderous disquisitions on ethics and religion flowed from his pen for more than thirty years. As the extraordinary if rare fiction from these years, *The Death of Ivan Ilyich*, illustrates, Tolstoy's own grappling at middle age with his mortality—though he would live a long time—lurked among the causes of his philosophizing. Along the way, Tolstoy became not only the most renowned pacifist in the world, and the best-known vegetarian, but also an idiosyncratic holy man who changed the spiritual face of the twentieth century.

Tolstoy's whole ethics drew substantially on the Christian vision

Americans had developed for opposing slavery and war alike earlier in the nineteenth century. Very quickly after his conversion, and working on his own, Tolstoy centered his interpretation of Jesus's message on the same passage that had inspired Ballou's nonresistance ethics fifty years before—Matthew 5:39: "But I say unto you, do not resist an evildoer." No church of which he could remain a member, Tolstoy insisted, could allow "approval and acceptance of persecutions, executions, and wars." When the son of the now deceased abolitionist William Lloyd Garrison read these initial religious writings, he was struck by Tolstoy's convergence with American prophets of nonviolence. And so he sent the famous Russian the biography of his father he was composing, which so impressed Tolstoy that he made a deep dive into his honored predecessors. He even inquired of his correspondent whether their pioneering Non-Resistance Society was still open for business.

Tolstoy settled for writing a preface to the condensed version of the biography of Garrison that a disciple produced at Tolstoy's direction, and he celebrated the reformer as "the first to proclaim" nonresistance "as a rule for the organization of the life of men." (Tolstoy didn't address Garrison's difficult and different choices when abolitionists faced the dilemma of violence.) Ballou's nonresistance theology made an even deeper impact. The Massachusetts reformer was still alive in Hopedale, and after a neighbor sent his books to Tolstoy, Ballou and Tolstoy began a lively correspondence that ended only with the American's death in 1890, which shattered Tolstoy "as that of a close friend." For the elderly Ballou, Tolstoy had gone mad in the monomaniacal extremes to which he took Ballou's own arguments. But Tolstoy didn't mind. The Cornell University founder Andrew Dickson White, a long-distance visitor to Tolstoy's estate, was shocked when Tolstoy insisted in conversation that Ballou was the "greatest of all American writers."

Never one to avoid the opportunity to pen a lengthy tome, Tolstoy was so affected by his Americans that he started writing a commentary that became his most influential statement of his philosophy of nonviolence, *The Kingdom of God Is Within You* (1894). Citing the Americans copiously, Tolstoy also gave his thinking free rein. He gratefully followed Ballou's biblical interpretations, since—Tolstoy said—"no aspect of the question" of nonresistance had escaped Ballou's gaze. And it was no accident that the Americans had been led to oppose slavery and war simultaneously, and through it discovered the general principle of nonviolent politics in response to evil. When requested to address the American people as a whole in 1901, Tolstoy decided to "thank them for the great help" that their peace advocates had afforded him. "And I should like to ask the American people," he added mischievously, "why they do not pay more attention to these voices (hardly to be replaced by those of financial and industrial millionaires, or successful generals and admirals)."

Ever since his conversion, Tolstoy's readers have been divided by his ethics. The Russian sage never fully worked out its implications. He coveted a morality of pure intentions rather than judging by results. "To many people of our society it would be impossible to torture or kill a baby, even if they were told that by doing so they could save hundreds of other people," he wrote to a New York correspondent in 1896. "And in the same way, a man who has developed a Christian sensibility of heart finds a whole series of actions have become impossible for him." But he sometimes appealed to results anyway—as he would when it came to the likely effects of making war humane.

And he didn't ever precisely explain whether and why all violence was really proscribed. Tolstoy once diffidently acknowledged that killing a mosquito was allowable. Setting a mousetrap, even if immoral, was less momentous an act of violence than injuring a horse, he added. But he never did offer a persuasive answer to why, even in the face of a violent attack, violence was never acceptable (other, of course, than that Jesus had said so). At the end of his life, asked about Lincoln on the centenary of his birth, Tolstoy called him the "only real giant" of modern history because "he loved his enemies as himself."

He didn't mention that the U.S. president had gone to war with those enemies, too, however reluctantly.

But as his late texts washed over Russia and then the rest of the world, bands of "Tolstoyans"—and later nonviolent activists such as Mohandas Gandhi and Martin Luther King, Jr.—mobilized in response. Americans such as Jane Addams and William Jennings Bryan were far from the only ones to make a pilgrimage to Tolstoy's estate, and many more consulted him by post. And it was popular to found communes, as Gandhi did in 1910 outside Johannesburg, to live out Tolstoy's ideals. (One of his last American disciples, taken by his depiction of Christian life in its early decades, set up a still-existing Tolstoyan farm outside Spokane, Washington, originally as a refuge for Vietnam-era conscientious objectors.)

Others ruefully concluded that Tolstoy had allowed the worst part of himself, his philosophical tendencies, to overwhelm his writerly gifts and especially his genius for character and detail. "It is the greatest misfortune to the human race that he has so little power of reasoning," the philosopher Bertrand Russell remarked contemptuously. Tolstoy's own biographer chastised him for becoming a "denouncer of obvious evils in an obvious way," deeming his pacifist outpourings "simplistic." Intending to save him from a century's worth of knowing verdicts, the craggy-faced Oxford don Isaiah Berlin repeated such criticisms when he called Tolstoy a fox who was confused about who he really was and tried to be a hedgehog instead.

In debates around Tolstoy's legacy, however, it has never been noted that he was concerned in pioneering and still-pertinent ways with how legally humanizing vile practices risked entrenching them. It did so in two fundamental ways. First, reformers came to tolerate an enduring evil when they chose to make it more humane. Second, their audiences risked fooling themselves: they came to believe that striking a blow against the cruelty of a practice made their continuing involvement in it noble. Call the first the advocate's compromise and the second the beneficiary's bad faith. It is even possible that nothing of Tolstoy's self-made religion survives except his astute and prophetic attempt—a small part of his grandiose if not megalomaniacal undertaking to finally save the world from sin—to denounce the contradictions and risks of humane war.

PRINCE ANDREI'S ARGUMENTS IN *WAR AND PEACE* NO LONGER MADE sense, by the converted Tolstoy's lights. Those arguments had revolved around the likely consequences of humanizing or intensifying a conflict, speculating that the one would worsen outcomes where the other might improve them.

The later Tolstoy's most inspired move was to develop a comparison of humane war to the more obvious evils of humanizing other violent corporal practices. He started by recalling the example of chattel slavery, charging that making it more humane had been a gross moral error. What if reformers humanized an institution they could and should have eradicated?

Not that Tolstoy's outrage at human bondage was immediate. As a count and landowner, Tolstoy had enjoyed help from his 4,000-acre estate's serfs for decades. He had once commented in his diary, "It's true that slavery is an evil, but it is an extremely lovable one." But shortly after, during his military service, he read Harriet Beecher Stowe's *Uncle Tom's Cabin*, the bestseller of the nineteenth century (after the Bible). Soon Tolstoy—like Pierre Bezukhov in his greatest novel—was attempting to free his own serfs. In 1861, he helped administer the abolition of serfdom in his home province, shortly before Abraham Lincoln's Emancipation Proclamation called for an end to American slavery in the midst of the nation's Civil War.

Tolstoy felt that slavery's transformation from inevitable to intolerable provided lessons for targeting all human wrongs. Tolstoy never ceased likening things he did not like—including government itself—with chattel slavery. "Slavery has long been abolished. It was abolished in Rome, and in America, and in Russia, but what was abolished was the word and not the thing itself," he contended. "Where violence is legalized, there slavery exists." But in his activist phase, Tolstoy also referred much more specifically to the lessons that chattel slavery bore for the indictment of military violence. And his most explosive argument was to suggest that the very same compromises that reformers countenanced before gathering to abolish the practice were now being trotted out to rationalize the endurance of war. Humane slavery? That had been a sham. The idea of humane war was, too.

There had been a time, Tolstoy explained in a letter reported all around the world, when no one believed slavery could ever end. "Not only the ancient pagans, Plato and Aristotle, but the men nearest to us in time and Christian, were not able to conceive of mankind as existing without slavery," he reported (accurately). Once the extraordinary possibility of an emancipated society had been glimpsed, a great many nonetheless concluded that the enormity of slaveholding made it ineradicable after all, or that its end was distant and speculative. If so, why not deal with its cruelty for as long as it lasted? That dreadful mistake, Tolstoy cautioned, was now being repeated with war, too. Under the headline "Tolstoi Writes of War, Says It Must Follow Slavery and Disappear," *The New York Times* reported his message: "The partisans of error then pretend to understand the enormity and the cruelty of the system they defend . . . [but] declare that for the present its destruction is impossible." Humanizing looked like a horrendous mistake when it came to chattel slavery in the past. Why not save ourselves from repeating the error when it comes to war in the present?

Tolstoy's example is exceptionally interesting. For a long time, the cause of reform, when it came to chattel slavery across the Atlantic, tended in the direction of humanizing it, a project that coexisted comfortably with the strengthening of plantation discipline. Organizing movements and framing laws, reformers did not challenge property rights in slaves so much as attempt to ameliorate their treatment. If not human liberty, then humane treatment was what the humanity of slaves required. The choice was not entirely new at the turn of the nineteenth century. In the French and Spanish empires, often in the name of "Christian justice," legal codes constrained what masters could do with their human property, without challenging their right to it. But in the 1790s, and especially after the fearful specter of slave revolt in Haiti, planters across the southern United States and the British West Indies accelerated a turn to a rhetoric of "amelioration," which ended in the same place.

This amorphous term could mean many things. In the island sugar colonies of the British Empire, especially in the quarter century between the ban of the slave trade in 1807 and the Slavery Abolition Act of 1833, most planters had understood the need to answer moral criticisms of human bondage. They therefore asserted that their slaveholding was changing in form, and taking the sane path between stagnation and revolution. Production was made cheaper and more efficient, to demonstrate its modernity (and increase profit); slaves were better fed and treated—not worked to death and replaced so frequently, as in decades before.

Everyone understood such "amelioration" to serve the long-term endurance of the slave economy. And activists worked to find reforms slavers would accept, urging legal reform to enforce limits on treatment, such as the 1826 Slave Code. In his epistle to the Corinthians, Paul recounted that he was given thirty-nine lashes by the Jews, and masters disciplining slaves through flogging were sometimes limited to that number as an upper limit for each day (or in each session). And reforms often ruled out whipping slave women altogether. One law in Berbice, in British Guiana, explained that slaves needed to be treated "with such humanity, that Love and not Fear may operate, as motives for their good conduct to their Masters."

Amelioration occurred in British North America, too, and (after the American Revolution) the southern states of the new republic. Indeed, the West Indies retained a reputation for cruelty and mortality to the end of enslavement while the United States took humanization to the hilt. As a result of its own sense of Enlightenment and modernity, the slaveholding class adopted a sometimes fervent principle of humanity that dictated treating their chattel less cruelly though never equally. As in the European empires, American slave codes bore on the decency required of masters, and case law authorized judges to determine if limits were transgressed. Just as early humane societies did not threaten the right to own pets, slave owners did not see the slightest contradiction between new limits to what they could do to their property and their eternal right to own it. Though struggling with each other, humanitarians and slaveholders shared the same goal: humane slavery.

The assumption of many reformers was that, because the possibility of abolition seemed a long way off (if it was available at all), humanization was the best policy for now. Occasionally they entertained the hope that the humanization of slavery would lead to its eradication—precisely the perspective that Moynier was to take, decades later, toward war. Was there a case to be made that transforming slavery in a more humane direction could or did prepare onetime advocates of the practice to become its enemies? Perhaps. The British pivot from humanization to abolition occurred in the space of a few decades. Focusing on the American case, however, Tolstoy stressed and worried about the reverse possibility: humane slavery could become endless slavery.

As the decades passed in the United States, the slave power was extended across the Cotton South and the number of humans held in bondage—however they were treated—skyrocketed. And everywhere it spread, humane slavery was insulated against criticism in the bargain. With "inhumane treatment" of chattel property increasingly under a cloud, slavery emerged "more tolerable for the slaveowner and the abolitionist," wrote one of America's greatest historians of slavery. "Victories over brutality left the real enemy more entrenched than ever. As slavery became less brutal there was less reason why it should be abolished." The compromises that "humanity" made with slavers along the way were profound. No wonder that by the 1830s radical abolitionists in the United States inferred that the British example of ameliorating slavery had only entrenched the institution. For them, this stoked "a sense of urgency" about the need for immediate abolition, and "a mistrust of palliatives." If they had been correct in retrospect, Tolstoy asked, why was the attempt to bring about humane war now different?

BUT TOLSTOY'S FAVORITE OBJECT LESSON OF A VIOLENT CORPORAL practice that, if humanized, could endure more malignantly than ever was not human bondage but the slaughter of animals. This example allowed him to explore not advocates and their debatable and perverse compromises but entire societies and their bad faith. What did it mean when societies took modest acts that allowed their members to think they were good people while merely humanizing a systemic evil central to their way of life?

From his youth, Tolstoy had eaten animals with gusto. His years baiting and killing them were memorialized in *War and Peace* both in Pierre Bezukhov's evening carousing with a bear and in an aristocratic wolf hunt. Even then, Tolstoy knew that "man feels a sense of horror" when "seeing a dying animal," for a being "similar to his own is perishing before his eyes." In "The Bear Hunt," a later story, Tolstoy fictionalized his own brush with death after he hit his target in the head with a gunshot but only maimed the beast before it rushed him and his face was nearly chewed off. But not long into his conversion process, Tolstoy commanded his sons to stop bringing their prey from their routine country expeditions into the house; and shortly he was to stop eating animal flesh.

Concerns about animal cruelty had surged in the nineteenth century, together with the attack on slavery and then the campaign to humanize war, all with few precedents before. The Society for the Prevention of Cruelty to Animals, a British outfit, appeared in the 1820s, and parallel groups appeared across the Atlantic over the middle of the century. But some reforms were more popular, while others were unthinkable. Pride of place was given to animal cruelty protections, including bans on the fighting or torture of animals, blood sports such as bullbaiting and cockfighting that had once been common as popular entertainments. An enormous campaign against vivisection, in spite of its medical uses, surged later. The treatment of animals in slaughterhouses lagged far behind, and the main reform in that arena was to move sites of killing from urban view rather than regulate their internal workings. Nonmeat diets, meanwhile, were still regarded as crackpot.

Given his anxieties about movements against "brutality" (a crass misnomer to describe animal mistreatment), Tolstoy was not above attacking the coming of "humanity" in this realm. As with war, Tolstoy emphasized how it could function to enable and entrench more violence than ever. By the 1860s, when Americans got around to starting their own American Society for the Prevention of Cruelty to Animals, its founder could explain that "already it is *fashionable to defend the friendless dumb brute*." But that defense prettified enduring and even increased violence, especially since the stigmatization of some outrages to animals coexisted with the skyrocketing of their murder for food. Prince Andrei in *War and Peace*, as part of his speech, captured the hypocrisy brilliantly. Making war more humane, he says, is exactly like "the magnanimity and sensibility of the lady who turns sick at the sight of a slaughtered calf—she is so kind-hearted she cannot see blood—but eats fricasseed veal with a very good appetite."

In 1885, Tolstoy met William Frey, an itinerant mathematician who had served as a soldier in the Russian Empire during the Napoleonic Wars before moving to central Kansas to take part in an ill-fated Russian colony. A vegetarian, Frey had also given up salt entirely. And over a few days of intense conversation, he convinced his new friend that the structure of human teeth and the length of our intestines proved eating meat was unnatural, in case the moral reasons a preacher renowned for nonviolence might have to abstain weren't enough. Tolstoy's daughters and his—initially rather grudging—wife conformed to his new vegetarian diet; a cookbook of their recipes traveled the world.

Unlike many early vegetarians of the era, who were often linked to other kinds of counterculture but saw no connection between diet and war, Tolstoy constantly sustained Prince Andrei's analogy between slaughtering animals and killing men. "As long as there are slaughterhouses there will always be battlefields," he had remarked already the year before his decision to stop eating meat.

When he wrote a preface for an early treatise of vegetarian ethics in 1892, Tolstoy returned to his analogy of animal slaughter and humane war. His visit to the slaughterhouse in Tula, the town near his estate, in order "to see with my own eyes the reality of the question raised when vegetarianism is discussed," called forth—one more time—his denunciation of the sinister dynamic of humane entrenchment. On arrival, Tolstoy remembered, the "disgusting, fetid smell" suffused the area. As he entered the red brick building, he was able to watch as a butcher stabbed an ox into immobility before cutting its throat and beginning to dismember it before its life was gone, even skinning its skull "while it continued to writhe." "All the time this was going on," Tolstoy noted, "the ox kept incessantly twitching its head as if trying to get up." The next victim, a bull, required much more violence even to subdue, for the initial blow went awry.

What interested Tolstoy in this scene was not merely the grisliness of slaughter, an immemorial practice, but the novelty of acting in the name of humanity to make it kinder and moral. He went to Tula, rather than a local shop in the countryside, in order to witness "the new and improved system practiced in large towns, with a view to causing the animals as little suffering as possible." In the great cities of the transatlantic world, slaughter was being centralized and quarantined in new ways, before the vast new zones of death were transplanted far away. Tolstoy's grim expedition revealed, however, that the amelioration of meat production primarily served to help its audiences manage their consciences, telling themselves they were better people while in fact they sponsored as much violence as ever, if not more.

At the end of his visit to the slaughterhouse, Tolstoy revived Prince Andrei's thinking from almost three decades before, almost citing his former character. The aged guru imagined "a kind, refined lady" who "is so sensitive that she is unable, not only herself to inflict suffering on animals, but even to bear the sight of suffering." No wonder that a more humane mode of production—if preferably out of sight—suited her. Yet "she cannot avoid causing suffering to animals—for she eats them." Indeed, thanks to the amelioration of slaughter "she will devour these animals with full assurance that she is doing right."

There is little debate to be had over whether making animal slaughter humane helped raise consciousness over time, to the point of sparking a drive to abolish an atrocious practice altogether. And Tolstoy only glimpsed the early stages of the humanization of meat production. In the case of animals, humanization was clearly a path not to pacification but to much more violence. The slaughterhouse showed how "humanity" worked when its pursuit was entirely unrelated to an abolitionist goal. Did making war humane risk a similar result?

TOLSTOY DIED IN 1910, IN A REMOTE TRAIN STATION IN ASTAPOVO, on a bizarre flight from his home and his long-suffering wife. Ironically, it was within a few weeks of Dunant's own passing. It would soon become clear—if it wasn't already clear during the Russian sage's lifetime—that his worries about Dunant's project were expressed too early. *Hadji Murat*, Tolstoy's posthumous novella recounting the difficulties of maintaining imperial control in the face of Muslim terrorism, could not seem prophetic to Americans for decades. For a long time, his warnings about making war humane were inapplicable as well.

Indeed, the inhumanity of wars would remain and even worsen, even as they broke out too regularly and lasted too long. The fact that killing was nasty and brutish did not make it either infrequent or short. That some wars would become more humane, toward the end of the twentieth century, could never undermine the ethical importance of pushing for even more humanity. Even so, Tolstoy's anxieties about the risks the ideal of humane war poses to an elusive peace still apply.

Tolstoy went too far and, like many prophets, spoke too soon. He had a premonition of a fearful syndrome that had not yet come online. He understood that humanity in warfare, for all its virtues, opened up the possibility of a new vice—facilitating and legitimating war rather than controlling its outbreak or ending its continuation. Humanitarianism led advocates to compromise in pursuit of humane war and publics to feel good enough about themselves in the bargain to permit it to go on and on.

In his great post-Vietnam book *Just and Unjust Wars* (1977), the political theorist Michael Walzer concluded with a respectful critique of the Russian sage. "It is no service to the cause to ridicule the rules of war," he wrote, "as Tolstoy did." Humanizing conflict, Walzer surmised, itself makes possible further resistance to it: ungoverned violence, after all, might leave no one left to criticize it. The "restraint of war" through the humanizing of rules "is the beginning of peace." To which one might say: Sometimes, sometimes not.

In one of the most celebrated scenes in *War and Peace*, Prince Andrei, his back on the ground after being wounded at Austerlitz, becomes enraptured by the sky, which symbolizes justice and tranquility, compared with earthbound carnage and strife. "All is vanity, all falsehood, except that infinite sky," Andrei meditates. Tolstoy died shortly before war began to colonize the heavens, and he could not have imagined our age of drones. But his warning has never been more pertinent than it is now. Today, Tolstoy is being proved right, and Walzer wrong: the humanization of America's wars has become a part of the syndrome of their perpetuation, not a step beyond them.

CHAPTER TWO

Blessed Are the Peacemakers

IN 1891, LEO TOLSTOY READ *LAY DOWN YOUR ARMS*, A NOVEL PROclaiming the need for peace. The book, written by the Austrian noblewoman Bertha von Suttner, had taken America and Europe by storm and made its author the second-most-famous woman in the world. (Queen Victoria was the first.) Suttner would win the Nobel Peace Prize, which she had helped inspire, in 1905. She was the first woman to do so. In the previous two decades, no one had done more to broaden and popularize the transatlantic movement for peace.

Tolstoy didn't think much of Suttner's artistry, he told friends; but the moral importance of her cause led him to write to her with a tribute anyway. The novel was "a happy augury," he enthused. "The abolition of slavery was preceded by the famous book of a woman, Mrs. Beecher Stowe; God grant that the abolition of war may follow upon yours." If they were lucky, Tolstoy hoped, Suttner would raise consciousness of war's evils so that the old law protecting war would crumble and a new one prohibiting it—God's law of love—would take its place.

Forgotten today, Suttner and her fellow peace activists ushered in a new moral order in which politicians at least have to pay lip service to the ideal of peace, even when they wage war. Her flaws and foibles were many. Yet the peacemakers were the true seers of our world today, one in which war is deemed immoral and illegal, with infuriating but narrowing exceptions. And though few could have predicted it during her time, it was Suttner more than anyone who made imaginable a new American-led peace that would guarantee Europeans a paradise beyond the age-old imperial strife that culminated in two gargantuan world wars. Indeed, the goal of institutionalizing peace surged, while the agenda of making war humane dithered in the century after Tolstoy first warned against it.

Tolstoy kept abreast of the burgeoning transatlantic peace movement as it expanded through the era of his ethical preaching, praising its goals and voluminously propagating the message of its members in his much-read writings. Suttner and Tolstoy agreed that peace had to become an expectation and norm before anything else. But they differed about how advocates for peace should proceed. Tolstoy insisted that refusal to serve states alone would do the trick. "For the disappearance of war there is no need of conferences," he warned her. "As long as every man at the age of twenty or twenty-one abjures his religion—not only Christianity but the commandments of Moses ('Thou shalt not kill')—and promises to kill all those whom his superior orders him to kill, even his brothers and parents, so long war will not cease; and it will grow more and more cruel, as it is already becoming in our day." Suttner loved conferences.

Individuals who heard Tolstoy's call across Europe—in books, articles, and letters to sundry correspondents—struck their blow for peace by refusing to serve. Tolstoy himself also championed the pacifism of whole communities such as the Dukhobors, a Christian sect in the Caucasus persecuted by the tsar. (Tolstoy later helped fund the mass exodus of the Dukhobors to Canada.) But his refusal of compromise with states struck many who shared his goals as pointless. If there was any opportunity to make states take war off the table in their dealings with one another, why not seize it? The perfect could not rule out the good. "If the policy of Tolstoy had been followed," some admirers in the American movement put it diplomatically on his death, "we should probably have had no organized peace movements at all, and certainly none of the great results which have been brought about."

With the era of world wars already looming at his death, it wasn't clear that Tolstoy was wrong. The results of coaxing states to the peace table were not great and were about to get much worse. Citing an old peasant saying, Tolstoy told an interviewer that trying to get governments to settle their differences was as futile as trying to catch a bird by sprinkling salt on its tail. He criticized Suttner for taking Nobel's money. When he passed away, she nonetheless praised him as "a high priest" of her cause. Yet her version of their religion involved chasing a lot of birds with salt.

BORN IN 1843 AS BERTHA SOPHIA FELICITA COUNTESS KINSKY VON Chinic und Tettau, Suttner escaped genteel poverty through marriage. Her mother was a commoner, and her father, a Bohemian aristocrat with an ancestor who had been involved in the defenestration of Prague, had died at seventy-five before she was born. It was after she began work as a Viennese governess in the Suttner household that she fell in love with her charges' older brother. The family's disapproval was such that she had to decamp temporarily to Paris—where she fatefully served as the Swedish chemical magnate Alfred Nobel's private secretary—before she became Baroness von Suttner in a clandestine wedding in 1876.

Suttner dedicated herself to writing, both in the couple's first romantic decade together in the Caucasus and from her husband's family's modest castle near Vienna thereafter. No one knows what sparked her investment in the cause, but she decided to write an antiwar novel. Suttner had heard of the fledgling European peace societies in her salons—and succeeded in raising them to a new level of visibility in the novel she dashed off quickly. She later explained that it was mainly a matter of saying the right thing at the right time: "The stroke of lightning is only possible if the air is loaded with electricity." Like Stowe's sentimental fiction, the familial melodrama of the story and the feminine protest against the effects of brutal violence on domestic virtue added a supremely popular new perspective to Christian and male reform alike.

Lay Down Your Arms is the heartrending story of a young Austrian wife. She loses one husband to the Battle of Magenta—an engagement in Lombardy in the Austro-Sardinian War two weeks before the Battle of Solferino, which had led to the Red Cross's founding. Then Suttner's heroine finds domestic bliss with a second mate repeatedly called to Austria's wars, especially its failed wars against Prussia in the course of German unification, culminating in the bloody 1866 Battle of Königgrätz. In Suttner's dramatization of antiwar politics, the dead and wounded were not faceless and faraway. They were the husbands, brothers, and sons of modern women no longer resigned to their losses.

Artlessly didactic in its message, the novel was effective for its hundreds of thousands of readers because it staged a moral awakening through the experiences of its characters. Martha, the narrator and protagonist, long shares the "dark and awful conception which the majority of mankind have of war." Before her enlightenment, however, it was as if the clash of what is "really two masses of men who are rushing to fight each other" were someone else's doing, with responsibility for the butchery "lying beyond the will of individuals."

After a war, there were always recriminations about its consequences. But when it started, the haze of militarism, pride, and virtue obscured the possibility of moral choice—or even awareness that, in the end, you could lose. "The mere mention of a shadow of a doubt" when it comes to war "is in itself unpatriotic," and when Martha casts one in public discussion before her husband marches to his death, she is "ignominiously hissed down." But what is her alternative? When she volunteers for "Patriotic Aid" to minister to Austrian troops, she feels a certain virtue herself. After all, there is no better course than to make the inevitable less disastrous. It makes no more sense to talk of the end of war than of "the abolition of earthquakes."

Remarried to a cerebral and compassionate aristocrat, whom

Suttner modeled on her own husband, Martha is not above snide wit as they live together through the wars to come. On hearing that the cure for depression is "a jolly rattling war" but that "the peace threatens to last as far as we can see," she replied that it is "an extraordinary collocation of words" to equate war with happiness and peace with disturbance.

The couple's most convincing answer to militarism is to insist that progress has meant a new sensibility. When her father says his ardor for killing has never cooled, Martha's husband remarks that he goes to war "not with pleasure, but with resignation." In the father's generation, "the warlike spirit is livelier than in ours," and lacked "the feeling of humanity, which is zealous for the abolition of all misery, and which at this time is extending in ever-wider circles." When the father protests that misery in general can no more be abolished than war in particular, the response comes on behalf of all those who have moved from necessity to possibility:

> In these words you are defining the only point of view (one now much shaken) from which the past used to regard all social evils—i.e., the point of view of resignation—as one looks at what is inevitable . . . But if ever, at the sight of a great evil, the doubtful question has forced itself on one's heart, "Must this be so?" then the heart can no longer remain cold; and, besides pity, a kind of repentance springs up. Not a personal repentance indeed but—how shall I express it?—a *protest from the conscience of the age.*

As a result, and under Martha's tutelage, her husband abandons all investment in war. In an extended analogy with the primitivism of religion, he gives up fealty to "the war god," and resolves that he will "no longer kneel" or even "enter the now desecrated temple," hear "the mighty organ-voice of the cannon," nor inhale "the incense-smoke of the powder."

The true religion was peace among states, not humanity within their wars. "What is the flag of the Red Cross compared with the white standard of peace?" asked Suttner's novel *The Machine Age*, published in 1889, the same year she published her masterpiece. "To heal a fraction of the wounded was possible under the former—but for the victims of a coming war, to make all the impoverished rich again, all the sick healthy, all the dead alive was what the latter symbolizes, by nipping the possibility of the coming war itself in the bud." In *Lay Down Your Arms*, even Martha's once-militaristic father converts to her pacifist cause on his deathbed. Unfortunately, even as she discovers and joins the cause of the "war on war" of the new peace associations of Europe, Martha's second husband perishes in the midst of the Franco-Prussian War in 1870, in spite of his attempt to steer clear of the fracas.

When *Lay Down Your Arms* appeared in 1889, it set fin de siècle Europe and the United States on their ears. After selling more than 200,000 copies in German-speaking lands, more than a million copies circulated in at least sixteen languages elsewhere. Before World War I, no document of Western civilization did more to turn what had been a crackpot and marginal call for an end to endless war into a mainstream cause. But it also helped that the cause itself was transforming, becoming more professional, realistic, and "scientific."

THE MOVEMENT SURGED IN EUROPE DURING THE SLOW BREAKDOWN OF peace between the 1860s and the outbreak of World War I. The reason was the crystallization of a new sensibility that despised exposure to occasional wars in the midst of progress and plenty. The same nations whose populations were learning to demand a European peace, of course, were at the height of an imperialist scramble to parcel out the world among themselves. States faced far less criticism at home when they committed violence on other continents, in perpetual counterinsurgent war to conquer new colonies or in the maintenance of ongoing overseas holdings. Still, the transatlantic expectation of peace among white people and Christians telling themselves they shared a common "civilization" was nothing short of extraordinary. For the first time, the inevitability of war in human affairs was not taken for granted.

Uncoordinated, new peace groups sprang up across the Atlantic, championing hardheaded approaches to the horror of war. Unlike some earlier Christian preachers of nonresistance, most peace advocates conceded the legitimacy of defensive war. Their focus was on devising realistic solutions that would control all the wars that were aggressive in intent, unnecessary for safety, terrible for soldiers, and wasteful of treasure. They were galvanized by an unprecedented burst of women's activism and new strategies of international mobilization. The Interparliamentary Union brought together elected representatives across borders. It, in turn, was dwarfed by the profusion of other nongovernmental organizations, both religious and secular, which the ideal of peace brought into existence like no cause before human rights a century later. After conference upon international conference, by the outbreak of World War I, the groups counted more than a million members.

With Suttner as its most famous propagandist, peace was commonly cast as a feminine agenda. In fact, men led all the peace associations and groups that were not exclusively for women—and the delay in Suttner's Nobel Prize was almost certainly due to the fact that she was a woman. One German militarist dismissed the German Peace Society as "a comical sewing bee composed of sentimental aunts of both sexes," and jibes about "bluestockings," educated women who strove for public and not merely private virtue, were common everywhere.

Suttner herself denied that peace was specifically a women's cause. "There is no reason to expect women *as such* to care about the peace movement," she wrote curtly. When addressing Americans the year she became an international celebrity, she explained: "Although it is self-evident that everything that a woman writes must be written from a woman's standpoint, it does not agree with my principles to treat the problem of peace and war exclusively, or even principally, in its relations to the feelings and lives of women." She added that, even when they did not fight, women were just as likely to glorify war as men. Others, however, were more forthright. The American Jane Addams and the Swede Ellen Key maintained it was not accidental that feminists were disproportionately pacifists and vice versa.

It was in part to counteract the peace movement's nagging reputation for utopianism (and feminism) that making it seem "scientific" became crucial. Advocating political change in modest steps, the movement could hold out credible hope for the future. Alfred Fried, the German peace leader whom Suttner inspired, kept his distance from her hectoring and sentimentalism, insisting that the end of war was not so much a moral demand as an inexorable necessity. The Polish financier Jan Bloch scored an international bestseller by combining prognostication and research in his seven-volume *The Future of War*, popularized in 1899, which claimed that technological change made traditional battles obsolete, and therefore war was not worth fighting. (He specifically predicted that, if fought, war would merely devolve into trench stalemates.)

And a good many peacemongers counted on economic interdependence alongside technology. Frédéric Passy, who shared the first Nobel for peace, was an economist by profession. War was no longer in any nation's economic or geopolitical self-interest, the English 1933 prizewinner Norman Angell claimed in his classic *The Great Illusion* (1909). It was precisely this reality, he contended, that could allow the case for peace to transcend the moral admonition that had failed badly so far. Selling millions of copies on publication and translated into twenty-five languages, Angell's analysis convinced readers that the material conditions for universal harmony were at hand.

The peace movement's proposed tool, legal treaty, looked better than it had in earlier decades, thanks to a fashionable new spate of international lawmaking after 1850 in other areas. Beyond all else, the movement put its weight behind the promotion of schemes to morally cajole or legally compel states to peacefully negotiate their differences so that they would never reach the point of war. The creation of a congress of nations seemed infeasible for the time being. And so it was arbitration that attracted most support among activists, especially Americans, and from governments, in the half century before World War I. Indeed, it was widely believed that a system of arbitration among states would avoid the trouble of setting up a more formal international organization of nations. Calls for disarmament also surged.

A universal system of binding arbitration among states had originally been proposed in the 1840s by an American, William Jay, who was a son of one of the country's founders and first Supreme Court chief justice. The idea was to encourage or force states into a system in which nonpartisan outsiders would adjudicate all or at least some of their differences. American enthusiasts saw it as a federalization of the world that would do for fractious nations what the Constitution had done for their previously fractious states in 1787. To gain traction for a multilateral system across the Atlantic, advocates of arbitration often proposed that individual states could agree to bilateral treaties with partners that called for arbitrating any disputes that arose.

In the late nineteenth century, they were astonishingly successful. They boasted more than 150 actual instances of arbitrated compromise between states, in circumstances that might otherwise have led to armed strife. By the 1890s, there were serious proposals not merely to establish a universal arbitration system but even to found an expert body or full-fledged court that would pacify the globe with the consent of once-warring states. Proposals differed about how compulsory to make the system. There was also disagreement over whether states could reserve the right to go to war, not merely in cases of self-defense but also when "national honor" or "vital interests" were at stake.

CALLS FOR ARBITRATION, LIKE THE ADVOCACY OF PEACE IN ALL ITS forms, were gifted an electrifying opportunity when a bolt from the blue struck at the languorous end of the summer of 1898. The new

Russian tsar, Nicholas II, called for a European peace conference to address the arms race of European powers and to deliberate on conditions and institutions of a durable peace. His premise was "the longings for a general appeasement" that had "become especially pronounced in the consciences of civilized nations" in "the course of the last twenty years." A "real and durable peace" was not only a new condition of popular legitimacy of governments, the tsar explained. It was in their essential interest, too. A conference on the topic would be "by the help of God, a happy presage for the century which is about to open."

It was an utterly shocking development, and not only because of the authoritarian and even reactionary politics of its main advocate. Why the conference had been called provided as much fodder for windy debate as what it could or should achieve. But it was clear that the cause of peace had achieved an unprecedented breakthrough. When he heard of Nicholas's rescript, his third cousin Wilhelm II, the sybaritic Kaiser of the German empire, reportedly exclaimed: "Holy Bertha!" Even a gruff Tolstoy momentarily warmed to the prospect of concord among states, through their own agreement when pressed by their own publics.

The tsar's interest in the conference was political as much as principled. The arms race had brought Russia to the brink of financial ruin, with the Anglo-German naval rivalry rushing toward its climax. But Nicholas's personal interactions with Jan Bloch, with his predictions of the obsolescence of war, also stood behind the tsar's call for a durable peace. Given that Western states had recently and unequivocally refused to sign on to more arbitration or disarmament schemes, the tsar's initiative was a providential surprise, and the peace movement stood to gain an advantage from it.

The European peace movement threw itself into furious preparations to redeem its promises, as the conference site was fixed in The Hague, a palace of the Dutch monarchy. W. T. Stead, the leading British newspaperman of his age, added momentum (or stole it, according to annoyed old hands in the cause). Founding a mass subscription magazine, *War Against War*, to chronicle the event, Stead publicly called for an international "peace crusade." States would have to be pressured to heed the tsar's call to abandon war for good, or at least to halt their frighteningly destructive and ruinously costly military buildups. (When Stead, who also popularized Bloch's thinking in English, died on the *Titanic* in 1912, not the least of the tragedies is that it deprived him of his Nobel Peace Prize, in what was said to be his year to win it.)

The peace movement moved into high gear precisely because the tsar's vision elicited unexpected public enthusiasm. Peace activists gathered hundreds of thousands of signatures (more than a quarter million from Denmark alone) supporting the conference agenda. It was a moment when, to Suttner and so many others, the final peace of which they had dreamed was suddenly there to be grasped in reality—if enlightened statesmen were forced into obeying public opinion.

Suttner's hotel flew a white flag to advertise her presence during the proceedings, and she kept the pressure on, publishing a diary of her activism in the formal sessions and in the wings. Machinations in the lead-up to the conference already showed that humoring Nicholas and placating the eager public were going to be the main agenda. As negotiations continued, it became clear that states (especially Germany) were not about to do more than pay lip service to the cause of peace. Suttner's worst fears were realized when it became evident that no constraints on the freedom to initiate hostilities were in the offing. Scandalously, delegates at the opulent House in the Woods, where the conference was held, moved sanctimoniously to Plan B: an agreement concluded with effusive pageantry and showy moralism to regulate how war is fought. Like Suttner, Tolstoy returned from his credulous stance to one of knowing skepticism. Always willing to castigate the immoral from his mountaintop, he inveighed against all "hypocritical institutions, whose purpose is not the attainment of peace, but, on the contrary, the concealment from men of that one means for attaining universal peace"—namely, his own ethics of nonresistance. Once so promising, the proceedings at The Hague were no more than a dodge.

True, there was one breakthrough: the creation of a corps of judges called the Permanent Court of Arbitration, which still exists to this day. And the possibility was left open that future conferences might obligate states to submit themselves to that court's arbitration on a compulsory basis. Yet it was now clear that the dream of peace would have to be realized another day and rely on a different embodiment. Unfortunately, the successor conference, which took place in 1907, also ended with little to show for itself other than more rules for humane war, and with dreams for a more powerful arbitration court dashed. Suttner, refusing to be defeated, took a long view. A decade after the first conference in The Hague, she called it "an epoch-making date in the history of the world." It marked "the first time, since history began to be written, that the representatives of governments come together to find a means for 'securing a permanent, genuine peace' for the world."

SUTTNER DIED IN SUMMER 1914, MERE DAYS BEFORE THE ASSASSINAtion of the heir to the Habsburg throne touched off World War I. On her passing, the editorialists of *The Nation* in New York City recalled Suttner's novel *Lay Down Your Arms* as the most transformational call for peace the world had ever seen. "No other brief for peace has won so many converts or exercised so great an influence on all quarters of the globe."

A minority of Americans were sure that their country was essential to Suttner's cause of bringing peace. "Law, the first daughter of the voice of God, asserts herself as civilization advances and will be heard," insisted a group of U.S. peace activists advocating arbitration who met every year at the beautiful Lake Mohonk in New York State, where their leaders owned a hotel that still draws visitors. And Suttner frequently returned the favor. "I wish to dwell for a moment on the subject of America," she had remarked on the receipt of her Nobel Peace Prize for 1905, to an overflowing crowd in the Hals Brothers Concert Hall in Oslo in April 1906. "This land of limitless opportunities is marked by its ability to carry out new and daring plans of enormous imagination and scope, while often using the simplest methods. In other words, it is a nation idealistic in its concepts and practical in its execution of them. We feel that the modern peace movement has every chance in America of attracting strong support and of finding a clear formula for the implementation of its aims."

She had visited the United States twice, in 1904 and 1912. The first time she came for the international peace conference that year and met with President Theodore Roosevelt. He owed his reputation to leading the Rough Riders in the Battle of San Juan Hill in Cuba in 1898, and thus for leading the United States into an imperial era. After extracting Roosevelt's promise to advance the arbitration movement, Suttner traveled as far as Cincinnati.

On her next trip, Suttner traveled to San Francisco at the invitation of women's activists. Omitting the annexation of Hawaii and the incorporation of the formerly Spanish Philippines, Suttner once again held out the United States as iconic. "America's glory and grandeur," she recorded, "consisted in having attained such proportions without a standing army, safe without defense, giving the world an example of peace." Celebrating the enfranchisement of Californian women the year before her visit to San Francisco, Suttner cast it as one more sign that America would "lead the lion of European militarism and the bleeding lamb of the people to a resting place."

The trouble was, for a long time it had been difficult to imagine the prospect of the United States playing the role of peacemaker. It may have been the state most identified with peace, but that was only because of its *refusal* to traffic in war outside its hemisphere. Yet there was no denying that by 1914, in spite of its Civil War and resulting late start, America boasted perhaps the richest peace culture of any transatlantic state. In addition to commonalities with Western Europe, the country's peace culture relied on two distinctive resources. The nation's unreconstructed Christianity and geographical isolation meant that Americans—especially in the agrarian Midwest—could make up for their lack of exposure to the bloodbaths of European war with a fervency for the cause of peace that Europeans could not always match.

The 1823 "doctrine" of the fifth U.S. president, James Monroe, forbidding new European colonization in the Western hemisphere was unclear enough to allow for warring interpretations throughout the nineteenth century. William Seward, secretary of state at the time of the Geneva Convention, even believed Monroe's framework ruled out U.S. ratification of the treaty for humane treatment of wounded soldiers. The Civil War nurse and philanthropist Clara Barton, who learned of the Red Cross in 1869 on a health cure in Europe, where she witnessed the carnage of the Franco-Prussian War, came home and faced resistance in coaxing her country on board. Seward's son Frederick, serving as assistant secretary of state, "regarded it as a settled thing" when Barton approached him in 1877. After five years of her agitation and under a new administration, Secretary of State James Blaine decided that "the Monroe Doctrine was not made to ward off humanity," and the United States became the last "civilized power" to join the treaty in 1882.

At the turn of the century, however, that same doctrine was still taken to mark limits to America's ability to enter binding international peace agreements. At The Hague, in 1899, the U.S. representative Andrew Dickson White organized a field trip to nearby Delft on July 4 to lay a wreath of silver and gold on the tomb of the seventeenth-century philosopher Hugo Grotius. The act was meant to symbolize the coincidence of America's role in the world with the aims of the tradition of international law that the early modern thinker had supposedly founded. But when it came to the conference's arbitration treaty, Europeans agreed that the United States *lacked* any global obligations. Nothing so far interfered with whatever action America deemed necessary in its hemispheric security zone, or required U.S. involvement in European affairs.

Indeed, as America's empire expanded across the Pacific starting in 1898, the country stubbornly refused any version of arbitration that placed any check on its freedom to stay out of European war. Arbitration was a good thing for European states, given their usual internecine violence. But Americans drew up short if arbitration meant they might get drawn into wars, especially ones pitting European warmongers against one another. In 1897, the U.S. secretary of state Richard Olney negotiated a treaty calling for submission of any disputes with the United Kingdom to binding arbitration. It was a sign of a growing relationship between the "mother country" and its once-rebellious child and was welcomed initially as "one of the greatest events of modern history." The Senate voted it down.

American elites still pursued the broader project of making such treaties in the aftermath of this bitter experience. The Republican secretary of state and later New York senator Elihu Root was a fanatic for arbitration in order to keep the United States out of European wars. (He did not believe the concept should apply to the colonial pacification of his country's new Philippines holdings.) Root even won the Nobel Peace Prize in 1912 for arbitration work. U.S. interest in international law exploded, with professional associations formed and new journals founded. For fifteen years, Root presided over an endowment for international peace funded by the steel magnate Andrew Carnegie, which touted the uses of international law. The new breed of practitioners in the field, operating in harmony with the new American empire, considered arbitration an important mission—but even they generally wanted its fulfillment to leave the United States free of hard new commitments.

In spite—or as a reflection—of America's traditions of keeping distance from European wars, an extraordinary flourishing of peace activism and sentiment occurred. Peace was a mainstream idea for Americans, who could not imagine themselves disrupting it (at least outside their own hemisphere). It sank into many sectors of national life, from Christians to feminists and from lawyers to workingmen. Carnegie, inspired by his Scottish uncle's devotion to the issue, became a "great apostle of arbitration and peace," as American activists exultantly put it when he came out for the cause in 1904. Alongside his American peace projects, Carnegie gave the enormous sum of $1.5 million—$50 million today—to build a peace palace in The Hague, which opened ten years later and still hosts the Permanent Court of Arbitration as well as other internationalist enterprises. He even offered Suttner a pension to the end of her days.

U.S. politicians were more authentic and more outspoken in pressing the peace agenda than politicians elsewhere. In between his second failed presidential campaign in 1900 and his third failed attempt in 1908, the peace advocate and Democratic Party politician William Jennings Bryan took the time to visit Tolstoy on his Russian estate. He became a Tolstoy nut, hanging a picture of the Russian sage in his home and proselytizing his message. Bryan didn't stave off U.S. entry into World War I (in spite of trying). But from the earliest days of his stint as President Woodrow Wilson's secretary of state in 1913–15, he concluded no fewer than thirty arbitration treaties between the United States and other countries, including the United Kingdom. As the Senate ratified treaty after treaty, Bryan distributed as souvenirs paperweights that had been created from War Department swords beaten into plowshares, inscribed with biblical peace promises. Notwithstanding the tsar's good press for calling the peace conference in The Hague, no comparable politician ever emerged from Europe nor ascended so high.

A YOUNG AMERICAN NAMED QUINCY WRIGHT WAS DETERMINED TO BE part of the American peace right away. A bespectacled political scientist with black hair parted in the center, Wright had a vision. When it came to him in 1917 as his country entered World War I, it inspired his lifetime task, which he never relinquished. From his decades-long perch at the University of Chicago, he picked up Suttner's baton and attended a lot of conferences, too. He was the Zelig of American internationalists between World War I and the Vietnam War. Involved in every major debate, he would witness the making of a Pax Americana—though it may not have been the peace of which Suttner dreamed.

Born in 1890 in Medford, Massachusetts, Wright grew up in Illinois. His father, Philip Green Wright, was a grandchild of the famed New England abolitionist and father of American life insurance, Elizur Wright. Philip Green Wright taught economics at Lombard College (now defunct) in Galesburg, Illinois, and his son Quincy grew up in a house steps from the college, where Philip and his wife, Elizabeth, received students in their prairie salon. The poet Carl Sandburg, a Galesburg native who returned to study at Lombard after joining the army during the Spanish-American War, was formed there. Philip Wright "was at home in either the hard-as-nails utilitarian fields or in the realm of the ethereal and insoluble," Sandburg recalled later. Sandburg was "frequently around our house," Quincy remembered. While they "discoursed on such subjects as economic reform and socialism," the younger Wright helped the poet put out early works using the printing press his father kept in the basement, a memento of an earlier career.

Quincy went to Lombard, too, and then earned a doctorate at the University of Illinois. After a brief spell in naval intelligence, he became the University of Chicago's authority on international law and one of its leading scholars. When he had his vision, his father had since moved from Galesburg for a brief stint in the Harvard economics department, then joined what would become the Brookings Institution. A few weeks after the United States entered World War I in summer 1917, Philip Wright sent his son a speech by Senator J. Hamilton Lewis of Illinois predicting that the war would force America to enter a "United States of World Government." It was "exactly the thing called for," Quincy wrote back.

Was it not realistic, he explained to his father, to do the same for the world—pushing it from loose confederation to strong federation—that the Constitution had done for the American states in 1787? An organization of polities under law was "the scheme of things which international law writers have thought, (not realized) for the past three hundred years," and the world was "very much nearer that desideratum than appearances would lead one to believe." In response, Philip Wright (who dabbled in verse when not studying sugar and tariffs) cited Alfred Lord Tennyson's memorable poem "Locksley Hall," which promised a day when "the war-drum throbb'd no longer." With "the battle-flags . . . furl'd," a "Parliament of man, the Federation of the world" would arise. Still, it was a prospect that hardly seemed imminent—and Philip worried whether the legalistic reform of which his son was so enamored would ever bring it about, especially given the grim news of Black people massacred by white mobs in East St. Louis and socialists protesting war beaten in the street in Boston.

The objection that "technical discussions on questions of the law of war, seem wholly futile when we hope to abolish war," Quincy acknowledged, struck him powerfully. (Nor was it novel. He and his new wife, Louise, were reading Tolstoy together that very summer, he explained.) Moreover, it would be wrong to proceed with small steps without keeping the ultimate goal of final peace in mind at the same time. But his father made a gross error in thinking that peace was utopian. "There is no problem so small that its solution in the better way is not worthwhile." War was the problem from hell. But it could be solved.

For every skeptic who said that the mounting political hostilities that had climaxed in World War I proved definitively that peace was beyond reach, there were droves of survivors of the horror who demanded that statesmen never loose such a blood-dimmed tide again. Certainly, in the summer of 1914 it had not seemed that pressure for peace would result from the war. Europeans on all sides were fervent for victory, a gory one if necessary. In spite of a generation of peace activism, patriotism surged in Europe to the point of swamping opposition. Even socialists who claimed to represent workingmen across borders and who had regularly stood for peace in international affairs in various crises ended up embracing the war when it came. Almost as floridly, the leaders and members of peace movements sided nearly unanimously with their respective countries' decision to go to war in August 1914. Even in the United States, the die was cast when some progressives and socialists took Wilson's rationale for one last war seriously in 1916–17, although Wilson soon engaged in a ferocious crackdown on dissent as the intervention began.

Perverse as it may seem to say so, World War I was also "the great war for peace." The death of ten million soldiers and forty million civilians, at a price tag of $200 billion (more than $3 trillion by today's reckoning), made the old warnings of the peace movement about the stakes of conflict seem both justified and prescient—once war fever passed. Over the course of its terrible four years of death, what had been a marginal agenda became central to national life everywhere and global diplomacy forever, beyond the wildest dreams of earlier generations of activists.

Ironically, in other words, the very failure of the peace movement to stave off World War I created the conditions for its eventual success. Many more European survivors of war, especially the victims of its worst depredations, were now ready to demand peace from their states. The overthrow of the Russian Empire and the birth of the Soviet Union portended a new equation. America's entry into the war in 1917 in the name of what Wilson gravely called "peace without victory" did so even more.

Even during the war, peace agitation occurred. Forlorn socialists of every nation, in the minority within their own movement, indicted the patriotic response to the call to arms—and were normally thrown in jail for their trouble, from Eugene Debs in the United States to Rosa Luxemburg in Germany. As in no war before, war resistance became rife across the Atlantic, far transcending minor religious sects and calling down the repressive tactics of states newly empowered by war itself. Women were once again frequent leaders. The founding of what became the Women's International League for Peace and Freedom, with its own conference in The Hague in 1915, epitomized the leading women's role in groups of all descriptions.

In her classic *War, Peace, and the Future* (1916), Ellen Key, the Swedish feminist, insisted that the cries of so many sons in their battlefield death throes—"Mother! Mother!"—showed that the time had come for women to wean the world from male nationalism. "When before has an educated man asked a woman how in her opinion war can be prevented," asked Virginia Woolf rhetorically of the novelty that women had entered politics not merely as voters but as peace activists to be taken seriously. (Woolf conceded by 1938, in her acidly pacifist *Three Guineas*, that women would have to do a lot more than they once thought to change the world.)

As a result, after World War I the peace activism of both mainstream elites and ordinary people exceeded in intensity and scale anything seen before. The seed planted by prewar activists blossomed from scorched earth, their ragtag idealism making mass movements possible, forcing the hands of statesmen—or at least loosening their lips to pretend allegiance to peace. F. Scott Fitzgerald, in his first novel, *This Side of Paradise* (1920), captured how many read "a great smattering of Tolstoy" and combined it with "intense longing for a cause," which drove them "to preach peace as a subjective ideal." The success of antiwar literature left far behind Suttner's one-hit wonder and altered the artistic canon. If anything, it has become easy to overstate how universal revulsion toward war became. The devastating skepticism of the English war poets Wilfred Owen and Siegfried Sassoon or the post-traumatic therapy A. A. Milne offered for his son in the stories of Winnie-the-Pooh hardly ruled out the German officer Ernst Jünger's passionate glorification of the trench experience.

Not that German-speakers had a monopoly on hypermilitarism. As Käthe Kollwitz's poignant woodcut representations of the costs of a culture of violence showed, their antiwar activism was sometimes the most authentic and moving. Erich Maria Remarque's later smash hit *All Quiet on the Western Front* (1929) unforgettably dramatized the human costs of World War I and cemented the case against militarism, though it by no means silenced clamor for another conflict. Milne's own pacifist bestseller *Peace with Honour* (1934) didn't either—

especially since Milne, like so many other pacifists, was ultimately to support war to put Adolf Hitler down. But like never before and to this day, cycles of cynicism and weariness toward international war became familiar features of the moral culture of elites.

Before debates about how much to "appease" Hitler set in in the 1930s, the peace movement had altered the conditions of legitimacy that governed states' relations to their own people—at least when it came to European wars that could hurt them the most. Supporters of European harmony were much less sure that they opposed the constant violence of empires, except if geopolitical jockeying threatened to engulf Europeans themselves in war. Indeed, some openly urged "white peace" for the sake of a more harmonious global rule over non-European populations. But a transatlantic ascendancy of peace was better than nothing.

With their distinctive peace culture, Americans kept pace with the activism of Europeans who threw themselves into the cause of peace after bearing the brunt of its implosion in World War I. A motley crew of liberals and socialists, and noninterventionists in both major American political parties, had delayed the country's entry into World War I. In spite of President Wilson's decision to persecute them viciously thereafter, most critics of interventionism regrouped. By 1933, as old outfits swelled and new ones formed, Americans could boast twelve million adherents to the peace movement and an annual combined budget of more than $1 million (more than $20 million today).

The old Tolstoyan Jane Addams, cofounder of the Women's International League and speaker at its first conference, and later second woman (after Suttner) to win the Nobel Peace Prize, continued her activism. The indefatigable and well-known feminist pacifist Lucia Ames Mead, a former piano teacher, had gotten her start before World War I with Suttner's endorsement. She kept the presses rolling long after, insisting that if Americans had banned "man-selling" in law in the nineteenth century, it was going to be the turn of "man-killing" in the twentieth. (She was crushed to death in the Boston subway in 1936, saving her from seeing the short-term routing and long-term consecration of her work to come.)

Outright pacifists remained inveterate in their cause but were dwarfed by those willing to minimize the chance of war at the price of compromise with states. In old and new media—with the best-selling compilation of photographs *The Horror of It* (1932) reminding audiences of World War I's depredations, Hollywood making a movie of Remarque's novel within a year, and World Peaceways taking to the radio waves—peace propaganda washed over the public. It was an extraordinary mobilization never to be repeated, except in the Vietnam years. The midwestern Christian socialist-turned-pacifist Norman Thomas took over the Socialist Party of America after its founder Eugene Debs died, and he began his six runs for president in 1928. Through the 1930s, Thomas agitated against the coming of another world war as fiercely as he had opposed the first as a conscientious objector. Joining this nationally famous rebel in the Keep America Out of War Congress in 1938 was Jeanette Rankin, the Montana congresswoman (still the only one in history) who had voted with forty-nine others against U.S. entry into World War I. Three years later, she would cast the sole vote against war after Pearl Harbor.

THE THORNY QUESTION WAS HOW TO FINALLY REALIZE SUTTNER'S dream of peace in the aftermath of war. It was here that Wright, a legal expert, could play a discreet but decisive role as her American heir and successor among lawyers.

For Wright, the glass was half full from the outset. It was a coup for peace movements that, after World War I, the idea of international law came to be identified with their once-lonely ideal, through the rhetorical feints of politicians and states under pressure from mobilized publics with new expectations. Peace had never been the purpose of international law before, even for its promoters. Making war humane had been attractive among buttoned-up lawyers because it seemed more feasible than peace—and for the same reason did not risk the reputations of professionals nervous to transgress the mainstream. After the massacres of World War I, however, humane war lost its relative importance as once-radical hopes for peace became mainstream themselves. "The fundamental problem of our time," intoned one who explained that pacifism had become the very purpose of his field, "is to civilize and demilitarize the state, so that men can become free, and true masters of their destiny."

Though progressive to his core, Wright was not a starry-eyed idealist, nor a naïve legalist who thought passing a new law would change the world. "The law is a term to conjure with as is the flag, the church or the home," he explained to one correspondent, merely a tool for "the effective propagandizing of particular beliefs" which have "no objective validity other than the fact that they are believed in." This didn't make it less useful, but more so. "Many people will approve of a decision rationalized in legal terminology simply because it represents that holy symbol, the law," Wright insisted. For that very reason, part of the internationalist's agenda was to canonize a new and superior arrangement of power in the world in a legal scheme, one shaped by enlightened public opinion, and shaping it.

One reform plan quick to take shape during World War I was to hold legally accountable despots and madmen who disturbed the peace. Already in 1918, calls were rife to try the German Kaiser for initiating the conflict—but not for the numerous war crimes of his forces in the field, starting with their atrocities in Belgium on the way to the trenches. One of Wright's first publications explained how it ought to be plausible under international law to hold Wilhelm II accountable for his biggest crime, which was starting a war, with all the catastrophes to which that decision led.

Most of the early public uses of the phrase "crimes against humanity," now associated with grave atrocities during war, allocated responsibility for war itself. They came from the British prime minister David Lloyd George and other *entente* politicians who intended to target the German leader (if not because war itself was illegal, then because of his violation of Belgian neutrality, guaranteed by treaty).

As the war closed, Lloyd George reacted to what he called "a growing feeling that war itself was a crime against humanity." "The war was a hideous, abominable crime," he thundered at one point, "a crime which has sent millions of the best young men of Europe to death and mutilation . . . The men responsible for this outrage on the human race must not be let off because their heads were crowned when they perpetrated the deeds." Similar cries of the Canadian prime minister and Italian president for postwar justice indicates how popular it was in 1918–19 to call war itself, rather than its attendant cruelties, a "crime against humanity." (The Kaiser fled to the Netherlands, which refused to extradite the queen's "Uncle Willy.")

As this rhetoric indicated, the war on war that peace advocates had initiated now became the premier goal of international affairs. More constructive were new institutions that would preserve the peace to which World War I finally led. The very first of the preambular purposes of the League of Nations Covenant worked out at the Versailles Peace Conference in 1919 marked "the acceptance of obligations not to resort to war." This first bid at international organization bound signatories "to respect and preserve as against external aggression the territorial integrity and existing political independence" of member states.

This high verbiage was easily the biggest diplomatic success the cause of peace had ever enjoyed in world history. But it masked a harsh truth—states still had considerable latitude to resort to force. And famously, the United States remained outside the League after the Senate failed to approve the Versailles treaty. For the Americans and others who supported binding legal arbitration and the pacific settlement of disputes, the war ended with their dreams not realized but smashed. Even within the League, the primary solution was to give each nation its own power to keep the peace rather than transfer authority or power to any international organization to do so. Nine new "nation-states" were created in Eastern Europe where three now-defunct empires had once ruled, with the hopeful assumption that contention would be replaced by harmony. But advocates of systemic peace were not giving up.

Another popular idea was disarming states. If they retained carte blanche to conduct war, reducing their weaponry would at least make the consequences less cataclysmic. This was not the same as ruling out certain kinds of weapons because they caused excess suffering to soldiers, as advocates of humane war had long argued. Instead, disarmament would place limits on otherwise legal weapons, or even reduce them, a proposal that was especially attractive to states that could not or did not want to spend on arms races—not least frightening naval buildups. The idea had failed before World War I, but Wright immediately volunteered to think through how disarmament would work now. Its promise continued for a decade—for some, to this day—but in spite of fervent advocates such as Albert Einstein, it failed again, most climactically at the General Disarmament Conference that dithered for two years after opening with high hopes in 1932.

Even before then, a system of prohibiting war under international law remained the real chance Wright and others saw to improve on the League of Nations Covenant, in effect by strengthening the terms of the pact and undoing America's calamitous withdrawal. This goal was earnestly pursued by internationalists who inherited it from the prewar peace movements and the early transactions of states going through the motions. Arbitration remained a popular means to this end. But its credibility was dealt a grievous blow when the Geneva Protocol of 1924, which proposed to make it compulsory for all states, failed to win British acceptance.

Wright was a fan of international arbitration, and he would spend the rest of his career looking for a functional equivalent to it. Before the frost of the late 1930s overtook them, however, various flowers had sprouted from its grave. Outside the League, in an instrument negotiated among Europeans at the Swiss lake town of Locarno in 1925, Germany's border with its western neighbors was set, with Britain promising to guarantee it against alteration or incursion by either side. The agreement was the high point of optimism for European peace. It left much undone, including arms reduction and the status of Germany's eastern borders. And even at this bright moment, the continuation of the sorts of alliance blocs that had brought about World War I threatened disputes, and so were a bad omen of a darker future.

Most significant, leading powers replaced arbitration with a system of collective security under international law that allowed for identifying aggressors and policing them for the sake of peace—what the United Nations does, in theory, to this very day. This functional replacement for arbitration rose through a brilliant exercise in rebranding known as the "outlawry of war" proposal. It resurrected a binding scheme for peace among states from its grave but made it political rather than judicial. It worked by proposing to federate states in a League powerful enough to deal with rowdy members when they arose. A jury of the states themselves, rather than independent judges, would pass a verdict on warmongers and stop them.

Not only would this outlawry plan require the United States to step up, but also it would demand the abandonment of the idea that a state could be neutral toward aggression elsewhere. Either the world got together to keep the peace, combining forces against aggressive states that interrupted it, or war would continue forever. "Voluntary methods are doubtless most important in preserving domestic peace, nevertheless, states also use coercive methods," Wright explained in 1925. The only solution was to establish enough governance internationally to define wrongdoing and police it—just as states did at home.

Audaciously, Wright started his intellectual activism with a bow toward the outlawry project's new popularity: he insisted that war was already illegal quite apart from the new attempt to suppress it once and for all. The idea that states still had a legal right to use force beyond their borders, including the settlement of disputes, was already old-fashioned, he boldly suggested in 1924. "There has apparently been a tendency," he explained, "to assume" that "war is lawful," merely because states accepted some rules applying once war broke out. But that didn't follow. You might need a new law to save victims from an already unlawful practice. All that was required now, really, was to make more explicit and formal what most lawyers already believed, and legally institutionalize a system for policing those states that broke the prohibition of illegal force. The rules themselves would have to allow for self-defense, as in domestic criminal law. But once again that very analogy showed that preventing war was possible. It was just a matter of deciding what could count under law, what would not, who would decide, and who could become the globe's constable.

The hard part would be to get states—starting with Wright's—to agree to a system of policing to check aggressors. "King Canute did not increase his prestige by commanding the tide to recede," Wright conceded, referring to the medieval Danish king renowned for trying to do just that, "and international law will not gain in authority by commanding wars to cease if they do not cease." Even before the Geneva Protocol arbitration project went south, Wright knew it was going to be hard to federalize power to back up words. But there was no alternative, since "the hopelessness of outlawing war by treaties alone becomes evident when we consider that a large proportion of war has been begun contrary to the terms of some treaty of 'perpetual peace and amity.'"

The most famed of the peacemongers' efforts was the Kellogg-Briand Pact of 1928. Named after Frank Kellogg and Aristide Briand, respectively the American secretary of state and the French prime minister who proposed it, the treaty was negotiated quickly, in the mid-1920s era of good feeling on the European scene following Locarno. "The High Contracting Parties solemnly declare," states its first article, "that they condemn recourse to war for the solution of international controversies, and renounce it, as an instrument of national policy in their relations with one another." But there was no enforcement provision: the treaty contemplated the pacific resolution of disputes, though to do so was like saying eating too much food is illegal, then gesturing to the fact that people will need to figure out how to stick to their diets.

To placate public opinion demanding no recurrence of World War I, states scrambled to affirm in the name of eternal peace approximately the same obligations they had accepted at The Hague decades before in the form of voluntary arbitration. As one astute observer insisted, the Kellogg-Briand Pact "does not outlaw war but approves it," for anyone who had eyes to see, for states conditioned their acceptance of the treaty on exceptions, far beyond the claim to self-defense that still permits force today. Wright and others who saw beyond the hype understood that the treaty's true meaning was not the immediate victory of peace. Instead, it anticipated the paramount responsibility of the United States in advancing that cause. "The historical significance of this treaty, if it can still be said ever to have possessed any," one wise observer of the situation remarked, "resided exclusively in the association of the United States in the campaign for the maintenance of peace."

Capitalizing on its victory at The Hague a generation before, the United States insisted that nothing done pursuant to the Monroe Doctrine could in principle qualify as a violation. Kellogg told the Senate that the treaty did not forbid self-defense, which extended to "any interests or rights the United States may have." In response to the United States conditioning its signature on its birthright of hemispheric intervention, Argentina, Bolivia, Brazil, and El Salvador all refused to sign. The British foreign secretary, Austen Chamberlain, was not to be outdone in brazenly reducing the treaty to meaninglessness. He had won the Nobel Peace Prize only three years before for negotiating the Locarno treaty (his more notorious half brother, Neville, would serve as appeasement prime minister in the next decade). Now Chamberlain reserved his nation's right not simply to defend itself but also to deploy armed force in "self-defense" wherever the British Empire's interests were at stake—which is to say, anywhere.

How did the solemn renunciation of war succeed in garnering

the assent of the United States—including the notoriously skittish Senate—where arbitration had failed? The success was due principally to the fact that the Kellogg-Briand Pact left open the room for maneuver that advocates of a compulsory form of arbitration were trying to close. By the 1920s, Americans who had refused to join the League itself were willing to join in hallowing European peace rhetorically. The outlawry of war became completely mainstream for Americans. It was endorsed by Calvin Coolidge in accepting the Republican Party nomination for 1924 and figured in the Democratic Party platform the same year.

William Borah, a Republican senator from Idaho who offended some by wearing a ten-gallon hat around Washington, D.C., had been one of the "Irreconcilables" at the end of World War I, keeping the country from joining the League of Nations. He became a "crusader" for the outlawry of war five years later without missing a beat—even before the Kellogg-Briand Pact—and he saw no contradiction in doing so. The League peace had committed the United States to something far worse than a defensive pact with any particular ally. It entangled his country in obligations to an international organization, potentially to keep global peace. As Borah saw it, the Kellogg-Briand Pact, by contrast, merely involved the obligation to abstain from war. No wonder that Borah loved outlawry, understood in these terms. At best, Kellogg-Briand could keep Europeans from descending into their own strife; at worst, it made no more difficult America's project of keeping itself from being sucked into it again at all costs.

Wright knew the hard part was going to be inciting Americans to interpret the commitment they had now made in his way rather than Borah's. When an aggressor rose anywhere, Wright wrote, it violated the rights of *the United States* under treaty no matter what the country chose to do about it. No uninvolved bystander anymore, America was an injured party. "Wars of aggression," Wright explained in 1930, "are no longer moral offenses against the victim alone, but legal offenses against every state party to these multilateral treaties." The only question remaining in the face of bad behavior by another was: "What will the United States do about it?"

THIS WAS NO MERELY HYPOTHETICAL QUESTION, FOR HITLER ROSE TO power in Germany three years later.

Even before, Wright had cause for encouragement when the Republican Henry Stimson, a Wall Street lawyer and Herbert Hoover's secretary of state, responded to Japanese "aggression" in invading Manchuria in 1931 by saying the United States would not recognize this brazen act of colonialism as lawful. Stimson's announcement, Wright celebrated, "is likely to go down in history as of greater significance in the development of international law" than any other "of recent or even more distant years." International law had once "converted violence into legality, robbery into title, might into right." The idea that it would consecrate peace instead was not new in content but had suddenly moved from books into practice. Of course, this didn't solve the real problem. Somebody would have to boot Japan out rather than deem its annexation illegal alone. That the United States now withheld recognition from the fruits of someone else's war hardly meant it was committing to keep the peace.

Wright knew, of course, that reinterpreting words was not the same as inciting deeds. The question remained: Would the United States step up to guarantee eternal peace after its missed opportunity when World War I ended? Already the greatest world power, would it not have to accept the risk (however hypothetical and unlikely) of seeing its own wars condemned as illegal? Either way, wouldn't the United States also have to help put down any newly recognized aggression—or even lead the way in doing so? "The collective system for preserving peace, which has developed in spite of the initial abstention of the United States," Wright noted in 1933, "has received rude blows during the past year and its fate may in a large measure depend on the attitude of the United States."

Skeptics, like the elderly then-dean of American international lawyers, John Bassett Moore, felt it was not a good idea for their country to renounce its birthright in exchange for the pottage of endless war to keep other countries from fighting one another. The low dishonest decade of the 1930s convinced most Americans that, with Europeans at one another's throats again, Wilsonianism had been catastrophic and global entanglements were not a dream but a ruse. Wright replied that the world had changed, as ultimate American entry in World War I already proved. Why not arrest the coming of faraway unwanted conflict early rather than get swept in again? "If it is practically certain that we will become involved in any war between great powers which lasts for a considerable length of time, whatever we do," he observed in 1935, "then a policy of co-operation to prevent war could add little to the risk."

Unfortunately for an internationalist vision of peace, not many Americans were buying it. Suttner, dead twenty years, had left a bequest in the form of a new ideal but without any guarantee of its realization. Now the next terrible blow to that dream—World War II—was on the way. Had Suttner lived in vain? Had Wright wasted his time? War remained endemic, or even worsening, its brutality increasing along with its frequency. It was hard to take seriously Tolstoy's warning that making warfare humane could postpone peace—yet.

CHAPTER THREE

Laws of Inhumanity

IT WAS AN OUTRAGE. WHEN BERTHA VON SUTTNER LEARNED THAT HENRY Dunant might win the first Nobel Peace Prize for the year 1901, she sprang into action. Why was the founder of the International Red Cross even being considered? "In Nobel's will there is not one syllable about 'humanitarian' things," Suttner wrote to her friend Alfred Fried, a fellow Viennese who had decamped to Germany to run the most important pacifist newspaper of the era, and who would himself earn the Nobel in 1911.

Suttner was in a position to know. Years before, she had worked briefly for Albert Nobel, the Swedish chemist and magnate who had invented dynamite, and she had also advised him on what purposes his vast wealth could serve after his death. "Instead of aid for current misery," the prize "demands and supports abolition of future conditions of misery," she insisted. If the very first prize recognized a "welfare tendency" when it came to war rather than honoring those who planned its extinction, the message would be disastrous. "I would regard it as a misfortune for the cause (even though I would not begrudge the old man)," Suttner explained, "if a Red Cross man, that is a war humanizer, were to be called the most deserving element in the peace cause."

Dunant won anyway. He was chosen along with the Frenchman Frédéric Passy, a onetime schoolteacher who had founded a

French pacifist league and was the foremost (male) European peace activist. The joint awards gave the impression of some indecision on the Nobel committee about the compatibility of the campaign to end war and the desire to make it more humane. Suttner, a close associate of Passy's, liked to cite his dictum on that question: "You do not humanize carnage—you condemn it because you are in the process of becoming more humane."

Once Dunant was chosen, Suttner turned to damage control—attempting to promote Dunant as a peace activist while downplaying his contributions to the campaign to humanize warfare. Suttner and Dunant had been in correspondence for five years, ever since Dunant reemerged and was made iconic for his role in the Geneva Convention three decades earlier. When she first wrote to him, Suttner confessed she had assumed he was dead. Now that he had won, it was time for image management.

In fact, Dunant had explicitly observed in his epoch-making memoir of the Battle of Solferino that the project of making war humane was based on the assumption that there was no way to end it. "Men continue to kill each other," he had written in 1862, and one must "renounce" the hope for eternal peace. Suttner explained to him that she saw things differently: humane war, with its international conventions, could, as certain Red Cross affiliates had privately hoped, prove "a step along the path toward a possible convention *not* to wage war." That concession hardly minimized the risk in Dunant's victory. Suttner implored Dunant: "Give me a few lines, please, in which you prove that you are a bearer of the white flag"—not merely someone who "humanizes war" but "one of those who (after war has been humanized) wants to abolish war."

Advocates of peace like Suttner worried from time to time that humanizing warfare would rule out its elimination. And the sniping back and forth between proponents of the two goals was far more open and vivid before World War II than in any era since. The truth was, though, that the peace movement need not have worried, since for all its failures the cause of making war more humane was faring worse. Humane war did not get off the ground, so it could not yet threaten peace. States began to engage in more international law-making after Dunant's Geneva Convention, but they took advantage of Geneva's reputation to push forward protections that were compatible with almost any form of military force. Far more gallingly, the protections did not even apply to the most atrocious forms of combat—colonial and counterinsurgent warfare, especially against racialized foes. And in World War I and long after, what rules did apply were almost universally ignored.

Like Leo Tolstoy's, Suttner's anxieties that the idea of humane war would entrench war itself were creditable—but they had been expressed far too early to apply. The laws of war were not humane. In fact, the essentially limitless war they allowed reveals that it is only the partial humanization of conflict in our own time, with new rules propounded and new observance of old ones, that incurs the risks of which moralists had warned from the first.

IT WAS THE FRANCO-PRUSSIAN WAR OF 1870–71 THAT DROVE EUROPEAN statesmen to begin forging more treaties about how to fight war—so that it could be fought with maximum forcefulness. On both sides of the Atlantic Ocean, it was an age of writing rules in domestic codes and international treaties. In the case of war, most of the law that emerged remained permissive—a trend reinforced by the frightening reemergence of armed partisan warfare and civil resistance on the European continent.

In fall 1870, Prussia won a quick victory at Sedan over Emperor Napoleon III, who was sent packing by a new French republic that went on to fight for another five months. As the Prussian forces advanced, the French population did not greet its occupiers meekly. Both sides had signed the Geneva Convention, yet across northern France, they both disrespected it while charging that all the blame fell on the other side. When the American nurse Clara Barton and other humanitarians sought to ameliorate the suffering, they could not easily get their neutral rights respected by peasants in hot zones who had never heard of international law, though Prussia's wounded received great care from its own Red Cross society.

Worse was what happened to those left unprotected even on paper. The French citizens of Strasbourg held out for weeks under bombardment, earning for their trouble the allocation of their historic town to the new German empire formed under Prussian auspices. Hundreds died while cannons razed libraries, and the main cathedral—at the time, the tallest building in the world—was set on fire. Across the north of France, the Prussian armies encountered irregular and sniping enemies. After Paris fell, the city's National Guard refused to disarm, sparking an intermittent citizens' uprising that required several months and unparalleled violence to suppress.

The Prussian Army was not happy about the disorder, though its efforts to contain it never became a full-scale anti-guerrilla war. The extraordinary siege of Paris in the fall and winter of 1870–71 killed up to fifty thousand noncombatants, many intentionally starved to death. It was one of the most extreme bouts of repression on the European continent in the nineteenth century, driving the city's inhabitants to eat even the elephants and kangaroos in the zoo (the hippo was spared only because butchers suspected that even starving Parisians would not stoop that low). But the violence was not over: no sooner had the siege ended and France surrendered than the Commune seized power in Paris, incubating radical democratic ideals as it faced down the gruff rejection of France's newest republic. In May 1871, when the French Army entered Paris amid pitched battles, thousands died and no rules for combat were seen to apply in one "bloody week."

In this new era, civilian resistance confronted occupying armies but also ruling governments everywhere. States feared that struggles on foreign territory could make their occupations complicated. They also increasingly worried that *their own* citizens might rise up and make revolution. In response, the 1874 Brussels Declaration on the customs of war set out on a very different trajectory than the Geneva Convention ten years before. The Swiss plan for humanity in warfare would remain marginal for a century.

In Brussels, representatives of European states excluded nongovernmental actors such as Red Cross functionaries and codified what they said were existing rules for war, beyond the Geneva Convention protection of wounded soldiers and those who set out to heal them. The results strove to give states maximum control over potential chaos, licensing harsh occupations so that they would not devolve into partisan wars. The point was to protect soldiers from enemy civilians, not the other way around. As for internal wars like the suppression of the Commune, international laws of war were not relevant by design.

Swiss and other philanthropists who claimed humanity would suffuse war through the operations of international law were blind to the fact that their initiative was co-opted by European governments. For states, international law proved useful, making it more legitimate to suppress new challenges to their authority. It was definitely not what Dunant—who scraped through in Parisian exile during the Prussian siege and the no-holds-barred French suppression of the Commune a few months later—had had in mind.

International lawyers, who emerged as a profession in the 1870s, accepted the sham and sometimes prettified it. In their sundry treatises, the new crew looked back to a mythologized prehistory that stretched from the ancient Greek Amphyctionic League to Hugo Grotius (the seventeenth-century Dutch theorist of the law of nations), foreseeing a civilized world order that agreed on a more humane form of war until humanity became good enough to give up war once and for all. And, in a spirit that blended Christian reform and scientific pretension, they looked forward to days when particular states, if they still existed, would obey a universal morality. The spokesmen for law could hazard mystical prognostications in this regard. "While the inert matter of the earth always loses its heat, and the expansive power of its interior fire diminishes," speculated Gustave Moynier, the Swiss Red Cross chief, "an inverse revolution occurs for its inhabitants, whose hearts are slowly learning to warm themselves, substituting care and kindness for that animosity and egoism that once determined the relation of peoples." He was fooling himself: international law cajoled states only so far and no farther.

Most international lawyers were not so much co-opted as strategic in presenting their field as high-minded while knowingly going along with the lower-minded agendas of states. They rejected pacifism outright. If peace activists proposed relying on an international law of the future, international lawyers themselves knew such law developed only with the consent of states, volunteering (as they still do) to try to bring about a better world through whatever compromises might be required. They knew that any regulation of war would require military representatives in the room, and those representatives were likely to budge only in small steps, counting on rising civilian militarism to overcome any public wish that war become less cruel. For decades, talk of "humanity" could not conceal the churn of ideologies of military force.

Moynier put the best face he could on the dispiriting situation. He hoped the Geneva Convention, in spite of its original restriction to a narrow cause of wounded soldiers, would open the door to "a general codification of *war law*." And there was much opportunity to generate law that militaries and states would embrace. A great deal of it simply could make more formal customs of war that militaries already respected, at least in normal circumstances (such as good-enough treatment of one another's prisoners of war). It could also ban weaponry they were happy to relinquish if there were credible guarantees their potential foes would do the same, or if technology had already evolved beyond the means of war in question.

In exchange for their blunted idealism, international lawyers got no love from the warrior class. In 1880, the leading European international lawyer Johann Caspar Bluntschli wrote to the longtime chief of the Prussian General Staff, the field marshal and Reichstag member Count Helmuth von Moltke, architect of victory in 1870–71 and at the time the most famous soldier in the world. Bluntschli showed Moltke the law-of-war manual that the new Institute of International Law had devised and planned to propose for adoption by states. In a notorious response that scandalized pacifists everywhere, Moltke curtly dismissed any attempt to eliminate war legally. "Eternal peace is a dream—and hardly a beautiful one," he said. Indeed, "war is part of the world order that God ordained." Regular violence was the font of virtue for males, without which humanity would "sink into materialism."

In the face of resistance like this, the Red Cross project of humane war mattered mainly because it cloaked the agenda of states as they followed up its 1864 convention with new moves to codify rules of war without any intended or express humanitarian goal at all. It may have been true that Dunant's humane concern kicked off a tradition of modern international law around how war is fought. But the century that followed showed that states took that law seriously only when it served purposes militaries already had in mind. It helped states that a sense of vague humanitarianism was attached to the endeavor, in the fluffy verbiage that even legal treaties can include. But the actual rules were often reduced to meaninglessness by the insurance that "military necessity" could override them—a proviso that the Prussians boasted about out loud but that no army truly rejected.

How did international lawyers fool themselves? Mostly through a combination of complacency and self-regard. They assumed that if the existing customs of war were written down and raised from national policy and law to international treaties, it would necessarily improve the world. Over the course of a few "well-catered days" of "Flemish feasts" in Ghent in 1873, Moynier cofounded the Institute of International Law with the Belgian Gustave Rolin-Jacquemyns, who hypothesized that the project should lead to a result "not only *as* humane but *more* humane" than otherwise. (One year before Suttner won the Nobel Peace Prize, the institute won the first such prize awarded to an organization.) There was little reflection on what it meant that international law generally left war its old self or licensed new cruelties.

It was true that many international lawyers understood themselves, even when they worked as diplomats, to be speaking for an evolving civilization that transcended states. The lawyers did not disdain national sovereignty, but they assured themselves that an enlightened public opinion spoke to and through their profession and went beyond the self-regarding dictates of merely local interests. The depressing truth was that Bluntschli and his European colleagues provided a new ethos for the law of war while barely humanizing its content. It courted progress at the risk of glorifying the law's intentions, while still serving the ends of states. Having received Moltke's reply, Bluntschli did not see the institute's further proposed reforms enacted.

YET THE PROMISE OF HUMANE WAR REMAINED APPEALING ENOUGH THAT statesmen would offer it up as a consolation prize when their peace negotiations failed. Humane war was cast into the role of Plan B when statesmen needed image management. Suttner angrily concluded in 1907, after rounds of false promises, that so far there had been only "conferences for consolidating war."

Her worst experience had been in 1899, when the bait-and-switch occurred in The Hague after Tsar Nicholas convened the self-styled civilized powers of the earth to seek peace. To introduce "the humanizing of war," Suttner recalled of her preparations for the event, was already "a wedge (surely not without purpose)" to divide and mislead before the delegates even gathered for the negotiations. As the conference went on, Suttner grew horrified. In a letter to Alfred Fried, Suttner dismissed humanizing war as a "trap that opens up in front of the feet of the pacifists," and "when the goal lies in the south, we should not pave the way to the north."

It did not help that the admirals in attendance who championed the rise of sea power ridiculed the prospect of regulating war. The American advocate of naval supremacy Alfred Thayer Mahan derided not just the conference's first goal of eternal peace but also the second, of humane war. Britain's naval leader, First Sea Lord John Arbuthnot Fisher, happily assured the diplomats in the room who were going through the motions of imposing constraints on fighting that it was a fool's errand. Like Carl von Clausewitz before him, Fisher insisted that those who cared about peace should not constrain but unshackle their forces, for "moderation in war is imbecility." As his biographer explained, Fisher "grasped firmly and ruthlessly tore off the virginal garments in which idealists had wrapped the vile hag of war and exposed her true loathsomeness." But his supposed hatred of war led him to insist on raising its stakes to the maximum extent—up to and including the worst depredations of civilians—so that conflict would not break out in the first place. "Torture the women and children, and then people will keep clear of you!" he remarked. And even if it was undesirable, humane war was impossible, Fisher concluded. "The humanizing of War!" he declared at The Hague to the horror of fellow delegates. "You might as well talk about humanizing Hell!"

With the original conference goal of peace off the table, the delegates pretended to humanize hell to save face. Suttner wasn't buying it. Insisting on giving peace a chance, she flew into a rage. Suttner immediately warned Dunant. In "the hands of the retrograde," she explained, his whole idea of humane war was now serving as a consolation prize and functioning as a moral compromise. "All the military men, diplomats, and government officials, who do not want to hear a word about the end of wars," she fulminated, "entrench themselves behind the Red Cross and the Geneva Convention," turning to "the evils of future massacres, in order not to deal with the means of avoiding the massacres themselves." "See how good and humane we are," she feared statesmen would assure their publics, garlanding themselves in the humanity of war they had brought about as the best outcome compared with the utopian renunciation of war. "We are too sensible not to regard war as unavoidable," they would say, "and we will come to an arrangement about how it can be mitigated."

That was precisely what in fact ended up occurring. No wonder she was so concerned when Dunant was awarded the first Nobel not long after. The presence of militarists in delegations, such as Mahan and Baron Carl von Stengel (whose main qualification for leading the German team was his glorification of war and hatred of the peace movement), was derided by some as "sending butchers to a conference in the interests of vegetarianism."

The Hague treaties of 1899 and 1907 on rules for fighting were in some places more than cosmetic. "At least," Fried observed, "no one can now say that no rules apply to war." However paltry, it was a real victory. The original Geneva Convention's protection for the wounded in battle was now extended from armies on the ground to sailors at sea. Disfavored practices such as denial of quarter and killing prisoners of war—Prince Andrei's proposal—were absolutely prohibited. There was even some early civilian protection (again, with emphasis on property), especially in situations of military occupation. As they had at Brussels, delegates also affirmed in the treaty that there was *some* limitation to the means armies could use to win, leaving it vague what they were ruling out.

They did get specific when it came to weaponry. Soft-tipped bullets that caused grievous injury by expanding in flight were banned. Years before at St. Petersburg, in 1868, all the great powers of Europe had agreed not to use exploding bullets. Suffusing their acts with humanitarian rhetoric, militaries were sometimes willing to outlaw old weapons if they had assurances that the other side would not use them either. Tolstoy wasn't impressed: "Why are a wound and death from an explosive bullet any worse than a wound caused by the simplest kind?" he asked. "It is incomprehensible how mentally sound adults can seriously express such strange ideas." Now, at The Hague, states agreed to ban the "dum dum" bullets that, with their hollow points, expanded while traveling and caused much more grievous injury than mantled ammunition: "splintered bones, rent skin, and severed muscles" that "often required amputation as the only remedy." Of course, self-interested regulation hardly kept militaries from developing new weapons, while the solemn treaties they agreed distracted people from the fact that technological innovations made new firepower deadlier and deadlier to more and more people.

Fedor Martens, the Russian lawyer who worked out most of the reforms proposed by the successive tsars, succeeded in inserting into the Hague treaty of 1899 a provision clamping down on the risk that ruling out some vile practices might rule others in. Everything about war, the treaty says, remains "under the protection and empire of the principles of international law, as they result from the usages established between civilized nations, from the laws of humanity and the requirements of the public conscience." But no one could say for sure that such eloquent verbiage imposed extra requirements on states, which have never yet recognized it. In the successor conference in 1907, the most novel development was the agreement to proclaim the illegality of means of war that inflicted "unnecessary suffering"—once again, without defining what counted.

But the lion's share of the new Hague rules in 1899 and 1907 had nothing to do with humane war. Instead, they codified military customs and definitions of military necessity. Provisions for occupation gave enough wiggle room for armies facing civil disorder to crack down. For those in the know, Dunant's Geneva Convention was beginning to look more and more like the rare occasion when the interests of militaries and the goal of reducing suffering coincided. "Humanity" was hardly a credible description of the laws of war as a whole. Tolstoy had worried about the compromises advocates would make to work with militaries, the same way prior do-gooders had compromised with slaveholders not to abolish slavery but to make it more humane. For a long time, there was no space for compromise, and instead plenty of humanitarians were fooled into giving away the store to militaries. As a result, there was no humane war in sight. The Geneva Convention aiding wounded soldiers had already involved a strategic agreement outsourcing military responsibilities. After the ink was dry on it, states accepted few serious constraints.

Two years after the disaster in The Hague, Suttner mobilized. With the doddering and elderly Dunant's partial connivance, she rehabilitated him not only as an emissary of peace but also as one who had always aimed to achieve it rather than humane war instead.

Though Dunant had been interested in proposals to set up international arbitration as an alternative to war for some time, her browbeating drove him to openly embrace the goal of peace.

Dunant pretended retroactively that his call for humane war had been issued to "instill" in people "a sacred horror of war in order to make them into friends of peace." With enough to go on, Suttner advertised to any takers his assurance that he did not want to be remembered as an advocate of endless if humane war if there was a chance of peace. "Dunant has been honored chiefly as a friend of peace and not for the Red Cross," she assured one intimate, "and I will give the world proof of this." It is "something the world at large does not know," Suttner wrote, conceding almost grudgingly the exclusive reason for Dunant's fame. (Dunant's commitment to peace was something "the Nobel committee may have known," she added wishfully.)

Defenders of humanizing war increasingly insisted, like Dunant in 1901, that from the beginning the whole point of their enterprise had been peace. In the opening speech to the Red Cross's annual international conference, held in the United States for the first time in 1910, Secretary of State Elihu Root insisted that its humanitarian vocation should never limit itself to managing war or picking up the pieces after. It would bring peace someday. "I believe there has been a feeling in the United States for many years that, although the aim of the Red Cross was to lessen the horrors of war and to alleviate suffering, its ideal was necessarily antagonistic to the idea of war; the programs of the Red Cross, its powerful organization, its compassion, its love of others, would not cease to turn men from the spirit and revenge and cruelty which causes war."

Humanitarians connived with and played on the hopes of peace advocates. Gustave Moynier occasionally invoked the nineteenth-century novelty of treating war as "an unnecessary evil," and presented an antiwar strategy with two prongs, "seeking to render it less and less frequent" and "less and less disastrous"—a strategy "more or less avowed," as he delicately put it, depending on the audience. And in an utterly extraordinary moment, Moynier prophesied a disturbing future of endless humane war—only to reject it in advance. "If these laws made the abominations that occur in war disappear from it and made war so harmless that it would no longer have to be regarded as a terrible mischief," he noted, "I would not hesitate to declare those laws fatal and to fight them." For the moment, that possibility understandably seemed so remote—"too improbable to fear," Moynier called it—that humane war was definitely worth pursuing. If states ever signed on, that would be the time to deal with the risk not of brutality but rather of humanity.

BUT THE SITUATION WAS WORSE THAN IT SEEMED. IT WASN'T JUST that the effort to make war more humane failed on its own terms. It was that most laws of war didn't apply or were ignored when it came to counterinsurgent and colonial war. Advocates of humane war concentrated on the dreadful clash of great powers clustered around the Atlantic Ocean. Like the organized peace movement, the exponents of humanity spoke for white and increasingly wealthy populations outraged that war brought so much ruin to modern societies boasting the greatest accumulation of power and riches ever seen. Few proposed that ending war or making it more humane pertained to the globalization of the European empire, already centuries old, that continued into the twentieth century—or that they applied to American overseas expansion in the same years. After all, the very era that saw the rise of the peace movement and the early steps toward humane war also saw the height of global expansion and the hardening of what has been called a "global color line."

The peace movement itself was always the affair of white men and women, not only in terms of who participated but also in terms of who was supposed to benefit. As "clearly as the ultimate destiny of our planet is manifested in the progressive conquest of the globe by the English-speaking race," W. T. Stead wrote in 1891, so, too, did they "possess the secret of the salvation of the world." A deep influence on the peace advocacy of Andrew Carnegie—"I am as you are a Race Imperialist," the steel magnate wrote to the newspaperman a decade later—Stead propagandized a coming American peace in the form of an Anglophone union.

The "murder of men by men" that peace advocates such as Carnegie wanted to stop did not rule out bloodcurdling atrocities beyond the European and transatlantic space. Those few voices who might have demanded a global peace transcending human difference would have been abandoned by comrades who thought that a white peace established by force in a world of racial hierarchy was the entire point. As late as the 1930s, many American and British observers thought the Kellogg-Briand Pact—the famous attempt to outlaw war for good—portended the Anglophone or white ascendancy that had partly motivated peace politics for decades.

Yet the regulation of how war was fought remained even more profoundly racialized. Colonial war was forced into a nether zone of asymmetrical if sometimes conventional conflict, counterinsurgent suppression to restore order, and imperial provisions licensing emergency measures and martial law. In all these versions of global fighting, rules were even less significant a constraint than on the transatlantic scene. One reason humanitarians and peace advocates alike gained more traction when it came to great-power conflict across borders was that few people found anything wrong with counterinsurgency—the suppression of the irregular forces of enemies—within empires. It was hardly by accident that international law regulated war between states, not within colonies. As a result, the "progress" that the campaign for humane war embodied did not interfere with the global designs of states.

Counterinsurgent war also had a North Atlantic history, and it showed that a second set of standards also applied to white enemies when they failed to fight with an organized army. Breakaway Americans facing down the British Empire in the 1770s, like the doomed 1790s insurgents in the Vendée suppressed by the leaders of the French Revolution, had certainly used irregular tactics to fight better-armed or more numerous foes. But it required Napoleon's mass armies and new modes of organization for a second track of counterinsurgent warfare to emerge clearly in response to his ragtag opponents. It was immortalized forever as "guerrilla war," after the resistance during Napoleon's Peninsular War in Spanish lands. Tolstoy captured something of how norms went out the window in such situations when he portrayed the Russian people destroying Napoleon's conventional forces in 1812. "War was being carried on contrary to all the rules," the narrator of *War and Peace* remarks of the scene, with a blend of dread and snark, "as if there were any rules for killing people."

A century of counterinsurgent "small wars" followed around the world. A border war in America between bushwhackers and jayhawks—as irregular forces contending with each other in Kansas and Missouri before and during the Civil War were known—and the Franco-Prussian War five years later showed that not all counterinsurgencies were in faraway colonies. But most were standoffs of white empires against nonwhite foes. As a result, militaries developed—most famously in the British colonel C. E. Callwell's manual for small wars—counterinsurgency theory for global violence that they would apply into the twentieth century.

Asymmetry, unlike counterinsurgency, went back in time as far as anyone could study. Lopsided conflicts were routine in the colonial wars of conquest and control that raged the world over from the fifteenth through the twentieth centuries, with vanishingly rare non-European victories. In 1896, Ethiopia decisively won the battle of Adwa against Italy, fielding a force that may have topped 100,000 rifle-bearing and often horse-borne soldiers, crushing the smaller Italian army. But far more often, the arrestingly total victories were of the West over the rest.

For example, consider the long-running "Dervish wars" in the Sudan. A two-decades-long counterinsurgency against the Mahdi, a Muslim rebel leader, climaxed in the extraordinary Battle of Omdurman on September 2, 1898. There, more than 50,000 Africans armed with swords and spears—with some of the emirs leading them wearing chain-mail armor—faced the famed Victorian soldier Herbert

Kitchener's riflemen. When the fighting started at dawn, none of the opponents of the British could get within a half mile of their lines before being mowed down.

By the end of the morning, the Dervishes had lost half of their forces, while Kitchener reported a mere forty-eight of his own men dead. The disparity was either awe-inspiring, sickening, or both. The future prime minister Winston Churchill, who had fought in northwest India at age twenty the year before in the aftermath of the Afghan War, was a lieutenant at Omdurman, deeming it "the most signal triumph ever gained by the arms of science over barbarians." The laws of a scientific age did not prohibit asymmetry and still do not. Only occasionally more ticklish was the fact that whenever Europeans treated non-Europeans differently while fighting counterinsurgent wars, they blew past limits whether old or new. Most notably, they declared war on whole populations.

For most of its history, international law was generally in tune with imperial and increasingly racialized projects. Even when racist assumptions were lacking, the liberal idea of international law was that global peoples needed to be brought under the stewardship of the civilized. Martens, the great Russian international lawyer, is still famous for his clause in the Hague treaty holding that what the law of war prohibited specifically did not necessarily exhaust the general obligation to treat enemies humanely. Speaking for his profession, however, he stated bluntly that "Muslim peoples and pagan and savage tribes" were not admitted to the society of nations, or covered by international law, though by keeping their commitments to one another civilized states could "set a scrupulous example" for their inferiors. The very fact that the rules of humane war were routinely said to symbolize "civilization" meant that those peoples considered "uncivilized" were beyond the pale of the protection of the rules by their very sponsors.

A rare exception to such patterns, the Swiss international lawyer Joseph Hornung proved the rule. In the 1880s, he urged his colleagues to save international law from its hypocritical restriction to

Christians and white people, which was making "selfish interest and, too often, unmitigated violence" the global norm. The world's barbarians and savages were "children," Hornung acknowledged, in a paternalist streak, but children needed to be treated with care. "We burn their poor towns, we chop their trees down, and we massacre their women . . . Is that the best way to make them love civilization?" It may have been a rhetorical question, but for a long time it received no answer.

Moynier spent most of his working life trying from Geneva to make war Christian and humane. But on the side, he supported European imperialism in general and worked on behalf of Leopold II's notorious Congo adventure in particular. In 1879, Moynier founded a newsletter for the imperial project, *L'Afrique explorée et civilisée* (Africa Explored and Civilized), which made the case for Leopold's potential role as votary of civilized values. After the Berlin Conference of 1884–85, which parceled Africa out among the great powers, and gave Leopold the vast territory of the Congo, Moynier served as the Belgian king's representative in Switzerland.

Moynier expressed the hope that both Europeans and their wards abroad were finally ready for progress. "The men of the white race, after having hated and cruelly exploited men of the Black race for centuries, refusing to see them as their fellow human beings, have now come to their senses," Moynier reported. To begin with, white people could and must end the slave trade among Black people. Unlike the usual imperial enterprises, in which the national interest inevitably got mixed up with the "tutelary" one, Leopold's personal rubber colony in the Congo, Moynier believed, could become a model of bringing Christianity and civilization where it was lacking. Yet at the apogee of European empire, even greater horror followed in the Congo than elsewhere. Secretly, and for a long time, Leopold's henchmen amputated arms and hands of native workers when rubber quotas were not met, and what historians now estimate to be as many as ten million deaths took place. Moynier never mentioned any of this. Always omitted among those who lionize Moynier and the Red Cross for inventing the project of humane war, his imperial interests reflected mainstream opinion among the new breed of international lawyers.

With expansionist and imperialist politics firmly in the mainstream, the new international rules developed in the century after 1850 applied uncertainly to global violence. They governed—and were developed to govern—the paradigm case of conventional battle among white people. But standards were different when the other side was composed of irregular fighters, or there were "uncivilized" peoples, or both. The self-styled civilized "have not recognized in those they call barbarians the right of belligerents," Hornung protested, to say nothing of according them the protections under law that might have followed.

It will not do, of course, to homogenize European military action around the world and over several centuries into a picture of complete disregard for all moral and legal constraints on using force against nonwhite people. Agreements such as the Geneva Convention of 1864 or the Hague treaties of 1899 and 1907 were never framed to exclude global peoples explicitly, and they operated on top of customs of engagement, or even underlying principles of natural law, that a few took to be applicable everywhere. But the rules—and especially their interpretation in policies and on the ground—clearly were different in spirit and especially in practice when it came to counterinsurgent and colonial war.

An older tradition of treaty-making with non-European peoples actually waned as modern times progressed. By the nineteenth century, few believed that the "uncivilized" peoples of the world could even join treaties. In the very century when the law of war solidified, racial theory more and more defined the understanding of human difference, including religious diversity, across the world. The "semi-civilized" Ottoman Empire ratified the Geneva Convention protecting wounded soldiers in 1866, but no Asian country did for another thirty years. As for Africa, its few existing states at the time, notably Ethiopia and Liberia, did not join—though, presumably under Moynier's influence, Leopold ratified the treaty for the Congo when it was his private estate.

By the early twentieth century, the rest of Africa, like much of Asia, had been made part of the domestic space of empires, including America's in the Philippines. It was, theoretically, a huge breakthrough that the Hague treaty implied that any force fighting conventionally—under responsible command, with open arms and a visible insignia, and following the rules of war—earned protection of the rules. But conventional engagements happened outside Europe much more rarely than within it. More important, the overwhelming majority of colonial violence took place *within* empires. As such, it was not subject to any international law, which did not purport to regulate the "domestic" affairs of private ranches like Leopold's Congo or even of far-flung polities on which the sun never set.

A DECADE INTO HIS CAREER OF WRITING TALES OF SHERLOCK HOLMES, and already immortal, Arthur Conan Doyle decided that the British armies in South Africa fighting the Boer War in 1899 could use his services. It was a ticklish situation, with the Hague treaty just negotiated and whites at war against whites at the end of the earth.

Doyle had enthused, in the beginning of that year, over the galvanizing and uplifting proposals of Tsar Nicholas II for peace that led to the Hague conferences. Doyle even chaired a London meeting for the cause. But with his investments in mining in South Africa, with its diamonds and gold, Doyle shared the widespread sense that the Afrikaner, or "Boer," misrule in the Transvaal justified military intervention, if not another expansion of the British Empire.

When Britain's troops massed on the border of its colony of Natal, the neighboring Transvaal's Afrikaner president Paul Kruger ordered a preemptive invasion, and war began. After dropping his wife and children with friends in Naples, Doyle—a trained physician, like Holmes's sidekick John Watson—arrived in Britain's Cape Colony in early 1900. Just then Lord Frederick Roberts took command of the British campaign there. The situation had devolved into military dithering as white settlers disputed who should rule the majority Black territories. Doyle hoped to minister to wounded British troops in South Africa, which he did once Roberts took over the Boer Orange Free State on his way to the Transvaal to the north.

After a typhoid epidemic broke out, Doyle had work to do. He was present as Roberts—victor of the Afghan War—waged a successful imperial war as the first year of the new century began. But Roberts's campaign was harsh in the extreme. The overwhelming force he deployed—400,000 men—meant that he quickly won the conventional battles for the cities of his enemies, forcing Boer political and military leaders into hiding. What followed for the next two years, under Roberts's assistant, then successor, Kitchener, was a vicious contest across the veldt as organized British forces pursued Boers fighting elusively in small bands. It was a counterinsurgency that resembled many asymmetrical partisan wars before and since, with the familiar difficulties of finding and identifying military enemies and suppressing them amid an opaque and unfriendly rural population.

Doyle left by July 1900, and Roberts not long after. The campaign against Boer guerrillas and snipers had already begun. The escalating controversy about Kitchener's tactics became so white-hot on Doyle's return to Britain that he put his talents at the service of his empire in a new way. For all but a few "pro-Boers" and peace activists in London, it was acceptable that the British treated their enemies unsparingly in the asymmetrical conflicts of the South African veldt. Internationally, including in the United States, where sympathy with the Boer republicans prevailed, outrage at British tactics was intense. With Afrikaner farms burned and their farmers rounded up and put in some of the world's first concentration camps, and then a no-holds-barred counterinsurgency, Doyle understood that the morality of the war—at least among white people—required comment.

Doyle insisted that the British had been driven unwillingly into the conflict, yet even so, had gone on "to wage it with humanity." The world did not see the affair the same way. Leaders of the peace movement, including Suttner and Tolstoy, inveighed against the outbreak of the Boer War. Not long before, the Hague peace conferences had led statesmen to issue sententious paeans to the goal of avoiding war. Now those paeans were put to the test. In Britain itself, W. T. Stead, fresh from his peace crusade, summarized the case for acknowledging the extent of British atrocity. His mission was to hold up "the mirror to the face of War" so that his nation would have "a vivid picture of the kinds of deeds for which as a nation and as individuals who have approved of the policy of the nation we shall have to answer at the Day of Judgment." He creatively pointed to legal violations—at least when they involved crimes against fellow white people.

Like a ragtag assortment of "pro-Boers" in British politics, Stead had attacked the war openly from its outbreak. His compilations of wartime atrocities were made in the name of ending the violence rather than making it humane for its own sake. If Stead ever felt—like other peace leaders—that insisting on a more humanely conducted war might inadvertently abet its endurance, he did not complain of that risk once counterinsurgency was raging. "The difference between barbarism and civilization is," he insisted, "largely to be measured by the extent to which nations, when they appeal to the dread tribunal of war, abide by the rules which the experience, not of philanthropists, but of soldiers, has found to be indispensable." Far from treating humane war as an unholy substitute for no war at all—as Suttner and especially Tolstoy had done—Stead relied on the fruits of the Hague conference to build his bill of particulars against British violations of the new international laws of land warfare. A breakthrough speech by the opposition Liberal Party leader, Henry Campbell-Bannerman, in June 1901 denounced "methods of barbarism" in the field—reviewing many outrageous tactics that shamed the self-styled magnanimity of the British public.

It was less revealing that Doyle's views proved more popular than Stead's than that neither thought Black lives mattered. Part of the reason for Doyle's confidence in the face of the affecting stories told by critics of the war (most of which he dismissed as propaganda) was that the bar for fighting counterinsurgent war humanely was low in the first place. Indeed, Doyle insisted as much right from the start, to set expectations properly. "When a nation adopts guerilla tactics it deliberately courts those sufferings to the whole country which such tactics invariably entail," Doyle began. "They have been the same in all wars and at all times. The army which is stung by guerillas strikes round it furiously and occasionally indiscriminately." As a matter of fact, Boer civilians themselves celebrated the gentlemanly humanity of British soldiers. That Boer soldiers were interned at all, Doyle insisted, was proof of British humanity, in spite of troublesome obligations in the new Hague treaty to require quarter and internment of surrendering enemies in conventional battle. The British even went beyond the requirements, Doyle added, when they voluntarily imprisoned Boer partisans whom the Hague regulations did not protect and who had regularly been put to death as brigands in European wars through the Franco-Prussian War of 1870–71.

Admittedly, farms had been burned in Lord Roberts's advance. The burnings continued as the counterinsurgent phase of the war kicked off. And it had been done neither against orders nor sporadically but as a matter of official policy. But, Doyle insisted, Roberts was careful to limit this act to what the situation required. He was actually being forbearing, especially since Boers had destroyed property themselves in British colonies. True, the Hague treaty, concluded just before hostilities broke out and ratified by the United Kingdom in April 1900 while they intensified, barred property destruction. But there was also an exception when military necessity required it, which—Doyle insisted—it sometimes did to clear territory infested by brigands or to deprive shadowy forces of food sources. Worst, farmhouses were frequently used as snipers' nests, in unacceptable violation of oaths taken by disarmed Boer "burghers" to remain neutral as fighting continued. It was right that they were treated harshly.

In February 1901, Churchill was just back from South Africa himself as a newly elected member of Parliament. When he had arrived in South Africa as a journalist, he was caught with a weapon as part of an English company and interned by the Boers in a prisoner-of-war camp near Pretoria. But he was treated well as an aristocratic prize—before he daringly escaped a few weeks later. He had been fortunate not to be shot as a civilian partisan—and almost convinced his captors to release him as a noncombatant. Even so, he argued that counterinsurgency permitted harsh conduct. "His Majesty's government would not have been justified," he opined two years after his brush with death and salvation thanks to humane treatment, "in restricting their commanders in the field from any methods of warfare which are justified by precedents set by European and American generals during the last fifty or sixty years."

More troublesome for Doyle was what was done to those white people deprived of their homes when they were put to the torch, since it had become scandalous across the world that up to 100,000 white women and children had been herded into concentration camps. Of the 28,000 who died, most were children, many of whom perished after a runaway measles outbreak. Concentration camps had been used before—by Spain in its last-ditch attempt to control the Cuban outpost of its declining empire—but this episode gave them notoriety, even while making them a model for counterinsurgency in other situations. (When challenged about Nazi practices before World War II, Hermann Goering reportedly took an encyclopedia from his shelf and under "concentration camps" found: "First used by the British, in the South African War.")

News of the camps was undoubtedly a public relations disaster brewing. But Doyle wondered: What was the alternative? "It was the duty of the British, as a civilized people, to form camps of refuge for the women and children where, out of reach, as we hoped, of all harm, they could await the return of peace." As for the children, the fact that they perished was largely the fault of the "ignorance, perverseness, and dirty habits" of their mothers, who sometimes refused the ministrations of British doctors. The death lay "heavy, not upon the conscience, but upon the heart of our nation."

Doyle's defensive posture anticipated a time when the public judged how warfare was conducted, even counterinsurgent war. But it mattered more that he barely mentioned the indigenous Black population because not enough of his opponents considered their treatment relevant. More than 100,000 of them had been forced into a separate camp system, and 20,000 died, most of them children. On both sides of the international struggle over the morality of the war, pro-Boer and pro-British, the treatment of Africans went almost entirely ignored, though it was generally far worse. The most famous British activist to address the treatment of Boers in camps, Emily Hobhouse, referred the problem of Black people to the Aborigines Protection Society. It was far more opportune for peace activists to focus on the plight of white people. But doing so reflected and reinforced the commonsense view that the argument about rules of war and the value of human life depended on race.

The African presence in the war surfaced only briefly for Doyle. Interning white women and children might look bad, but, he offered, it would have been an even more "ineffaceable stain" to leave defenseless white people "without shelter upon the veldt in the presence of a large Kaffir population." "No woman on a lonely farm was safe amid a Black population, even if she had the means of procuring food," he explained. Without mentioning Africans in camps, Doyle remarked that it had been exceptionally high-minded of the British to keep it "a white man's war" and to do so "wisely and well."

Had native Africans been given a bigger role in the conflict, Doyle explained, there would have been no pretense of generosity. It turned out that at The Hague Britain hadn't, after all, joined its fellow European states in banning expanding bullets (the United States didn't either). Fortunately for the Boers, Doyle suggested, it was a matter of policy for "these two enlightened and humanitarian powers" simply not to shoot the expanding bullets "in a war with the white races." Regrettably, there had been some mix-ups in South Africa and some ammunition meant for target practice had snuck into a few pouches during live exchanges. If the rules of war were flexible in counterinsurgency against white people, they were inapplicable to colonial wars against nonwhite people. Doyle was quite open on this point: "Fighting desperate savages, the man-stopping bullets could still have been used."

A few years later, Doyle penned a screed denouncing Leopold's atrocities, *The Crime of the Congo*, that helped crystallize international public opinion against the evil there. He didn't comment on the distance between his apologetic attitude toward his country's conduct in the Boer War and his passionate denunciations of the immoralities of Leopold's rule.

FOR AMERICANS IT WAS MUCH THE SAME STORY. FIRST IN THEIR OWN continental expansion, and then later abroad, rules of war were generally deemed inapplicable to "savage" enemies.

"The Indians' fight far differs from Christian practice," dryly remarked Captain John Underhill, the "eccentric daredevil," in his account of the Pequot War of the 1630s, the largest early contest that English settlers fought in America with a native people. It was hardly the last. And it was no-holds-barred on both sides. It was precisely because the Pequots had observed no constraints in killing and kidnapping that they had to be exterminated. The settlers' commander John Mason led Underhill and others in the massacre at the Pequot stronghold near today's Stonington, Connecticut.

In a two- or three-acre fort, the Pequots were completely surprised in late May 1636 when Mason barred one door, and Underhill the other. In less than an hour it was burned to the ground, with anyone approaching the exit shot; 695 of the 700 Pequots present died. "It was the end of the Pequot nation," a late nineteenth-century historian reported. "The tribe which had lorded it so fiercely over the New England forests was all at once wiped out of existence." No one should be so squeamish as to think any rules of God or men were broken either. "As a matter of practical policy, the annihilation of the Pequots can be condemned only by those who read history so incorrectly as to suppose that savages, whose business is to torture and slay, can always be dealt with according to the methods in use between civilized peoples," he continued. Actually, it was a forward-looking act: "The world is so made that it is only in that way that the higher races have been able to preserve themselves and carry on their progressive work."

Crystallizing in the early eighteenth century, "Indian war" fought by teams of white "rangers"—as some of the special forces of the United States are still called—became the monotonous rhythm of the continent's life. Especially in the early days, it did not rule out co-existence and collaboration. But that frequently broke down. While their own practices by no means conformed to later notions of humanity in warfare, native peoples actually learned many techniques of exterminating violence from settlers rather than the other way around. What Europeans called *petite guerre* in the eighteenth century to refer to aberrant and dishonored modes of engagement became routine for Americans, affecting their thinking about conventional wars.

Patterns of settler counterinsurgency left a deep mark on American war-making far beyond the domain of war proper, because conquering and clearing territory helped to define national identity and expansionary zeal. According to James Kent, one of independent America's earliest legal gurus, Indians were still "in a savage state" with "continual war" as "the natural instinct and appetite." And when the law was taken to be relevant, it was because Indians, themselves not following the rules, did not get the protection of any.

America's default way of war—honed in the imperial encounter with native peoples and lasting into the twentieth century across the globe—recognized no limits. There was no protection for noncombatants, since the people were the enemy; prisoners, if captured instead of killed by choice, were entitled to no respect; and torture, eventually the most important taboo in an age of more humane war, was rampant. "Will it not be strictly just and absolutely necessary," one newspaper asked in the eighteenth century, "that we . . . make some severe examples of our inhuman enemies when they fall into our hands?"

If justification was needed—and the point is that it usually wasn't—the new Americans were just punishing their predecessors for having taken the low road first. "The known rule of warfare with the Indian Savages is an indiscriminate butchery of men, women, and children," Thomas Jefferson maintained in 1779. It was scandalous when white men visited such cruelties on fellow white people. But it was noble or at least necessary when the "Savages" themselves needed to be cleansed from the land, and Jefferson cheered two years later when seven hundred Virginians burned and terrorized Cherokee country, as if no limits applied.

Two centuries after the Pequot War, the First Seminole War, in 1816–19, was conceived as one episode in an endless and inhumane war by necessity. Hillis Hadjo, leader of the Red Stick tribe, known by white people as Josiah Francis "the Prophet," raided Fort Sinquefield in Alabama before his men were decisively beaten and fled into the Florida Panhandle wilderness. Apprehended a few years later by Andrew Jackson, leading U.S. forces in a reign of terror at the head of the Tennessee militia, Hadjo was hanged without any legal proceeding—not deserving one, in Jackson's estimation.

In the midst of America's Civil War, the Prussian American Francis Lieber issued Rules for the Union Army that purported to codify the unwritten rules of war. His project shared almost nothing of the aspiration for humane war that Swiss gentlemen breathed deeply across the ocean at the same time. And he restricted the code to conventional rather than counterinsurgent war. Each of "the Marauder, the Brigand, the Partisan, the Free-corps, the Spy, the Rebel, the Conspirator, the Robber, and especially the Highway Robber," Lieber concluded, was no more than "a simple assassin." Essentially no limits applied to their treatment. "They know what a hazardous career they enter upon when they take up arms," he offered, trying to come off as avuncular.

In the Civil War itself, the general practice of Union forces in the field (who didn't need Lieber's advice in this regard) was harsh. They shot on sight anyone deemed a partisan. As for anyone suspected of falling into that category, the most rudimentary trials approved their execution. If Lieber didn't bother to mention "Indian war" in his learned survey of how European examples of irregular partisan war could inform American rules, it was because it was so obvious that no rules applied to it. In the Civil War, a controversy arose over how to treat bushwhackers and John Singleton Mosby's Virginian cavalry battalion, which maddeningly crossed Union lines in secret. All were found fair game for harsh treatment. No such controversy about the applicability of the law occurred when it came to nonwhite foes.

Unlike Hadjo, the Modoc chief known to white men as Captain Jack got a trial fifty years later, but not because it was legally required. Born around 1837, Kintpuash—as he was called among his own—was hanged on October 3, 1873, at Fort Klamath, just over the Oregon border from his tribe's Northern California home. From the U.S. government's perspective, Captain Jack had violated the most sacrosanct of the laws of war when he shot down a U.S. general in a peace talk. Kintpuash had not technically killed Edward Canby. The Modoc faced a campaign of extermination. In the tribe's holdout in the lava beds of the area, Kintpuash and fifty Modocs lived for more than five months eluding capture and confrontation, assenting to a chat on Good Friday, April 11, 1873, about how to resolve the standoff. After screwing up his courage, Kintpuash followed through on his plan for premeditated killing, shooting Canby at point-blank range. His weapon misfired, and his second shot caromed off Canby's cheek, before one of Kintpuash's men executed their foe in the melee that followed.

George Henry Williams, attorney general under President Ulysses Grant, solemnly affirmed that the military could do whatever it wanted with Captain Jack. A New Yorker who moved to the Oregon territory as a judge and then, after switching parties, became a one-term Republican senator for the newly spun off Oregon state, Williams almost became Supreme Court chief justice. (Grant withdrew his nomination as rumors flew that, as attorney general, his man had spent government funds on his wife's fancy horse-drawn carriage and footmen). In summer 1873, in an opinion endorsing the propriety of an ad hoc commission later cited by President George W.

Bush's lawyers, Williams said the law allowed the drumhead court that General William Tecumseh Sherman proposed.

"It is difficult," Williams suggested, "to define exactly the relations of the Indian tribes." Once they had been seen as external treaty partners; now they were an internal presence and threat. But since native peoples were different from white settlers, the "laws and customs of civilized warfare may not be applicable to an armed conflict with the Indian tribes upon our western frontier." Even if they had applied, of course, Captain Jack had violated the most solemn requirements of civilized warfare, which—Williams speculated—probably applied to the way savages fight. The confederates of Abraham Lincoln's assassin, John Wilkes Booth, had been tried by commission, too, as wartime enemies. Modocs were eligible for sure.

The proceeding that followed was a sham in retrospect. Knowing little or no English, the accused were forced to represent themselves, their translators served as star witnesses against them, and their bitter enemies sat in judgment. Williams's note was revealing for its vision of an international law that didn't apply to how white Americans treated their native enemies in war. Even when it was invoked, it was to permit whatever outcome between death and forbearance that policy dictated.

"I want the world to hear my side of this trouble," Kintpuash said to a visitor while awaiting hanging. From Kintpuash's perspective, international law was little more than a euphemism for the destruction of his people. And there were two critical facts left out of the American story and the attorney general's reasoning. First, the United States wasn't true to its word when it purported to make peace agreements with native peoples—legal treaties were deceptive to begin with (as Kintpuash felt of one he signed), or disregarded as soon as expansion and settlement demanded it. Second, both before and after this extraordinary breach, Americans had themselves recognized no rules of conduct in hostilities. It was a law of war that allowed punishment only of enemies.

Kintpuash's father had died when Ben Wright, a settler in Yreka,

California, rounded up volunteers and rode out to Modoc lands to discuss peace terms, on his own authority. At the meeting, Wright drew on the Modoc chief and shot him dead—just what Captain Jack was to do to Canby two decades later—killing scores of others in the melee for good measure. "Had he slain the entire tribe in fair battle, no just condemnation could have been pronounced against him," remarked one observer, *"but to violate a flag of truce, under pretence of peace-making,* was a wrong that fair-minded men, everywhere, condemn as an *outrage against humanity and civilization."* As, indeed, they did a generation later—but only when Captain Jack committed that wrong.

Following his father's slaughter, Kintpuash became chief, and in 1864 he signed a treaty restricting the Modocs to the Klamath Reservation in Oregon. There they would live amid their longtime foe and far from their historic lands, accepting a pittance in exchange for them. Under army escort, the Modocs moved in eight caravan wagons with mules the fifty miles north to their new home. But relations with the Klamath Indians broke down, with mistreatment of the Modocs tolerated under the supervision of the reservation's government agent. "I just as well die in my own country," Kintpuash concluded grimly. He moved many of his people back south in 1870, setting the stage for the hostilities that followed when the U.S. secretary of war sent a directive to enforce the peace treaty by expelling the Modocs from California.

"The treaty was a lie," Captain Jack explained to one friendly white contact—though people differed as to whether he had been deceived at the start, was angry that the government failed to protect his people, or simply didn't like his new life, compared with his old one "free from restraint." It wasn't a unique situation, with "Indian war" often starting because Americans broke false promises in peacemaking. "How many times were the treaties a hypocritical mask covering embarrassing corruption beneath the pretense of legality?" wondered Jean Pictet, a Swiss gentleman responsible for renovating the laws of war in the later twentieth century, while writing American history on the side. "It is hard to understand how men who were respectable in their own society could show so much duplicity when they dealt with the natives. But then, why should pens have been less mendacious than forked tongues?"

As skirmishes escalated into war, Americans conducting hostilities recognized no limits, for no law—written or not—applied. The ill-starred peace conference where Captain Jack committed his treacherous assassination had been arranged after army forces with scores of volunteers could not beat him and his men, holed up in their natural fortress in the lava. In furious response, Sherman ordered the "utter extermination" of the tribe, and Canby's successors started to attempt just that. Both army forces and private militias began killing any Modocs they could find, including women and children. And if they stopped, it was not because any law required them to do so.

After Captain Jack and his confederates were captured, the octogenarian but still passionate Quaker feminist and pacifist Lucretia Mott and her fellow leaders of the Universal Peace Union implored Grant to offer something better than sham justice for the Modocs, or at least clemency if they were convicted. In a petition, Mott reminded Grant that he had promised a new age of peace after the Civil War led the nation into bloody fratricide. "We feel confident," Mott explained, "that were pure peace principles applied in the case of the persons in whose behalf we address you, it would show the civilized and uncivilized worlds that there is in the soul of man a far mightier and more enduring power than any of the nations of the earth have yet brought into use."

Feeling ignored, Mott later burst in on a fine dinner Grant happened to be enjoying with her Philadelphia neighbor. In response to her plea for clemency, Grant promised her that not all the convicted Modocs would die. One of the two fighters who was shipped to Alcatraz instead of being hanged nonetheless perished from scrofula within two years. As for Captain Jack, once he was pulled down from the hanging rope, his head was severed from his body and sent to Washington in a box as a trophy. It was the last act of California's wars with the Indians, unless you count the exile of the Modoc remnants to eastern Oklahoma, almost two thousand miles away, where the entire population—including children—was held as prisoners of war indefinitely. "We have never considered the wrongs of the Indian as our own," Mott observed the next year. "We have aided in driving them further and further west, until, as the poor Indian has said, 'You will drive us away, until we go beyond the setting sun.'"

A QUARTER CENTURY LATER, ACROSS THE PACIFIC OCEAN IN ITS burgeoning overseas empire, the United States found itself embroiled first in a conventional war and then a decades-long counterinsurgency. It received the Philippines in the peace treaty following America's brief, decisive, and glorious war with the mother country of Spain in 1898. There was just one problem: Spain's bitter opponent in the Philippines, the diminutive former mayor Emilio Aguinaldo, wasn't buying it.

On his return from exile, Aguinaldo, still only thirty years old, declared a republic after taking control of most of the country during the imperial handoff. He then fought his new master tooth and nail. After the United States put down Aguinaldo's armies in their stronghold in and around Manila, a protracted rebellion followed. Aguinaldo, with no previous fighting experience, succeeded in leading a guerrilla resistance, which sprang up across the islands. Even after Aguinaldo's own capture in March 1901, it lasted for years, especially in the Muslim Moro provinces.

For Americans, the legal situation was clear from the start. As with "Indian war" before, they were simply putting down resistance in their justly claimed lands. It was not an international war. Where the United States had waited decades on the original Geneva Convention of 1864, the Senate promptly ratified the new Hague rules of 1899 in 1902. But even after it did so, the international treaty governing the fighting of war wasn't formally applicable, since the conflict was not a war between nation-states but between the United

States and its disorderly imperial subjects. Still, the hot contest and the deployment of a humongous military presence meant it could be conceived as a war, and some rules of fighting might matter. In the Boer War, the United Kingdom had faced opponents such as William Stead, who cited chapter and verse from a new treaty calling for restraint (for white people). By contrast, the United States waged its biggest campaign outside Europe before World War II under the old Lieber Code from the Civil War, which was not replaced until 1914.

The most common assumption from the start, though, was that there were no laws or customs—or that the Lieber Code offered license rather than limits in counterinsurgency. The few courts-martial that did occur were exceptions that prove there were no rules or only permissive rules. With newfangled theories of race approaching their global apogee and older stereotypes persisting, Filipinos almost by definition could not count as honorable enemies. "Murder is almost a natural instinct with the Asiatic, who respects only the power of might," remarked Adna Chaffee, a U.S. general and Indian War veteran fresh from helping put down the Boxer Rebellion in China. "Human life all over the East is cheap. One life more or less does not matter, and it is only the fear of prompt, immediate, and unfailing punishment that holds the population in check." Chaffee would put those assumptions into practice as a military governor of the Philippines in 1901–1902. Though Lieber himself had been explicit that his rules applied regardless of color—the boundaries of the law depended on conduct—the fact that the Philippines campaign was a "race war" meant to most that the law of war said there were no limits.

From the first days of fighting, Americans violated even the new rules—such as the requirement to accept surrender—that would have applied had they recognized the Hague treaty as relevant. Worse, from the early phase in and around Manila, Americans assumed that most of the people they met were hostile, and shot many without a second thought. The French minister filing reports commented mordantly that "American soldiers are the true savages," adding that their very "brutality, provocation, and excess surely have served the cause of insurrection." Once its writers got word of what was going on, *The Nation* agreed. "The war of 1898 'for the cause of humanity' has degenerated in 1899 into a war of conquest, characterized by rapine and cruelty worthy of savages." Trying to be nice, the magazine conceded that it was "to the credit of our soldiers that while in the heat of battle they carry out the orders to take no prisoners, most of them inwardly revolt at the idea of such barbarism, and want to come home."

Whether or not that was true, the commanding general and first military governor in the Philippines, Elwell Morris, having honed his craft in Indian engagements in the Montana Territory after Little Big Horn, approved harsh tactics from the start. Anyone with the potential to resist was fair game. And unconditional surrender was the goal, which justified nearly any act. These were "methods which have proved successful in our Indian campaigns in the West," Elihu Root, secretary of war in the period, explained (a view of no pertinence to his later Nobel Prize as enthusiast for transatlantic arbitration). And practices worsened when General Arthur MacArthur, Jr., succeeded Morris as governor, as the U.S. effort devolved into the kind of counterinsurgency farther south that MacArthur had personally led on the northern island of Luzon before his promotion.

For a brief period, before MacArthur proclaimed all resistance—and in practice, anyone the army wanted—beyond the pale of legal protection, there was an internal debate within the military about limits. There had been rhetoric from the start that not only was the situation a war, but also applicable constraints on war among civilized nations applied. But in practice, this verbiage took one of three forms: assurances for public consumption and legitimacy (which testifies to changing expectations if not changing war), justifications for the harshest treatment of Filipino enemies, or warnings to them to heed limits themselves or live with the consequences. Almost no evidence survives in which a legal interpretation of the Lieber Code or unwritten international law called for constraint on U.S. force or tactics. It is true that in the first, conventional phase of the war Americans captured rather than killed prisoners, though many were eventually shot. Once the counterinsurgency intensified, less radical policies were shelved as whole populations were treated as potential enemies. Doing so did not demand a new legal framework in which bandits and outlaws deserved any treatment they got. The existing one sufficed.

When he succeeded MacArthur as military proconsul in July 1901, Chaffee faithfully continued the approach that lay behind the Lieber Code—intense wars were best in the long run, as they would convince restless opponents to submit and end the conflict more quickly. He escalated the policy options farther along the continuum of intensity, in the tradition of "Injun warfare," without ever meeting a law he didn't like. This often meant burning crops, killing animals, and leaving nothing behind—including humans. After an alleged Filipino massacre of U.S. troops, the most sadistic counterinsurgency operations raged on the island of Samar. "I want not prisoners, I wish you to kill and burn, the more you kill and burn the better it will please me," commented General Jacob Smith, Chaffee's subordinate and another Indian War veteran, promising to reduce the area to "howling wilderness."

No one was legally safe from U.S. counterinsurgent violence. The rules imposed no limits, either because the Filipinos were unprotected by law or because those generously distinguished as noncombatants under the law were still eligible for reprisals, which the Lieber Code did not ban (and almost encouraged). "I want all persons killed who are capable of bearing arms in actual hostilities," Smith commanded his forces, specifying he meant males ten years and over. People who failed to understand that the rules did not cover irregular fighters and permitted brutality for the rest were "ignorant of what constitutes the laws of war," explained General S.B.M. Young at a New York Chamber of Commerce dinner in 1902, after returning from overseas. "To carry on war, disguise it as we may, is to be cruel, it is to kill and burn, burn and kill, and again kill and burn." (He added reassuringly to the monied guests in the room that the "the American army is the most humane that ever waged war.") The overall death toll reached as high as a seventh of the population—and intermittent hostilities continued against Moro "fanaticism" in the far south for another decade.

At home, public discussion of the Philippines War did suggest that an early public ethics of punctilious obedience to the laws of war could come someday. It was revealing that, when he ceremonially ended the war on July 4, 1902, President Theodore Roosevelt could wax eloquent about the army's "humanity and kindness to the prisoner and non-combatant," with "our soldiers" bound by "the laws of war." Even so, he allowed that American "friendship" proved difficult when "it was impossible to distinguish friend from foe." The hypocrisy of the statement, its pretense that the efforts in the Philippines signaled a rising consciousness of the laws of war, counted for little. It is best understood as a distant anticipation of those laws' centrality to U.S. politics later. The same could be said of the fact that Smith was caught up in a court-martial, receiving a light sentence before Roosevelt pardoned him altogether.

After September 11, 2001, a few observers recalled that many Americans had been furious about reports of imperial violence in the Philippines a century earlier. The first to raise the alarm were Democrats backing William Jennings Bryan's pacifist candidacy in the 1900 presidential campaign. Philippine insurgents, for their part, cast an eye on an election they hoped would lead to their independence, and they also wanted the war to seem unsavory to American audiences. But Bryan and his allies were less concerned with brutality of conduct than with openly stigmatizing global entanglements and military empire. Many of them were advocates of white American isolation rather than humane war.

After Bryan's loss, an early version of a "torture debate" over the ethics of wartime infraction occurred in 1902. That year, the Republican Senate willingly investigated and substantiated some of the more toxic rumors swirling around the use of the "water cure," an early euphemism for waterboarding. As in the Boer War, atrocity consciousness was an open tactic of political opposition. Once again, it failed. Roosevelt's damage control and public relations efforts helped pave the road to his landslide victory in 1904, as accusations of malfeasance were excused and whitewashed.

"I believe in God who made of one blood all races that dwell on the earth," the African American intellectual W.E.B. Du Bois prayed in 1904 in his prose-poem "Credo," anticipating a world without aggressive conflict or race war. "I believe in the Prince of Peace. I believe that War is Murder," he continued. "I believe that armies and navies are at bottom the tinsel and braggadocio of oppression and wrong; and I believe that the wicked conquest of weaker and darker nations by nations white and stronger but foreshadows the death of that strength." But it would take a long time. "Finally, I believe in Patience," Du Bois concluded. He would need it.

AS THE TWENTIETH CENTURY BEGAN, THE CAUSE OF HUMANE WAR HAD little to show for itself. The few provisions that might have imposed serious limits on the conduct of fighting were simply ignored in practice. It was not just that humane war was a consolation prize for the failure to constrain the resort to force in the first place. It was not merely that the rules of humane war were inapplicable to most conflicts because they were counterinsurgent and colonial fights. The last indignity was that, even when they were applicable, the few concessions that states recorded on paper had little real bearing on military practices, and were ignored or abandoned even in conventional warfare when hostilities broke out. As the great advocate of aerial bombardment of civilians was to note, international legal constraints were always "swept away like dried leaves on the winds of war."

The trampling of the original Geneva Convention as the Franco-Prussian War spun out of control into counterinsurgency ought to have been sobering. A half century later, the Balkan wars of 1912 and 1913, now regarded as crucial preludes to the outbreak of World War I in 1914, were simply too anarchic and atrocious for the idea of humane war to be credible. Imagining the impact of the mutual defense pacts that nations were signing, Tolstoy speculated, "Idle ladies and gentlemen will fuss about, entering their names in advance for the Red Cross and getting ready to bandage those whom their husbands and brothers are setting out to kill—imagining that they will thereby be doing a most Christian work." Those looking backward on the enterprise were just as skeptical. "It was no coincidence," the French intellectual Jean-Paul Sartre later noted in indicting the U.S. war in Vietnam, "that jurists and governments should have been increasing the attempts to 'humanize war' on the eve of the two most frightful massacres mankind has ever known."

World War I dealt a serious blow to the hope that someday humane war might come. Not only were the laws of war violated without a second thought, but also the worst acts of war, the ones that met with the most moral outrage, were not illegal. Atrocities in Belgium committed by the German Army executing the Schlieffen Plan, though dismissed as propaganda for decades, were horrendous. The burning of the Belgian university town of Louvain as collective punishment was an affront to civilization, though not clearly in violation of any standards, which were regularly offset by allowance for "military necessity." In some episodes, Germany did violate the laws of land warfare, but not with entirely distinctive zeal.

In the eyes of contemporaries, the most undeniable German lawbreaking, and the infraction that mattered most, was the violation of Belgium's neutrality guaranteed in various nineteenth-century treaties. If Britain fared better in perception or practice as the war dragged on, it was because the constraints on its sea power were much less robust: the British Empire had made sure of it. International law such as it was permitted the most gross moral wrongdoing of the period, besides the Armenian genocide: the British blockade of the Continent, which caused half a million civilian deaths through starvation.

Not that the Red Cross got bad press. It won its first Nobel Peace Prize in 1917 for its noble practice of keeping prisoners of war in touch with their families, even though it wasn't until 1929 that states agreed on a new Geneva Convention. Where the first convention governed care for the wounded, this one added rules for the humane treatment of detained soldiers. Where the rules failed profoundly was the fighting itself. The Armenians were driven to slaughter, and the eastern front was a nearly ungoverned zone where the Hague rules went almost entirely disregarded. Even on the trench-ridden western front, atrocities anticipating World War II's excesses, from camps to rapes to reprisals, have barely begun to have their stories told. The category of "civilian" offered little protection; a civilian could be defined as a kind of victim in waiting, in part because the formal rules did precious little to protect him or (usually) her.

Even so, humane war did not inspire the civic activism and moral consensus that ending war did in the era around the turn of the twentieth century. With new insight into the death drive that no law could eliminate, the psychoanalyst Sigmund Freud was blunt about the futility of humanization. In 1915, when World War I was only in its second year, he wrote: "Not only is it more bloody and destructive than any war of other days, [but] it is at least as cruel, as embittered, as implacable as any that has preceded it. It disregards all the restrictions known as International Law, which in peace-time the states had bound themselves to observe." "It is more utopian to hope to make war humane than to eliminate war," one German international lawyer concluded two years later, at the depths of the carnage.

In the years that followed the 1918 armistice—agreed to in the eleventh month, on the eleventh day, and at the eleventh hour of that year—it was simply no longer credible to argue that making war more humane would contribute to staving off its outbreak. How had that worked out in World War I? "In four brief years," the English novelist and seer H. G. Wells insisted in 1919, "Europe was compelled to develop a warfare monstrously out of proportion to any conceivable good which the completest victory would possibly achieve for either side." If that was so, "all Geneva Conventions and such palliative ordinances, though excellent in intention and good in their immediate effects, *make ultimately for the persistence of war as an institution*. They are sops to humanity, devices for rendering war barely tolerable to civilized mankind, and so staving off the inevitable rebellion against its abominations."

Another commentator was brutal about where the demand to end brutality had led: "The failure of international law," he glumly recorded, "is due to the failure of the statesmen and jurists of the last century to use the moral forces of their day for the development of international law along the lines of true progress; and this, in turn . . . is due to their preoccupation with the laws of war." If international law was to be relevant again, it would have to be a law of peace. A young Quincy Wright did not go as far as to blame humane war for endless war. But it was clear to him that if international law did not institutionalize peace, it was not worth much. "The war has . . . shown that international law can not greatly reduce the destructiveness of war," he observed in 1920. If so, "the effort of international law to regulate war" was "of slight practical value," and "international law must more seriously devote itself to the regulation of the conditions which lead to war and the elimination of war itself."

World War II would have to be the war for peace that its predecessor had turned out not to be. As it turned out, the American-run peace that took hold in Europe after 1945 would lead the very people for whom humane war was devised—white Europeans—to stop slaughtering one another. But in those same years, Americans would commit to fighting all around the world. If their wars were ever to become humane in intent or effect, it was, alas, not going to be anytime soon.

CHAPTER FOUR

Air War and America's Brutal Peace

WORLD PEACE THE AMERICAN WAY WAS BRUTAL WHEN ESTABLISHED IN the 1940s, and for a long time after. One of the biggest reasons was airborne weapons, which would do more than any development to make dreams of humane war incredible, even as—in our time—they would indicate the possibility of hostilities that are less cruel. Falling from Prince Andrei's sky, free of the rules of warfare, the bombs that killed civilians by the millions and on purpose in World War II contributed mightily to the intensification of brutal war. They also helped bring about the establishment of a Pax Americana that has existed ever since.

From the 1930s to the 1950s, Americans lived through the most transformational era in their foreign affairs. Swept into conflagration after Pearl Harbor, they assumed responsibility for global affairs despite previous decades of skittish doubts. Yet the consequences of World War II were ambiguous. With America's help, European dreams of a continent beyond military strife were finally realized. But the militarized standoff that counted as the Cold War's version of peace in Europe coexisted with American wars in Asia and elsewhere. American internationalists such as Quincy Wright had argued for their country to be involved in the struggle for global peace. Perpetual war was the price. And it was pitilessly violent. The United States guaranteed the European peace by exporting to

Asia the total-war tactics Europeans had previously used in colonial wars, and that Americans themselves had employed against Native Americans and Filipinos. On the land and in the air, U.S. power was deployed ruthlessly not just to end World War II but also to hold the line against communism in Korea five years later.

It was no accident that American peace and brutal war went together; it was a matter of fervent belief. "I am a one hundred percent disbeliever in war," General Douglas MacArthur remarked at one point. Some might have seen it as a peculiar claim, coming from the most celebrated U.S. soldier of the middle of the twentieth century, famous for his brave acts, corncob pipe, and dashing ways. Yet it was precisely war's brutality, MacArthur thought, that would guarantee peace on acceptable terms. If Americans now embraced global order as their mission, it was at first as ardent foes of humane war.

MacArthur hoped to be remembered, as he famously put it when arriving in Tokyo in 1945, "not as a commander engaged in campaigns and battles, even though victorious to American arms." Instead, he was an emissary with a "sacred duty" to "carry to the land of our vanquished foe the solace and hope and faith of Christian morals." Christian Europeans were finally pacified and the Japanese bombed into surrender, but there was still an unimaginable amount of work to do. Alongside the new rules of peace propounded by the fledgling United Nations, the Geneva Conventions of 1949 produced a new international law for regulating hostilities just as the Cold War dawned. The laws of war, however, remained as irrelevant as ever, especially when it came to U.S. air power. Humanized versions of war were not yet a sacred duty.

Five years after he arrived in Japan, MacArthur made a fateful decision to break the new rules of peace. In the dreadful winter of 1950, he made the rash choice to send troops across the 38th parallel. In response, Communist troops streamed over the Yalu River, which divided Mao Zedong's China from the Korean Peninsula, prompting MacArthur to let U.S. air power off its leash. Amid the greatest ideological struggle in world history, the new peace in Europe would depend on a lot of war outside Europe. And global American belligerency would remain inhumane for a long time to come.

IN THE 1930S AMERICANS CONDUCTED A "GREAT DEBATE" ABOUT THEIR country's global role. Both sides stood for a kind of peace. Those who came to be dismissed and reviled as "isolationists" believed in maintaining hemispheric security, coupled with neutrality toward the wars of the great European powers. It was a policy they thought had always served the country well—even as the United States became a great power itself. Self-styled internationalists, meanwhile, insisted that America had to commit to a globalized peace scheme. It would only emerge slowly that this option meant committing the country to global war.

At this critical moment, Quincy Wright began ruminating on the consequences of the fall of the comparatively peaceful British ascendancy: "The *pax Britannica* had given Europe the best two centuries it had had—at least since the *pax Romana* a millennium and a half earlier." It was a long-established fact: empires brought peace, too. "The excessively brutal civil and imperial wars which characterized the last century of the Roman Republic were followed by such a will to peace that most of the western world submitted to the Pax Romana of Augustus and his successors for two centuries," Wright mused. Could the twentieth century offer something similar, he wondered, without requiring the humiliating subjugation of vassals and ceaseless violence at the savage frontiers of empire? Could a world organization under international law keep aggressors from bringing ruin to liberal democracies at peace? Would peace come, if it did, under the auspices of another empire or in some unprecedented guise?

Following World War I, internationalists such as Wright had earnestly sought a new answer to the problem rather than a new empire. But he knew there was a crucial instability in Woodrow Wilson's historic "internationalism." To enter World War I, the president had united progressives with a promise to "end all wars" that portended a global order beyond power politics. It wasn't supposed to be a scheme for American hegemony. But what if it was precisely such hegemony that would allow skittish conservatives to support an American-led peace? And what if that hegemony required precisely the militarization of the globe that progressives had once denounced?

As the great debate raged through the 1930s, those who had objected to U.S. entry into World War I were no longer seen as vindicated by events; now they entered the ranks of the disastrously shortsighted. A broad consensus about the arms industry's nefarious role in history, and in the outbreak of World War I in particular, gave way. Now the industry was glamorized as crucial to the defense of democracy across the ocean. Six months before the Lend-Lease program and a year before Pearl Harbor, President Franklin Roosevelt devised a scheme to "sell" the British fifty destroyers—and Attorney General Robert Jackson justified it in a remarkable opinion. The deal brought down accusations of an executive power grab in violation of the Neutrality Act and international law. Along with other "internationalists," Wright contended it was legal.

The spat over the destroyers was just one episode in a broader campaign to bring the United States into global conflict. Wright fulsomely supported broader interventionist policies, working actively in the Committee to Defend America by Aiding the Allies. In early 1941, he celebrated the Lend-Lease program because it signaled that the United States had edged to the brink of putting German aggression down. The peacemonger was arguing for American war. To what kind of internationalism would it lead? Air war was going to be central to the answer.

THERE WAS NO GREAT DEBATE OVER CIVILIAN BOMBING BEFORE OR during World War II—or even after it. At The Hague in 1899, when only the century-old possibility of bombing from hot air balloons existed, aerial bombardment of any kind was banned for five years. Before those years were out, the airplane had debuted at Kitty Hawk.

Astonishingly, it was imaginable from the beginning that aerial targeting might someday become humane and precise. At The Hague, the U.S. delegate and army captain William Crozier, with a record of fighting the Sioux after graduating from West Point, had anticipated this development, with the prospect of dirigible balloons in mind. He foresaw that air power would eventually allow for "localizing at important points the destruction of life and property and [permit] sparing the sufferings of all who are not at the precise spot where the result is decided."

The immediate question for those tinkering with the rules of war was how—and against whom—air power was to be used in its originally indiscriminate form. Since the introduction of the Zeppelin in 1900 made dirigible ballooning more plausible, the same consensus did not exist to ban aerial bombardment at the next Hague conference in 1907, though a majority supported another temporary ban. Never again did international law specifically prohibit it.

The rules updated at The Hague in 1907 did exclude "bombardment" of "undefended" towns "by whatever means." But in practice, this modification ruled out very little. It all depended what "undefended" meant. Meeting at Oxford in the halcyon summer of 1913, some urged reading this provision as "not being defended in fact" rather than "capable of being defended in theory," to restrict aerial wrath to towns fighting back. But these progressive voices were drowned out. Lawyers wrangling the rules for states reasoned that the small payload of airplanes compensated for their imprecision. Aerial bombing, they reasoned, would not necessarily be more brutal than accepted conduct like the famously cruel daylong British shelling of Alexandria in 1882, amid a nationalist uprising against the ruling Egyptian khedive (a European client).

Across the Atlantic, peace activists mobilized against the prospect of weapons being released with high-altitude immunity and causing indiscriminate carnage. In 1911, Italy dropped the first bombs from airplanes, on Arabs in Libya, with the French and Spanish following suit elsewhere in North Africa the next year. It was immediately clear that aerial strikes had their uses in extra-European violence. More important for the peace movement, they raised the prospect of even greater scandal in conventional European war. "What aerial war will mean," wrote W. Evans Darby, secretary of the Peace Society in London, "is beyond our imagination." ("The invaded Arabs of Tripoli might tell us," he added.)

Those—including Arthur Conan Doyle!—who signed a "Memorial Against the Use of Armed Airships" in 1912 agreed that regulating this means of war was inseparable from the drive to eliminate war itself. "There never yet has been a moment when it was practically possible to ban the war machines of earth or water," the signatories insisted. "There is a moment when it is practically possible to ban those of the air."

That same year, the world's leading peace activist, the elderly Bertha von Suttner, published her impassioned pamphlet "Barbarization of the Air," in which she continued her campaign against war now that it ominously threatened the skies. In bestselling novels, H. G. Wells was imagining what airships would do to war, and Suttner hoped to stop it—invoking the colonial victims of the first bombardments—before it was too late. She recorded that, in the early days of aviation, penniless inventors would come to the cash-strapped peace movement for funds, given the widespread expectation that air travel would create a race of cosmopolitans who would never fight. Now, she rued, they had gotten more money than they needed from states willing to arm themselves for doomsday.

The limited but real use of bombs from the skies in World War I was widely understood to be a dry run for a future age of air power. Aviators had had only a short time to prepare, and the logistical difficulties of dropping bombs from dirigibles and planes were almost insurmountable. A few frightening runs in the sky were all that the European powers conducted against one another—but enough to convince everyone below that if World War I did not end all wars, the future would be terrible. Air attacks in "the present war," *The New York Times* reported in 1914, "violate no law, however much that might offend the world's sense of humanity." Although the fifty Zeppelin raids over Britain in 1915–16 and twenty-five plane sorties in 1917–18 caused little damage, they were portents of the nature of future war that everyone could read.

While Europeans struggled to end war with one another, new practices of "strategic bombing" to sap the morale of populations were used with abandon in Europe's colonies. Following its use in North Africa, air control became a fashionable means of pacifying resistance across the colonial world. In World War I, the British used it on India's Northwest Frontier in 1915, where Pathans were bombed, then in Darfur and Egypt in 1916. Three years later, Mohammad Abdullah Hassan, dubbed the "Mad Mullah," saw his long-running and tenacious Somali insurgency easily terminated by a squadron of twelve DeHavilland aircraft. The planes singed him while killing his entourage on the first strike and eventually drove him into the wasteland, where he would die of influenza months later.

The practice came into its own in Iraq (the part of the former Ottoman Empire given as spoils to the victorious British after World War I). Arthur "Bomber" Harris, later the hero of Britain's destruction of German cities in World War II, earned his wings there. He boasted that no Iraqi enemies would resist if they knew their forces would be "practically wiped out" and "a third" of nearby villagers "killed or injured by four or five machines which offer them no real target, no opportunity for glory as warriors, no effective means of escape." The bombing of peoples who were usually imagined as "deserving" such treatment replaced more costly and older armed expeditions across forbidding landscapes. As in other kinds of counterinsurgency, the targets were of a different race and religion, and they either posed a grievous threat justifying extreme treatment or required the shock of fire from the clouds to shake them from their fanatical resistance.

The method also allowed maximum fear and terror to be spread with minimum cost and effort. Its defenders were not above justifying "the great humanity of bombing" because it also lowered casualties among the target population, theoretically at least. It was the old idea that intensified war left everyone better off, updated for an aerial age. Along with Hugh Trenchard, the father of the Royal Air Force, Winston Churchill—by 1920 secretary of state for war and air—was instrumental in dreaming up the new system of imperial order.

Though aerial technology did not allow a modicum of precision from the sky for many decades, Churchill praised gas bombs in February 1920 as if humane control were already in prospect. The new tools would police "turbulent tribes" without killing most of their targets and merely "inflict various degrees of minor annoyance" enough to bend the savage will. In the same spirit, the British international lawyer J. M. Spaight mused soon after that air power "is capable of transforming the whole face of war almost beyond recognition. It can turn the old, crude, hideous blood-letting business into an almost bloodless surgery," to "the immeasurable advantage of mankind." There was no reason not to turn to humane war, he insisted, though it would profoundly change war's meaning, making it completely unrecognizable in a new form. "War, after all, is only a means to an end."

But Churchill's plan for humane control proved unlikely to work logistically. It was also feared to provoke ire among Europeans who had lived through gas shelling on the ground in World War I, so standard bombs were used to pacify native resistance from the sky instead. There was never a very clear distinction between civilians and combatants, especially in insurgencies. The hope was to burst the morale of enemies by using the terror from the air pioneered in the colonies.

Not many were very concerned with whether such tactics broke any laws intended to make war more humane. For all its success in pressuring for a peace politics for Europe, the transatlantic movement against war did not prevent the rise of air control in the colonies, with grievous consequences later. As air power came to the fore, states rested content with the failure of attempts at The Hague to specifically regulate aerial bombardment.

In Washington in 1922 and The Hague again in 1923, states met to consider regulation, tentatively agreeing to limit air power to "military objectives." Though the term was easy to define broadly, some authorities were willing to interpret "military objectives" narrowly and anticipated today's prevailing notion that real military gain is prohibited if disproportionate to civilian harm. The draft rules on aerial sorties specified that where military objectives were "so situated that they cannot be bombarded without the indiscriminate bombardment of the civilian population, the aircraft must abstain from the bombardment." If taken seriously, that provision would have imposed an enormous legal check on aerial practices, forbidding the destruction of cities in Britain, Germany, and Japan that occurred during World War II. The draft rules also prohibited bombing "for the purpose of terrorizing the civilian population." But after finalizing the wording, states did not ratify the agreement, leaving it on the drawing board as a hypothetical bar to mass death from the sky.

One reason was that bombing had become essential to maintaining colonial order and meting out punishment. Having initiated the tradition of bombing the savages in Libya in 1911, Italy returned to it after World War I. The new Fascist government used bombing to establish control over the Libyan interior, a campaign that lasted until 1931. After raining fire down on the town of Tetuán in their colony of Morocco in 1924, the Spanish pursued a ferocious counterinsurgency in 1925 against rebellious Berbers in the Rif, the mountainous area that bordered French Algeria and extended into it.

The Rifians "come of a white race," as one chronicler of the events acknowledged at the time. Unfortunately, however, they had been "warped by generations of suffering and hate." Worse, intermarriage with Semitic invaders had corrupted any innate virtue the Rifians might have boasted. "From childhood," their boys were "taught to make war" and "have the look of frightened eaglets, suspicious but 'out for blood.'" With their fathers, they responded to enemies with "the innate cruelty of a primitive race."

Spain answered the mayhem with more than hyperbole. The poison gas bombs that fell from the sky onto the Rifians starting in June 1924 certainly gave Spain's fury a bit of international notoriety. The action came on the brink of Geneva Protocol meetings in 1925 that would prohibit gas weapons delivered from ground or sky. The ban was agreed. This breakthrough was the sole real advance for international law governing the conduct of military hostilities in the era, even if it occurred not because of outrage over the Rif War or extra-European bombing but because of memories of European gas in World War I.

France helped Spain finish the job of putting down the Berber rebellion in 1925–26, this time with conventional bombs, and extended its empire in the bargain. In 1936, Italy's invasion of Ethiopia and seven-month bombing campaign caused an international uproar—though it was the use of gas rather than its aerial delivery that sparked outrage. With European war brewing, it also mattered that Italy's acts were in clear violation of the 1925 protocol. Only the international hue and cry over the aerial destruction of tiny Guernica by Germans helping Francisco Franco win the Spanish Civil War in April 1937 suggested that there might be something more outrageous about conventional bombing than about conventional ground weapons.

As its own era of global warfare approached, the United States was no less enthusiastic about bombing, and for the same reasons. "Among savages, war includes everyone," wrote the U.S. army captain and literature aficionado Elbridge Colby in 1927, in a contribution to the country's leading organ of international law. He was miffed that Wright had dared to criticize the French for their indiscriminate bombardment of Damascus, Syria, eighteen months earlier, in the midst of the "great revolt" against European rule under a League of Nations mandate there. Colby, whose son William later directed the Central Intelligence Agency, was perplexed that anyone could think foes who were not Christian or white deserved any protections under international law. It was "essentially a Christian doctrine," meaning that no limits applied to others, as the example of Richard the Lionheart showed. Though the pope himself had condemned the use of the crossbow in Christian war, Richard "freely and unperturbedly" used it against "Saracens" during the Crusades. In modern times, Colby wrote in his immortally entitled "How to Fight Savage Tribes," custom showed that the disparity in forms of warfare still applied.

Since its first use to pacify savages, Colby recalled, bombing served as "a more modernized and more effective version of prior British bombardments with field artillery against native Asian villages, a casual type of incident against native tribes in the story of British colonial enterprise and mastery." Now it was time for Americans to follow suit, extending to the sky "the long list of Indian wars in which the troops of the United States have defended and pushed westwards the frontiers."

And fortunately, there was no law to ignore, since Colby agreed that any military objective nearby placed cities "actually and geographically, as well as legally, on the battlefield." It was well to learn from European imperial control that "to a fanatical savage, a bomb dropped out of the sky on the sacred temple of his omnipotent God is a sign and a symbol that that God has withdrawn his favor." Colby stressed that even those who made the category mistake of thinking there were nonwhite innocents ought to buy in: "If a few 'non-combatants'—if there be any such in native folk of this character—are killed, the loss of life is probably far less than might have been sustained in prolonged operations of a more polite character."

Hard as it might be to accept, Colby concluded, "there were no non-combatants" anymore in an age of looming total war. What had always been true of war against savages was now true about war of nation against nation. "There is a popular fallacy to the effect that with the passing of time and the adoption of international conventions war has become more and more humane," he recorded, almost gleefully. "It is actually true that warfare has become more and more vicious and vigorous as time goes on." Nor should states move to punish individuals for infractions of whatever rules there were, Colby added. "When airplanes destroy towns occupied only by noncombatants" or "when atrocious acts are committed on a large scale and with universal frequency," it is normally because "governmental policy or General Staff strategy have so prescribed."

AS A RESULT OF THIS PREHISTORY, THE PAX AMERICANA CAME TO THE world umbilically linked to air war. The fall of France in the summer of 1940 sparked an astonishing transformation in intellectual and policy circles. If a future peace could be established, it would need to be guaranteed. As war loomed, the world was going Wright's way. But with the Japanese attack on America's Pacific empire on December 7, 1941, the meaning of "internationalism" began to drift beyond Wilson's apparent commitment to the equality of democratic sovereigns—at least in states of white peoples. As the war went on, and the postwar order was planned, internationalism became a commitment to an arrangement in which the United States would intervene on condition of becoming first among equals, a new empire in all but name.

For liberals and socialists, internationalism had once suggested world government among equal states, but now it came to be nearly synonymous with armed if seemingly beneficent supremacy. Noninterventionist socialists had died out since World War I, and liberals writing at *The Nation*, *The New Republic*, and elsewhere followed a twisted path that ultimately swerved toward intervention and supremacy. Critical to the lingering leeriness of war among progressives was the influence, often subliminally, of the Soviet Union's public relations. For years, that country presented itself as a peace power, in part out of weakness, as it struggled for survival behind the *cordon sanitaire* with which the West kept communism at bay. But by the late 1930s, with Josef Stalin fully engaged in the Spanish Civil War, burying the hatchet with Hitler in 1939 and then dividing Poland with him, the equation of progressivism and peace seemed obsolete.

A few, like Wright, believed that it was still possible to create a new international law that put down aggressors. "A transition from a hegemonic to a democratic organization of the world could only rest on a firm structure of international law, but that law proved too weak to bear the load . . . There seems more hope in a federal organization of the world." The truth was that America's choice for armed supremacy after Pearl Harbor dealt as humbling a defeat to internationalist visions of peace through law, especially the dream of arbitration, as to "isolation." World War II enshrined a European peace through the ascendancy of one great power. It wasn't what Wright had intended. He was a charter member of the World Citizens Association, founded in 1938, and joined his Chicago colleagues in drafting a world constitution after 1945.

World War II, as he saw it, was a war fought on behalf of the rule of international law, for "the ramparts to defend are the ramparts of law, and the place to defend them is the place where lawlessness begins." Totalitarian states, Wright explained in summer 1941, were so perverted that their existence was simply incompatible with the new destiny of international law to abolish recourse to force. The Soviet Union's move from peace policies to the offensive invasion of Finland in November 1939 proved that point long before Hitler moved west and then east, rupturing his erstwhile alliance with Stalin and invading his lands. To Wright, "Totalitarianism both in principle and practice rejects all standards above the legislation of the totalitarian government."

WORLD WAR II WAS THE MOST BRUTAL WAR YET, AND NOT ONLY BECAUSE the Axis powers disregarded all constraints. America's reconquest of the islands of its Pacific empire proved so costly and difficult that it shaped a still-debated endgame to the conflict. The recourse to aerial bombing in 1944–45 lessened the more symmetrical horrors of close-range engagement, but only in favor of mass death of civilians, first as Japanese cities were razed by fire and then as two nuclear bombs were dropped with no thought about the rules of international law.

The propriety of morale or strategic bombing, with openly advertised roots in colonial counterinsurgency, was already secure enough by the early 1920s to inform a doctrine of the United States Army (of which the United States Air Force was formally part until

1947). According to one 1922 manual, "The effect of bombing . . . is generally very great upon the morale of an irregular enemy. The objective of irregular operations . . . may be the capital of the people, their main source of supply, their prominent leaders, or, if a fanatical people, the seat of their religion." General Billy Mitchell, father of the U.S. Air Force, propagandized for air power. He promised in 1925 that "it will cause a whole people to take an increasing interest as to whether a country shall go to war or not, because they are all exposed to attack by aircraft, no matter if they live in the remotest interior of the country." Winning control of the air was the first imperative geopolitically and strategically. A willingness to bomb could guarantee that "if a nation ambitious for universal conquest gets off to a 'flying start' in a war of the future, it may be able to control the whole world more easily than a nation has controlled a continent in the past."

Such exciting prospects, of course, were initially speculation. Air superiority promised relative immunity from harm for whichever states achieved it, but airplanes were persistently inaccurate and not invulnerable (especially on the ground). Enduring worries about whether strategic bombing was worth the financial and moral costs were not banished until the success over Japan in 1944–45. And outside the circles of enthusiasts, there was apprehension about what it would mean for those who might lose the contest for air supremacy.

In 1937, the Japanese bombing of Nanking was overshadowed by Japanese atrocities on the ground: the massacre of tens of thousands of civilians, the execution of prisoners of war, and the mass rape of women. In a widely remarked event in May 1939, however, the Japanese air force rained terror on the improvised Chinese capital of Chongqing, setting off a wave of anxiety and nausea worldwide about the coming war. Madame Chiang Kai-shek's heartrending report from the scene vividly depicted the "raging infernos" leaving the sky "crimson with fire and, indeed, with the blood of thousands of victims" as "mothers watched their children burn alive."

Only European bombing, however, provoked a last-ditch insistence on the need for humane legal constraint on the practice. On September 1, 1939, with World War II on and the Luftwaffe bombing Warsaw, Franklin Roosevelt publicly condemned the "ruthless bombing from the air of civilians in unfortified centers of population" that "shocked the conscience of humanity." "If resort is had to this form of inhuman barbarism during the period of the tragic conflagration with which the world is now confronted," he added, "hundreds of thousands of innocent human beings . . . will lose their lives." He pled to "every government" to affirm that "in no event, and under no circumstances" would any power bomb civilians or "unfortified cities." The "rules of warfare" prohibited it, Roosevelt insisted, repeating his plea two months later with the Winter War in Finland under way and the Soviets pounding Helsinki from the sky. If Roosevelt knew that his own air forces had long since determined that there were no unfortified cities—and that the morale of populations counted as a fair target—he did not mention it.

Americans in the European theater mainly flew daytime targeted sorties, while the Royal Air Force bombed areas and destroyed German cities by night throughout 1942 and 1943. The American Curtis LeMay, a major in the European theater in 1942 who piloted dangerous missions himself, strove to make bombing more precise there—though the Americans and the British had agreed from the start that it was not necessary to be too discriminating. They divided their tasks between military targets and strategic bombing because only the Americans had the Norden bombsight, which allowed a modicum of control. In the second half of 1944, both air forces unleashed firestorms on urban centers in tandem. One U.S. officer worried that it would "absolutely convince the Germans that we are the barbarians they say we are, for it would be perfectly obvious to them that it is primarily a large-scale attack on civilians as, in fact, it of course will be." As, of course, it was.

If there was a moral calculus in the mix, no law figured into it. In the U.K. House of Lords, in February 1944, the Anglican bishop of Chichester, George Bell, gave an impassioned speech doubting these acts comported with any legality, earthly or higher: "The Allies stand for something greater than power," he explained. "The chief name inscribed on our banner is 'Law.' It is because the bombing of enemy towns—this area bombing—raises this issue of power unlimited and exclusive that . . . it is of supreme importance that we who, with our Allies, are the liberators of Europe should so use power that it is always under the control of law." In a nation that had been pushed to the brink of defeat, with air raids on London and the destruction of Coventry burned in memory, Bell's insistence on the law was an enormously unpopular view.

Only misgivings around the superfluous firestorm in Dresden in February 1945 caused Winston Churchill to bring strategic bombing to an end. The cultural capital of a beaten enemy was devastated with no regard for the presence of thousands of refugees, who would make up a substantial proportion of the tens of thousands dead. His reputation tarnished as a result, an unrepentant Arthur "Bomber" Harris could rightly claim in his memoir that "in this matter of the use of aircraft in war there is, it so happens, no law at all." Should there be? *The New York Times*, in the outcry around the English former nurse, writer, and pacifist Vera Brittain's coruscating ethical critique of the bombing of Germany, took the tack that no law could make bombing salubrious, and only a durable peace mattered now. "Attempts to humanize [war] have utterly failed," its editorialists conceded in March 1944. "Let us not deceive ourselves into thinking that war can be made more humane. It cannot. It can only be abolished. Let us resolve that this war shall be so conducted and so concluded that no city shall ever be bombed again."

No international lawyers rose to prominence in ethical resistance to urban holocausts, perhaps because the law gave them no basis to do so. No matter their positions in earlier debates, some even championed bombing as the means to the end of a peace beyond the need for humane warfare. J. M. Spaight, the Englishman who had promised in the 1920s that air power would transform hideous bloodletting into bloodless surgery, was cheerful in retirement from the British air ministry when things did not turn out precisely as he had foreseen. Even amid World War II's carnage, he now judged that "the prophets of calamity who fixed their thoughts on the menace of the air were really the slaves to an *idée fixe*." Having complained in the late 1930s that no one listened to him when he argued that air war needed rules, he realized now, with the end of the war in sight, that the bomber had "saved civilization." Indeed, the bomber would prove the guarantor of any postwar peace: "It is the ideal weapon for smothering aggression."

But Japan had to fall, too. Many Americans greeted a Carthaginian peace in the making, requiring not just total defeat but utter destruction. Sent to the Pacific as a general to command the bombing of Japan in 1944–45, Curtis LeMay had a number of reasons for sending his B-29 Superfortresses on low-altitude runs at night to burn wooden cities and the civilians living in them. Scores of cities and hundreds of thousands of civilians were incinerated well before Harry Truman's climactic decision to nuke Hiroshima and Nagasaki. More people likely died in the destruction of Tokyo on the night of March 9–10, 1945, than from Fat Man and Little Boy, the two nuclear bombs that the B-29s *Bock's Car* and *Enola Gay* dropped on Hiroshima and Nagasaki in August of that year. LeMay himself sought the most destruction possible because it was predicted at the time that a ground invasion would require 750,000 U.S. troops, at least a third of whom might die. (Numbers were subsequently exaggerated way upward in rationalization.) Thanks to LeMay's innovations, he recalled, "the war was over before the atomic bomb was dropped." As the inferno raged, never was the law of war deemed relevant, nor was any lawyer asked whether it was.

Like earlier colonial struggles, World War II was a race war—for Adolf Hitler in the European theater, most of all, but also for Americans in the Pacific. It was certainly a racialized war for the Japanese, who presented themselves as both antiracist and pan-Asian, whitewashing their severity in the annexation of Korea in 1910 and their colonization of much of China, beginning with Manchuria in 1931. The Americans ended their war in the Pacific in the way the Japanese had started it, with death from the sky. But Americans also drew on their own traditions from the ground, as the leading historian Allan Nevins commented in 1946. "Emotions forgotten since our most savage Indian wars were reawakened by the ferocity of Japanese commanders," he reported—and drove Americans to atrocious war without limits.

With the rest of the Axis, the Japanese committed the clearest violations of the laws of war on the books when World War II began. After Nanking came the infamous mistreatment of prisoners during the Bataan death march of 1942, which killed some Americans and tens of thousands of their Filipino colonial subjects. Americans were appalled by the dreadful fate of U.S. flyers captured during Lt. Col. James Doolittle's impetuous raid over Tokyo in April 1942. But it was a little rich for anyone to seek the high ground in these years. The Doolittle raid openly aimed at civilian targets—though it was only a pinprick compared with LeMay's cheerful decision to burn the city to the ground two years later.

The straits of island warfare in the Pacific led U.S. marines and GIs to descend to the lowest levels. Few Japanese prisoners were taken, and not because they would never submit. There were especially routine violations of applicable rules about the treatment of the dead; skull collections were especially popular, alongside necklaces of harvested gold teeth. And the nonchalant execution of civilians, including "gook" women and children—the epithet had its origins in a slur on Filipinos forty years before—was familiar.

For Americans in the Pacific race war, it was universal to ignore, or treat as unreal, whatever limitations in warfare may have existed. It was "Indian country" all over again. Freely indicting their enemy as a race, and persecuting their fellow citizens of Japanese descent, Americans normally exempted the German people from opprobrium for Nazi crimes against non-Jews and continued to look down on Adolf Hitler's chief racial victims. Both in and beyond the air war, the ambiance for the conduct of hostilities was very different in the Pacific theater. It wasn't "fair" to suggest that the Japanese deserved the fate of ancestral native foes at home, *The New York Times Magazine* commented. They had earned worse, for sometimes their corpses were armed to explode, a risk that rangers in the West had never confronted. "Even a dead Jap isn't a good Jap" accorded a posthumous virtue to onetime indigenous foes. Whether or not Indians were better than Japanese, traditions of exterminatory warfare honed to deal with the former were adaptable to the latter.

On August 10, 1945, two days after Nagasaki, the government of the Japanese empire, through the intermediation of Switzerland, protested the American holocaust. "The use of atomic bombs . . . surpasses the indiscriminate cruelty of any other existing weapons and projectiles," it insisted, citing the Hague rule against "arms, projectiles, or material calculated to cause unnecessary suffering." Legal principle was (and largely remains) too vague to prohibit nuclear weapons, and Japan was not in a good position to invoke it. Five days later, Japan surrendered. The Americans never wrote back.

THE MOST EXTRAORDINARY FACT ABOUT THE AFTERMATH OF WORLD War II is that anyone thought they could piece back together again the dreams of a peaceful world or a more humane war. The Axis had smashed the first and both sides had done grievous harm to the second. As in World War I, the Red Cross got good press and a second Nobel Prize (in 1944) for monitoring prisoners of war. The organization's wholesale failure on the Eastern Front, where Nazis executed upward of three million captured Soviet soldiers, and its even deeper failure to respond to European Jewry's destruction—scandalously, its leader Carl Jacob Burckhardt harbored sympathies for the Nazis out of his greater fear of communism—have become common knowledge only in the decades since.

But if anything, these tragedies masked a much more comprehensive and significant catastrophe for the project of humane war, which was the failure of the law to make the conflict less cruel for anyone. Strategic bombing alone, in Western Europe and over Japan, accounted for millions of civilian deaths. The lesson was not that total and totalizing wars were uniquely immune to humane regulation. It was never clear that the laws of war were more effective in the case of limited strife, and it was precisely unlimited carnage that most required their application and respect. Clearly, the circumstances for taking the dictates of humane war seriously, even among the conventional forces of transatlantic armies, were going to be a long time coming.

In part the reason was that the laws of war had had no priority after World War I. Even as World War II began to loom, few put much stock in the revival of those laws after their embarrassing irrelevance the last time around. Even Hersch Lauterpacht, a Galician Jew who became a Cambridge don, could acknowledge in 1935 that "rules of moderation may, even if they are observed, prove to be insignificant when compared with the devastation wrought by war." And they were generally not observed. "Law ought not to abdicate its function" in the face of the worry "that by devoting attention to the laws of war, we not only create an unjustified belief in the possibility or likelihood of their observance, but also deny by implication the reality of the renunciation of war as an instrument of national policy." But for the time being, international law could do little more than save face.

No wonder that Wright and other American internationalists labored to the point of exhaustion to ensure that international law played some role in the final peace of World War II. He guarded the possibility even before World War II that, as one of his honored predecessors in the field had put it, "times in which international law has been seriously disregarded, have been followed by obligations in which the European conscience has done penance by putting itself under straighter obligations than those which it before acknowledged." It would require organization and law to institutionalize that result. Based on the work of his long-running Committee to Study the Causes of Wars, it was complacent to assume that economic or technological progress would do the job on its own; if anything, the reverse was true.

Outright pacifism almost died as a result of the coming of World War II. In Germany, it was one of Hitler's first targets. Carl von Ossietzky, the renowned German pacifist, had been rounded up as a political threat after the Reichstag fire and sent to Spandau Prison before spending his last years in concentration camps (in spite of his 1935 Nobel Peace Prize). But after years of debate over appeasement, most agreed that meeting Hitler's threat required bellicosity. The techniques of pacifism did survive World War II, especially in anticolonial efforts around the world as well as in the American civil rights movement, thanks to the Dutch Reformed pacifist minister A. J. Muste, the "American Gandhi." But the pacifist cause itself has never lived down accusations that the "isolationism" to which it led was part of the problem—"objectively pro-fascist," as George Orwell described it in 1942. A genuine mass option during World War I, pacifism was far more marginal during World War II, and it met with even more massive public revulsion even so.

Still, American intervention hardly connoted American empire. Activists and experts like Wright seeking to institutionalize peace through state agreement had achieved mainstream prominence due to World War I's costs. Now Wright hoped that World War II could lead to a breakthrough to an internationalist rather than an imperial peace. The meek might not inherit the earth. But it was by no means a foregone conclusion, Wright thought, that the war would bring about American empire instead of the workable system for world peace he had long sought.

In 1939, in deep conversation with the Department of State's own planners, Wright cofounded the Commission to Study the Organization of the Peace, a private organization that threw itself into imagining a postwar world. Keeping hope alive, Wright still believed that the war would bring about a federalization of world affairs, especially when it came to nixing the ability of states to disrupt the peace. Even before Pearl Harbor, he proposed that the new federal structure would have an executive, a legislature, and a judiciary. It would also need a police force (which Wright preferred calling a "peace force") that could nip war in the bud rather than merely intervene when it broke out. The most urgent need, once the United

States was finally in the war in 1941, was keeping it in the peace, to avoid repeating the errors of 1919. "We should . . . assume our share of responsibility for ordering the world of which we are inescapably a part," Wright urged his fellow Americans in a magazine. If not, "we may expect the catastrophic decline of civilization to continue."

After the decisive battles of Midway and Stalingrad, Wright watched as the Allies began planning the peace in earnest, at a series of summits at Tehran, Yalta, and Potsdam. Plans to transform the United Nations from a military alliance into a treaty organization devoted to ending "the scourge of war," as its 1945 charter proclaimed, were debated and finalized. Uppermost in Wright's mind was the task of providing "institutions to determine, whenever hostilities occur or are threatened, which belligerent is the aggressor and which is the victim defending himself." And to cure the central defect of the Kellogg-Briand Pact and the League of Nations, "it must provide itself with means for preventing and stopping the fight." Outlawry would leave behind the inadequate carapace of the League of Nations that caused it to fail, and allow the world to enjoy eternal peace under new arrangements that would identify aggressors and put their aggression down.

And then punish them. The ultimate goal, Wright recorded in his epochmaking *A Study of War*, had to be moving from a world in which enemies "like a wild beast, could only be hunted but not tamed" to one of world citizenship. But getting there required opprobrium for Nazis once they were hunted down. Even as the United Nations met in San Francisco in summer 1945 to finalize its arrangements, the victorious Allies in Europe met in London and finalized their wartime plans to try National Socialist criminals. From early in the negotiations, the charge of "crimes against peace" had pride of place, because the thing the United States agreed most about with the Soviet Union was that starting war was the worst thing Hitler and his henchmen had done.

The trial commenced in November 1945 in the Bavarian city of Nuremberg, a picturesque medieval town where some of the fiercest urban fighting in the war had happened that spring. The city's imposing and spacious Palace of Justice had providentially escaped intensive Allied bombing, and Wright traveled there to work as a technical advisor. Earlier in the year, he had already cleared away objections to trying individuals for acts of state in apparent violation of international law. There was no legal barrier, Wright urged, to holding high-ranking National Socialists to account for offenses against peace, since the events of the 1930s had rendered aggressive war illegal. Some objected that no one had ever proposed to make individuals legally accountable for aggressive war, or precisely defined aggression—but whatever it was, Wright was sure Hitler's henchmen had perpetrated it.

Nuremberg unfolded, indeed, as a trial against aggression first and foremost, with inhumanity demoted to the consequence of that gateway crime, a kind of included lesser offense. "This inquest," the chief prosecutor, Supreme Court Justice Robert Jackson, announced right at the start of his opening statement, "represents the practical effort . . . to utilize international law to meet the greatest menace of our times—aggressive war." Having missed its chance at the end of World War I, the world would now try enemies of peace. "War is essentially an evil thing," the judges wrote the next year in their judgment, emphasizing the absolute priority of banning it. "Its consequences are not confined to the belligerent States alone, but affect the whole world. To initiate a war of aggression, therefore, is not only an international crime; it is the supreme international crime differing only from other war crimes in that it contains within itself the accumulated evil of the whole."

The Soviets, insisting that Kellogg-Briand had not gone far enough, led the way in making war not merely illegal but criminal and punishable. The United States agreed with its then ally's prioritization of curbing aggressive war. As Roosevelt's attorney general, Jackson had been instrumental in circumventing the U.S. Neutrality Act while the great debate over intervention raged. At Nuremberg, his "main preoccupation" was to justify both bending the law in the past and establishing America's armed but nonaggressive role in keeping the peace for the future. But there was also an unanswerable moral case for punishing aggression.

After generations of peace activism and the experience of conflict, it was obvious that there were terrible consequences to war *other than* its almost inevitable inhumanity, which was but one feature of war's toll. The legal death of combatants by the tens of millions and the broadest accounting of the costs of the fight that statesmen had committed their people to pay mattered, too. "Once the evil of war has been precipitated, nothing remains but the fragile effort . . . to limit the cruelty by which it is conducted," Herbert Wechsler, perhaps the greatest American legal scholar of the time, observed in explaining why Nuremberg slighted such cruelty, including European Jewry's destruction. "Of these two challenges," he asked rhetorically, "who will deny that the larger offense is the unjustified initiation of a war?" If you criminalized and stigmatized war, you made it less likely for crimes *in* war to occur.

As the history of our time shows, the reverse is not true: you can make war humane, while war continues. But it made no sense to those in the 1940s that war ought to be cleansed of its crimes; it *was* the crime. Home from Nuremberg, Wright definitely agreed it had been a good thing to rank aggression the premier evil. In effect, it was an auspicious sign for a federation to come that there was so much agreement to try individuals for war after the fact—as the Allies did in Tokyo for Japanese perpetrators, too. "Sanctions to be effective must operate on individuals rather than states," Wright explained. "International law cannot survive in the shrinking world, threatened by military instruments of increasing destructiveness, if sanctioned only by the good faith and self-help of governments."

Many war crimes were punished at Nuremberg, in later trials in the occupation zones of Germany, and in the successor trial that was held in Tokyo for Asian crimes. "Crimes against humanity," the term introduced into international law on an August day in London in 1945 between the obliteration of Hiroshima and that of Nagasaki, concerned killing civilians. But at Nuremberg and Tokyo, the charge was only allowed in connection with the primary infraction of aggressive war, which Americans were sure they did not fight. As for aerial bombardment, all powers had conducted it, and no one was punished.

THE MAIN QUESTION FOR THE FUTURE WAS WHETHER THE PRINCIPLES espoused at Nuremberg would extend to all war, and therefore which wars—and which American wars—would be deemed illegal. Jackson had insisted that the new regime for punishing aggressive war had to be universal rather than a smokescreen for victor's justice. "The record on which we judge these defendants today is the record on which history will judge us tomorrow," Jackson pronounced eloquently, insisting that the United States take seriously in its future conduct its punishment of the aggression of other states. "To pass these defendants a poisoned chalice is to put it to our own lips as well." And even more important than the risk of hypocrisy in the future was the interdiction of aggressive war—including in the name of self-defense. Nuremberg implied that aggressive war must be stopped before the fact, instead of merely punished after the fact.

At San Francisco in the summer of 1945, the United Nations Charter was finalized. Even as the Pacific War continued, internationalists such as Wright appeared to get what they wanted—but with provisos that risked reversing everything, leaving the rictus of ongoing war behind a smiling mask of peace in good times. The Charter instituted a Security Council with a monopoly on legal force, except when nations act in self-defense. And it was empowered to deem lawless false or pretextual claims to acting in self-defense. Yet the devil was in the details. Everyone understood that American internationalism mutated in the course of World War II. Wright's form was marginalized by those who wanted the United Nations to look like a federation but function without any constraint on its most powerful members—most definitely including the United States itself. "International law has a secondary position in the Charter," one

American commented just after its promulgation. "The pendulum of political thinking has swung," he added, from an idealist vision of internationalism "to the other extreme, the 'realism' of . . . San Francisco."

Where the text of the League of Nations Covenant had explicitly made room for the Monroe Doctrine in hopes of winning U.S. support, the "ghost" of the doctrine remained in the United Nations Charter. With its specific references to regional security, the charter was understood by Americans to recognize the validity of the Monroe Doctrine and their country's primacy in its hemisphere. Taken as a whole, the compact went further: it verged on making the entire world the security zone of one country, which could act to uphold its conception of international order without formal obligations. As one who helped negotiate the charter, the Michigan senator and Republican internationalist Arthur Vandenberg remarked ebulliently, "We have retained a complete veto—exclusive in our hands—over any decisions involving external activities." That allowed even onetime critics of Roosevelt's war such as the gruff Senator Robert Taft of Ohio to vote to approve it. Much more important, the veto rules agreed to at the last minute with the Soviets at San Francisco—the touchy issue that almost wrecked the scheme—allowed for any of the permanent five members of the Security Council to keep any state, not least themselves, from being branded an aggressor. The arrangement exempted the United States, which would go on to hundreds of military interventions after 1945, from ever being named a legal aggressor. After all, it could veto any suggestion that it strayed from peace.

It is "unlikely that sanctions would ever actually be voted against a great power or its friends," Wright glumly admitted in 1947. No, it definitely wasn't what he had had in mind. It meant that, early and often, the United States could use the exception of "self-defense" to the otherwise absolute prohibition on force. But the hypothetical potential for American endless war was not the only problem. With the coming of the Cold War and the Communist takeover of Eastern

Europe, it was clear that the defeat of Hitler had still left a totalitarian onetime ally around to disturb the peace.

Now a nuclear power, the Soviet Union, after all, was also on the Security Council and possessed a veto. It used that power routinely in an era when the United States and its allies controlled the body (after Mao Zedong's 1949 revolution, China lost its seat for three decades). With the Soviet Union playing spoiler in the face of American mastery, the organization was deadlocked. There was a peace in Europe, armed to the teeth at the Fulda Gap, with no federation relevant to it: not much to write home about and hardly the stuff of which Wright had dreamed. It was the balance of power of two empires, not international comity under law.

THE QUESTION OF HOW WARS WERE FOUGHT WAS NOT IGNORED IN THE late 1940s. But at Nuremberg, and at its sister trial in Tokyo, and in a new attempt at rulemaking, the question was distinctly subsidiary to the quest for peace. The middle of the twentieth century saw the war with the most victims in history: at least twenty million soldiers died legally, and five million prisoners of war died in violation of the laws of humane protection, with fifty million civilians perishing because they were directly targeted or collaterally killed, or they suffered from disease and disorder during the war or after. Of these, six million Jews died in history's most notorious crime. The main priority for world affairs was the establishment of international peace. But a few turned their attention to changing the rules for fighting war.

The year 1945 might not have seemed like a propitious time to pick up the laws of war, dust them off, and try again. After all the wretched things that had been done in the war, wasn't that idea among its fatalities? Yet it was precisely during the interval between the end of U.S. hostilities in one area of the Pacific and their beginning five years later that the most famous rules of war—the Geneva Conventions of 1949—were framed. What lessons had been learned? That depended, as always, on which options states were forced to take off the table under the pressure of public opinion, and what options they sought to retain in view of the wars they still expected to fight. Even with a nervous and tentative European peace in place, few expected the great powers to stop fighting globally. One reason was that European empire was far from dead. And the United States, the new titan, was on the way to taking its place as ultimate guarantor of order.

Decades later, once the Geneva Conventions became central to far more widespread aspirations for humane war, they would take on new significance in culture and law. In their own time, they registered the horror of World War II only selectively. Most important, while they were slightly more humanitarian in content than any previous laws of war, the Geneva Conventions were designed to be largely inapplicable to colonial and counterinsurgent war—and if they did apply, to be unenforceable. At the time, West Europeans anticipated anticolonial opposition they were not yet above callously suppressing, while Americans were soon to embark on globalized war—in Korea, for example.

The International Committee of the Red Cross drove the process of cajoling states to support the reboot. The ICRC emerged from World War II a profoundly damaged institution, and almost lost custodianship of the laws of war altogether before putting its energy behind the new convention project. It was remarkable that, with the Cold War approaching and then taking hold, the ICRC convinced the sixty states of the time of the need to act at all, and the treaties were no doubt honorable in the steps they took. It was especially revolutionary that the Soviet Union—along with the states of its empire in Eastern Europe—participated, after bitter recriminations kept it out before World War II. Indeed, the Soviet self-presentation as a humanitarian force shaped the U.S. negotiation posture, not least efforts to fend off proposals to ban atomic and other bombardment.

Beyond some revisions to historic agreements concerning injured soldiers and sailors and prisoners of war, there were two novel achievements in coverage in 1949. Now at last there was a separate treaty that protected civilians, especially under circumstances of foreign occupation. There was also Common Article 3—"common" because it figured in all four of the new Geneva treaties—which protected combatants and civilians in circumstances of internal or "non-international" armed conflict. Some rules against taking civilians hostage and their collective punishment were strengthened because the Nazis had made those acts radioactive. The same was true of mass deportations, which during World War II had also affected non-Jews, who were far likelier to return to tell their stories of internment.

The treaty process had few implications for the actual fighting of war, which the spotty old Hague rules still governed. Even the new civilian convention did not clearly provide new protection from aerial bombardment by conventional or nuclear weaponry, and it didn't challenge the idea that any amount of military gain could justify any amount of innocent death. What today seem the worst cruelties of World War II were not the problem the delegates were there to solve. Part of the reason was that the Holocaust of European Jewry had not become central to public consciousness. And the power of states to deliver death from the sky was viewed at worst as a necessary evil.

It was a large achievement to ban civilian punishment, individually or collectively, of the kind typified by Hitler's decision to order the Czech town of Lidice razed in 1942 as a reprisal for the assassination of his trusted aide Reinhard Heydrich. But the new treaty did not prohibit the mass starvation that had killed most civilians in World War I. It had recurred in World War II in Nazi Germany's Hunger Plan—but also in the U.S. attempt to induce mass famine via Operation Starvation in Japan and its shrinking empire of islands. Humanitarians tried for more, but the treaty prohibited only the interdiction of foodstuffs destined for children and expectant mothers, unless there was reason to believe someone else would eat them: "humane blockade."

As a default, growing clarity that civilians mattered still meant something. And this spirit also affected Common Article 3, which held that in "armed conflict not of an international character," those "taking no active part in hostilities," including captured or wounded soldiers as well as civilians above the fray, had to be treated "humanely," no matter their "race, colour, religion or faith, sex, birth or wealth." Specifically, humanity barred killing, torture, and other "cruel" or "humiliating and degrading" treatment. And no punishments were allowed, especially executions, without "judgement pronounced by a regularly constituted court" with "judicial guarantees." After many battles in the negotiations to the treaty, a rather awkward alliance of the Swiss humanitarians and the Soviet Union overcame opposition to any such article. But the relevance of this article to the war on terror more than fifty years later was entirely unforeseeable, because the intent at the time was to place constraints on internal armed conflict, especially civil war. Even there, it was primarily a symbolic victory, given that any state could always dismiss its opponents as terrorists rather than belligerents—an option routinely relied on by the European imperial powers fully expecting to engage in counterinsurgency on their own territory.

Worst of all, the new rules were toothless. It was not only that the treaties left to states themselves the obligation to punish "grave breaches" of its rules for international conflicts. There was also no obligation to try violations of the minimal rules in Common Article 3 for internal armed conflict, and when it came to the more robust framework for international law, the task was generally left by states to self-protective militaries themselves. More fundamentally, no law could magically enact a culture in which a new kind of humane war mattered to militaries or populations. World War II did not bring about that culture. As the Red Cross leader Jean Pictet acknowledged in 1954, in a cautious stocktaking on what he had achieved so far, "In times of war, legal stipulations—especially today, when warfare is especially ruthless—are liable to be wholly disregarded." The results illustrated a sobering fact: everyone anticipated that many more ugly conflicts were on the way. In light of the atomic bomb, J. M. Spaight caustically observed, "the humanitarian Conventions read like hypocritical nonsense."

Once again, after World War II as after its predecessor, nobody mobilized in the name of humane war, though undoubtedly the few around the world who heard about the long-obscure Geneva Conventions sympathized with their spirit. There would not have been such a diplomatic struggle around the Geneva Conventions had parties to the negotiations expected them to be eternally meaningless, but that does not mean states expected to worry about widespread outrage over the continuation of brutal war anytime soon. European empires learned sooner than they would have liked that anticolonialists could make hay of counterinsurgent violence. In the long run, however, European empires were on the way out, and what would matter more was whether and how America's global wars were going to be affected by the new rules.

While there was no humane war movement of note for decades—outside of the realm of Swiss patricians—peace movements survived after World War II. Yet in the United States they had almost disappeared, compared with their presence before. Those that survived were comparatively disabused. They existed in the shadow of decades of global death, and amid self-styled realism about the need for violence on both sides of the Cold War and decolonization struggles. With the midwestern Henry Wallace cashiered in 1944 as vice president and losing an independent run for president in 1948, the American tradition of Christian pacifism was almost dead. The declaration by the Soviet Union (which infiltrated Wallace's campaign) of "a peace offensive" in 1948, as the hallmark of its own empire's foreign policy, calling for coexistence rather than conflict, made it exasperatingly difficult for Americans to articulate their own pacific visions. "Peace propaganda and agitation have a disarming effect on those nations, which are intended victims of communism," screamed the chair of the House Un-American Activities Committee. The Cold War shifted what the United States said it stood for globally, from peace to freedom. Fledgling movements targeted the fearful threat of the atomic bomb, some Christians retrieved their traditions from before World War II and adjusted them in the face of globalized conflict, and women's groups continued their hopes of softening international affairs in a man's world—to little effect when it was the order of the day to defend and spread freedom violently.

In August 1949, the Soviets detonated their own first test nuclear weapon in the desert of Kazakhstan and the arms race began. As Albert Schweitzer, the Alsatian historian of Christianity turned medical humanitarian, noted when he received the Nobel Peace Prize in 1954, treaties on the laws of war may have made some difference, but "these advantages are trifling when set beside the immeasurable harm which has been inflicted by modern methods of death and destruction." He spoke for the few peace activists of the early Cold War: "There cannot, at the present time, be any question of 'humanizing' war."

THE EUROPEAN PEACE COEXISTED WITH A NEW BOUT OF CRUEL GLOBAL war. And this time, it was Americans who waged that war. Its most decisive moment came on October 1, 1950, when General Douglas MacArthur weighed an extraordinary choice on which the future of the world order turned.

The United States had helped divide the Korean Peninsula after the Japanese were expelled in summer 1945, and helped the local strongman Syngman Rhee consolidate power in the south. When the Communist leader Kim Il Sung crossed the 38th parallel in the summer of 1950, the United States quickly committed to assist South Korea against the onslaught. MacArthur's troops were driven to the last hills around Pusan, in the extreme south of the peninsula, beyond hope or rescue. But with an amphibious landing of 270 ships bearing 80,000 marines in the barely guarded harbor of Inchon, not far from the largest Korean city of Seoul, MacArthur daringly snatched victory from the jaws of defeat. In one of the most miraculous reversals of fortune in military history, MacArthur drove Kim Il Sung back beyond the 38th parallel from whence he had come.

The status quo before North Korean aggression in June 1950 had been restored. Would MacArthur keep going? It was momentous:

besides the extraordinary brutality and death in the Korean War, MacArthur's decision to step beyond the 38th parallel destroyed the prospects of a Pax Americana under international law. MacArthur's choice meant that America's age of ascendancy in world politics would be not only a merciless one of endless war for decades in the global south—but also one in which the rules of peace that the United States had crafted in 1945, and enforced at Nuremberg against the Nazis, did not apply to its own acts across a long arc of territory in the Asian "rimland" of bloody contest between two systems.

When Kim first invaded the south in June, the United Nations Security Council had met and condemned the Communist aggression. To that point, the plan of internationalists was working: not that eternal peace would take hold magically but that its disturbers could be identified and interdicted. An accident helped: the day the Security Council met in Manhattan to authorize restoring the peace that Kim breached, the Soviet Union's representative, Jacob Malik, stayed on Long Island, supposedly in protest that Communist China had been deprived of its council seat. With no spoiler's veto, the plan remained in force, and the U.S. confrontation remained legal under United Nations auspices.

The United Nations Charter had not exactly envisioned a single country taking the lead in the way that the United States now had. But thanks to the Security Council resolutions, the U.S. intervention was broadly perceived as a good-faith act of keeping the peace. In the memorable phrase of the country's D-day hero and now joint chiefs of staff chair General Omar Bradley, the resolutions could make the Korean War one "under the guise of aid to the United Nations" rather than the act of a capitalist empire opposing Communist expansion. The new script of peace had not been torn up in favor of the old one in which powerful nations angled for advantage and might in a lawless world.

Yet those same United Nations resolutions that authorized response to the aggression of the north against the south gave no authority for crossing the 38th parallel, let alone for regime change or "rollback" above it. By the time of MacArthur's decision, Malik had returned to the Security Council to foil further action. The former Vermont senator Warren Austin, serving as U.S. ambassador to the United Nations, now dismissed the parallel as an "imaginary line."

In an era before decolonization multiplied its membership, the United States controlled the UN General Assembly. On October 7, the United States organized a General Assembly resolution to bless MacArthur's move north past the 38th parallel as a prelude to a democratic unification of Korea, and then proposed a further "uniting for peace" statement in a vain hope that dreams associated with the United Nations could somehow survive Cold War division. The resolutions passed. But by U.S. design, the General Assembly, unlike the deadlocked Security Council, did not have powers to identify aggressors and organize collective security. It was like a teenager pretending her friends could give her permission to drive the family car, after her parents couldn't agree to let her—and then crashing it. MacArthur's fateful step was the first U.S. abuse of the rules of peace the country had laid down in 1945. It was not the last.

The war that followed was anything but humane, and the laws of war—even the new ones—were largely irrelevant once again. The new Geneva Conventions were hot off the press and no involved state had ratified them in time. (The United States would do so in 1955.) Not only the United States but North and South Korea, too, promised to observe the new provisions, or at least large parts of them. MacArthur informed the press that his "present instructions" were to abide by "the humanitarian principles" of the treaties. The former proconsul of Japan who had sponsored the Tokyo trials of Japanese war criminals warned "Reds" to follow the rules. For U.S. forces, however, the war showed that what MacArthur meant was that "present instructions" were to be ignored or rendered inapplicable.

In practice, it was another "Indian war." Truman had formally integrated the army two years before, and the United States was beginning to lift the Asian restrictions that defined its immigration policies. But racial egalitarianism was not yet central to American identity, or to geopolitical strife. In MacArthur's family traditions lay not only the governance of Pacific colonies; further back, Douglas once recalled, his father had been one of many who shouldered "the onerous task of pushing Indians into the arid recesses of the Southwest and of bringing the white man's brand of law and order to the Western frontier." Now the frontier had moved farther west, in a rising contest against barbarism with an Asian face. (Lt. Gen. John Hodge, whom MacArthur sent in September 1945 to occupy Korea, told his superior on arrival that "Koreans are the same breed of cat as the Japanese.")

General Lawton Collins, army chief of staff throughout the Korean conflict, told *The New York Times* that the "reversion to old-style fighting" required by the conflict was "more comparable to that of our own Indian frontier days than to modern war." The journalist Walter Karig made the same allusion that year in a report in *Collier's* magazine, explaining that U.S. pilots and soldiers were ordered to kill in an environment where their enemies recognized no limits and there was no distinction possible between foe and friend: "Our Red foe scorns all the rules of civilized warfare." The *Harper's Magazine* correspondent observed that the experience took Americans back to the very beginning of their military traditions in a rerun of the Pequot War of the 1630s, where no rules could apply to natives who recognized none themselves.

Even before the war formally began in the summer of 1950, southern Korea had at times reached near civil war conditions, as the U.S. client Syngman Rhee strove to extend and stabilize his rule, notably by carrying out vindictive repression and slaughter in Cheju Island off the tip of the peninsula. The Korean War, like Vietnam later, internationalized an ongoing civil war; indeed, as many may have died in the south in the three years before official U.S. intervention in June 1950 as in the fracas after. Atrocities were committed by all parties to the war, notwithstanding promises to adhere to the laws of war in their new guise—including by Americans, who routinely shot civilian refugees. The machine-gunning of hundreds of civilians at No

Gun Ri in July 1950 became the most notorious of such incidents, after finally being reported in 1999 and confirmed in the controversies that followed.

After MacArthur crossed into North Korea, he operated under a National Security Council directive issued the previous month that called for "liberation" rather than "retaliation," forbidding the United Nations troops he led from "reprisals against the forces, officials, and populace of North Korea, except in accordance with international law." As MacArthur pushed north, Rhee's men followed behind, hunting down suspected Communists and executing their family members, especially after Chinese troops were on the march southward. "We cannot execute them," one American said of captured Koreans who turned out to be Communists, testifying to honorable concern for already old prisoner-of-war rules. "But they can be shot before they become prisoners," he added with a wink—an early example of how minor legal constraints around detention could drive states to kill. Another voice added the proposal to turn prisoners over to Rhee's men to do the dirty work, which broke one of the new convention rules without ceremony.

Then there was the aerial bombardment. There is some evidence that the United States Air Force was ordered under protest to be more discriminate in its targeting in the early months of the war. While more care was taken in fall sorties compared with the winter armageddon, however, it was "precise" only in comparison with what followed. And early air control often involved direct participation in atrocities, like the strafing of hundreds to add insult to the injury of the No Gun Ri massacre.

When Mao Zedong sent his Communist troops across the Yalu River to save Kim's regime, the United States still continued to enjoy absolute air superiority, and used it with no further constraints. The air force bombed the north mercilessly throughout the winter as U.S. troops and their allies retreated south. More tonnage was dropped than had been used over Japan five years earlier, and also more napalm, which was greeted by Americans who witnessed its effect as a miracle weapon. Unlike fifteen years later, no one protested.

Curtis LeMay, now head of the Strategic Air Command back home, later claimed credit for the ashen burnscape. From the beginning of the Korean War, he had advised the use of incendiary bombs, which had worked so well in 1944–45. When MacArthur finally let the air force do its worst, every town and even village of note in the north was reduced to smoking ruin, as fighters strafed those who tried to put the fires out. "The city I'd seen before," one American testified, "wasn't there anymore." During the retreat south to the 38th parallel, meanwhile, ground forces torched farms and foodstuffs. Many of the Korean civilians who survived were left without shelter or sustenance in temperatures so cold that an untold number who did not perish in the bombing froze to death on the road.

Korea was the most brutal war of the twentieth century, measured by the intensity of violence and per capita civilian deaths. In three years, four million died, and half of them were civilians—a higher proportion of the population than in any modern war, including World War II and the Vietnam conflict. As Korea showed, World War II did not end the tradition of inhumane war, especially against "savages." The winter of 1950 was a bleak parody of what was supposed to be a new age of peace.

The American Harry Summers, Jr., had enlisted in the army in 1947—falsifying his birthdate so he could join at fifteen. After serving in Korea and Vietnam, Summers became the sage of the "revisionists." He brazenly downplayed the civilian harm and lawless fighting in Southeast Asia—by comparison with the baseline of Korea. "To antiwar protestors it was axiomatic that the war in Vietnam was the most awful, most barbaric, most terrible war in the history of mankind," Summers grumbled. But he knew better. He had experienced massive change since Korea, where he manned an M-24 tank.

"Nothing in my Vietnam experience came even close to the horrors of the 'scorched earth' policy during our retreat from North

Korea in the winter of 1950," Summers explained. "All houses were burnt, all livestock killed, and all food supplies destroyed to prevent the Chinese from living off the land. Millions of civilians, mostly old men, women and children, were forced to flee their homes in sub-zero weather, and the sight of those poor souls dying in the snow during that terrible trek south still haunts me." By comparison, "the Vietnam war was an exercise in gentility." Summers's goal of minimizing the hell of Vietnam hardly means that he was wrong that Korea—and the whole history of American war before it—was far worse. And not just for victims but also for the idea that a law calling for humanity might matter to their fate.

At the time, almost no Americans complained about the new inhumane war in the name of global peace. But if Korea began a history of flouting new international rules of peace, it was also just another episode in a long history of no-holds-barred violence. For Americans, such harsh tactics were continental before they went global, culminating in Korea before going into decline even by the time the Cold War moved to Vietnam's killing fields. True, a war with less atrocity than Korea—more rules against inhumane fighting and some internalization of them—is hardly setting a high bar. But if American war over centuries sent many soldiers and civilians to the grave, the current "humanity" of America's wars could arise only on the grave of their historic forms.

IN 1942, WITH THE REALIZATION THAT HIS DREAM WAS BOTH CLOSER than ever to being achieved and moving in an unforeseen imperial direction, Quincy Wright had published his summa. *A Study of War*, a fifteen-hundred-page behemoth, sought to bring the science of the causes of war and the foundations of peace onto a new plane. Wright showed no reason—he found barely a leaf of paper in his forest of prose—to mention the value of making war humane. After 1945, he was only half-satisfied that his search for the conditions of durable peace had ended.

In the aftermath of the Korean War, Wright was still hopeful.

The United Nations remained a work in progress. A decade later, in the chilling winter of Cold War antagonism, he was less confident. Material conditions might allow "world government," but—Wright commented in 1960—"the *moral* basis for such government is still lacking." Thirty years after his campaign for a new U.S. foreign policy in the 1930s, he wondered: Was the long peace across the Atlantic that the United States achieved after World War II the internationalist one Wilson had portended, or an imperial one with the familiar afflictions of degradation at home and violence abroad? Wright, who now wore up-to-date glasses and a shock of white hair with the same part in the middle, never said.

That America could bring world peace, by whatever means necessary and beyond the borders of Europe, looked like an ever dimmer possibility by the time Wright reached old age. Before passing away, he joined a small band of lawyers to devise arguments for why the United States, in escalating its military presence in Vietnam, was now reneging on its own commitment never to begin an aggressive war. Outside Europe, shouldn't the United States have to drink from its own chalice? That a war in Vietnam was likely to be inhumane was a near certainty in 1965. But Wright did not prioritize making the conduct of the conflict more law-abiding. Instead, he pinned everything on the hope that the internationalist structure and legal claims he had championed still had enough force to restrain the new hegemon his country had become.

After Wright died in 1970, just shy of his eightieth birthday, and with global peace as elusive as ever, his allies in the movement against the Vietnam War organized a prize in his honor. It was first awarded in February 1972 to a dissident analyst in the Defense Department, who after years of misgivings had concluded that—for the moment, at least—American peace was still an oxymoron. That honoree was Daniel Ellsberg.

PART II

HUMANITY

CHAPTER FIVE

The Vietnamese Pivot

TELFORD TAYLOR SPENT 1969 IN CAMBRIDGE, ENGLAND, THAT MOST secluded grove of academe. It was a welcome respite from his home campus of Columbia University in Morningside Heights in New York City, where during the previous year students had occupied buildings and protested against the military-industrial complex, and the faculty had become divided against itself. As 1969 ended, back in his Upper East Side apartment, Taylor found in his mail a note from a family friend, Marjorie Schell. Enclosed with it was a *New Yorker* article published in March 1968 about the realities of U.S. counterinsurgency in Quang Ngai Province, Vietnam. Its author was Schell's twenty-five-year-old son, Jonathan. Taylor sat down and read it. He was floored.

Born in 1908 in Schenectady, New York, where his father had resettled his old New England family to work as a General Electric engineer, Taylor enjoyed an enviable reputation as an American patriot, liberal internationalist, and responsible lawyer. After Williams College and Harvard Law School, he had gotten his start as a New Dealer and then worked in army intelligence during World War II, assisting British codebreakers at Bletchley Park.

In his most visible performance, Taylor became chief prosecutor at the U.S. trials held in Nuremberg, Germany, when Robert Jackson decided to return to his day job in Washington, D.C., as a Supreme

Court justice. Later, after retiring as a one-star general, Taylor settled into academic life. Dashing in his uniform at Nuremberg, he aged gracefully and always dressed traditionally and sharply, even as his students let their hair grow longer and their skirts shorter. In 1970, a latecomer to criticizing his country, Taylor also changed. Forced to revisit everything he had believed and taught about how American global power, the rule of law, and moral progress went together, the former chief prosecutor became an innovator in the use of international law to launch a public attack on a misbegotten war.

On November 12, 1969, weeks before Taylor had read Jonathan Schell's article, a freelance reporter named Seymour Hersh published a newspaper report that revealed the My Lai massacre. In March 1968, a platoon of "Charlie Company" slaughtered hundreds of Vietnamese civilians, including women and children, in a village in the central highlands. In the weeks that followed Hersh's exposé, the Cleveland *Plain Dealer* and *Life* magazine published photographs of the horrifying scenes of the slaughter, leaked by the ex-army photographer Ron Haeberle. As a result of the lurid photos of dead bodies by the side of the road, Charlie Company's commander, Lt. William Calley, eventually stood trial for murder.

The winter of 1969–70 was a turning point in U.S. history, but not because the Vietnam War became terminally unpopular after the disclosure of war crimes at My Lai. It already was. In 1968, Lyndon Johnson had decided not to run for reelection, and Richard Nixon won the presidency by promising to end the war, after years of popular opposition to its alleged immorality and stupidity. There had even been some claims the war was illegal—but not because of war crimes.

Before My Lai was revealed, most of the controversy had raged over a different question: whether the war should have even taken place. It was stoked by ethical concern that the Cold War had led American elites astray, while a small but stalwart band of lawyers insisted that international law forbade the intervention. News of atrocity added fuel to a campaign against an American war that was already increasingly unpopular, and the blaze scorched what little support was left. The news eventually brought Taylor to the front lines, where he made novel arguments that distinguished him from almost every other attorney friendly toward the antiwar movement.

In our time, atrocity and appeals to international law have worked very differently. After its invasion of Iraq in 2003, the U.S. military set up a makeshift prison at Abu Ghraib, one of Saddam Hussein's old detention facilities, and photos taken there showed U.S. troops inflicting sickening cruelty on captives. At the end of April 2004, CBS News broadcast the first Abu Ghraib torture photos in the lead-up to *The New Yorker*'s online publication of Seymour Hersh's nauseating article about them.

At first glance, American inhumanity and the protest it elicited might seem very similar in Vietnam and Iraq—and why not, because the very same reporter broke the single most scandalous and high-profile story about crimes in both wars. In fact, the comparison fails. A campaign to make the fighting in Vietnam humane did not follow from the My Lai revelations. Far from providing legitimacy and stability to an endless war, the passionate response to My Lai helped end it.

What commitment there is now to legal restraint in the fighting of war is very largely the result of a period of clarity in the early 1970s, when many people, far more than ever since, were prepared to see government officials and U.S. citizens themselves as potential and actual evildoers. But that crystalline moment of insight, in which concerns about how the United States fought were explicitly linked to what justification the country had to fight at all (and what role it ought to play in the world), has since passed. American concern with war has become focused on ensuring it is humane—not on whether it drags on and on, or even should be fought in the first place.

Telford Taylor's activism after My Lai was the harbinger of that turn.

U.S. INVOLVEMENT IN VIETNAM HAD ALREADY LASTED MANY YEARS when President Lyndon Johnson decided to escalate the war, seizing on allegations of North Vietnamese attacks on the U.S.S. *Maddox* and

Turner Joy in the Gulf of Tonkin in August 1964. Under its charismatic leader Ho Chi Minh, a Communist and nationalist icon, Vietnam had declared independence in 1945. But the restoration of the French empire in the region led to a bloody and protracted war that culminated in 1954 in the Battle of Dien Bien Phu, where the French were dealt a humbling defeat.

The Geneva Accords that followed divided the Vietnamese territory in two at the 17th parallel, pending fair and free elections to determine which government would rule both the north and the south. Those elections never happened, and the United States spent the following decade assisting the government of the south in maintaining control in the face of insurgent attacks and disorder. Johnson's decision to escalate radically, after Congress passed the Tonkin Gulf Resolution, transformed the situation. U.S. forces in the country grew from a baseline of 15,000 to 500,000, and along with hundreds of thousands of Australians and South Koreans, among others, they fought bitterly against Viet Cong insurgents to ensure the survival of the Republic of Vietnam (as the southern regime was called). Beginning in February 1965, in retaliation for insurgent attacks on the U.S. Army's Camp Holloway near Pleiku, the U.S. Air Force began massive aerial bombardment of North Vietnam.

As a matter of international law, the American situation in Vietnam was different from that of European empires in which anticolonial war erupted. After World War II, European powers waging counterinsurgent warfare against breakaway nationalists—whether the British in Malaya or Kenya or the French in Algeria—could claim they were fighting inside their own territories. Yet the United States could not treat Vietnam as part of its domestic space. The Johnson administration offered no detailed legal rationale under international standards at the start of the escalation. Both Secretary of Defense Robert McNamara and the White House explained that attacks on North Vietnam were "reprisals," an old category from a more permissive age of international law. And that argument made no sense with respect to Viet Cong attacks on Camp Holloway, since the legal relationship between the state of North Vietnam and the southern insurgency across the border was never altogether clear.

One thing was from the start: the United States fulsomely agreed to conduct its hostilities in the new war legally. The State Department advised the International Committee of the Red Cross that it saw the Geneva Conventions as fully applicable to what it took to be an international conflict. The United States "has always abided by the humanitarian principles enunciated in the Geneva conventions and will continue to do so," Secretary of State Dean Rusk noted in a public statement in 1965.

The Geneva Conventions divide war into two categories: international and "non-international." U.S. lawyers after September 11, 2001, were to make use of this distinction, arguing that the campaign against "enemy combatants" who did not represent a state represented a third category of war that the law simply didn't cover. In amazing contrast, during Vietnam the United States took no advantage of any fuzziness in the law to escape its applicability. At the time, academics wondered if counterinsurgency efforts in South Vietnam, even when they took on an insurgency aided by external intervention, could fall under the weaker rules for non-international conflict, which imposed only the few limitations of Common Article 3 of the Geneva Conventions. (The Supreme Court would later impose the article as a necessary constraint on the war on terror.) But instead of embracing this less strict standard, the U.S. government even forced its ally in Saigon to comply with its interpretation of the events as a full-fledged international war—though that meant more full-spectrum formal obligations for both patron and client.

This remarkable development might have suggested that U.S. governmental attitudes toward humane constraint on war had developed since World War II. The commanding U.S. general, William Westmoreland, went even further—and was met by strong praise from the International Committee of the Red Cross for doing so. He directed his forces to treat Viet Cong captives as prisoners of war under the full sway of the Geneva Conventions, though their failure to fight as an organized army and their unclear relationship to North Vietnam could have given him the latitude to withhold such protection.

As it turned out, the policy generosity in both Washington and Saigon was feasible because—as in Korea—levels of American popular support for the war were strong at the start of the conflict, whereas traditions of public debate around the laws of war were weak. Given the American brutality that followed escalation, Rusk's affirmation and Westmoreland's directive suggested not that American allegiance to powerful humanitarian norms was high, but instead that it never occurred to them that anyone would regard the international law on combat as a barrier or taboo. They believed they could bask in the glow of the rule of law while liberally violating its terms. For a long time, they were right.

AND SO, THE INTERNATIONAL LAW CALLING FOR HUMANE WAR WAS ALL too frequently broken by U.S. troops, due to converging forces: cavalier attitudes, cultural preconceptions about savage foreigners, counterinsurgent realities, strategic policy—and, not least, the lack of an ethic within the military itself that humane war mattered. How far the brutality went remained impossible to know, yet a surprising amount of information was available, and from early on. In an age-old story, few stared the known facts of their country's activities in the face.

The everyday excesses of a counterinsurgent war were appalling and grievous though also normal and routine. The requirement to discriminate between combatants and noncombatants became exceptionally difficult if not impossible to sustain. The Viet Cong's insurgent philosophy guaranteed this. In his counsel to rebels the world over, Mao Zedong had preached the moral propriety and tactical utility of combatants living among civilians. "The relationship that should exist between the people and the troops," he explained in a guerrilla manual influential the world over after his smashing conquest of his country in 1949, "may be likened to water [and] the fish who inhabit it."

No less opaque were the loyalties of many Vietnamese. Whole communities such as Vinh Linh (in Quang Tri Province on the border of North Vietnam) participated fully in abetting the Communist cause, and they found the favor returned in the form of relentless U.S. bombing day after day. Farther south, counterinsurgency made applying rules devised for organized battle—the very rules the United States accepted as binding on the war—difficult.

American rules of engagement were also to blame for the excesses, for they were not adequately designed for the realities of counterinsurgent war. They required that Americans make "every effort . . . to avoid civilian casualties." But troops in South Vietnam were ordered into situations that were recipes for systematic violations, notably when it came to civilians. Until 1968, Westmoreland stressed the importance of body counts: the higher, the better. It was not a strategy likely to lead to humane war. "Search and destroy" missions throughout the late 1960s commonly involved shooting at targets on the barest suspicion of Viet Cong involvement. More sweeping techniques, like the destruction of "hooches" and villages, frequently for dubious reasons, or extraordinary population displacement in the name of clearing the water to find the fish, were also renowned. Worst of all were free fire and free-strike zones created after "fair warning" and population displacement. It was an approach pioneered by the British in the successful Malayan counterinsurgency of the late 1940s, in which soldiers and pilots often shot at anything that remained, on the presumption that the innocent would already have left.

In jungle- and village-level combat, close air support from helicopters and airplanes—including the C-52, aka "Puff the Magic Dragon"—assisted ground operations, taking little care for civilian harm. After September 11, 2001, lawyers were deeply involved in pinpointing the targets of American wrath, but such efforts were unimaginable in the Vietnam era. Many observers felt that incontestable war crimes, such as My Lai, or the infamous gang rape and murder case reported in *The New Yorker* by Daniel Lang just before news of My Lai broke, were expectable outcomes. There was just no interest in distinguishing soldiers from noncombatants.

One reason was racism. "War," W.E.B. Du Bois remarked in the 1950s, "tends to become universal and continuous, and the excuse for this war continues largely to be color and race." By the time of Vietnam, U.S. forces had been racially integrated for two decades. Endemic discrimination remained within them, but it paled beside the extraordinary racialization of the enemy in Vietnam, as America's own increasing internal egalitarianism collided with the low value of Vietnamese lives. One observer caustically spoke of the "M.G.R."—the "mere gook rule."

Americans—including Asian Americans—fought in an international coalition, alongside fifty thousand South Koreans and six thousand Filipinos at the peak, and the South Vietnamese they were officially advising. But race was still a factor in the killing of enemies and mistreatment of civilians. "Would we have pursued quite such policies—and quite such military tactics—if the Vietnamese were white?" one former White House official asked openly in 1968. "I think it is uncontestable that the Vietnam war reflects the fact that we are fighting and killing a nonwhite race," observed the foreign policy realist Hans Morgenthau. As in America's earlier Pacific violence, soldiers routinely compared what they were doing with "Indian war." Compared with 57,000 Americans, four to six million Vietnamese died in the conflict. The toll on the local population was not as grievous as in Korea, in relative terms, and it took place over more years. But that was not saying much.

In testimony to the House Armed Services Committee in April 1970, a few months after the My Lai revelations, Westmoreland insisted on the importance of one-hour classes on the law of war as part of basic training, and he reminded his audience that all soldiers were supposed to carry a pocket card that called on them to behave humanely. But in one investigation, the Charlie Company member Herbert Carter remarked under direct examination that the class about the law of war ended up communicating that soldiers could "do what you want to do."

My Lai led to a recognition within the military that education in the laws of war for troops and commanders had been woefully insufficient. Despite an essentially functional system of military justice, the military culture of the day—including among lawyers in the Judge Advocate General corps—excused callous and deadly treatment of civilians and frowned on allegations of wrongdoing. One reason no one will ever know how prevalent such crimes were is that the Defense Department began systematically collecting information about alleged violations, through a Vietnam War Crimes Working Group, only after the My Lai cover-up failed and the exposure of violations finally became a central concern of the antiwar movement.

Meanwhile, the U.S. use of napalm and phosphorus in everyday counterinsurgency became particularly controversial. On the West Coast there were demonstrations around Dow Chemicals, whose products "burned babies." Indictment of napalm started comparatively early during the war, especially after photographs of victims began to circulate, long before the publication in 1972 on the front page of *The New York Times* of the bone-chilling image of Kim Phúc fleeing burning death. But almost no lawyers thought these weapons—or defoliants that some tried to cast as "ecocide" later—were illegal, though many felt that the Hague regulations ban on excessively cruel means of warfare had to mean something when it came to their deployment.

The other major domain of alleged illegality was the air war—not the air force's assistance to army and marine activities in the south but rather the bombing that took place there and throughout the north. That air war began in 1965 with the "Flaming Dart" and "Rolling Thunder" campaigns and soon expanded to sometimes even more massive campaigns in Cambodia and Laos. At first, in spite of the living memory of the razing of Japan and Korea, the assumption was that only military targets were being chosen in fierce air activity in North Vietnam. Johnson picked the targets himself at Tuesday lunches, and he faced rage from the military when he seemed unwilling to exploit air power to the fullest, as Americans had in earlier wars. General Curtis LeMay, mastermind of the infernos in previous Asian wars, backhandedly acknowledged Johnson's limits with a famous comment. He counseled his branch in 1965, the year of his retirement from the air force, "to bomb them back into the Stone Age." It had worked before, he thought.

Rolling Thunder was so massive that it readily seemed excessive, even without LeMay's bravado. The *New York Times* correspondent Harrison Salisbury received an invitation to visit and tour the northern capital of Hanoi in late 1966. His reporting challenged the credibility of the U.S. government's promise to restrict its aerial wrath only to military targets. The devastation of the north that Salisbury described could not plausibly be ascribed to honest mistakes. Salisbury's claims were subsequently given extraordinary scrutiny, and some skeptics alleged that he had been taken in by North Vietnamese propaganda. But the initial impact of his reporting was enormous. The most remarkable thing is that, if there were more policy constraints on aerial bombardment than in Korea, the question of what was legal in such warfare had occurred to no one.

Though startling to some, news about the air war did not lead to an outcry as loud or relentless as what would follow My Lai, and so did not meaningfully transform aerial practices. Nevertheless, a few critics began to document the effects of the air war on the North Vietnamese landscape, and distressing evidence accumulated, though to this day no one can estimate how many tens of thousands of civilians died. As with napalm used in the south, there was no specific law prohibiting aerial bombardment, and no real standards to define excess, even as B-52s were raining destruction from on high daily.

Activities that would scandalize many after September 11, 2001—torture and other detainee abuses—were also routine. Through most of the conflict, U.S. forces handed over all captured enemies to South Vietnam. Eventually, American holding facilities were opened, partly in recognition that its ally—which also held a huge number of "political" prisoners frequently captured in and outside battle zones—engaged in routine violations of the law of war. Even so, no one wanted the U.S. forces to take over detention completely. That remained the case the summer after the My Lai story broke, when word of the "tiger cages" of Con Son Island (where the regime's political prisoners were held) hit the news accompanied by lurid images in *Life* magazine.

As for the U.S. military itself, as the war ground on, more and more evidence surfaced about nonchalant attitudes toward the requirement to treat captured prisoners humanely, or even to leave them alive. Evidence accumulated of incidents of simply shooting prisoners, a practice abetted—though not, he insisted, intended—by Westmoreland's demand for higher body counts. And sometimes the military was directly involved in torture. In the army's 173rd Airborne Brigade, Lt. Col. Anthony Herbert shockingly recalled after My Lai that between twenty and thirty soldiers acted as "interrogation specialists," committing heinous acts like electrocution and waterboarding to gather information. (As with Salisbury, Herbert's credibility was strenuously attacked.)

Torture could be an everyday affair—but it occurred in special circumstances, too. Most glaringly, beginning in 1967, the CIA's infamous Phoenix program led to the assassination as well as detention and interrogation of suspected subversives. Targeting insurgent National Liberation Front, or Viet Cong, leaders for torture, other forms of harsh treatment, and summary execution, and apparently exceeding fifty thousand in the number of mortal victims it claimed, the program became known in stages after 1969. Yet even once war crimes became an issue, there was no torture debate in the Vietnam years, at first because the practice was tolerated and then because it was folded into dissent over the war in general rather than being singled out as a uniquely heinous transgression.

For those few who came to grips with the scene, the extent of the violations in Vietnam could make law seem not a necessary tool but a laughable irrelevance. "Charging a man with murder in this place," says Captain Benjamin Willard, Martin Sheen's character in *Apocalypse Now* (1979), "was like handing out speeding tickets in the Indy 500." In spite of mounting evidence of exceptional brutality, few spoke out at home before My Lai brought many over a critical threshold. For most Americans, war was still necessarily hell, for better or worse. And it was easy to emphasize the truth that allegations proved useful for Communist propaganda designed to undermine the American cause. The fact that the far left was almost exclusively the source of war crimes allegations also made their dismissal easy—until it was impossible.

The earliest forum for critics was Bertrand Russell's international war crimes tribunal, which first met in Denmark in 1967 to arraign the American war. Thanks to the personal intervention of the existentialist French philosopher and Russell's fellow "judge" and juror Jean-Paul Sartre, the court went so far as to find the United States guilty of genocide. Yet like most of those who would eventually raise the specter of U.S. war crimes, Russell and his associates were most concerned with U.S. aggression; war crimes were not a separate or distinct matter but the expectable consequence of a larger violation—war itself—that the United States had once done so much to criminalize. As at Nuremberg before, inhumane war was not an independent problem or the main one.

In the United States, however, the Russell tribunal was broadly scorned. It was even ridiculed as the sad mutterings of a great thinker gone senile, or as another Communist show trial. Ogden Nash contributed a poem entitled "You Are Old, Father Bertrand" that also took a swipe for good measure at his French sidekicks "Sartre and Simone," referring to Sartre's paramour Simone de Beauvoir, and dismissing both as "a voluble French intellectual crew." "The only relevant figure missing," opined the *New York Herald Tribune* in 1966 of Russell's dramaturgy, "will be Kafka, and he will be there in spirit." Though a show trial without any of the classic hallmarks of procedural justice, the Russell tribunal faithfully reflected Nuremberg's original prioritization of the crime of war itself over crimes within war.

IN THE EARLY GOING, THE MAJOR LEGAL DEBATES AROUND THE VIET-nam War had little to do with how the United States fought. Rather, they bore on whether the war itself was legal to begin with.

The Lawyers Committee Concerning American Policy in Vietnam was organized in 1965 after the Tonkin Gulf Resolution and the escalation of U.S. military involvement. The two central figures were both New York lawyers in private practice: William Standard, an expert on the law of the sea who served as chairman; and Joseph Crown, a tax specialist who as secretary and treasurer stood at its center. Carey McWilliams, editor of *The Nation*, served as honorary vice chairman, and soon after its founding the Lawyers Committee formed a consultative council of law professors, which eventually took on the main legal analysis.

Founded prior to the crystallization of a massive antiwar movement on campuses and the streets, the Lawyers Committee adopted an elite model of agitation, directed toward highbrow readers and governmental policymakers. Its members worked especially closely with friendly congressmen, notably the Democratic senators Wayne Morse of Oregon and Ernest Gruening of Alaska, who had cast the sole votes against the Tonkin Gulf Resolution, and J. William Fulbright of Arkansas, once he became the most prominent congressional critic of the war. The lawyers' main weapon was the letter to the editor, though the committee certainly attempted, by reducing its legal memoranda to pamphlet form and widespread newspaper advertisement, to make its views known to as wide a circle of Americans as possible.

Crown and Standard drafted an initial memo disputing the grounds of intervention and alleging violation of the United Nations Charter, the Geneva Accords of 1954, and the Manila Pact of the Southeast Asia Treaty Organization. Turning the tables on widespread rhetoric of Communist aggression, including Dean Rusk's public justification for the war, Crown and Standard used the memo to argue that, judged by its treaty obligations beginning with the United Nations Charter, the United States was the aggressor.

Where the Johnson administration cast Vietnam as an international conflict (in spite of the far greater burden in terms of the law of war that theory imposed), the Lawyers Committee insisted it was a civil war in which outside parties were not welcome. They did not care that this theory left the conflict under the sway of the weak Geneva Conventions provisions for non-international conflict, which later governed the war on terror. Senator Morse read the Crown and Standard memo into the *Congressional Record* in September 1965; it attracted only 700 signatures from the 178,000 lawyers and 3,750 law professors to whom Crown and Standard had sent it. In January 1966, the Lawyers Committee resent it to the president, with some amendments and news of the response it had received so far.

The truth was that the anti-interventionist position was legally dicey. Besides the United Nations Charter of 1945, debate swirled around the exact meaning of the Geneva Accords of 1954, which had settled the French war after Dien Bien Phu. Besides calling for elections, the accords had prohibited the introduction of new troops. However, the United States had not signed the accords and eventually claimed it had merely replaced troops until North Vietnam's own cavalier attitude toward the agreements justified further escalation.

As for broader international law, the United Nations Charter prohibited illegal uses of force. An anticolonialist General Assembly Declaration of 1965 held that "no State has the right to intervene, directly or indirectly, for any reason whatever, in the internal or external affairs of any other State." But these propositions did not apply if it turned out that South Vietnam was its own state rather than part of Vietnam. If it was its own state, attacks on it by North Vietnam could give rise to rights under the United Nations Charter to self-defense, including the right to invite other states to assist. And it could also invite friends to help it suppress armed opponents. No wonder the Lawyers Committee spent most of its time arguing that South Vietnam was not truly a state.

The White House Counsel's office initially asked academic allies to respond to such claims; when Attorney General Nicholas Katzenbach decided it was unworthy of official reply, the White House then prompted the leading Yale Law School professor Myres McDougal to organize a fuller response. The White House was also involved in a unanimous American Bar Association resolution affirming the legality of the war, to which the Lawyers Committee reacted angrily. Its antagonist in 1965–66 was Leonard C. Meeker, who served as the State Department's legal advisor, and who finally made public the government's legal rationale for war only after the Lawyers Committee argued there was none.

Born in 1916 in New Jersey, Meeker attended Deerfield Academy, Amherst College, and Harvard Law School before serving during World War II in the Office of Strategic Services. A veteran of multiple Democratic administrations, Meeker lived to the ripe old age of ninety-eight, swimming every day at his home on Ocracoke Island, North Carolina. His landmark memo of March 1966 concluded that the Geneva Accords gave rights to South Vietnam to defend itself, and to invite the United States to help put down internal rebellion.

After law professors came to the administration's defense, and Meeker offered his main memo, the Lawyers Committee turned to its own handful of academic experts. Among them was a now elderly Quincy Wright, retired from his post at the University of Chicago but still an icon in the field, and who pitched in until his death in 1970. John H. E. Fried of the committee's Consultative Council was born an Austrian Jew, immigrating to the United States in 1938 and serving as an advisor at Nuremberg. But in the Vietnam era, he came to rue his adopted country's descent into what he saw as an evil comparable to the one he once fled, and he served the Lawyers Committee by drafting what became a book-length memo. The committee then arranged to publish it with a marginal New Jersey publisher; in spite of their low visibility, Meeker did reply publicly to these arguments in a speech.

For all its legalism, the Lawyers Committee's basic purpose was a political one, and it freely and openly announced its ulterior goal of encouraging a settlement that would include the southern rebels. The lawyers were surely not above protesting what they saw as immoral techniques. Crown and Wright argued that the Rolling Thunder bombardments of Hanoi and the nearby harbor city of Haiphong were "demonstrations of military might against a small people and a small country" that "only demean the American people and affront the conscience of mankind." They also cited the Hague treaties' prohibition of bombing undefended towns—a prohibition that had long since proved meaningless. But most of all, they relied on the horror to press their case for the illegality of the whole enterprise. "Collective self-defense does not bring the right," they maintained, "to bring systematic destruction upon a whole people."

Having failed to influence administration policy, the Lawyers Committee took its case global. Its leaders attended European conferences of activists and lawyers in 1966–67 and urged the International Court of Justice to pronounce on international law violations by the United States (it didn't). After furnishing the principal arguments about the illegality of the war, the Lawyers Committee and its members also became active in selective service cases. They fondly hoped for the unlikely outcome of seeing a U.S. court declare the war illegal—which never occurred even once the enterprise became even more unpopular. The Lawyers Committee also organized the publication of academic work on the subject and participated in related invocations of the arguments as rationales for acts of civil disobedience. In 1969, it offered a five-point peace program.

Despite these efforts, the Lawyers Committee's moment of prominence and relevance had already passed, as elite debate about the war was overtaken by the rise of a mass antiwar movement. Speaking to the group in New York in October 1969, a month before the news of My Lai broke, Crown expressed his hope that the attendance of more than five hundred lawyers reflected "the turn of the tide." But campus and public activism proved the true agent of transformation in U.S. politics.

The Lawyers Committee considered proposing Johnson's impeachment and, two years later, did urge Nixon's. Crown and Standard also attempted to put the issue on the agenda of the Supreme Court confirmation hearings of William Rehnquist in 1971—wondering why no one cared about the fact that Rehnquist, while a senior Justice Department official, had written legal justifications of the Cambodian incursion as a matter of presidential prerogative. In spring 1971, members of the Lawyers Committee testified at congressional hearings in which what became the War Powers Resolution, intended to check executive militarism, was first debated.

As for war crimes committed in violation of the Geneva Conventions or other rules governing the fight from the air or on the ground, targeting them was hardly the Lawyers Committee's priority at any point. After My Lai, the Lawyers Committee certainly paid attention to the issue, along with many other Americans. When Crown attended a major international conference of lawyers in Toronto in 1970, much more emphasis fell on war crimes than before, but still as a rationale for a politics of ending the war. Even when Crown visited Hanoi for a week in October 1971, movingly testifying to the ravaged landscape and the massive death of civilians due to aerial bombardment, the Lawyers Committee remained focused on seeking an end to the conflict.

NO ONE ILLUSTRATES BETTER HOW THE INVOCATION OF INTERNAtional law worked for the few concerned about it than Richard Falk, the Lawyers Committee's leading academic advocate and later critic and pal of Telford Taylor, once he belatedly entered the fray.

Falk was born in 1930 in New York City, the son of a corporate lawyer, and named after an admiral. In 1962, he had ascended to a storied position teaching international law at Princeton University, and the Vietnam War made him famous as the "professor whose cause is peace," as *The New York Times* dubbed him. Birdlike, railthin, and tall, Falk had philosophical leanings and wrote poetry on the side. Ironically, he had become a critic after breaking not merely with his conservative father's politics but also those of his own teacher the Cold Warrior and Yale Law School éminence grise Myres McDougal, whom the Johnson White House had tasked with organizing the legal justification of the war. According to no less a figure than Leonard Boudin, the leading draft case lawyer of the era who later defended Daniel Ellsberg, Falk had an "unchallengeable preeminence" among those trying to bring international law to the Vietnam conflict.

When the Lawyers Committee wrote to him in 1965, in a large mailing to solicit his agreement with its initial memorandum, Falk signed on with alacrity. Soon after, he set to writing a classic *Yale Law Journal* article on the illegality of the Vietnam War, which sparked a contentious academic debate. In the same period, Falk helped Fried prepare a book-length memorandum as chair of the Lawyers Committee Consultative Council that expanded the legal case against the war. None of Falk's early initiatives mentions any crimes of war—other than the war itself.

Falk's early attempt at academic activism, like that of the Lawyers Committee, at first attracted very few supporters. The Harvard Law School professor Richard Baxter took Falk to task in the pages of the London *Times* for his wild arguments and insisted that British readers know how unrepresentative Falk's views were. They were, Baxter wrote, "*not* the view of the matter entertained by the great majority of American international lawyers." As if to alert people to the centers of opinion that truly mattered, he added (correctly) that Falk's Consultative Council did "not include a single member of the law faculties of Harvard, Yale, Columbia, Michigan, Chicago, California, or Pennsylvania." (Late in his life, Quincy Wright had departed Chicago to teach at the University of Virginia.) Another Harvard international law professor, Louis Sohn, responded to the Lawyers Committee with a memorandum justifying U.S. engagement in the conflict.

As the years passed, Falk's own reasons for engagement as the most prominent international lawyer in the antiwar movement were consciously political and proudly so. While he surely championed international law, it was in recognition of its possible use as one political tool among others. When Katzenbach, once a teacher of Falk's at Yale Law School, moved from the attorney general's office to become undersecretary of state in late 1966, Falk wrote to him as a "dissenter" in hopes of opening a dialogue. "Needless to say," Falk explained, "I regard the legal interpretation of United States policy to be of secondary importance in this setting." What mattered was "a policy that satisfies more general considerations bearing on the welfare of the country and on the prospects for global stability and justice." By those tests, not legal ones in the first instance, the Vietnam War was a disastrous mistake.

In fact, Falk's overridingly political aims in using law as a tool to end a mistaken war could, on dark days, lead him to conclude that the law had little role in the movement and had shown its limits precisely as a tool. Because the strategy he and the Lawyers Committee had adopted—asserting the illegality of the war—seemed to make no discernible difference, he confessed to a colleague the next year that "an appeal to legal reason does not have much relevance either to the policy-forming process or to shaping of public attitudes." He added: "It remains important not to create a legal vacuum to be filled by official positions, but legally oriented arguments aimed at the public assume a legalistic quality by virtue of their irrelevance." In the hands of Meeker and the Johnson administration's supporters among academics, international law was "less a fig-leaf than a see-through garment."

In the banner year of 1968, Falk visited Hanoi and then, with Crown, attended the Conférence mondiale des juristes pour le Vietnam, held in Grenoble, France, that July. Falk agreed with the dominant approach, which focused on American aggression and illegal intervention, and with North Vietnamese representatives in the room championing the right of self-determination as the basis of struggle. Reporting on the effects of his trip as a "representative of international juridical conscience," Falk described his "general shift in orientation." He was no longer interested in resisting the U.S. government as one of its citizens. Falk became a "third-worldist," affiliating with Vietnamese desires for liberation as part of a global struggle against empire. This coincided, he reported, with "a very sharp shift in priorities with respect to the legal issues." This shift had nothing to do with making war humane if it broke out. "The primary issue," he argued, is "that the war is at its deepest level a war fought for the fulfillment and expression of Vietnamese national self-determination; this war is a continuation of the colonial struggle."

In 1967, interdenominational clergy including Daniel Berrigan, Robert McAfee Brown, William Sloan Coffin, Abraham Joshua Heschel, and Martin Luther King, Jr., had banded together to make a strong statement about the war. Drawing on mainstream press coverage, they documented what seemed to be massive and intentional cruelties. They released their book-length compilation and argument a month before the My Lai slayings, and Falk pitched in by explaining the legal reasons for caring about the moral wrongs the clergy denounced. But while he took the by now horrific reports seriously, Falk knew they were easily contradicted and that no serious mechanism existed in the American landscape at that time for creating a culture of legalism around military conduct. He reminded readers of the overriding importance of the debate he had been trying to spark about the legal propriety of the war itself, adding that the laws of war the clergy wanted to bring to the public were "not to encourage legal debate as much as to provide benchmarks for a searching moral reappraisal."

As for Leo Tolstoy's greatest American heir, Martin Luther King, Jr., he decried not merely American inhumanity but the entire enterprise of the war. Young Americans, Black and white, were in "brutal solidarity burning the huts of a poor village" but still "would never live on the same block in Detroit." And violence hardly weaned Vietnamese victims from a Communist alternative. For a Christian (especially one who had won a Nobel Prize three years before), the necessity of "the making of peace is so obvious that I sometimes marvel at those who ask me why I am speaking against the war." King finished:

> A true revolution of values will lay hands on the world order and say of war: "This way of settling differences is not just." This business of burning human beings with napalm, of filling our nation's homes with orphans and widows, of injecting poisonous drugs of hate into veins of people normally humane, of sending men home from dark and bloody battlefields physically handicapped and psychologically deranged, cannot be reconciled with wisdom, justice and love. A nation that continues year after year to spend more money on military defense than on programs of social uplift is approaching spiritual death.

Never was Tolstoy's vision for an American idealism of peace more amply fulfilled than in Riverside Church in Manhattan when King delivered his words in April 1967, exactly a year to the day before his Memphis slaying.

As time passed, the political circumstances changed rapidly. With the Tet Offensive and Lyndon Johnson's decision not to seek reelection in 1968, the nature of the war shifted profoundly. It did so even more as Richard Nixon and Henry Kissinger famously sought through extraordinary measures an "honorable" settlement. The "Vietnamization" of the war meant the departure of American boots on the ground coupled with the escalation of fierce bombardment everywhere in the country, not forgetting the massive expansion of bombing in Cambodia and Laos and a brief but furious 1970 Cambodian ground incursion. The Cambodian intervention, though justified by Rehnquist under domestic law and by Meeker's successor John Stevenson under international law, finally prompted the legal denunciation that critics like Falk had urged for the war from its beginning.

After My Lai was revealed, Falk certainly invoked rules of humane war far more often, initiating precisely the legal debate about brutal crimes he had once hoped to spark around the intervention itself. Following the My Lai exposure and public disappointment that Nixon's promised "withdrawal" made the conflict more intense, Falk reoriented his activism around war crimes. The Nuremberg precedent now mattered not simply for the charge of aggression but for the principle of command responsibility—and its imperative to trace how high up accountability went.

As Falk wrote soon after the My Lai revelations in a classic article in *The Nation*, "The Circle of Responsibility," "It would . . . be misleading to isolate Song My [Lai] from the overall conduct of the war." At the moment when his attention was most focused on war crimes, however, Falk—who had once dismissed it as a "juridical farce"—now followed the Russell tribunal in insisting that such attention was not possible to isolate from the overall legality of the war itself. "The Nuremberg principles suggest a broader human responsibility to oppose an *illegal war* and *illegal methods of combat*," he explained. It was not a matter of dropping a focus on the one in favor of a new agenda. It was a new tool with which to pursue the old agenda.

Public reaction to My Lai was convulsive, and moral opprobrium about war crimes spiked in the winter of 1970–71, in tandem with outrage that Nixon was expanding a conflict he had promised to end. As always, the inhumanity of a war became both visible and (for some) objectionable mainly to the extent the consensus around the propriety of the war itself shattered. The timing of atrocity consciousness is everything, and in this instance its rise added fuel to the fire of a case for withdrawal that was suddenly becoming mainstream. The Russell tribunal proceedings, once marginal, were republished by a trade press. *The New York Times Book Review* took the radical step of asking the celebrated war correspondent Neil Sheehan to review the antiwar literature professor Mark Sacharoff's entire bibliography of materials on war crimes, in a catalytic intervention for highbrow readers.

On the ground, Vietnam Veterans Against the War staged the

most visible appeal to the idea that rules should govern hostilities. They held a mock trial in Detroit in which they described their own shameful transgressions in the once well-known Winter Soldier investigation. Never one to be left out, Falk joined in a Washington, D.C., popular inquest in October 1971 to brand the whole U.S. leadership class as "war criminals." Falk also participated in the creation of the Citizens Commission of Inquiry into U.S. War Crimes in Vietnam. (Begun by American affiliates of the Russell tribunal, it took on a life of its own after the My Lai news.) Last but not least, Falk joined with the leftist historian Gabriel Kolko and the celebrated psychologist Robert Jay Lifton to edit a mass-circulating compilation, *Crimes of War*, to inform and spur the debate. (Falk, still living today, reunited with old collaborators to produce a similar volume on Iraq in 2004, which received considerably less attention.)

Like others in the antiwar movement, Falk hoped to take advantage of My Lai as a moment of breakthrough, in which Americans would come to grips with the evil of the war from its beginning and in its totality. As Kolko put it, "Song My [Lai] is merely the foot soldier's direct expression of the axiom of fire and terror that his superiors in Washington devise and command from behind desks." In their compilation, Falk cited the international law of war not to exonerate but to indict the generalized culpability of U.S. soldiers, generals, statesman, and the people as a whole.

At the trial of Karleton Armstrong, Falk called for amnesty for the University of Wisconsin student who had set off a bomb in Sterling Hall to destroy an army research center, inadvertently killing a thirty-three-year-old postdoc and father of three. All war resisters deserved amnesty, he insisted, on the grounds that even violent tactics were permissible in the face of an "illegal, immoral and criminal" war. In the preface to *Crimes of War*, Falk and the other editors agreed "with Jean-Paul Sartre and others in conceiving of the entire war—or any massive counterinsurgency campaign by outside forces relying upon modern weaponry—as one all-embracing war crime."

That the war was the crime meant that crimes of war were folded into the opprobrium it deserved.

MORE THAN ANYONE ELSE, IT WAS THE NUREMBERG TRIAL VETERAN Telford Taylor who went where Falk did not, and he framed the case against the Vietnam War exclusively in terms of war crimes. In the most vicious periods of American war, a concern with atrocity was absent among elites and the public and first stressed by the international far left. And yet the subject was now discussed by the establishmentarian Taylor with the fullest doctrinal rigor, and made an extraordinary impact. If one had to choose a single cultural document that marked the beginning of the coming of humane war in our time, Taylor's bestselling and widely reviewed *Nuremberg and Vietnam: An American Tragedy*, which appeared in late 1970, is undoubtedly it. At the same time, Taylor also epitomized how, after My Lai, atrocities became the index of a consensus—belatedly mainstream—that the war had to end.

Taylor mattered because he was so morally serious—and made allegations of war crimes "respectable" by moving them from the far left to the liberal center and offering a judicious discussion of why Americans had violated international standards. Unlike Falk, who was the main target of criticism in *Nuremberg and Vietnam*, Taylor castigated the irresponsible left and excused a great deal of American conduct in Vietnam on the way to his extremely sobering conclusions about what had gone wrong.

Taylor offered a sage account of American transgression that avoided the most radical indictment. He agreed with his colleague Herbert Wechsler, who once snarkily remarked, "Professor Falk makes up a lot of law that I don't think exists and then expects the judicial system to apply it." In this moment, the journalist Neil Sheehan published a highly public indictment of American war guilt that came with a standing the left lacked. Six weeks before, Sheehan had attacked the propensity of the antiwar movement to fabricate atrocity stories. At just this time, after receiving the Pentagon Papers from the dissident defense analyst Daniel Ellsberg, Sheehan was preparing to publish them. His grave and wide-ranging *New York Times Book Review* essay on whether to hold war crimes tribunals for Americans normalized talk of national guilt. "Do you have to be a Hitlerian to be a war criminal?" Sheehan asked. "Or can you qualify as a well-intentioned President of the United States?" But he also recognized that atrocities mattered to Americans now because their war had gone awry. "The resort to force is the ultimate act. It is playing God. Those who try force cannot afford to fail."

Taylor focused on war crimes as a proxy for reckoning with a far larger disaster. But in doing so, he not only severed legal claims from the political movement that had first inspired them; from the start he also separated concern with the inhumanity of the Vietnam War from any case for its illegality. A former supporter of the intervention, Taylor could draw on his stature as a moral voice above politics to make an impact. As Falk was to put it, Taylor might have been "the only person alive who was in a position to change the public climate sufficiently to make the issue of war crimes [one] which would be taken seriously."

Before My Lai broke, Taylor had participated in the defense of the "Boston Five," a group of prominent protestors, among them the pediatrician Benjamin Spock and Yale's chaplain William Sloan Coffin, arrested for picketing a selective service center in 1968. But Taylor was moved to intervene at book length because of disturbing parallels some were beginning to draw after My Lai between American and Nazi terror. And he attended a congressional conference on war crimes as the news of My Lai was debated in the winter of 1970. There, he was already distinguishing himself from Falk, commenting, "Those to whom the Vietnam war in its entirety is an abomination may find any consideration of the laws of war, and what may or may not be done legitimately in military operations, to be questions of small account." It was true.

Taylor wrote his book quickly in the summer of 1970. Throughout, he made clear that the United States and its legal system were strong enough to deal with the atrocities and misdeeds the country seemed to have tolerated. It is illustrative that Falk frequently dedicated his books to Vietnamese victims, whereas Taylor dedicated *Nuremberg and Vietnam* "to the flag, and the liberty and justice for which it stands." When Taylor's book went into paperback and the publisher designed a cover with a swastika imposed on a U.S. flag, Taylor protested and had it changed.

Taylor's patriotic attitude to the nation matched his refusal to "trash" the law simply because it was a mixed bag. Allen Ginsberg beseeched Taylor to see that the law was deeply compromised, but Taylor shot back at the Beat poet, saying he had "fallen victim to a mistaken attitude about the law, which is prevalent both within and without the bar itself. The mistaken attitude is the idealistic belief that the law is worthless unless it is consistent, and administered with the courage and impartiality of that blind marble goddess holding the scales." All that mattered, Taylor continued, was whether Americans would take the chance after My Lai, not to make the law perfect but to give it the tools to right some of the wrongs it had so far helped to inflict. "Doctors often fail to cure the sick," he observed, "clergymen fail to save souls; poets fail to work the magic of their art; lawyers and judges, alas, often fail to do justice. Perhaps the fact that our judicial system is ill-adapted to test the legality of what the Congress and the White House are doing means that we are losing law, and that lawyers are just a bunch of hams. But if that is so, it has been so for a long time; it is nothing new."

What some found to be cynical world-weariness in the face of evil, others could embrace for moderation and wisdom. Taylor's first move in *Nuremberg and Vietnam*, after historical preliminaries, established a clear contrast with prior American agitation: he cast doubt on the very idea of aggressive warfare, and he treated claims that Vietnam had been an illegal intervention skeptically. The malleability of "aggression" did not mean the concept could never have legal clarity, Taylor insisted. But unlike at Nuremberg, where it was obvious who had started World War II, the Vietnam era showed that one man's aggressor was another man's victim (and vice versa). The debate of the late 1960s over the legality of the Vietnam War, for Taylor, led nowhere. To Falk's insistence that if it stood for anything, Nuremberg stood for criminalizing aggression, Taylor responded revealingly that Nuremberg "was a long time ago. Nuremberg is now two quite different things: It is what happened there, and it is also what people think happened there"—not aggression trials but atrocity trials. "Perhaps the second is rather more important than the first," he finished.

In particular, Taylor continued, Falk was wrong in suggesting that domestic courts could and therefore should responsibly adjudicate whether the United States was guilty of aggression. Rejecting Falk's arguments for an extremely expansive circle of potential liability, Taylor observed that Nuremberg never conferred a right—let alone a responsibility—to avoid military service on the grounds of personal opinion about a war's illegality. Nuremberg judges who acquitted generals and industrialists had been willing to hold only the highest leaders to account for aggressive war. In compensation, Taylor's attention fell squarely on the means and methods of war, of which he provided a damning account. What may be most impressive about his analysis is Taylor's isolation of the American actions he felt were unquestionably criminal. For there were a lot

Beyond My Lai, Taylor indicted routine and massive civilian reprisals, which were obviously not justified when there was no suspicion of enemy presence, and not justified even if any evidence suggested some. Shocked by Jonathan Schell's reporting, Taylor was also concerned about the use of air power in South Vietnam, especially the use of free-strike zones; and he expressed considerable doubt about the legality of displacing civilians with no intention of bringing them back. Taylor also indicted the cavalier attitude toward prisoners of war. In the trial of Lieutenant James Duffy in the spring of 1970, embarrassing testimony had surfaced that the imperative to achieve high body counts sometimes overrode the rules of war, including even the rule against the denial of quarter.

At the same time, focusing on the highest directives of General

Westmoreland, Taylor deemed the army's rules of engagement "impeccable," ignoring how their ambiguities licensed rather different interpretations. And he was surprisingly dismissive of worries that Rolling Thunder—the aerial bombardment of North Vietnam—had gone too far. It did not seem to Taylor that U.S. bombing involved wanton cruelty against civilians sufficient to qualify as a failure to distinguish civilian from military targets. Even if one conceded, as Taylor did, that the bombings of Dresden and Nagasaki had probably been illegal because they were redundant and not required for inevitable victory, in Vietnam there had been "no urban holocausts." In any event, no one had been punished at Nuremberg or other postwar trials for deliberately bombing civilians, in part because all parties to World War II had engaged in the practice.

Taylor changed his mind on this critical point when, with the folksinger Joan Baez, he traveled to Hanoi in winter 1972–73 in order to deliver holiday mail to prisoners of war. He happened to be present during the wrathful Linebacker II bombing of Hanoi and Haiphong, which Nixon and Kissinger hoped would coerce a favorable settlement of the conflict. Before the Christmas bombing began, Baez recalled, "legally, I was of no use, especially because of my deep-seated opinion that war itself is a crime; that the killing of one child, the burning of one village, the dropping of one bomb sinks us into such depths of depravity that there's no use bickering over the particulars." In their mission, Taylor behaved differently: "Telford was a terribly conscientious man and was carrying out his duties to the last detail with endless questions about logistics, dates and so forth. [I was] fascinated with the way his mind worked."

When Taylor emerged from the bomb shelter near his Hanoi hotel, reporters asked him whether he had been deliberately led to the destroyed Bach Mai hospital and devastated residential areas rather than elsewhere because of a public relations gambit. He responded: "We might not have seen some things that we would have liked to have seen, but nonetheless we did see the things we saw." Instead of saying that such aerial fury was tragic but legal, as he had in his book two years earlier, Taylor commented that no court was ever likely to bring a great power to justice for such enormities as the Christmas bombings. No treaty yet outlawed aerial bombardment. Still, he allowed, what the United States had done—though no comparison with the World War II immolation of cities—likely violated an emerging understanding of the 1960s and 1970s that attacks should be allowed only when collateral harm wasn't disproportionate to the military advantage sought.

For a patriot, it was a shocking denunciation of his country. And it suggested how far even such a patriot could go in the early 1970s when the atrocity of Vietnam—and by extension, the excesses of the entire Cold War era—had become plain to so many. It was also a generative moment for future struggles to make war more humane. Of course, opinions differed at the time about how much credit Taylor deserved for grasping a truth that had applied all along, and not just in cities, a truth many had seen before his accidental personal experience led him to it. Boudin, the civil libertarian lawyer who had led the Boston Five defense, wrote in a hard-hitting review, "It is hardly a tribute to objectivity in legal circles that few other than Taylor could have had such an effect today, and that not even he would have had the same audience, much less taken the same position, five years ago."

Precisely because of that evolution, Taylor's intervention in *Nuremberg and Vietnam* on war crimes was extraordinarily consequential. As Falk noted in his laudatory review, "Despite Taylor's conservative stance he reaches radical conclusions." His legal caution and his liberal patriotism, Falk recorded, meant that even though Taylor avoided indicting the United States except in cases of absolutely clear wrongdoing, the remarkable thing was that he had gone so far. The book was "a *minimalist indictment* in the sense of being the minimum conclusion that an honest, conservative, and well-informed man can make about the criminal status of American war policies." Falk celebrated Taylor's conclusions that the inquest over My Lai—even if Charlie Company's murders were exceptional—

should reach as high as evidence could lead. World War II's legacy, Taylor had written, implied that military accountability should go all the way to the top and perhaps into civilian corridors of power, too. Soon after Falk's review, Taylor stated clearly on *The Dick Cavett Show* that Westmoreland was liable for war crimes, and then he went further by adding that, while he reserved judgment on such a tricky question, Johnson might be, too. This appearance caused an uproar. (Westmoreland later dismissed it in his memoirs as an "emotional outburst.")

After Falk reviewed Taylor's book so fulsomely, the two barnstormed around American universities for several debates on how to bring law to bear on the war, and they struck up a friendship playing squash. Falk didn't engage the legal analysis of Taylor's book. He bridled only in response to Taylor's belittlement of the antiwar movement. Where Taylor chided popular demonstrations as counterproductive, Falk wrote, in a remarkable moment of direct rhetorical address: "But what, General Taylor, is 'productive' given the circumstances of a continuing criminal war that is being carried on by individuals you yourself characterized as seeming criminals?"

Taylor's moderation epitomized the isolation of war crimes from the broader Vietnam War: the conversation moved from concern with aggression to one with atrocity. Yet the finale of *Nuremberg and Vietnam* made clear that if law could play no role in ending the war, Taylor hoped politics would. Indeed, he considered his own post–My Lai reflection inseparable from a political stance against a war he now viewed as ill-conceived if not immoral. Taylor noted: "To say judges should not answer the question [of whether Americans were aggressors] is not to deny the reality and significance of the question itself." Whether enormities like the Christmas bombings were crimes was "of small moment to the victims." Only one question mattered: "Why are we doing what we are doing?"

U.S. intervention in Vietnam had been idealistic in the beginning. However, Taylor concluded, the rationales for war had been shown to be comprehensively ideological: "Whatever peace-keeping and protective intentions may have governed our initial involvement in Vietnam have by now been so completely submerged under the avalanche of death and destruction that they no longer are credible descriptions of the operation as a whole." If so, then the Nuremberg charge of aggression, though unviable as a legal claim, still did matter as a political instrument to undermine the war itself.

Taylor's hopes for legal accountability for war crimes went unrealized, and he steered clear of popular mobilization against war. But his intended contribution to the political deployment of law for the sake of ending war was ultimately self-evident; he balanced a legal indictment of war crimes with political opposition to the war itself. Focusing exclusively on the illegality of the conduct of the Vietnam War was openly an attack on the war itself by other means. Taylor was living in a different world, even as he prepared the way for ours.

AMERICAN DISPUTES AROUND VIETNAM NEVER MADE THE INTERNAtional laws of war central. "It is a humbling realization of no small moment," Falk observed bitterly in 1973, "to acknowledge that only international lawyers have been paying attention to the international law arguments on the war." The very fact that the United States had formally accepted that the rules of the Geneva Conventions governed the conflict—unlike after September 11, 2001—helped inoculate the legal propriety of the war from scrutiny, even as more and more Americans expressed their doubts in a moral or strategic register. Even after My Lai, Taylor's activism in indicting atrocity led nowhere in the short term.

Yet in the long term, Taylor, who died in 1998, was the prophet of a new attitude. After September 11, 2001, international law came to occupy the center of national debate about the nature of American war-making. What's more, with many people now paying attention, the part of the law that Taylor prioritized would receive almost exclusive attention. The rules forbidding war itself that many in the Vietnam era had taken most seriously—standards forbidding the extension chronologically and expansion geographically of American military intervention—were given short shrift. In compensation, rules for more humane war controlling how troops fought in the field and even how bombs were dropped from the air were the ones increasingly heeded.

From the ashes of Hanoi and the darkness of My Lai, the possibility of humane war would come into view.

CHAPTER SIX

"Cruelty Is the Worst Thing We Do"

WHEN IN THE 1990S THE PRINCETON UNIVERSITY LITERATURE PROFESSOR Samuel Hynes surveyed stories about twentieth-century wars, he noticed something momentous. From World War I through Vietnam, the prototypical story was about the fighters doing the fighting. Whether dead or alive, Kilroy, and only Kilroy, was there. "The helpless, the sufferers, the unarmed, the captive, the weak," Hynes reported, "have had no voice." And then they did.

It wasn't that civilian atrocities were new or becoming more traumatic, Hynes emphasized. Since the Hebrew Bible and the Homeric epics, they have been endemic to war's ravages, yet for a very long time stories about them were marginal. First-person accounts of civilian sufferings, as well as narratives of the treatment of captive soldiers, were even scarce during much of the twentieth century. Although World War I raised the frightening possibility of war as an aerial assault on civilians, and World War II realized the fear of an urban holocaust, neither event prompted many stories written by or about the bombed, as opposed to the many reports about the bombers. The same, of course, was true of Europe's wars of decolonization, in spite of the massacres visited on ordinary people, including from the sky: if their victims spoke, they were not heard.

Hynes was near the end of his forty-year career as a professor when he published *The Soldier's Tale: Bearing Witness to Modern War*

(1997). His expertise wasn't limited to the archive. Hynes had been a bomber pilot during World War II. Awarded the Distinguished Flying Cross for his exploits in the Pacific in 1944–45, he had told his own war story a decade earlier in *Flights of Passage* (1988), but it was rooted in an antiquated moral world. As late as the 1980s, he could focus resolutely on the camaraderie of young men learning to fly together; there was bearing witness to horror, but the horror was that of brothers-in-arms falling.

In *Flights of Passage*, he writes of grieving for two fellow Pacific airmen when they were blasted from the sky over Okinawa. *The Soldier's Tale* is dedicated to their memory. The bombarded did not yet count for much. "In an air war," Hynes recalled of his seventy-eight combat missions, "you are not very conscious of your enemies as human beings." They were targets, not people. You never took them prisoner—and did not think about collateral damage. Death from the air, Hynes went so far as to record, was an art form, and the killing of enemies its medium. "I grieved for the dead men," he explained of Japanese soldiers he killed (without mentioning any others in harm's way), "and I hated the unnecessariness of their dying. But the images that the mind cherishes remain beautiful."

Another reality snapped into place shortly after, and a new set of assumptions and expectations quickly prevailed. The age-old experience of victimhood, once mute and unmourned, found audiences and authors. For Hynes, the example of Holocaust memoirs and testimonies drove the change most of all. Ignored after World War II, they helped redefine the new moral culture. In the 1990s, Hynes's recognition of the plight of "the helpless and the innocent" decreed "the end of war stories." Those who had been "caught up in war and killed or maimed or imprisoned or starved simply because they were powerless or were there" had come to occupy the foreground of depictions of armed strife.

The new moral reality would have been unimaginable for millennia of fighters' stories—including long into the twentieth century. It was now vividly clear—the epitome of the meaning of war, even—

not to kill as a soldier on the ground or from the air, but to suffer in detention or experience the depredations of passing armies or planes. Such stories "have radically altered the geometry of the modern soldier's tale," Hynes concluded, expressing confusion about why the change had happened, "adding to the usual story of army against army a different war story—of armies against humanity."

Hynes's perception tracked the evolution of American war and matched new attempts to regulate it in law. Not that American war ended between Vietnam and September 11, 2001. The country continued to fight Cold War and post–Cold War proxy wars worldwide. Stung by defeat in Southeast Asia, the United States slowly recovered its confidence to intervene globally, especially when the passing of a bipolar world in 1989 left the country with fewer self-imposed limits. Between Vietnam and September 11, most of the other conditions for the humane war America would come to fight in the new millennium coalesced. In the new moral world Hynes described, the imperative was to avoid or at least minimize the old and tenacious scandal of wartime suffering. It did not occur to anyone that once the suffering was edited out, the worst thing about war could still remain.

International law changed to suit the era of recognizing victims. But in this era, the longtime Swiss custodians of the laws of war found themselves competing with others for the credentials of humanists. Americans had their own reasons to evolve. There were new monitoring groups concerned with the fate of the innocent in war. And the government, too, got involved. Angling for importance in a defense community humbled by defeat in Vietnam and stung by accusations of atrocity there, lawyers in the U.S. military agreed to occupy themselves with something called "international humanitarian law."

Together, the different groups converged around and acted to humanize the laws of war, previously ignored and permissive, and even to apply them to killing operations themselves. As for the ideal of peace, it fared far less well. September 11 did not "change everything." It set in motion a fulfillment of the fondest hopes for the coming of more humane war, hopes that had been cherished in the period immediately preceding it.

Beyond all the other factors in the emergence of America's novel and shocking form of belligerency, it was the cultural transformation that Hynes registered that made humane war imaginable. Concern for military excess, culturally peripheral before, gave the laws of war an importance they had never acquired under their own power. Yet while those laws would cleanse war of its historic brutality, their legacy would be not eternal peace but endless control.

ONCE AGAIN, IT FELL TO A SWISS GENTLEMAN TO DRIVE EFFORTS TO make war more humane through law. But this time, unlike in the nineteenth century, his moment proved to be quite propitious. He was a pioneer in advertising the laws of war as humanitarian through and through, and in getting states—including the United States—to accept that killing itself had to become humane.

Born within a month of the outbreak of World War I, Jean Pictet was easily the most important twentieth-century lawyer to drive the "humanization" of the laws of war—even if his success depended on factors over which he had no control. Pictet descended from the second-oldest great Genevan family, a dynasty of patrician wealth and power that succeeded in placing its name on a crater of the moon even before one of its branches would found what is still one of the largest Swiss banks. A lawyer, Jean Pictet had joined the International Committee of the Red Cross at age twenty-two in 1937, and he spent fifty years there.

Back then, as with so many in the late 1930s, Pictet had had pacifist leanings. Like his nineteenth-century Swiss predecessors in the organization, Pictet hoped he could "fight war by endeavoring to humanize it." Aware of the darkest events of World War II, Pictet had drafted a protest in late 1942, and proposed to issue it publicly, breaking the group's usual practice of working discreetly with states. Though the statement was "anodyne" in its tone given the horror, he later reflected to the Holocaust filmmaker Claude Lanzmann in an interview, his superiors quashed it.

Pictet played a role in the drafting of the Geneva Conventions in the late 1940s. Disabused by World War II of hopes for peace, he now concentrated on ameliorating wars. Through the hinge period of the 1960s through 1980s, whether that approach would work remained an open question. "You know those people who make predictions?" he asked in the late 1990s, after his retirement from propagandizing for humane war, when he wrote histories of Native Americans in his spare time. "They used to say, 'The year 2000, the golden age of humanity'; well, here it is and it's not the golden age." But perhaps it was a silver one. While humanizing war hadn't ended it yet, people like him had made it less grievous.

Pictet, who died in 2002, rallied from the beginning to the Christian premise of his Swiss forebears: rules minimizing suffering and death in war enacted Jesus's parable of the Good Samaritan for a modern and more secular age. But the obstacles to lessening the depredations of war were forbidding. Monitoring the compliance of states with the Geneva Conventions in the decades after 1949, Pictet knew the process was faulty and weak. It was not just that the laws of war were generally ignored. In spite of the noble original Geneva Convention of his Swiss ancestors, most of the laws of war were not humane in purpose at all. And when it came to the elemental realities of combat, there were virtually no limitations, not least in aerial bombardment, which caused some of the worst suffering. To add insult to injury, the civil wars that were increasingly preponderant among armed conflicts were also left practically unregulated. "It is even open to question," Pictet worried in 1950, though flush from the success of the new Geneva Conventions the year before, "whether new kinds of war leave any room for legal control."

In the face of these difficulties, Pictet spent three decades on a rebranding exercise that happened to coincide with a new popular concern for wartime carnage. He set in motion events that succeeded in giving the laws of war an unprecedented level of significance in fighting around the world and popular moral consciousness. Starting in the mid-1950s, Pictet relabeled the whole field of regulating the conduct of hostilities "international humanitarian law," or IHL. The acronym is now routine among humanitarians, militaries, and observers alike, implying consensus about its purpose.

Besides marketing, there was substance. To deal with the absence of limits on actual killing, including the death toll from the sky so vivid for those who had lived through World War II, Pictet and his Red Cross colleagues started to agitate in the 1950s for a new limiting principle. Attacks once justified as militarily necessary, they proposed, ought never to be allowed if collateral harm would outweigh the advantage they would reap. Pictet also hoped to see fuller rules for internal armed conflict. The 1949 Conventions offered only the lonely Common Article 3, which guaranteed a very minimal humanity—embarrassing compared with the detailed rules for war among or between states. Pictet succeeded here, too, and his work would have an impact on America's humane war after September 11, 2001. Counterterrorism would eventually be placed within a framework originally devised for internal war.

Pictet also recognized, unlike his forebears, the realities of a newly decolonized and diverse world. He hoped to overcome a dark past in which reformers had focused on making war humane only for Europeans who no longer fought one another, and—after losing their empires—almost stopped fighting altogether. Europeans, after all, had led the way after World War II in reconceiving the state from the belligerent actor they had made it for centuries into one committed to respecting and protecting the humanity of citizens and (at least sometimes) strangers. Silently transposing his Red Cross inheritance from the imperial age into a world that allowed for no official distinctions of coverage founded on race or religion, Pictet assumed the eternal and universalistic applicability of humane standards in war. "Young people," he worried in 1962, "can be inclined to reject the idea of the Red Cross as some European affair along with everything else they are repudiating, simply because they inherited it." But "the whole world can rally to the Red Cross," he insisted, because "it fits the educated interest of all peoples." Indeed, he observed, the goal of humane war "is permanent," the "expression of a long-term wisdom indifferent to passing opinions and momentary ideologies."

Pictet had initially dreamed of connecting the postwar revisions of the law of war on which he was working to the contemporary innovation of outlining international human rights, most famously in the Universal Declaration of Human Rights adopted by the United Nations in 1948. This came to naught at the time—the great powers involved did not want newfangled notions such as human rights to interfere with whatever "humanity" required in wartime settings. In fact, in spite of a certain amount of talk about the possibility in the late 1960s, human rights were not brought to bear on war until after September 11, 2001. But as Pictet angled to undo his defeat, he was more successful in proselytizing for what he called "international humanitarian law." This law would elevate a few isolated principles in the laws of war and make them the humane essence and purpose of the entire field.

This astonishing leap forward began in the 1970s. The years before were hardly promising. The 1960s had been a crisis time for Pictet's project, and he knew it. It was not just the era of decolonizing violence and the Vietnam War, the scene of the kind of "massacres, torture, and brutality that mankind, in its hope of progress, had believed were forever banished from the face of the earth." The 1960s had also seen the last surge of a peace politics that had always haunted the humane war project. Doubtful that the Geneva Conventions would abet peace, and aware of their critics, Pictet had been anxious as far back as 1951. The Red Cross founder Henry Dunant's original handiwork had "struck a shrewd first blow against the Moloch of war," Pictet insisted, but it was true that "disappointment" had reigned since. He was sure at least that "the existence of humanitarian Conventions does nothing to promote war," even if it was hard to make the case that they had improved the world yet.

His vision of humane war would seem more plausible, Pictet concluded, only if the laws of war actually demanded greater humanity on paper and finally made a bigger difference in practice. All the laws of war had to become humanitarian in spirit: even the incredibly permissive standards governing killing itself. In the face of the new antiwar sentiments of the 1960s, Pictet cautiously welcomed his own group's flirtation with peace ideals. But he forthrightly prioritized a different project: humane war must move beyond old concessions to militaries to be credible. "Revision of the law of war is urgent," Pictet insisted.

Vietnam's end was a moment of opportunity. Assembled by Pictet, with negotiators from the United States open to a deal because of the public relations hit their nation had taken, diplomats from all the world's states met for three years from 1974 to 1977 and did something extraordinary. Before the humbly titled "Additional Protocols" to the Geneva Conventions, one could say with only a bit of exaggeration that there were no laws of war, humane or not. Dunant's Geneva Convention of 1864 had largely outsourced care of soldiers to nongovernmental organizations for states that didn't want to shoulder their responsibility, and the rest of the nineteenth-century law of war had incurred the risk of being mistaken for humanitarian while legitimating militarism.

Then and since, there had been laws on the margins of war—what happened to the captured and wounded, and finally, in 1949, to civilians who suffered occupation by enemy armies—but they were barely taken seriously before. Aside from banning certain weaponry and exempting some targets under narrow conditions, the militaries of the world could always cite "necessity" to do nearly anything they wanted within the fight. Pictet's ambitious rebranding project was to reverse polarities: the laws of war would become constraining rather than permissive. Humanity would define the terms of violence rather than eking out minor exceptions on the margins of its reign.

Remarkably, the Geneva protocols of 1977 enacted his vision, driven by decolonized new states, East European Communists strategizing to accuse their Cold War enemies of inhumanity, and West Europeans finally done with colonial violence. (The empire with Europe's last African colonies, Portugal, fell while the delegates negotiated.) The documents not only clearly formalized the immunity of civilians from targeting for the first time but also imposed the newfangled prohibition against fighting that risked excessive collateral harm, even when the targets were fair game. Equally important, they called for precautions in targeting so that militaries could not shoot first and ask questions later. Even to get these provisions down on paper, after years of state resistance, was epoch-making.

The biggest controversy in the negotiations was about whether and in what circumstances to extend to national liberation movements the privileges of combatants under the laws of war—including the protections for soldiers that lawyers had worked out for conventional wars back into the nineteenth century. In the 1960s and 1970s, the new states of a now postcolonial world tired of great-power intervention in their lands held out the most hope for restraining war itself. They all put the most effort into more rigorous controls on force in the international system. In their view, World War II had enthroned a peaceful internationalism beyond strife in the global north—but further perpetuated war under the euphemism of Pax Americana in the global south. But these states cared about regulating hostilities, too. The most brutal final battles of decolonization were being fought against the Portuguese empire in Angola and Mozambique; bitter memories of Vietnam were fresh.

Earlier, the extraordinary repression of irregular fighters for "national liberation" had been the norm, on the premise that they existed outside legal categories or were ordinary criminals. The history of overseas colonialism, like the American treatment of native peoples, was a grim record of the consequences of such treatment. Before—and during—the wars that led to so many new states after World War II, counterinsurgent empires and genocidal settlers had regularly played by no rules. Now those states had a vote on the laws of war. In the 1977 protocols, there was much confusion over what sort of compromise with their old imperial masters had been made. But the postcolonial states succeeded—with the Soviet Union on their side—in guaranteeing guerrilla fighters some entitlement to prisoner-of-war protection in international armed conflict, even if they were not organized armies obeying all the rules themselves. The African National Congress and the Palestine Liberation Organization, decades from assuming any power, were even involved in the negotiations to push through such protections. And the protocols went far beyond the Geneva Conventions' minimal concern for internal armed conflict to provide more rules than the old Common Article 3 for such situations.

With the Cold War still going, postcolonial states lost in their attempts to establish a more peaceful world with less great-power intervention. The new states succeeded mainly in protecting struggles for "national liberation" that were already becoming a thing of the past. Pictet's idea that "humanity" must characterize the fighting itself would prove more consequential. For the first time in the history of international law, these documents affirmed that the point of war was to weaken military capacities on the other side, absolutely prohibiting the direct targeting of civilians. And excessive collateral damage was also condemned for the first time.

Strategically if sanctimoniously, delegates in the mid-1970s pretended that they were only reaffirming ethical precepts laid down long since. They wanted it to seem as if the laws of war had always been humanitarian—even as they papered over how inapplicable or permissive those rules had been. The new rules prohibited urban destruction, previously justifiable if there was any military target nearby. Many progressives hoped that states would accept a ban on targeting choices that threatened collateral harm that outweighed anticipated military gains. This requirement of "proportionality" didn't make it into the text. Still, the taking of civilian life and collateral damage now mattered enough that they were allowed only if not "excessive" in comparison to the military advantage gained through an attack. Though the requirement of proportionality was dropped during negotiations, it was soon taken to be in the treaty in spirit.

Now there really were—finally—laws of humane war. Now, for the first time, the brutal essence of killing itself was a legally constrained activity. It was an enormous breakthrough on paper for a world of persistently atrocious fighting. But if states complied, it opened the possibility of unforeseen risks, too. What if those who initiate, moderate, and tolerate more humane war consider the results ethically legitimate precisely because they are following the new rules?

The laws of war since the nineteenth century had failed to achieve humanity, not being designed to do so. Now they had a chance to succeed. The costs of failure could decline, but the costs of success could begin to mount. Even so, this possibility would have remained hypothetical and remote had not activists other than the Swiss, including the U.S. military itself, joined in.

HEWING TO ITS TRADITIONAL MISSION, LEADING ON THE EVOLUTION of the laws of war and discreetly advising states when they were in violation, Pictet's Swiss group could never make the laws of war a public cause on its own. It increased its staff in the 1970s threefold but remained limited in its tasks. It was utterly crucial that new groups intervened to denounce governments publicly for their transgressions. They would make a new politics of shame about wartime atrocity essential to our conscience.

In the United States, the group that became Human Rights Watch began to name and shame states for violations of the newly updated international humanitarian law. In response to the election of Ronald Reagan as president in 1980, the group that had begun as Helsinki Watch chose to balance its anti-Communist work by also condemning the right-wing regimes it rightly feared the new administration would support. To do so, its founders spun off the parallel Americas Watch, which quickly adopted the tactic of reporting on violations of the new international humanitarian law. Being an NGO that also did hard-hitting reporting on wartime atrocity was its "most significant innovation," the group's leader Aryeh Neier later observed.

In the pioneering international human rights activism of the 1960s and 1970s, the animating concerns had been free speech and false imprisonment in authoritarian states in South America and totalitarian ones in Eastern Europe. But as Americas Watch began its work in the Central American war zones of El Salvador and Guatemala in the 1980s, a new calculus emerged. It was unclear how rights standards applied in wartime when deprivation even of civilian life was legalized. Enter international humanitarian law, which now purported to define which deaths and how many of them were beyond the pale. In internal and proxy wars in Central America, human rights activists would appear biased if they reported only on governments, as they had done before. In Nicaragua, the political enemy of the human rights groups, Reagan, was backing the brutal Contra paramilitary opponents of the leftist Sandinista regime.

The human rights movement broke with the discretion of the Red Cross. It went public to dramatize the fate of civilians in wars, where the Swiss group had kept its demands to states secret in hopes of pushing them without the opprobrium of public shame. Yet the human rights movement would officially remain "apolitical." Starting in the early 1980s, Human Rights Watch first reported on violations of the laws of war without a great deal of ceremony or even officially reflecting on the fact that it was doing so. With the new Geneva protocols as its backstop, it attempted to raise consciousness of "violations of the laws of war on both sides" in Central American wars.

Committed and gruff, Neier had gotten his political education on the democratic left. Born in 1937 in Berlin, before his parents fled to the United States two years later, as a young man Neier was inspired by Norman Thomas, pacifist opponent of American entry into both world wars and Socialist Party candidate for president six times, until 1948. But Human Rights Watch was not pacifist. The outfit remained neutral not merely on who was in the right during a war but on whether a war was justified before it broke out. Neier's successor, the current Human Rights Watch leader, Kenneth Roth, later reflected, "We weren't against war per se. We never took up the issue of who is the aggressor, who is the defender, who was at fault for starting the war, who's in the right, who's in the wrong. We always did stay neutral on those issues."

It was a reasonable position for a progressive humanitarian group that took up some causes while leaving other tasks to self-consciously political groups. But what was the effect of demanding humane war if there were fewer and fewer left demanding no war? The intervention of humanitarian advocacy in the most brutal settings was to have unexpected implications.

As Human Rights Watch embraced the humanitarian laws of war more formally after the Cold War ended—and expanded the scale and scope of its activities all over the world—it stepped back and, with some pride, accounted for its approach. "By far the largest number of victims of severe violations of human rights worldwide are the noncombatants who are killed, injured, deprived of food and other necessities, or forced to flee from their homes because of the manner in which opposing forces seek to prevail militarily," it explained in 1992. "War-related abuses of human rights were largely neglected by the worldwide human rights movement before Human Rights Watch determined to assume this role. International humanitarian law was hardly ever mentioned in the reports of human rights organizations until Human Rights Watch began doing so." All that was true.

Even so, the group also faced an interesting moment of pushback from its own funders. When the Ford Foundation expressed skepticism about the group's decision to double down on incorporating the laws of humane war into its monitoring, Neier was indignant. "We think we are developing a role that is complementary to that of the International Committee of the Red Cross," he explained in 1991. "That is, they provide humanitarian services and advise the parties confidentially of abuses; we report publicly on abuses."

Ford commissioned a study of whether it was a mistake for human rights groups to stray into the territory of humane war. Understandably, its main objection was that it would be difficult to clarify standards for wartime monitoring. No one pondered one possible consequence of abstaining from political criticism of warmongering in order to offer nonpartisan description of abuses within the fight: that it could help bring about a world characterized by less-atrocious conflicts with fewer limitations in space and time. The conditions for that result were accumulating, but the result itself was far away and indeed unimaginable. With the Iron Curtain down and Yugoslavia imploding, Neier chastised his funders. Far from demanding caution, the 1990s and after would "accelerate the human rights community's shift to focus on humanitarian law issues." He was right.

Around the same time as the breakup of Yugoslavia unleashed armed strife in Europe, Human Rights Watch also moved to apply the same strategy to cross-border war. The group continued to dramatize the horrible costs of internal conflict and ethnic cleansing. But then it took a giant step. After visiting with the U.S. military to receive instruction on what the law required, Human Rights Watch also shone its spotlight on American excesses during the Gulf War in 1990–91. The U.S. bombings of Iraqi territory while the dictator Saddam Hussein's forces were being driven from Kuwait—including arguable illegalities in target selection, with hundreds of needless civilian deaths—were the first deaths from the sky to attract such denunciation for breaking the laws of war. They were not the last.

"UNTIL THE TIME THAT HUMAN RIGHTS GROUPS BEGAN TAKING ON IHL," Roth recalled, "there were only a handful of people in the world who had any idea what this specialized body of law meant." The situation, he added, "was very comfortable for militaries because military lawyers interpret IHL in a way that is deferential to the military." In the 1990s, his advocacy group, along with Amnesty International and others, vaulted the laws of war into the headlines by publicizing their violation. "Suddenly," Roth gloated, militaries "had lost their monopoly over the interpretation of humanitarian law."

But militaries had never really exercised the power of their monopoly: it did not matter much to them what rules were on the books or how they were interpreted. Now militaries began to insist on following the rules—out of a combination of moral education and post-Vietnam public relations. What one might call the self-humanization of the military under law was probably the most important factor in paving the road toward humane war after Vietnam. After all, when the military lost its monopoly on interpreting the laws of war and acceded to a new ethos of humane conflict, it gained something, too. There was now a space for compromise between new generations of activists cut off from an antiwar past and a military newly concerned about the ethics and optics of fighting. They would agree to contend with each other not over whether the United States went to war—a question the new humanitarians were actually less concerned about than militaries interested in avoiding losses—as over how.

Vietnam changed the U.S. military in a host of ways. In the long run, it was probably most pivotal that conscription ended with that war. The draft had made American conflicts, with the exception of World War II, endemically controversial. The proposal to get rid of the draft had percolated before, but it gained traction after Richard Nixon made it one of his election promises in 1968, mainly to "quell the restless students" on American campuses. As the idea percolated through policy circles, the former defense secretary Thomas Gates headed a commission weighing pros and cons for the president. The group supported the end of the draft unanimously, before the institution formally ended in 1973.

A coalition of strange bedfellows fought to end the draft. Libertarian economists such as Martin Anderson and Milton Friedman helped devise the step. Left-leaning economists such as John Kenneth Galbraith joined the cause, with Galbraith insisting that the draft involved a "shift of the cost of military service from the well-to-do taxpayer who benefits by lower taxes to the impecunious young draftee." Creating an "all-volunteer force" would require the better-off to abstain from supporting wars for which they would have to pay in treasure, since they rarely paid in blood.

Some draft foes hoped that ending conscription would make it harder for the United States to fight war, not easier. "Immediate draft-provided reserves of men make it possible for U.S. foreign policy to be based on military might and subject to military adventurism," observed one peace activist testifying before Congress in 1971. As conscription continued amid opposition, the antiwar Senator Mike Gravel of Alaska defended filibustering its renewal. "Ending the draft," he explained, "will also cut off an administration's ability to engage in future military adventures which do not have the support of the American people."

Conservatives took this line of argument seriously. They opposed the plan to end the draft because presidents might need a conscript army in emergencies. Meanwhile, their liberal allies such as Senators Thomas Eagleton and Ted Kennedy worried that the move would make it easier, not harder, to raise armies, while forcing the burden of American war even further onto poor communities, especially racial minorities. "It could make it too cheap and easy for national leaders to make the initial decision to wage war," Joseph Califano, Jr., a domestic policy advisor for Lyndon Johnson and later cabinet secretary, predicted in 1971 as debate raged. "An all-volunteer force that subjects only the ones at the bottom to military service will effectively reduce the need for future leaders to be concerned about the more affluent majority of America and its judgments about foreign adventures," he added two years later, after the draft was gone, "at least until those adventures are so far along that they will be virtually impossible to stop."

Over time, these voices proved prescient, if not entirely in ways they predicted. The end of the draft would make it next to impossible to mobilize an antiwar movement, because "volunteer" service in America's wars immunized the well-off even more than before. Sam Brown, antiwar activist in the 1960s, saw the writing on the wall in the mid-1970s. The movement to end Vietnam had long suffered from "overdependence on upper-middle-class, draftable young men." Now immune from service, they were suddenly less concerned about American wars, leaving "a predominantly poor and increasingly Black 'volunteer' army" whose exposure to harm aroused less ire. It was imaginable now that the rage might spike among the country's own troops and veterans when future wars went south, without generating anything like the antiwar sentiment of prior history.

As the draft ended, something remarkable happened: the U.S. military embraced the now humanitarian laws of war—a self-humanization of armed force without precedent in the history of any great power. That outcome required generational change. The army colonel Harry Summers, Jr., was the loudest voice among those unrepentant about the conduct of hostilities in Vietnam—preferring in the early years to blame bad press on American leftists and North Vietnamese propaganda. For many such officers, the lesson was that civilians should only send U.S. forces to fight winnable wars. They blamed the public relations disaster of My Lai on failures of nerve and patriotism, and they were incensed not by the massacre but by the single court-martial that had followed.

A younger generation of officers in the military went in a different direction entirely. They welcomed the newly humane laws of war. Adherence to these rules was not only honorable; it would also help militaries avoid the hit to their reputation that atrocity stories caused. The opprobrium of activists and publics was establishing new standards for America's global violence. This result could prove both moral for its own sake and useful to the legitimation of military affairs.

Judge Advocate General lawyers in the different service branches were in the forefront of this change, leading a legalization process in government that broke decisively with prior military traditions. Previously they had engaged with international law only to deal with foreign claims, work out status of forces agreements when the United States stationed troops abroad, and formalize and interpret the old rules over how to treat prisoners of war and civilians under occupation. These lawyers were also responsible for training all members of the armed services in the laws through Vietnam, but the training was light and there was no commitment to a culture of education and enforcement. In 1974, by contrast, the Department of Defense established a "law of war program," recognizing the faulty inculcation of basic principles in training U.S. forces. But the self-humanization of the military after the Vietnam War did not stop there. After all, there were brand-new rules that intruded into operations and had to be imparted.

AMERICA'S ROLE IN THE DEVELOPMENT OF THE GENEVA PROTOcols anticipated a self-humanization of the military inconceivable before Vietnam. When the diplomat George Aldrich led the U.S. contingent to Geneva in 1974 to negotiate the new protocols, one of the JAG officers who accompanied him was the general and lawyer George Prugh, Jr. Aldrich was a St. Louisan trained at Harvard Law School who had worked out of the State Department on prisoner-of-war issues during the Vietnam War (and as Henry Kissinger's assistant at the Paris talks that ended it). Aldrich made common cause with Prugh, a Virginian raised in San Francisco who had served twenty months in-country in Vietnam as the leading legal authority before ascending to the pinnacle of his corps. Though both acknowledged how hard it had been to apply even existing law in Vietnam, Aldrich and Prugh arrived in Geneva with a striking willingness to renovate it.

The main reason was that U.S. prisoners of war had been harshly treated by the Hanoi regime. The military was open to beefing up rules in order to guarantee better protection of its own in future wars. Beyond their narrower ends, Aldrich and Prugh understood that in Vietnam the U.S. military had suffered a public relations disaster of the first magnitude. It now had to interpret self-interest to include far more humane conduct—including humane fighting—on its own part. "Every evening for years," Aldrich later recalled of Vietnam, "the horrors of war were displayed graphically in every living room and the suffering of the civilian population in a war of guerrillas and high technology was often emphasized."

Aldrich clearly identified the Vietnam experience as the one that mattered, embarrassing a national security establishment that had once been more immune to shame. Even if allegations of atrocious conduct were not always fair, the United States "became sensitive to charges of indiscriminate bombardment, attacks on civilians, attacks on dikes and the environment and similar charges," he wrote. Ethics—or at least optics—required innovation: "A pervading sense of defensiveness, if not guilt, about the suffering caused by the war, and by aerial warfare in particular, resulted, I believe, in an increased American willingness to participate in the review and improvement of that part of international law that deals with the conduct of hostilities," Aldrich emphasized. "We want, of course, to mitigate the terrible scourge of war," Prugh explained before going to Switzerland, "to protect noncombatants to the extent possible."

Though the larger military hardly turned on a dime to embrace humane war under international law, a growing phalanx of military lawyers after Vietnam was on board with Pictet's rebranding of their field as international humanitarian law. But had Aldrich and Prugh conceded too much in the process? Their participation in the Geneva protocols allowed for the United States to legitimate wars, while also responding to criticisms of prior excesses, by accepting new requirements to fight humanely. But had they also exposed the United States and its allies to the now legal violence of their potential enemies? The first American debate over the Geneva protocols alleged as much.

A young administration official named Douglas Feith denounced the treaty at the Pentagon and then went on the offensive in the inaugural issue of the neoconservative godfather Irving Kristol's *The National Interest* in 1985. Feith served as special counsel for Richard Perle, assistant secretary of defense for policy in the Reagan administration. For such neoconservatives, and a few like-minded soldiers figuring out what to do with what Aldrich and Prugh had negotiated (and less given to guilt than many Americans), what stood out in the Geneva protocols were not the opportunities. Feith equated the postcolonial agenda of the 1960s with a terrorist one, and he decried the risks to the United States in granting more legal recognition to insurgent forces. He reviled the extent to which U.S. negotiators had placated new states by granting "national liberation movements" more protections than they had enjoyed from Algeria to Vietnam. The result, Feith complained, was "a pro-terrorist treaty masquerading as humanitarian law."

It was revealing, all the same, that Feith justified his florid opposition on the grounds that it "would undermine the Conventions' protection of noncombatants," inadvertently testifying to how much humane warfare now mattered rhetorically. Reagan did the same when he worried that the protocol—in spite of introducing legal constraints on killing itself for the first time—would "undermine humanitarian law and endanger civilians in war." In late–Cold War America, the argument had considerable appeal, to the point that the *New York Times* editorial board applauded when the president decided not to send the now radioactive first protocol for Senate ratification. (He did send the second, but it was not ratified either, tarred with the ignominy of the first.) Enhanced "protection for prisoners of war and civilians" was not worth it, the newspaper said, when it involved "new legal protection for guerrillas and possible terrorists." Feith's activism, and remnants of a skepticism about humane war in defense circles, created a political atmosphere that would make it impossible for the United States—to this day—ever to formally sign on to the new regime.

Feith later bragged that his pushback against the Geneva protocols anticipated his involvement with a much broader U.S. attempt to exempt itself from the requirements of humane war after September 11, 2001. In the long run, however, it was more important that the U.S. military wanted to self-humanize, and it had already committed to doing so long before the war on terror. It was not just that, starting with the Reagan administration Feith served, the United States began accepting the substance of the Geneva protocols as largely consonant with the unwritten international law it claimed to honor, whatever the Senate's fecklessness. Initially, Human Rights Watch had been the lone supporter of the view that the new law of humane war bound all states, even those who hadn't signed on, but over the years its heterodox position became dominant—including within the U.S. military itself. Indeed, it had no trouble assenting to the basic commands to distinguish civilians from combatants and to avoid disproportionate collateral harm. The aerial operations Aldrich had most wished to limit, in order for America's morality to remain publicly intact, were now formally covered.

Neoconservative opposition to the new rules of less-brutal war dealt those rules only a temporary setback—mainly because so many in the military wanted to obey those rules. In the imaginable future, the U.S. military was likely to be involved in minor interventions and proxy wars, not major interventions against foes who required the harshest measures. It was an astonishing outcome relative to an American past in which the country accepted few rules of conducting hostilities except those it made itself, and ignored those it accepted.

The military also developed a culture and institutions that took the old rules seriously, and inculcated them far more conscientiously than ever before. Paradoxically, a state that had always been skittish about binding itself to venerable international arrangements now did so when it came to newly humanitarian laws of war. Aside from concerns for honorable and upright soldiering, the main reason was that there was another side to the ledger. After My Lai, profound institutional and legal immunities remained in place to safeguard U.S. troops from trouble. And owning the rules meant the country could interpret them its own way.

Indeed, Aldrich had assumed that the whole point of involvement in the project to update the Geneva Conventions was that it gave the United States a voice in writing the rules, without relinquishing its latitude to interpret them to its advantage later. To the objection that the U.S. military was co-opting the laws of war devised for humanity's sake, the only fair response is that those laws were designed from their nineteenth-century beginnings to locate compromises that militaries would accept. And military interpretations of the rules that humanitarians might consider beyond the pale of plausible legality were not a blemish but a design feature.

Still, the concession to accept new rules for humane war—and greater obedience to old rules, too—transformed possibilities. Within the military, the shift gave unprecedented power and responsibility alike to military lawyers eager to do their jobs, angle for bureaucratic turf, seek the sweet spot between permissible violence and terrible press, and legitimate war before a public with evolving sensitivities. It helped that one provision of the protocols called on states to "ensure that legal advisers are available, when necessary, to advise military commanders" of their obligations.

RULES OF HUMANE WAR HAD BEEN BUILT, AND MILITARY LAWYERS CAME. David Graham graduated from Texas A&M University at the height of Vietnam and studied law. Eventually an army colonel, he formed a long association with the JAG school in Charlottesville, Virginia, where he helped train generations of warrior-lawyers. Establishing within the military a kind of think tank for the laws of war, Graham exemplified the efforts of other post-Vietnam officers to raise the profile of the field. Abetting larger forces, he achieved spectacular success.

Graham started out in the early 1970s thinking about American prisoners of war in Vietnam, working on how to ensure their repatriation as conflict still raged. But the exciting thing, he wrote as the conflict wound down, was the prospect of full-scale reform, in spite of skeptics. At first, Graham warned (as Feith would a decade later) against an agenda at the negotiations for the Geneva protocols that favored national liberation alongside humane protection. But by the 1980s, Graham began to proselytize for far fuller involvement of military lawyers in war, especially now that "international humanitarian law" actually spelled out rules of humane fighting. Because branding matters, he coined the concept of "operational law," which purported to organize the inherited and new tasks of military lawyers, its very name implying their essential relevance to every element of war. Agonizingly, this relevance remained mostly theoretical before the Cold War ended. When Reagan ordered Operation Urgent Fury, invading the tiny Caribbean island of Grenada in October 1983, lawyers were left out of the planning. Once the invasion began, military lawyers were overwhelmed. They knew they were unready for the future.

There was a stunning coincidence. With the Gulf War in 1990–91, Human Rights Watch moved to monitor its first international conflict. Meanwhile, for the first time U.S. military lawyers inserted themselves in the process of picking targets humanely. It would take two to tango, as humanitarian and military lawyers entered simultaneously into an activity from outside and inside the state. Each engaged with the other over whether American war had become humane enough, a tango that continues to this day.

That the post–Cold War military accepted an unprecedented intrusion of legality into fighting, and not merely into the niceties of detention or occupation, was especially remarkable. For many years after Vietnam, legal advice still played no role in combat decision-making, and especially not in air force targeting. From Hiroshima to Hanoi and Haiphong, U.S. presidents and policymakers had chosen to strike from above with a sense of political opportunity and constraint, but no concern for legal rules, let alone with lawyers nearby. The end of the Cold War finally changed this default. "War looks messy," one reporter conceded in November 2001 of the new conflict afoot. "But behind the scenes, meticulous lawyering shapes nearly every strategic maneuver—even those made in the heat of combat," she rejoiced. What had happened?

Lawyers in the air force had begun training for this eventuality as far back as 1980. In 1989, JAG officers took a role in planning the intervention that ousted the Panamanian strongman Manuel

Noriega. And then the Gulf War gave them a chance to extend their presence. Overnight, they became fixtures of air operations centers, advising when dual-use targets—with both civilian and military purposes—were fair game and when limits on disproportionate collateral harm were likely to be violated. When Saddam Hussein's generals placed their jets strategically next to the Temple of Ur, one of the earliest remnants of human civilization, the U.S. military lawyers had to decide whether to allow their destruction. (They said no.)

The air force wasn't alone. An unprecedented 350 judge advocates across all branches deployed to fight the first Iraq war—anticipating the thousands who would deploy when American war returned to the same country a decade later. "Desert Storm was the most legalistic war we've ever fought," bragged the chief advisor on the law to "Stormin'" Norman Schwarzkopf, Jr., the four-star general with two tours in Vietnam behind him who commanded the campaign to liberate Kuwait from Iraq. In spite of the kinks to work out, Colin Powell—African American chair of the joint chiefs of staff who was elevated into a national icon thanks to his Pentagon briefings during the war—agreed that lawyers had become "absolutely indispensable to military operations . . . Our best lawyers are activists." For some military lawyers, the mood was downright celebratory. Their application of "lessons learned" was leading the military from a depressing nadir of grotesque horror to the sunlit uplands of humane war. "My Lai must never be forgotten," two army JAGs insisted in 1993. "From its engagements in Grenada in 1983, to Panama in 1989, to Kuwait in 1991, the United States military can take full credit for its commendable record in adhering to the law of war." The enormous success—popular as well as strategic—of the first American war waged with lawyers at its very heart made clear that "savvy American commanders seldom go to war without their attorneys."

Yet the wars they go to are not chosen by attorneys. Never did the victory lap for "operational lawyering" involve judging the legality of America's choice to initiate hostilities abroad in the first place. After the exemplary victory in the Gulf War, Powell famously insisted on new guidelines for when the United States should go to war. According to the Powell doctrine, there had to be concrete objectives, popular support, vital interests—and the military had to be allowed to deploy overwhelming force with an exit strategy. Indeed, the Powell doctrine came close to demanding guaranteed success. Powell's goal may have been "never again Vietnam." Clearly, it didn't work. Aspirations to infrequency and success slid into endlessness and quagmire. Notably, Powell and others in the military did not look to international law to impose limits on getting involved in war or staying in it, even as they insisted on the value of international law in humanizing the fight.

Like humanitarians, then, the new culture of military law focused not on keeping American force from deployment but on making its force more humane when unleashed. Compared with antiwar forces of the past, humanitarians were a far preferable foe, occupying more common terrain. U.S. government lawyers would never be able to control the meaning of the rules. Nevertheless, a few observers began to ask: Did the military's self-humanizations since My Lai entrench violence more than they regulated it? Either way, it was of the essence that so many officers high up in the military would protest so loudly and successfully when, after September 11, word came down that the laws that they regarded as legitimate and legitimating no longer applied. Like humanitarians, they had neither the ability nor the aspiration to keep American wars from going on forever, even as they rebelled when invited to make them more brutal.

BY THE 1990S, A NEW CULTURAL IMPERATIVE HAD BEEN ESTABLISHED for humane war, one that did as much to account for the agendas of humanitarians and militaries as anything else. The reorientation went furthest among West Europeans, long since relieved of most imperial obligations and far more reluctant to deploy force globally than they had been in the prior five centuries. It helped that they were sheltered by America's security system. Now not only publics but also leaders were apt to think like the Swiss: humanity in global warfare was one of the most attractive exports of European civilization, like chocolate bonbons or classical music. But ordinary Americans also lived through a profound shift toward a morality attentive to human life ravaged by war.

Americans rethought their wars in the past and other people's in the present. The aftermath of Vietnam retroactively changed the way Americans remember earlier wars their country had been involved in. A representative World War II novel, Sloan Wilson's *The Man in the Gray Flannel Suit* (a smash bestseller in 1955), portrayed a hero who—like Samuel Hynes—kills Japanese soldiers with gusto but can still fit in on returning home because the horrors of war "were simply incomprehensible and had to be forgotten." Tim O'Brien's Vietnam novel *In the Lake of the Woods*, published in 1994 at a very different moment, depicts a veteran who witnessed atrocity and cannot slough it off.

The new sensibility placed Jewish death at the moral center of World War II decades after the fact. Atrocities affecting foreigners and strangers now plucked at heartstrings in the white Christian communities across the Atlantic that once had done the most in modern history to orchestrate such deeds. This rise in moral concern occurred in tandem with the rise of new and often repressive postcolonial states, where strangers were seen to suffer most at the hands of their own leaders. The carnage of World War II had made the creation of a peace architecture a first priority, for Americans and others. The new Holocaust memory coincided with the aftermath of decolonization, and a skepticism along with it that others were up to the challenge of ruling themselves. The result was not a demand for peace but for interventionist justice. These trends were confirmed by the end of the Cold War and the outbreak of civil war on the territory of the composite state of Yugoslavia, which was on European territory but involved unprecedented concern for Muslim victims.

It was no accident that, across these same years, the International Military Tribunal at Nuremberg was rehabilitated in memory—

falsified, really—as an atrocity trial rather than the aggression inquest it had really been. It was a misunderstanding that war crimes in Vietnam and calls to try them had first made imaginable. The far-left Russell tribunal staged its own mock Nuremberg, and there were later and less-radical invocations of the precedent by Telford Taylor and others. In the 1990s, it was as if Nuremberg's stigma on starting wars had never been. In a new mantra, the "legacy of Nuremberg" was taken to be the warrant for a contemporary struggle to hold perpetrators of atrocity crimes to account.

After the Cold War, a new vision for international criminal law arose, first from the strife during the breakup of the former Yugoslavia, and partly as Western atonement for doing too little in the face of it. The International Criminal Tribunal for the former Yugoslavia was established in 1993. Peripheral in moral consciousness before, "ethnic cleansing," culminating in genocide, became the defining evil of war past and present. Not aggression among peoples but atrocious slaughter of groups singled out for their "race" or religion emerged as the scandal that mattered and the wrong to right, as the specter of a new Holocaust reared its ugly head on European territory. Alongside such evils, the ignored experience of rape victims endemic in all prior wars (during Japanese colonialism in East Asia in the 1930s or the Soviet conquest and occupation of Germany in the 1940s, for example) achieved notice and attracted opprobrium, too. The former Yugoslavia's agonies even activated a once-marginal concern for punishing genocide.

An even worse slaughter of innocents in Rwanda followed in 1994, and the statute governing its tribunal named rape a war crime for the first time. In an era of apparent interstate peace associated with "the end of history," there was no urgency to ask who started the brutal civil wars in Europe and Africa. Climactically, a new International Criminal Court was founded thanks to a 1998 treaty. It fulfilled the legacy of Nuremberg, except in omitting its signature accomplishment of criminalizing illegal war itself.

The international recognition of new victims that climaxed in the 1990s was a breakthrough for both cosmopolitanism and care. But it also represented a narrowing of focus that no one exactly defended, in spite of the long-run consequences. With war between great powers a thing of the past, it was the fate of innocents suffering elsewhere—and perhaps in need of great-power rescue—that legal innovation now concerned. The agenda to extirpate not war itself but excess within it—"ending impunity," as a rampant phrase had it—reflected the fact that self-styled cosmopolitans experienced revulsion at the death and injury of the unknown abroad. A prior generation of Americans and Europeans had accorded overriding importance to laws that barred starting wars, after peace movements since the nineteenth century demanded them. Those advocates were gone. Now, as one liberal thinker put it to general agreement as the Cold War ended, cruelty was "the worst thing we do." No one asked at the time whether that implied that war itself—especially if it could be purged of its cruelty—was not that bad.

It was not just that atrocity had become the primary evil to abhor. Within atrocity, a new taboo on the horror of torture was consecrated. As with the concern for victims in general, it was noble to single out torture as the acme of transgression. But it did allow for a consequence no one intended: singling out torture meant that, if it occurred, prohibiting it could feel like expiation of the worst mistake, like the restoration of the very line between the sacred and the profane.

The kinds of practices that now count as illegal torture had once been routine occurrences that prompted no outcry in the United States or elsewhere. Against chattel slaves and criminals, and not merely in war, for centuries American torture was not abhorrent but normal. Americans were no different from others in this regard. Violent assaults on the body for amusement or information were especially common in centuries of colonial rule. Torture became a cause for new alarm at the twilight of European empire, its brutal practices finally inviting opprobrium when it was on the way out. America's misadventure in Vietnam involved far more torture than more famous episodes since.

True, America's homemade rules for its own armies had prohibited torture since the 1860s, and an article prohibiting torture had appeared in the Universal Declaration of Human Rights of 1948 (though the provision almost didn't make it into the text). Torture's illegality in international rules of war dated back to the 1899 Hague provisions, confirmed again in the new Geneva Conventions in 1949. Yet the practice remained disconcertingly widespread—more proof of how far these norms on paper had to go in practice, not least because they were neither inculcated nor taken seriously within militaries.

The equation had changed most drastically in the 1970s amid severe domestic repression in a series of places, including European locales such as Greece and Northern Ireland. Amnesty International wasn't ready to monitor war until Human Rights Watch showed the way. But Amnesty had taken the lead in stigmatizing torture, opening a "Campaign Against Torture" in 1973. The West Europeans who dominated the group came from countries that were leaving former colonies or long gone from them. Meanwhile, Jean Pictet's son-in-law, a former banker named Jean-Jacques Gautier, inspired by Amnesty's campaign, founded in 1977 what became the Association for the Prevention of Torture, and he worked for an international convention against it. In force by the late 1980s, the agreement prohibited torture in all circumstances—though it was not until decades later that its applicability in wars outside the borders of states became clearer.

As for the United States, it was leaving Vietnam. After her safe return from her visit to Hanoi during the Linebacker II bombings, the American folksinger Joan Baez participated in launch events for the Campaign Against Torture in London and New York as one of her country's first and most iconic human rights activists. Although the United States had used the vile practice since the start of the war, it was revelations that South Vietnam perpetrated torture that unleashed wrath. America's client had long kept prisoners in the "tiger cages" of Con Son Island. The crimes perpetrated there were revealed only in 1970, just as the United States was looking for a way out of the war, when Tom Harkin, soon to be a congressman, snapped photos of the scene that *Life* magazine published. It touched off a wave of revelations that provided antiwar fodder at the time—and left a legacy of making prisoner mistreatment outrageous even if American wars returned.

In 1988, even Reagan, whose staff was caustic about the third-worldist politics of the laws of war, solemnly signed and sent the Convention Against Torture to the Senate, which followed through and ratified it six years later. The makings of the taboo swept elite culture. "There may be no human event that is as without defense as torture," the American literary critic Elaine Scarry went so far as to remark in 1985, after traveling to London to read Amnesty's accounts of assault.

In this atmosphere, few noticed that loopholes remained open when some were finally closed. No one registered that America's Guantánamo Bay, Cuba, site was just enough outside U.S. territory for the treaty the country had ratified not to apply there, but just enough inside for the statute Congress had passed in 1994 criminally prohibiting torture abroad to be irrelevant. But whatever America's half-hearted treatment of the rules against torture in the international treaty, no one could disagree that the new statute applied to foreign war. And the military law that also banned torture was now taken seriously, along with the rest of the old and new rules of conduct in war. Two years after the federal anti-torture statute, Bill Clinton signed into law a criminal prohibition of war crimes, allowing civilian prosecutions when U.S. forces gravely breached the Geneva Conventions rules and the naturally self-protective military failed to take action. And another 2000 law finally got rid of an all-important exception to punishment that had allowed American war criminals simply to retire from service to escape justice. "We have come a long way since My Lai," David Graham observed in 2002, with glowing pride.

Torture, even more than other atrocity crimes, rose to the top of the list of immoral and even illegal acts, which was an enormous advance. But war fell off the list, and no one complained.

IF THE WITCH'S BREW OF HUMANE WAR WAS READY ON THE BRINK OF September 11, it was due to not only a preliminary but also a real commitment to humanity in warfare. It also required American war itself to be rehabilitated after Vietnam as legitimate or even progressive. And it required that the international law prohibiting illegal force be treated as advisory or obstructive rather than the most important of limits.

Following the 1940s, the circumstances were not promising for the United States to hew to its own constitutional rules forbidding presidential war, let alone to conform to weaker international law prohibiting unauthorized war—even though the United States had written the United Nations Charter itself. Democrats had led the way in initiating not just World War I and II but also the Cold War and the Vietnam War. And during the anti-Communist emergency, conservatives had thrown overboard their earlier suspicions of executive power and the massive federal state because they were necessities of a globalized war footing. For that matter, the destiny of the country long after 1989 was shaped by a ferocious battle among three factions of Democrats debating how to respond to Vietnam and set the country's foreign policy right.

The losing faction was the antiwar movement, due to the shipwreck of its standard-bearer, Senator George McGovern of South Dakota, whose 1972 presidential campaign was a disaster. Like the antiwar vice president William Jennings Bryan before him, McGovern—a former bomber pilot in the European theater—had stood for a plainsman's progressive Christianity, America's central pacifist tradition. Heir to that lineage, McGovern had seen "the nation's interventionist foreign policy as a historic aberration." Reminding Americans that foreigners were also made in God's image, he also proposed to deflate the military budget in favor of domestic social justice. "Come Home, America," the famous slogan of McGovern's ill-fated campaign, was a direct invitation to the United States to return to its pre-interventionist principles after an era of prodigality.

McGovern's humongous loss—he carried only one state, and it wasn't his own—led once-honorable American views to be deemed radioactive ever after. In response, Democrats constructed a firewall against any pacifistic inroads into the mainstream consensus around military power. In the long view, McGovern's candidacy proved the last gasp of an old tradition of pacifist Christianity in American life. Elite Christianity was dying, as the evangelical movement that had ended slavery and opposed empire and war was assuming a very different form. The effect of Vietnam may have been to create an enduring if small antiwar constituency in the party, but that faction also lost ground to the point that it seemed positively antique by the 1990s.

The two other factions—foreign policy neoconservatism and liberal internationalism—were closer to each other than their followers liked to admit. Hawkish Democrats such as Senator Henry Jackson of Washington, tired of dealing with a left they regarded as too soft on communism, schooled neoconservatives who moved into the Republican Party when Reagan won. The proponents of "liberal internationalism" emerged between the mid-1970s through the 1980s—when the very use of the phrase spiked—and stayed in the party.

Neoconservatives didn't think there were many lessons from Vietnam. They had no love for any kind of international law, especially not if it restrained American force. The most intelligent liberal internationalist, Richard Holbrooke, a young foreign policy analyst who had cut his teeth as a Vietnam pacification officer, argued against America's abandonment of its primacy and purpose, too. "The roll call of policies which liberals advocated" during the "ugly war" of Vietnam "turned out to be corrupt," Holbrooke observed in the trendsetting new magazine *Foreign Policy* (which he edited from 1972 to 1976). Certainly, it was "essential to understand our past in order to reshape our future" after "a string of revelations." But, he added, the worst mistake was to "accept the proposition that because America has done some evil things, America itself is an evil force in the world."

Holbrooke insisted that war fought with care and for good cause, not disengagement or noninvolvement, was what should emerge from the wreckage of Vietnam. Leftist congressmen elected during Vietnam such as Oakland's Ron Dellums attempted to sue Reagan for illegality in going to war, but such activism proved less and less plausible over time. McGovern had revealed antiwar politics to be an electoral dead end. More than this, even an ugly America still bestrode the world economically and militarily. Why not rehabilitate its force for humanity's sake?

After the fall of the Berlin Wall in 1989, with Republican George H. W. Bush in office and with the Cold War coming to an end, there may have been a moment of opportunity for a less-militarized American stance. There was genuine talk of less preeminence in arms and arms sales, less defense spending, and a "peace dividend." And indeed, the earlier invasion of Panama notwithstanding, fewer direct interventions and proxy wars occurred than under earlier or later presidents. Not accidentally, Bush's leanings were less neoconservative than realist. If a portal opened for American reset, however, it was slammed shut within two years. The reason was the very same Gulf War of 1990–91 that counted as America's first genuine attempt at humane war.

The Gulf War's military success gave new life to Cold War priors and even suppressed the complicated legacy of its worst disaster. The standard for America's unipolar moment would be not the agony of Saigon's fall, leaving a trail of humility and skittishness, but the thrill of victory. Bush himself crowed that "the specter of Vietnam has been buried forever in the desert sands." "The lessons widely drawn from America's victory in the gulf war contradicted in almost every respect the meaning that had been assigned to the end of the cold war," two conservatives explained. "Whereas the end of the cold war showed the declining utility of military force in the relations of the great developed states, the gulf war was widely taken as a striking refutation of this view." After the Cold War, U.S. presidents ordered not fewer but more wars: more than 80 percent of all U.S. military interventions abroad since 1946 came *after* 1989.

Why did an ultimately minor war to push Saddam Hussein's forces back across the Kuwait border to Iraq, however triumphant, so easily smash hopes across the American political spectrum for a post–Cold War pivot? Was it the accumulating dangers of a globalizing world? Was it that the unique circumstances of the Gulf War—a conventional conflict, and one that seemed easy to enter and exit—belied America's fifty-year entanglement in the Middle East and the Muslim world that allowed for no extrication? Or was it perhaps the pressure of a "military-industrial" complex that insisted on fighting enemies (albeit more humanely now) to justify its perpetuation?

Ultimately, the mature ideologies of foreign policy neoconservatism and liberal internationalism did much to bring about the humane war of our time. They agreed more than they differed both before and after the Cold War's end. Both, most of all, treated a unipolar world as an occasion demanding the ratification of American global might, not an opportunity for rethinking it. Together, the rival teams gave a new lease on life to American war after 1989, accepting its moralization not only in purpose but also in execution and style. If the portal before a more peaceful era had slammed shut, foreign policy neoconservatives and liberal internationalists took turns barring it for the quarter century that followed. Bipartisan arguments for ignoring legal constraints on going to war became more and more permissive as the regulation of war's humanity became ever more strict.

IT WAS BILL CLINTON'S PRESIDENCY STARTING IN 1993 THAT DID the most to drive the drift into militarism, no matter the legality of the wars involved. The same administration entrenched those wars' humane conduct so that it was difficult for his successor to reverse it. Early signs of this pattern came in June 1993, five months into the new regime, when Clinton sent twenty-three Tomahawk missiles from warships in the Persian Gulf and Red Sea to strike Iraq's Military Intelligence Headquarters in Baghdad. Three missiles went astray and killed between six and eight civilians in the process. But for those in the know, attention fell on the iffy rationale for the strike.

After authorizing Bush's ejection of Hussein's armies from Kuwait in 1990, the United Nations Security Council had approved what became an aerial interdiction regime that the United States imposed in the north and south of Iraq for security and human rights protection. But the strike in Baghdad received a different rationale. Madeleine Albright, speaking as the country's ambassador to the United Nations, cited self-defense, after an assassination attempt targeted Bush (now out of office) on a Kuwait victory tour that spring. Reprisals—the use of force as punishment for your enemy's past infractions—were no longer supposed to be allowed under international law. There was no huge outcry, but it was hardly clear that the missiles were lawful, judged by the United Nations Charter standard that acts in self-defense respond to an ongoing or imminent armed attack as well as meeting thresholds of necessity and proportionality. Under the clear blue skies of a post–Cold War world, it was like the first droplet of a coming storm as the United States treated "self-defense" not as a constraining limit on force but as an expansive justification for it.

The peacekeeping mission Bush authorized in Somalia in the last year of his presidency, after the country's dictator fled and civil war broke out, was authorized under international law. But the catastrophe under Clinton's watch of the Black Hawk helicopter missions in October 1993 put the United States off intervention for a while, legal or illegal. Clinton came close to intervention in Haiti a week after the Black Hawk Down episode (with neither congressional nor United Nations sign-off). And the more massive Haiti intervention that was planned the following summer with Security Council authorization—before Jimmy Carter brokered a deal as envoy to replace the island's military government—anticipated future acts of presidential unilateralism. As Yugoslavia continued melting down and ethnic cleansing continued in Bosnia-Herzegovina, Clinton became more sensitive to activists' anger and their charge that the United States was too slow to intervene. The cultural imperative to orient U.S. power toward innocent victims eroded Clinton's skittishness. At the opening of the United States Holocaust Memorial Museum in 1993, the survivor Elie Wiesel demanded action of Clinton for humanity's sake.

Worse straits for victims were to come. An inadequate United Nations peacekeeping regime allowed for a revolting massacre by Bosnian Serbs of more than 8,000 Muslim men and boys at Srebrenica in 1995—after Rwandan Hutus slaughtered 800,000 Tutsis with machetes in 1994. These events appalled a generation that resolved not to abstain from war but instead to embark on it to aid the innocent. As Samuel Hynes spoke of a new "literature of atrocity," many concluded that an America that stood idly by as more and more vile acts were perpetrated in war was delinquent to its moral duty. International law was good when it allowed for stigmatizing atrocity, bad when it obstructed the United States from stopping it. "For the purpose of stopping genocide," the political writer Leon Wieseltier explained in *The New Republic*, "the use of force is not a last resort; it is a first resort. The alacrity of the response matters as much as the intensity of the response." He didn't mention the law.

The memory of the Somalian intervention (and the Vietnam War) had passed. After NATO air strikes forced the belligerent parties to the table at Dayton in 1995, Richard Holbrooke's successful diplomacy to end that war was taken to prove the worth of U.S. "smart power": a combination of diplomacy and might for humanitarian ends. And by the end of the decade, Clinton was comfortable enough again with force to push the boundaries of legality. "When it comes to the use of the American military," a then-unknown law professor at the University of California, Berkeley, John Yoo, observed in 1999, "no president has a quicker trigger finger than Mr. Clinton." After all their cantankerousness under Reagan and Bush, he added, "the silence of these Democrats during the Clinton years has been deafening." Before authorizing torture two years later, Yoo scored a partisan political point—but it was not entirely false.

When Clinton launched fateful missile attacks against Al-Qaeda in Afghanistan and Sudan in 1998, the mood was permissive, across the U.S. political spectrum. With more rain in the forecast, the United States once again cited self-defense in explanation. Among others, the Democrat Abraham Sofaer, who had served as the legal advisor at the Department of State under Reagan, spoke out forthrightly in support of flexible rules for a new age of terrorism, making many of the arguments about what self-defense allows that would later become associated with George W. Bush's expansive rationales. Not merely imminent threat but speculative risk justified preemptive bombing, Sofaer explained in a *Newsday* op-ed. It was not known until after 2001, but Clinton even briefly authorized a secret exception to America's post-Vietnam ban on assassination to permit the killing of the group's leader Osama bin Laden. The lawyers approved, though Clinton decided to retract his own finding.

Yet the most extraordinary precedent set in the Clinton years lay elsewhere. From March through June 1999, the United States led the NATO bombing of Serbia to force Slobodan Milošević to halt threatened mass killings in Kosovo, a breakaway province, and to remove his troops from the area. It worked. The absence of United Nations Security Council authorization made it illegal, but it was publicly justified as moral *in spite of* this fact. Bill Clinton took to *The New York Times* in May to explain that the campaign he had ordered was a "just and necessary war." It apparently did not matter that it was an illegal one. To their credit, some American international lawyers who recalled why the United Nations system had been set up in the first place said that its charter ought to be respected, pending a better system of protecting victims. For most, however, right made might.

While Human Rights Watch had initially remained neutral on all wars, in the 1990s it actually decided to express support for some such "humanitarian interventions." It did not come out one way or the other on Kosovo. As it monitored and reported on the Serbian war crimes in Kosovo (as well as evil deeds by the Kosovar Liberation Army), it did the same for NATO actions. Human Rights Watch assessed not their legality in the first place but whether they violated standards of humane bombing. At the time, in fact, the Kosovo intervention was most controversial not because it violated international rules on the use of force, but instead because it ran afoul of laws governing how the war was conducted on all sides. It was clear what the now established priorities had become.

Nongovernmental organizations like Human Rights Watch that did not denounce the Kosovo War as illegal were nonetheless correct, of course, to make the complaints they did. No amount of humanitarian intent, they insisted, could exempt the United States from humane standards that now applied to fighting from the air. Without condemning the very activity of bombing from 10,000 feet, the group concluded that the United States understated how many people it might have killed (while the Serbian government overstated the number). In a series of instances, the Geneva protocol standards of distinction and proportionality—the very ones Human Rights Watch had pioneeringly applied and explicated—had been violated.

Military lawyers reached a different set of conclusions. Yet they picked their bone with humanitarians against the background of agreement that humane standards governed the war—and that prohibitions on force were someone else's problem. U.S. judge advocates had been involved in every aspect of Operation Allied Force for Kosovo, chiefly in classified chat rooms allowing quick decisions about picking targets. But by this point, according to one of David Graham's outfit's regular "lessons learned" postmortems, the truth was that there were not many lessons left: military lawyers had applied the right standards and applied them stringently, successfully humanizing American force from the air. There were, however, still some lessons to teach, since those carping from outside government sometimes seemed to think that civilian harm was itself illegal, even when it wasn't disproportionate to military advantage.

Anticipating justifications of drone warfare years later under President Barack Obama, another prominent military lawyer responded to the Human Rights Watch report on the Kosovo bombings by stressing that operations from on high actually served humanity best. What did humanitarians want? An even less humane ground war? "Frankly, it is puzzling to the military professional," this air force colonel wrote, "that anyone concerned with the sanctity of human life could conceive that such an operation would be less deadly than the air campaign that did take place." The mood after Kosovo was downright celebratory: "Of the more than 25,000 weapons used in Kosovo," he crowed, "only twenty resulted in collateral damage incidents, a phenomenal record in the history of warfare."

"THE LAW OF WAR HAS BEEN CHANGING AND ACQUIRING A MORE HUMANE face," the greatest authority on the topic of the time observed, with comparable ebullience, as the millennium turned. Not only did the phrase "international humanitarian law" now "signify the entire law of armed conflict," Theodor Meron explained, but also the growth of substantive protection in the wake of the 1977 protocols made a new age of human rights the setting for a more humane kind of war. It was incontestably a good thing, pending a time when "humanitarian norms" become "a part of public consciousness everywhere," with no brutal war left.

Such conclusions were the conventional wisdom of reform on the brink of September 11, 2001. Never mind that they would have looked like unacceptable despair to earlier generations who were bent on stigmatizing war and striving to prohibit it in law. If it involved forgetfulness, no one could fairly blame the new consensus for lacking foresight. It primed people not to resist America's coming war on terror, only its cruelty.

Not long after, some began referring to "the law of September

10," as if the United States had pivoted drastically from one regime to another. The reverse was true. A culture of adherence to new rules of how to fight, even as America slipped more and more the bonds of the prohibition of war itself, had already taken shape *before* the world supposedly changed from one day to the next. The humanization process had gone so far that the neoconservative abrogation of the laws of war after that date would find itself contained and reversed. But the illegal permanent war that foreign policy neoconservatives initiated was continued on a more humane basis not only by liberal internationalists but also by Donald Trump.

Still, no one ought to trivialize the fact that the road to humane war in its current form ran through the sickening experiences of a Manhattan inferno and a no-holds-barred response. The conditions for humane war before September 11 only go so far to explain its creation after. "To us their descendants, who are not historians and not carried away by the process of research, and can therefore regard the event with unclouded common sense, an incalculable number of causes present themselves," Leo Tolstoy wrote in *War and Peace* of the origins of another disaster. "The deeper we delve in search of each of these causes the more of them we find; and each separate cause or the whole series of causes appears to us equally valid in itself and equally false by its insignificance compared to the magnitude of the event." Our event, leading to America's final embrace of the humane syndrome, came from out of the blue.

CHAPTER SEVEN

The Road to Humanity After September 11

ON NOVEMBER 13, 2001, PRESIDENT GEORGE W. BUSH ANNOUNCED A NEW policy required by a new kind of war. Alleged Al-Qaeda terrorists were being captured on the battleground in Afghanistan and elsewhere; now they would be tried by military commissions that offered few protections for the accused. Ordinary courts with the standard full-dress guarantees and protections would be out of bounds. Detainees would have to be "treated humanely," the order stated, and the trials would have to be "full and fair." But no rules of treatment for accused "terrorists" reflecting international standards were specified.

Two weeks later, White House counsel Alberto Gonzales explained that such commissions were normal in U.S. history and that Bush's order was modeled on one from World War II, which the Supreme Court had approved in 1942. Of course the international law of war mattered, he hastened to add. That was the very body of law the *terrorists* had broken when they targeted civilians—and now they were to be held accountable for those violations, in fair trials adjusted to the special circumstances involved in trying such dangerous men with classified secrets.

"Well, this is fucked up," remarked the lawyer Joseph Margulies to his wife, sitting at their Minneapolis kitchen table reading the newspaper over breakfast. Bush's announcement stunk to high heaven. It seemed like a transparent attempt to create a second track of justice for terrorists, one that would not require the familiar safeguards of the criminal process, or even the wartime rules prescribed by the Geneva Conventions of 1949 for enemy treatment. "We should call Michael Ratner," Margulies's wife replied.

They did. Ratner, a onetime antiwar activist, was president of the Center for Constitutional Rights in New York and a storied litigator. He considered the order "the death knell for democracy in this country" and threw himself into action. Three years later, the desperate legal challenge Ratner led against the military commissions scheme paid off. Shafiq Rasul, a British citizen whom Americans rounded up in Afghanistan in 2001 and interned in the offshore facility of Guantánamo Bay, Cuba, had already been returned home and released, without being tried. But other plaintiffs in the case of *Rasul v. Bush* remained. And a few months after Rasul left, the Supreme Court held 6–3 that federal courts could exercise their power to issue writs of habeas corpus and thereby review the detention of accused terrorists being held indefinitely. Providentially for Ratner, just a few days after the Supreme Court heard oral argument in the case, scandalous photos of prisoner mistreatment by U.S. forces at the Abu Ghraib prison in Iraq were leaked, no doubt affecting the court's decision.

Such victories dispelled initial worries that the war on terror was going to be fought—as some still persist in thinking—in a "state of exception" without legal constraint. The same justice who authored *Rasul*, John Paul Stevens, followed up in 2006 with an epoch-making opinion in *Hamdan v. Rumsfeld*, which clarified that—at the very least—the Geneva Conventions Common Article 3 applied to the war on terror. And because that article requires trial of detainees by a "regularly constituted court, affording all the judicial guarantees which are recognized as indispensable by civilized peoples," the military commissions Bush had planned since 2001 were inadequate. The decision implied that a global and ongoing struggle against terrorism would have to be waged under applicable international law—because nothing less than the war's legitimacy depended on it.

Stevens's conclusions satisfied some of the fondest dreams of civil libertarians, but not theirs alone. Within the Bush administration itself, conservatives had already girded for battle with one another over this very same principle. As time passed, a lawyer named Jack Goldsmith was the intellectual leader of those who anticipated the result that the Supreme Court would reach.

By the time of *Rasul*, hostilities had expanded from Afghanistan, the home base from which Al-Qaeda had planned and executed the September 11 attacks, to Iraq, though the connection of its leader Saddam Hussein to the "global war on terror" was nonexistent. When *Hamdan* came down, the invasion of Iraq and capture of Saddam had given way to a failing bid to pacify that country, with hundreds of thousands of civilians dying in the carnage and disorder. If there was law that forbade the intervention, it was not a limit that activists decided to press, or that the Supreme Court ever enforced.

For a long time, it was not the decision to invade Iraq but earlier policy choices that occupied center stage of public debate. As the Iraq War began to go south, Americans lived through a bout of self-reflection around the mistreatment and even torture of prisoners. It may well have been an attack on the war by other means, but the results were not constraints on the war's expansion and extension. Instead, the torture debate gave rise to a newly humanized version of America's belligerency. For that reason, the early years of the war on terror were vital, but not merely as the time of a heroic assertion of law in the name of humanity by left and right. Unlike in Vietnam, consciousness of war crimes did not end a war but helped reset one. Humanity made war more durable.

In late spring 2004, Goldsmith, on the brink of leaving his post as head of the Justice Department's Office of Legal Counsel after tempestuous battles, withdrew the legal permission slips his predecessors had written for the harshest methods of interrogation (at the same time, he rewrote others authorizing unprecedented surveillance). In spite of their lesser role, U.S. allies such as the United Kingdom were wracked by much greater upheavals and ongoing recriminations for embarking on an illegal war. Legalizing the conduct of hostilities during the first phase of the war on terror, Goldsmith anticipated and helped bring about an endless new form of the ongoing enterprise.

For Goldsmith and even for Ratner, the question was not the legality of the war's beginnings and continuation but rather how to bring it within the pale of legality now that it was being fought. This vision of legality was broadly enough shared in American life—including within the military itself—that it ultimately prevailed against the fierce resistance of Goldsmith's opponents at the pinnacle of the Bush administration. And from late in Bush's first term until today, debates around interventions have been cast in the shade by concerns for their humanity under law.

Goldsmith and Ratner, from their respective posts inside and outside government, and as different in background, politics, and temperament as night and day, were working toward comparable ends. Ratner had given up as hopeless earlier campaigns to keep American wars from breaking out or continuing endlessly. After September 11, he, too, acted to make them legal in their conduct. For Goldsmith, whatever his misgivings about the expansion of executive power, the point that mattered was that in a democracy wars require public consent, and that in U.S. history the legitimation of war now demanded its legalization, which included a concern for humane limits.

The parallel acts of two gifted lawyers—one an activist suspicious of overweening government, the other its loyal servant bent on preserving its legitimacy—worked to bring the war within legal regulation. They led the country down a road to an endless war that neither lawyer might have envisioned or planned. Paved with their good intentions, the road was no longer to hell but instead horrendous in a novel way. Legalizing the manner of the conflict, Goldsmith and Ratner acted to remove the initial bug of inhumanity from what started out brutally. Together, they wrote the code of a war that became endless, legal, and humane.

THE BOEING 767S THAT AL-QAEDA TERRORISTS CRASHED INTO THE twin towers of the World Trade Center in New York, with a third plane slamming into the Pentagon in Washington, D.C., were of course the catalyst. From near the start, it was clear that international law—at least the half of it dealing with regulating fighting—was going to be at the center of debate, more so than in any American war before.

It was no wonder that the United States quickly responded by deciding to activate the armed supremacy around the globe it had enjoyed since World War II. The scenes from lower Manhattan, where nearly three thousand died, were nightmarish. Within ten days, Bush promised justice in response to an "act of war" by terrorists. The English war poet Wilfred Owen had once brought home the hellscape of the trenches in Flanders and the rictus of suffering on the faces of soldiers attacked with gas. Americans watched the live TV coverage of the smoky detritus of the World Trade Center and the ashen faces of its survivors with similar revulsion. Unlike for Owen's readers, however, the horror was the catalyst for patriotic ardor.

Like the collapse of the towers and the attack on the Pentagon, the years of argument that followed are burned into the memory of civil libertarians, human rights activists, government lawyers, and scholarly experts. People have dug into positions taken then—which still tend to divide neatly between assurance that all the law was settled before Bush so flagrantly trashed it and certainty that all the questions were open in a novel situation without precedent in the annals of civilization. But in retrospect, it's clear that far more important decisions were being made across partisan lines, casting the die for the future.

Before the embers of lower Manhattan had cooled, Bush's lawyers were poles apart from their predecessors during the Vietnam War on the question of how international law applied to the new conflict.

That earlier crew had feared the public relations implications of the brutal war to come so little that it could insist that the country would follow the rules—and it got no pushback for doing so. By contrast, Bush's lawyers were worried from the start about the costs of violating international law prohibiting brutality. As a result, their first move was to reinterpret that law so that it did not cover what they insisted was an utterly new scenario of global counterterror.

In a backhanded, revealing acknowledgment of the rising significance of international law, Bush's lawyers tried to lift its requirements. Their opponents, insisting on humane war, could point to the fact that much more of the law was on their side than ever before. Yet both those who crafted Bush's early legal positions and those who opposed them obscured what was genuinely novel about their situation. Humane war had become a cultural expectation and legal imperative for one side to push into full reality while the other sought an escape hatch at the last minute.

John Yoo, born in Seoul, South Korea, in 1967, was the key engineer of the escape hatch. On September 11, he was serving in the Department of Justice's Office of Legal Counsel, which renders authoritative legal opinions for the executive branch. He was five years younger than Goldsmith, who arrived to head the office after Yoo left. Yoo's parents, teenagers during the Korean War, became medical doctors before moving to the United States. They and their son landed in New Jersey when he was three months old. Yoo attended a Philadelphia prep school and from there went to Harvard College to study history. Harry Truman's salvation of South Korea, with all the expanded presidential power it required, sat at the root of Yoo's patriotism, alongside an immigrant family's gratitude in a land of opportunity.

Goldsmith's background was very different. Born in Memphis in 1962, raised by his beauty queen mother, he had an unusual family history. His paternal grandfather came from a department store dynasty in Memphis founded in the late nineteenth century by Jewish immigrants to the city; he served in the military in the 1930s and during World War II, and he passed on a lot of money to his son, who gambled it away. Though born his namesake, Jack Landman Goldsmith III was raised mainly by—and through his teenage years took the name of—his adoptive stepfather, Charles O'Brien, who married Goldsmith's mother when he was twelve. O'Brien was long the right-hand man of Jimmy Hoffa, the Teamsters president who disappeared mysteriously.

After military school in Florida, college at Washington and Lee in Virginia, and legal training in New Haven, Goldsmith taught at Charlottesville and Chicago before working for the Department of Defense while Yoo had the bigger job at the Department of Justice. They both had studied law at Yale, learning international law from Yoo's fellow Korean American Harold Hongju Koh. Their teacher, with whom Yoo co-authored an article early in his career, held international law posts in Democratic administrations, and he was to play an enormous role in the coming of humane war when Barack Obama ascended to power. His apprentices, however, each contributed in their own distinctive ways to that outcome, and they preceded the master in their hour on the stage.

Goldsmith and Yoo made their names by bolting from their teacher's stables and becoming international law skeptics within the expanding conservative legal movement after the Cold War. Their skepticism, alongside their intellectual gifts, made them eligible for appointments in the Bush administration. Good friends before events drove them apart, their divergence in the middle of the Bush administration only makes sense against their common background.

In the beginning, Goldsmith and Yoo took a consciously opportunistic view of international law: as they wrote in a 1999 co-authored piece, pouring caustic sarcasm on liberal fans and leftist skeptics of internationalism, the right approach to international law was to pick and choose. If international law served the United States, like the rulings of the World Trade Organization, it was a good thing; if not, not. When he and Yoo were attacked as "new sovereigntists" by critics even before September 11, Goldsmith shot back that "the idea that a nation can decide which international laws to embrace is not new and should not be controversial."

From the beginning, however, there were also shades of difference. Goldsmith had volunteered in his splashy early scholarship to argue for America's exemption from a burgeoning international human rights law. Yoo fastened on the domestic relationship among branches of government, offering a vision of the constitutional allocation of powers of war and peace that was strongly tilted to presidential power.

This meant that Yoo enthusiastically backed those in the Bush administration who not merely disdained international law but also magnified the president's authority in war-making. Koh and his other liberal Yale Law teachers had held the "standard" position after Vietnam that the power to authorize war lay with Congress. But Yoo pursued a different view, in part, as a profile noted in 2009, because he "saw Vietnam through the lens of Korea, imagining how life would have been for his parents under the savage dictatorship of Kim Il Sung."

It was hardly surprising, therefore, that one of Yoo's first acts in the emergency of September 11 was to explain that the president enjoyed essentially unconstrained authority to respond, as the founders had supposedly designed things and as history had confirmed. Pulling an all-nighter in Washington on the evening of September 11, Yoo affirmed that a state of war could exist between a state and its nonstate enemies, and that the president enjoyed essentially limitless power to retaliate. When it came to whether international law could get in the way, Yoo made sure to observe that presidents could override it even if it did. Yoo's theory of the presidency sounded in perfect harmony with a neoconservatism in power that embraced America's role in the world as conqueror and savior.

AS THE WAR ON TERROR BEGAN, THERE WERE ALREADY DIFFICULTIES under international law with Bush's first major decision—to invade Afghanistan in direct response to the September 11 attacks. Al-Qaeda, led by the bearded mastermind Osama bin Laden, was responsible for the outrages on the World Trade Center and the Pentagon. It was not at all obvious under international law that the United States could invoke "self-defense" under the United Nations Charter and resort to force against nonstate actors. And in intervening, America weakened the rules restraining attack on states involved with those actors.

When signed in 1945, the charter contemplated the use of force in self-defense only when a state had suffered an armed attack *from another state*. The day after September 11, the United Nations Security Council immediately met to decry breaches of the peace. It hinted at the novel possibility of authorized force against terrorists under its resolutions and made clear that America's own rights to defend itself under international law had been triggered. But the Security Council did not actually approve force. Nor did it say *against whom* the United States had a right to self-defense. The legal question left open was how close a terrorist enemy had to be to any state that hosted it to allow that state's invasion without consent. Still, no one complained when the United States intervened in Afghanistan anyway.

Before September 11, international lawyers had settled on the standard for when one could engage in legal self-defense against a state in response to an attack by a nonstate actor operating from its territory: the state had to exert "effective control" over the nonstate actor. As the world rapidly learned, however, the relationship between Al-Qaeda and the Taliban—the ruling authority in Afghanistan—was if anything the reverse. Al-Qaeda had killed the Taliban's principal enemy, Ahmad Shah Massoud, on its behalf and provided the regime fighters and weapons, rather than the other way around. It was obvious that the United States would need to bend the rules as generally understood. Of course, there had been exceptions in the past, mainly when Israel operated in neighboring countries to interdict terrorism. As with targeted killing later, the events of 2001 made the exceptional normal. Even so, after Congress rapidly authorized force against Al-Qaeda and the Taliban under its war powers, the United States offered almost no argument about the propriety under international law of attacking the latter to get to the former.

To object to U.S. intervention in fall 2001 would have been spitting in the wind. Almost everyone felt enough goodwill toward the victim of terror in the country's moment of bereavement and mourning to allow the first domino to fall toward permanent war. The world looked on tolerantly as the United States and the United Kingdom formally commenced Operation Enduring Freedom less than a month after September 11.

The campaign for Afghanistan started with air strikes on October 7. Marines were introduced less than two weeks later, with troop commitments rising to a peak of 100,000 in the waves of escalation and withdrawal that ebbed and flowed over the two decades that followed. There was no explanation of the campaign from the Bush administration's lawyers and no criticism stirred. It was a remarkable contrast to a few years later when memos leaked, and pushback occurred—not around starting and continuing the war on terror but instead around making it humane.

Yoo was given the task in winter 2001 of considering whether international law applied to how the war would be waged. In doing so, he faced the problem of what lawyers call "classification." To know what rules apply, first you have to know what kind of armed conflict is being fought, since the Geneva Conventions distinguish between international and "non-international" armed conflict.

All the detailed provisions regarding prisoners of war in the complex treaty of 1949 concern the first category of armed conflict and set a high bar of expectation for states to meet. The exception is the lonely standard of Common Article 3, which set a low bar for any "conflict not of an international character"—calling for fair trials for those detained and prohibiting torture and other outrages on personal dignity.

U.S. lawyers had defined the intervention in South Vietnam as an international fight, not a civil war, and therefore placed it fully under the sway of rules that it might have treated as optional. Yoo went to the opposite extreme. He interpreted Common Article 3 as giving to America's enemies none of the benefits usually granted to prisoners of war. Geneva's requirements for fair trials and humane treatment simply did not apply; in fact, no international law did, Yoo concluded, since he also denied the relevance of any unwritten international law to "unlawful combatants."

With brazen legerdemain, Yoo applied the same exemption to Al-Qaeda and the Taliban but for opposite reasons. Al-Qaeda was not a state, so it didn't fall under the regime for international war. But it also operated beyond borders, so the rules for "non-international" conflict didn't cover terrorists either. As for the Taliban, they were merely the outlaw warlords of a "failed" state, on Yoo's homespun theory, so their forces couldn't claim the privileges of states under Geneva. Bush eventually decided to extend Taliban fighters Geneva protections as a matter of policy. But Yoo's argument for why they didn't apply as law was strongly reminiscent of colonial-era assumptions that some peoples were simply not civilized enough to be party to international legal arrangements. The war on terror was a war but did not need to be humane, as international law defined it.

Yoo's allies in the administration—including Bush's Texas friend Gonzales in the White House—faced bitter opposition to the classification memo when it came to Taliban detainees. The Department of State, more solicitous of international law, pushed back against a more relaxed attitude toward legal requirements. The Department of Defense raised the objection that mistreating enemies could lead to mistreatment of U.S. soldiers. Secretary of State Colin Powell, prince of the post-Vietnam officer corps, worried that disregard of international law of fighting could "undermine U.S. military culture which emphasizes maintaining the highest standards of conduct in combat."

In the short term, such views lost, even if Bush decided to follow Powell and the uniformed Defense Department officials as a matter of policy. After all, as Powell and his associates observed, the fact that Taliban forces often fought as insurgents out of uniform provided an alternative rationale for denying them full prisoner-of-war protections. By the summer, Yoo had taken charge of a memo authorizing rough treatment of captives. This position depended on an interpretation of the Convention Against Torture, a treaty that the United States had solemnly ratified and implemented in its domestic law, including criminal penalties for those who violated it. Up to the point of bodily impairment or organ failure, Yoo wrote, the law did not prohibit such indignities, including such infamous "enhanced interrogation techniques" as waterboarding.

By the time anyone noticed that the United States was running roughshod over other rules prohibiting the use of force, it may have been too late to stop it. When second thoughts set in, the country was at war and there was little to do except rein in how it fought. But as activists within and outside the Bush administration girded to challenge inhumanity, a much bigger transition was occurring. In his findings, Yoo exempted both how America's wars began and how they were fought from applicable rules. He received pushback only on the latter point. Indeed, there was a huge outcry around the early inhumanity of the war on terror, in part *because* Bush's lawyers attempted to legally justify it. While there was little concern over the lawfulness of the invasion of Afghanistan, and not even much attempt by American international law experts to condemn the move into Iraq, Yoo played the starring role as he inadvertently unleashed an alternative debate.

Yoo's legal work has been widely denounced as incompetent or at least shoddy, and in 2009 it came near to being deemed unprofessional by a government investigation. As controversial as Yoo became, no one has been willing to acknowledge the diversionary effects of his sometimes zany stretches, which swept their critics into one controversy that masked the absence of another. After Yoo crafted legal arguments authorizing torture, the ensuing controversy about them led the nation's attention away from America's pivot into the war on terror in general, not to mention the flagrant illegality of the Iraq War that soon began. Much greater suffering was visited on more people through illegal war than illegal war crimes—in part because so much is legal once war starts. Americans forgot their onetime commitment against the Nazis to condemn war as a gateway to other crimes, and the results were predictably grave. That the all-consuming debate started where it did was itself revelatory of a public no longer oriented, as in Vietnam, to the propriety of going to war.

In a defensive memoir published in 2006, Yoo disdained as "simply ridiculous" the notion "that all the lawyers" in government service had "engaged in a conspiracy to twist the law" in order "to authorize an illegal war." But the truth was that he and his fellows faced no charges stating that they had signed off on starting any wars illegally in 2001 in Afghanistan or even in 2003 in Iraq. Rather, they were dogged by accusations that they had approved vile tactics in fighting. Yoo believed he was facing a novel and unprecedented situation and was castigated by his critics for doing novel and unprecedented things. The reverse was true: he resuscitated a type of brutal war that was beyond the pale of legality but already becoming obsolete. And the removal of those vile tactics from the equation made the propriety of the war on terror as such even more secondary in public debate, even more insulated from scrutiny. Yoo could mockingly ask, after popular discontent rose with the Iraq War and the Democrats won both houses of Congress in 2006 but did nothing to wind down Iraq or any other part of the war on terror, "Why are the pacifists so passive?"

Yoo became a pariah in his own profession. His critics called for his ouster as a professor at the University of California and for his punishment as a war criminal. But Yoo remained unrepentant. He was apoplectic after *Hamdan* overturned his memo deeming the Geneva Conventions inapplicable. The Supreme Court's "effort to inject the Geneva Conventions into the war on terrorism—even though the treaties do not include international conflict with non-states that violate every rule of civilized warfare—smacks of judicial micromanagement," he sniffed.

In the aftermath, however, Yoo could gloat that, through all the controversy, the Bush administration had strengthened a U.S. presidency confronting ongoing foreign threats that would require an energetic response—even if a Democrat was the next occupant of the White House. As history would prove, he may have been right to gloat.

IT WOULD BE GIVING YOO TOO MUCH CREDIT TO SUGGEST THAT HE intended to guarantee the propriety of the war on terror precisely by allowing one aspect of its conduct to be so vile that its critics were baited to remove it—ultimately leaving humane war behind. Nevertheless, that was the result all the same.

One reason for this outcome, whatever Yoo's intentions, is that his arguments gave some who supported America's wars a highly idealistic mission—to return virtue to a foreign policy globalism that had gone awry. In the critical years, a genuine longing for humane American war became widespread, especially among early supporters of the war on terror, and the disastrous Iraq intervention in particular, looking for a moral sequel to their mistake. As for those who opposed America's wars from the beginning, the dynamic and outcome of the fight posed the challenging question of whether opponents of the war were distracted into a misguided strategy. Michael Ratner offered an especially extraordinary—and perhaps tragic—example of this possibility.

Ratner's Jewish parents had immigrated to the United States from Bialystok, Poland, in the 1920s and settled in Cleveland, where their son was born in 1943. Ratner was a generation older than his Bush administration antagonists, and his consciousness was formed as a twenty-five-year-old student at Columbia Law School on a campus rocked by student activism against the Vietnam War. "Like so many people around the world," he later recalled, "I was politicized first in 1968." After he graduated, Ratner joined the Center for Constitutional Rights in 1972, where he would work on and off until his death from cancer in 2016. Less kempt than his conservative and straightlaced adversaries, Ratner was not above donning a suit for court, accepting the rules of the lawyerly game as the price of (sometimes pyrrhic) victory.

Ratner's brother became a wealthy financier, and his sister a Fox News commentator, but his identification with leftist causes remained unwavering throughout his life. He idolized Che Guevara, the Argentine hero of the 1959 Cuban revolution, and himself traveled to Cuba in the 1970s to work for the country. In the late 1990s, Ratner publicized a lawsuit filed in Havana against the United States for $181 billion in damages, to make up for forty years of "acts of aggression." Interviewed on September 12, 2013, Ratner remarked in passing that it was the day after not the anniversary of the attack on the U.S. homeland but of the coup against Chile's social democratic president Salvador Allende in 1973, with American connivance. Ratner became a follower of the famed radical lawyer William Kunstler, who would later marry Ratner's first wife. Kunstler, the shaggy cofounder of the Center for Constitutional Rights, defended unpopular agitators, from the rioters at the Democratic Convention in Chicago in 1968, to draft card burners the same year, to Black Panthers and Weathermen later.

As his storied career unfolded, Ratner was a pioneer in human rights litigation in U.S. courts. He sued perpetrators of atrocious and unforgivable acts under the once-exciting statute allowing foreign victims to collect damages from their oppressors. Ironically, this same law sat at the center of Goldsmith's early scholarship about international law running amok, and Goldsmith ultimately helped convince a conservative Supreme Court to clamp down on the venue Ratner had struggled to pry open. In his early years, Ratner teamed up with Koh—who had to overcome worries that Ratner was radioactive as a "radical leftist" to do so—in an early attempt out of Yale Law School to put students to work for the human rights movement. Most memorably, they lent their efforts to the cause of Haitian migrants, including ones interned at America's Guantánamo Bay site in a controversial use of the camp before the war on terror dawned.

Unlike the mainstream human rights movement, Ratner prioritized peace, not humanity in war. One of Ratner's greatest causes in his early career was the attempt to enforce the War Powers Resolution, a 1973 act that attempted after Vietnam to restore some congressional authority over foreign war. Among other things, the act mandates that the president may not continue "hostilities" abroad without legislative authorization after sixty days. Ratner joined the progressive Catholic priest and former congressman Robert Drinan—originally elected on an antiwar platform in 1970, he'd voted on the resolution when it passed—to sue to enforce the law in court after President Ronald Reagan sent "military advisers" to El Salvador in 1982. They lost the case, but they did not give up on the law controlling war. Ratner's activism on this front continued through September 11, because of expectations that the end of the Cold War could allow a reset. He helped another group of congressmen, led by Oakland's Ron Dellums, to sue George H. W. Bush in a test case to require legislative authorization for military intervention even before the first Gulf War formally began. Ratner lost again, but he persisted with such litigation under Bill Clinton's presidency.

Understandably, Ratner and the Center for Constitutional Rights behaved in this period quite differently from Amnesty International or Human Rights Watch. Those two humanitarian groups had long ago resolved to monitor whether wars were fought legally but never to take sides on whether they had a legal basis, or needed to stop. And Ratner trained his sights almost as much on American violations of international law's prohibition on force as on the damage he decried to the U.S. Constitution and statutes allocating war powers. In May 1991, he gathered with the dissident former attorney general Ramsey Clark and others to stage a rerun in New York City of Bertrand Russell's mock trial during Vietnam. Once again, Ratner followed the priorities of Nuremberg after World War II in condemning America's "aggression" as its worst war crime, rather than isolating violations of humane standards within the invasion.

Later, Ratner rightly complained that Bill Clinton had pushed far beyond the United Nations Security Council resolutions allowing inspections of Saddam Hussein's weaponry, resolving ambiguous permission to police it into carte blanche authority for armed attacks. America's "tendency to bypass the requirement for explicit Security Council authorization, in favor of more ambiguous sources of international authority, will probably escalate in coming years," Ratner and his frequent ally and Center for Constitutional Rights colleague Jules Lobel predicted. The article was being readied for print when the United States bombed Iraq for four days in December 1998, illustrating a "painful reality of superpower unilateralism." Yet for all Ratner's concern to invoke international law that forbids starting wars, the reality was that the cause was dying in the Clinton years, even among progressives. "Where Have All the Liberals Gone?" Yoo mischievously asked in one of his youthful writings, reviewing the abandonment of what was becoming a concern as idiosyncratic on the left as on the right.

Ratner wholly rejected any romantic view of violence as an idealistic and moral tool. Breaking with many fellow progressives, he was particularly upset by the rise of "humanitarian intervention" in the 1990s, protesting America's and NATO's illegal bombings of Kosovo in 1999, which the United Nations had never approved. Exceptions to the rule against using force were generally used as pretexts, Ratner insisted, and even if they were not, they would be abused by less high-minded powers, once precedents were set for breaking the law in a just cause. It had been Adolf Hitler, Ratner and Lobel wrote, who most notoriously claimed to "intervene militarily in a sovereign state because of claimed human rights abuses." Although "NATO is obviously not Hitler," they added, "the example illustrates the mischief caused when countries assert the right to use force on such a basis."

Through the late 1990s, Ratner's essential concern remained war itself. The worst was when war-makers claimed uplifting reasons for embarking on it. The United States in Kosovo had disdained even the pretense of compliance with international rules governing the use of force. In the international policing of Iraq in the 1990s, "at least the U.S. at that point was making a claim that had some kind of implicit authority from the United Nations," Ratner commented to Amy Goodman on a 1999 episode of the progressive television report *Democracy Now*. No more. "International law is a dead letter to a large extent with regard to intervention," he reported glumly. "We're living in Rome right now." On another episode, Ratner was not above denouncing the Kosovo intervention as a "crime of aggression."

Ratner was grim about the geopolitical implications. "What can you say except the United States is becoming a rogue superpower?" he asked his host. At the same time, in what some called the "virtual war" of Kosovo, in which NATO forces led by the United States Air Force bombed Serbia with total immunity from exposure to risk, Ratner chillingly anticipated the coming of a cleaner new form of conflict that would replace the dirty hands-on methods against which Ratner would soon campaign. "You can basically push buttons and bomb people."

RATNER WAS JOGGING PAST THE WORLD TRADE CENTER NEAR HIS LOWER Manhattan apartment on September 11 when the first plane struck. His brother was in 7 World Trade Center that day, and survived, and Ratner explained that he was hardly untouched by the mood "of obviously wanting to stop this, to never have it happen again, and to punish the people who did it." He wasn't as sure, this time, that there was a choice other than war. But the tragedy of his children's school friend losing her father also inspired the thought that, "unfortunately and sadly, people around the world have lost parents forever, whether that be in Israel or Palestine, or in Lebanon, or in Cambodia. And what it did really, in a way, thinking like that, actually deepened my resolve that we have to try and find alternatives to the use of military force."

Congress passed an authorization within three days to pursue Al-Qaeda and any and all "nations, organizations, or persons" involved anywhere, so long as there was some relationship to the September 11 attacks. Most members of Congress reassured themselves that at least some limitation had been imposed. Representative Jesse Jackson,

Jr., of Illinois, although voting in favor of the bill, remarked on "the similarity to the open-endedness of this resolution to the Tonkin Gulf Resolution," which Lyndon Johnson had used "to provide dubious legal cover for a massive escalation of an unwinnable war." A solitary no was cast by the Californian Barbara Lee, who warned that what Congress authorized would "spin out of control."

Ratner rued the day Congress approved force against not so much a foe as a method—terrorism—and did so without any end date. Three days after Congress voted, offering authority for a war on terror that has not been revoked since, Ratner appeared on *Democracy Now* to worry about the "rhetoric" of "revenge," of "pulverizing other countries" and "bombing them into submission"—and doing so without time limits. Congress had said "the president, under this resolution, can make war forever."

As lower Manhattan smoldered, even Richard Falk, the antiwar lawyer of the Vietnam era, endorsed a limited war in Afghanistan in the pages of the progressive American magazine *The Nation*. Skeptical of a "war on terror" from the first, Ratner shot back hotly that there was another way. He suggested it would make more sense for Bush to seek formal approval of any responses in Afghanistan or elsewhere from the Security Council, rather than simply invoking self-defense. Still, in spite of his earlier activism to highlight the limitations that international law placed on the use of force, Ratner did not protest when the United States stretched the rules of self-defense by entering Afghanistan and taking the Taliban out.

Instead, Ratner turned single-mindedly to the rights of those swept up abroad, sometimes innocently, in the conflict. What was the point of his old activism against war itself? There was no hope, as Ratner saw it, in returning to thankless earlier attempts to enforce limits to war itself in court. "We just gave up," he told one interviewer.

Not that Ratner's initially lonely legal activism on behalf of a more humane and legal global war on terror was much more likely to succeed. He faced opposition within his own outfit for doing something so controversial as to defend the rights of America's enemies, not to mention in the broader community of civil libertarians. When asked at the time by the lawyer David Cole, his disciple, if he thought his filing in *Rasul* had a chance, Ratner replied: "None whatsoever." Yet he doggedly and heroically pursued that tactic in the years that followed. Despite the long odds against making the conduct of America's wars after September 11 legal, Ratner enjoyed providential short-term success.

In part because of the bold extremity of Yoo's denial of the relevance of law to war, Ratner shockingly won in the Supreme Court in *Rasul*, after successive losses in lower courts. Before and after his breakthrough, Ratner led the creation of a "Gitmo Bar" that filed hundreds of habeas petitions for those interned at Guantánamo, and he publicized the depredations of his clients tirelessly. But Ratner's victories in cases like *Rasul* and *Hamdan* coincided with the increasingly popular move of fixing America's post–September 11 posture without undoing it altogether.

THE COMING OF THE MUCH MORE DISPUTED IRAQ WAR AND THE RE-sponses to it were the true crucible for endless if more humane war. Compared with the near unanimous Tonkin Gulf Resolution, and the complete support in Congress for the war on terror in 2001, the Iraqi intervention stoked more debate. In fall 2002, the Authorization for the Use of Military Force in Iraq garnered the votes of only about three-quarters of America's legislators. The Bush administration offered a grab bag of explanations for the need to invade, including Saddam Hussein's connection to international terrorism, the crimes of state against the Iraqi people epitomized by his "rape rooms and torture chambers," and—at the top of the list—his development of weapons of mass destruction.

A few doubted whether enough evidence of WMD existed, but most American experts, right and left, gave Bush the benefit of the doubt. By the time the spectacular invasion began on March 20, 2003, as Operation Iraqi Freedom, American popular support was running high. In fact, it took two long years to cross even into lukewarm territory. Ratner may have been right to conclude that his antiwar activism, which had now failed for decades, consisted of cries in an American wilderness.

Though he now generally prioritized making the war on terror humane, Ratner certainly did cite rules prohibiting going to war as Iraq loomed in the summer of 2002. Writing in *The New York Times* to remind its editorialists that the "prohibition on aggression constitutes a fundamental norm of international law and can be violated by no nation," he and his colleagues at the Center also circulated a primer against the coming invasion. Americans had taken to the streets, joining the world in what was, judging by the numbers of people participating, "the largest antiwar movement that has ever taken place." On February 15, 2003, coordinated marches clogged the streets of most U.S. cities, although they were dwarfed by the tens of millions outside the country, especially in European capitals, who decried the coming storm. As the historian Andrew Bacevich mordantly remarked, however, "the response of the political classes to this phenomenon was essentially to ignore it."

It wasn't until after April 2004, when CBS News broadcast the sickening mementos of abuse and torture that U.S. troops had taken with handheld cameras at Abu Ghraib, that a genuine phase of national soul-searching occurred. As the Iraq War itself started to fail, dreadful images of prisoner abuse, along with stories of the Guantánamo facility, proved more horrifying and persuasive than abstract and contested claims about the rights and wrongs of America's interventions. For many, denouncing mistreatment and torture was opposition by other means to an enterprise they had not spoken out against previously. But the timing of the critics' attempt to stigmatize its cruelties, and by doing so to undermine a war now under way, meant that their approach helped lead to its continuation.

Abu Ghraib, Guantánamo, torture: these became the watchwords of a generation. Barton Gellman and Dana Priest of *The Washington*

Post had reported on rumors of abusive U.S. practices as far back as December 2002. It was not yet credible that the United States could stoop to vile atrocity. Eighteen months later, it was due not so much to the contrast between word and image as to the fact that the Iraq "triumph" revealed itself to be another quagmire that the Abu Ghraib photos had the impact they did. Consciousness of American immorality and worries about the illegality of brutal war spiked. And leaks of memos confirming that Yoo and others had sidestepped the law cast gasoline onto the wildfire of moral insight. But it was a highly partial insight. What the *New Yorker* journalist Jane Mayer memorably called "the dark side" (following a saying of Vice President Dick Cheney's) came to refer across momentous years of moral panic not to war itself but to its means and methods.

The most important liberal journalist offering what became the conventional narrative, Mayer lionized "good conservatives" such as Goldsmith and the conscientious Department of Defense official Alberto Mora, who agitated against torture from within the government. Overnight, a mainstream consensus crystallized around the ethics of humane fighting, rather than the immorality of the entire enterprise of the war on terror. The weeks and months of revulsion after the Abu Ghraib revelations remain the moment of the most bitter and emotional public concern about the war on terror as a whole. But as a result—unlike after My Lai—that war was cleansed of stigma.

The new consensus maintained the fiction that America's descent into lawlessness was aberrant, to strengthen a selective agenda of humane war. "This country has in the past faced other mortal enemies, equally if not more threatening," Mayer assured her audience, "without endangering its moral authority." It was honest and right to decry Yoo's cavalier attitudes toward the Geneva Conventions. It was false and strategic to imply that until this transgression Americans had always fought good fights—that humane war under the law had long been central to American ideals before a cabal of neoconservative radicals came along. Speaking on the television show *Frontline*, even Ratner agreed that the United States "should be the absolute leader for human rights," having once "stood for something." The efforts to restore America's reputation, and to restore the taboo forbidding inhumanity in general and torture in particular, meant no taboo was constructed containing the war itself.

Once again, Yoo was stigmatized not for opinions declaring the war legal under international law but for opinions attempting to exempt the war's conduct from that law. Far more flagrantly than the Afghanistan intervention two years earlier, the Iraq intervention had been illegal under applicable international law prohibiting force. In defense of it, Yoo relied on the Security Council's prior authorizations to constrain Saddam—as far back as 1990—to justify full-on invasion. He took those authorizations as permission slips for a new war and indeed regime change. Unlike the memos permitting the country to conduct the fight without constraints, Yoo's memos explaining the legal justification of the Iraq War never attracted much controversy in the United States.

Yoo's claims were accepted by America's coalition partners, though it is now known that the British foreign secretary had to overrule the intense resistance of his government's lawyers. In the United States, the contrasting responses to the Bush administration's lifting of international law on the conduct of the war on terror and its twisting of the international law allowing for the Iraq War as such was extremely striking. One stirred national passions; the other went largely unremarked. Compared with the country's great debates around entry in World Wars I and II, none occurred after September 11. Judged by the numbers of people affected, and consequences for the world, it is hard to understand the glaring difference. Secretary General of the United Nations Kofi Annan openly insisted on the Iraq War's illegality. The claim eventually gained traction in the United Kingdom, where there was even an attempt that reached the country's highest court, after an official report on the catastrophe, to convict Prime Minister Tony Blair of initiating an aggressive war. As the longest war in U.S. history moved to its next stage, the most momentous debate, by contrast, was the debate that did not happen.

THE PRIORITIES OF THE MOMENT WERE A VAST DEPARTURE FROM MUCH of modern history, morally speaking. In the past, concerted attempts had been made to organize disgust and place a stigma around the outbreak of war and then to use law to preempt it in the future. After September 11, that did not happen.

To be fair, another possibility to consider is that critics of the Iraq imbroglio or the war on terror as a whole understood very well that it was strategic to make hay of torture. No one said so openly of course. But the timing of the struggle in 2004–2006 for a more moral and legal kind of war was too perfect not to interpret it as an early form of opposition to the Iraq intervention or the entire enterprise by other means, especially among those still unready to say openly that one or both had been a dreadful mistake.

Some were ready. "We're at war, endless war," Susan Sontag wrote in her luminous response to Abu Ghraib, published in *The New York Times Magazine* just a month after the photos were publicized. "To acknowledge that Americans torture their prisoners," she openly added, "would contradict everything this administration has invited the public to believe about the virtue of American intentions and America's right, flowing from that virtue, to undertake unilateral action on the world stage." Torture confirmed what such voices had long said, even providing vindication for skepticism toward American war as such. For many others, the connection between critiquing torture and rejecting war itself was unavowed and perhaps even unconscious. Either way, it did not work to curtail the country's longest war.

The aftermath of Abu Ghraib was utterly unlike the aftermath of far worse revelations about the Boer War, when critics of the war advertised their opposition to the whole intervention while complaining of its inhumanity along the way. It was poles apart, in U.S.

history, from the Vietnam era, when the revelation of My Lai added fuel to the fire of a massive ongoing attempt to end the war. If anyone in 2004–2005 turned to the laws prohibiting brutality in war as a strategy to oppose this war, their gambit failed. It would be implausible to say they are blameworthy for their attempt. But the unintended consequences of the legacy they left for making endless war legitimate, rather than ending war, are real.

One reason was that many in the U.S. military itself joined the chorus of horror. In November 2006, Patrick Finnegan, an army brigadier general serving as West Point dean, flew to Hollywood, where—with his medals gleaming and ribbons bright in the Southern Californian sun—he met with television producers after being mistaken for a cast member. His request: stop glamorizing torture. "Torture may cause Jack Bauer some angst," he commented of the hero of the popular show *24* who engaged in harsh interrogation routinely as "the patriotic thing to do." But for Finnegan, angst didn't cut it. Finnegan was a lawyer. He always found time in the midst of his duties to teach the laws of war, trying "to get his students to sort out not just what is legal but what is right." Aside from being offensive to military honor, Finnegan told the showrunners, war crimes were counterproductive. These new truths were hard to teach when popular culture purveyed old falsehoods. In the past, civilians had sought control over the military in order to curb wartime excesses. Now, with Finnegan's high mission to Hollywood, it seemed the reverse was occurring—perhaps for the first time.

By the time Yoo's central memo on torture was leaked in June 2004, it was increasingly clear that the invasion in Iraq had been conducted under false pretenses. The occupation was already deteriorating. But there was no antiwar movement of great significance, and Abu Ghraib's lurid exposure did not bring one about. In November 2004, Bush won a second term, in spite of his Democratic opponent John Kerry's emerging criticism of the Iraq disaster. In any event, the United States had agreed from the first that the Geneva Conventions applied to everything that occurred in Iraq (unlike the broader war on terror), because there was no doubt that with the move to overthrow Saddam Hussein, an international war between states was occurring. A debate around the detention and treatment of enemies in the war on terror was honorable in the extreme and understandable on its own terms. It backfired as a stratagem of containing the war, even in the short run or in Iraq alone, where further military escalations later occurred in hopes of salvaging the situation.

CONSERVATIVE LAWYERS INSIDE GOVERNMENT ALSO MOVED, IN A CRIsis of graphic inhumanity, to restore the rule of law. They, too, helped produce a more humane but endless war on the other side of the Rubicon they crossed.

Jack Goldsmith had qualified to serve in the Bush administration not merely through consummate skill as a lawyer but also by coming out for using military commissions to try terrorists even before Bush did in November 2001. When Yoo's nominal boss Jay Bybee was elevated to a federal judgeship in early 2003 (before word of his signature on Yoo's various memos leaked), Goldsmith became his successor at the Office of Legal Counsel.

Yoo had left in May 2003. Shortly after his arrival that October, Goldsmith decided that he would have to reset the legal framework of the war on terror, which he quickly concluded Yoo had gotten embarrassingly wrong. Goldsmith ultimately tore up Yoo's torture memo. He instructed the government not to rely on Yoo's other work, at the price of angry confrontations with White House Counsel Alberto Gonzales and especially Vice President Dick Cheney's enforcer David Addington, a maximalist in both his beliefs about the extremes that beating terrorism required and his willingness to scream at those who dared to take different views.

"The blood of the hundred thousand people who die in the next attack will be on your hands," Addington warned Goldsmith, who insisted that law applies to how war is fought even so. Most dramatically, when Attorney General John Ashcroft was ill, Goldsmith rushed to his hospital bed, with the like-minded Ashcroft deputy

James Comey, to keep Gonzales from reauthorizing limitless surveillance of U.S. citizens. No wonder Goldsmith resigned so quickly in June 2004, having prepared to do so twice before he ultimately followed through. But in an eight-month window, and through his actions, the conduct of the war on terror was placed within a legal framework.

Not that Goldsmith was any kind of humanitarian. At his job interview, Addington praised Goldsmith's scholarly work pushing back against the international human rights movement, assuming that meant they shared a no-holds-barred approach to American might. And he fully accepted the concept of a "war on terror." Before entering government, Goldsmith had found it reasonable to conclude that the Geneva Conventions applied to the fight with Al-Qaeda and the Taliban prior to Yoo's finding that they were irrelevant. But once in power, Goldsmith told his superiors he had no problem with Yoo's work in that regard. On duty as Iraq detainees mounted, he insisted that the full spectrum of Geneva Conventions covered them, but agreed that Common Article 3 did not apply at Guantánamo to protect terrorists captured elsewhere.

Goldsmith later wrote that his concern about Yoo's torture memo dated from his earliest days on the job. He acted early to rescind Yoo's separate March 2003 legal advice to the military justifying harsh techniques. But Goldsmith only formally withdrew the permission slip for the government in general and the Central Intelligence Agency in particular to go to extremes—a momentous act given traditional norms—once Yoo's handiwork had been leaked and become the topic of almost as much national consternation as the Abu Ghraib photos themselves. Goldsmith explained that the withdrawal of prior legal advice was so unusual that it required delay; given the timing, Yoo shot back that Goldsmith had caved to pressure and panicked in a crisis.

Where Goldsmith bolted most of all—leading to the high drama at Ashcroft's hospital bed—was not on rules of detention or treatment but Yoo's attempt to make the government's surveillance authority over U.S. citizens limitless and unreviewable. Having agreed at the start of his OLC tenure to work less slavishly for Gonzales than Yoo, Goldsmith was part of a cohort of rule-of-law conservatives, like Ashcroft and Comey at the Justice Department, who believed that the U.S. government at home and abroad lost strength when it overreached. Power required constraint.

In his short months of strife, Goldsmith was giving his honest view of the law. But in the meetings at which Addington accused him of disloyalty, it was the fact that limits mattered for power's own sake that counted most. "Why don't we just go to Congress and get it to sign off on the whole detention program?" he asked in one meeting, so that it would enjoy maximum democratic authorization instead of facing public crisis or Supreme Court rebuke. To no avail.

Goldsmith made his choices in what he understood to be a new historical situation. Moral expectations for war had been changing rapidly. Paradoxically, war was becoming more humane but seemed—especially to the novel human rights movement at home and abroad—more and more outrageous over time, just as the remnants of disease or poverty might seem outrageous once health and wealth were norms rather than exceptions. And law that had been newly imposed or newly taken seriously had become relevant. "War itself was encumbered with legal restrictions as never before," he reported. "Many people think the Bush administration has been indifferent to wartime legal constraints. But the opposite is true: the administration has been strangled by law."

Goldsmith was hazy on how this had happened, especially when it came to the Geneva Conventions themselves, which were hardly new. The comparisons he routinely invoked for Bush's dilemmas were good wars like the American Civil War and World War II—not Vietnam or other Cold War engagements. His points of comparison for George W. Bush were always Abraham Lincoln and Franklin Roosevelt, never Lyndon Johnson or Richard Nixon. But he certainly deferred to the brute fact of changing expectations out of recognition that the legitimacy of the presidency and of American war depended on keeping up with the times. Legitimate war required legality and therefore humanity.

Yet for all his sensitivity in this regard, Goldsmith missed another profound change: as the fighting became more and more legalized, *going to war* was less and less so. Even though he served in government in the direct aftermath of the illegal Iraq intervention, which was far more costly for all concerned than America's lurid inhumanity, Goldsmith simply did not have to defend war itself. The law may have strangled the Bush administration's early efforts. But no noose of law, none at all, was tightening around the necks of those Americans who chose belligerency—not least because critics of the administration had themselves opted to focus their ire not on its existence but instead on its tactics. Goldsmith volunteered to impose law on the fighting in the face of a new human rights movement and new expectations of humane war. But there was no old antiwar movement—none worth taking seriously, at least—that compelled Goldsmith to impose any constraint on endless or expanding war.

The results were an enduring framework of "law and the long war," as one of Goldsmith's like-minded friends called it. Initially blackballed by some Harvard Law School colleagues upon his arrival there in fall 2004 to teach—one called him "heartless" and others worried that he must have gone to the dark side himself—Goldsmith was soon feted by the mainstream for courageously acting to impose necessary limits on the war on terror. But Goldsmith's flight into endless war from the cockpit of the Office of Legal Counsel looks very different now than either the sniping critics or the grateful chorus were able to perceive in the immediate aftermath. Debates about letting him off the hook cannot obscure the real question about what that hook is. Was it Goldsmith's relation to the inhumanity that remained—or the humane war that future presidents, too, were to fight?

Of course, it was plausible to complain that the counterterrorist framework that Goldsmith and his successors constructed was nowhere near what civil libertarians and human rights activists demanded, even if it was better than before. To edit torture out was to clear a low bar. Goldsmith signed off on temporary transfer of Al-Qaeda terrorists captured in Iraq out of the country (and, critics worried, to "black sites") for interrogation, albeit with the proviso that Geneva protections still applied. He did not stay around long enough to update the law of interrogation after deleting Yoo's permission slips, but he did not forbid any specific techniques, warning only against more extreme forms of waterboarding than those previously authorized. The evolution of the policy after his departure moved the line so that interrogators were allowed some fearful practices, even as worse ones were forbidden. And his reworking of surveillance law, no doubt Goldsmith's paramount contribution, still left the United States as the most omnipotent snooping power in world history—when it came to foreigners, there were no limitations, and even with the country's own citizens, only minor ones.

But what even critics at the time missed, as divisive argument swirled around the *how* of the war on terror, was the cost of allowing the eclipse of constraints in law on *whether, for what duration,* and *where* it could unfold. There were long-term consequences to that eclipse. And the outcome of endless war, however improved its humanity and legality, was as much a tragedy for Goldsmith as for Ratner.

From the beginning, Goldsmith's skepticism of international law reflected the concern that it lacked democratic authorization. But this hardly meant that he endorsed Yoo's presidentialism, as if there were not another democratic branch of government, indeed one to which the Constitution appeared to give decisive power in war and peace. For a few years, Goldsmith expressed enthusiasm about the war on terror in principle, suggesting that it would bring something close enough to peace, in part through new surveillance technology. Eventually, however, he noted the irony that Yoo's vision of a less and less restrained executive came from Cold War liberals, who had bequeathed their ideology of war abroad to neoconservatives. Earlier conservatives in U.S. history had generally favored congressional prerogatives and been as suspicious of foreign entanglements as of an outsized presidency. Goldsmith edged closer and closer to that tradition.

Goldsmith had restored some modicum of the rule of law and was ultimately lionized by many liberals for doing so. But when it came to the country's move to a war footing without limitation, he had acted in service of a neoconservative crusade, however much he enraged its paladins by imposing law on its manner. Worse, under President Barack Obama, Goldsmith's effort to regulate the manner of the war on terror was inherited by the very liberal internationalists he found so objectionable—and who embarked on even more wars, once they could claim, thanks to a process he started, that their fighting was legal and humane. Goldsmith came to believe that America's democratic ecology could function to keep presidents within bounds. But by his own later acknowledgment, the accountability and constraint he found in—and helped impose on—the presidency after September 11 did not really place limits on continuing American belligerency.

NO MORE THAN GOLDSMITH WAS RATNER ESPECIALLY CONCERNED TO make American war more humane, though he certainly found some of the U.S. practices he learned about sickening. Ratner burned with rage over the "horror" of Guantánamo, but what he cared most about was not diminishing suffering in potentially endless war but ensuring that civil liberties did not die, and that the legal system remained a forum for challenging power. When his son studied the Magna Carta in high school, Ratner was struck by its promise that no man is above limitations. It was "about the king obeying the law, or the president obeying the law." Legitimation through law mattered more to Ratner, too, than the fact that some of the applicable law required wars to be more humane.

In the earliest days after September 11, Ratner agitated for placing the attack within a framework of crime rather than war. Seeing no hope for an antiwar stance, he concluded years later that his most agonizing failure was his failure to destroy the "war paradigm," which he characterized as "the biggest loss we've had." Within that paradigm, though coming from the far left, he occupied a position strikingly similar to Goldsmith's, except that he insisted on constraint not to buttress power and on legalization not to secure legitimacy but instead because power without limits is evil.

By the end of his life, Ratner was returning to the idea of constraints on using force abroad, the very constraints he had once hoped to give some teeth. As intervention loomed in Libya in 2011, he inveighed against the policy debate taking place in Washington, D.C., which failed to mention that "such an action would be illegal"—even conceived as a humanitarian intervention. Two years later, when President Barack Obama decided against intervening in Syria without congressional support, Ratner called it "the first time I've actually seen resistance to going to war in this country since 9/11." And he returned to the thankless task of seeking enforcement for the War Powers Resolution, shredded in the meantime.

There were signs all along that both Goldsmith and Ratner were anxious that the war on terror, even if fought legally, could have long-term effects in degrading American life. Ratner reported in 2005 that he was taken by the specter raised by the ancient Greek historian Thucydides of "Athens expanding its empire," bringing "tyranny abroad and eventually tyranny at home." What would follow, he wondered, for an America that had become "an incredibly imperialist nation right now, at war all over the world"? Allergic in the long run to a neoconservative mentality of messianic globalism, Goldsmith for his part harked back to phases of a conservative tradition that worried that foreign wars might spell the end of domestic freedom. Ratner was not the only one who witnessed the war party on his side of the political spectrum find uses for a now more humane war that he rejected. Having unbound indefinite global militarism by binding the U.S. presidency, Goldsmith, too, would be condemned to watch as the next two presidents hewed to the endless if legalized war he had helped bring about.

With fewer enemies captured, no one tortured, and the Guantánamo camp increasingly a shadow of its former self, the debates through which endless war was set on legal footing were increasingly things of the past. Neither Goldsmith nor Ratner touched subsequent thorny controversies regarding who was eligible for death from drones in the sky or special forces paying a visit, or how much collateral damage for those nearby was tolerable. But the legacy both men left for the future was immense.

The war, now debugged and legalized, would evolve in an increasingly humane form. If there had been a chance to put limits on the war itself, after Goldsmith's years in power and Ratner's years of filing petitions, it had been missed. And so it goes on, with no end in sight.

CHAPTER EIGHT

The Arc of the Moral Universe

ON MAY 23, 2013, THE PEACE ACTIVIST MEDEA BENJAMIN ATTENDED A speech by President Barack Obama at Fort McNair in Washington, D.C., where he defended his administration's use of armed drones in counterterrorism. In 2002, Benjamin had cofounded the advocacy group Code Pink: Women for Peace; at Fort McNair she posed as a journalist to gain admission. Thrown out after verbally attacking the president, she was dismissed in *The Washington Post* that day as a "heckler." Obama himself had been more reflective at the event, engaging with her criticisms, which led to even deeper self-criticism of his own. It was the moment of greatest moral clarity about war during a presidency that did more than any other to bring its endless and humane American form fully into being.

Nearing sixty at the time, her business-casual outfit belying her radical views, Benjamin had long supported left-wing causes. Born in 1952 to a middle-class Jewish family on Long Island, she changed her first name from Susan to Medea in college after reading Euripides. She liked how the name sounded, and she had heard a feminist interpretation of the Greek tragedy suggesting that Medea had never killed her children and was only blamed for it by patriarchal traditions. After college, Benjamin trained as a progressive economist and worked for the United Nations and mainstream internationalist groups. In 1979, she threw all that away and moved to Cuba, where she got married and worked for a Communist newspaper. She celebrated the regime in her journalism but was deported after four years for contesting restrictions on political dissent. On her return to the United States, Benjamin remarried and worked in radical causes, controlling a family grant-making foundation that funded her activism.

After Obama's election, support for antiwar politics cratered. Benjamin promptly put her energies into finding new support for the cause of peace by attacking Obama's drone empire. "Unless we shine a light on it," she told one reporter of his drone mania, "we're going to turn around and say, 'Wait, how'd we get involved in all these wars without knowing about it?'" Benjamin was convinced that attacking the aerial means of Obama's continuation of the war on terror was tantamount to an attack on American belligerency itself. The goal was "to push the arc of Obama's second term in the direction of peace and justice."

It was a reasonable hope. Obama had run as a kind of antiwar candidate in his fairy-tale 2008 campaign, and when it turned out that he was a hard-bitten pragmatist—in this and other areas—many of his supporters were surprised. Obama expanded the war on terror to an awesome extent, while making it sustainable for a domestic audience in a way his predecessor never did—in part because Obama understood the political uses of transforming American warfare in a humane direction.

Benjamin was right to have been suspicious. In just the first few months of 2009, after Obama took the oath of office, the initial metamorphosis of American war into humane form was achieved. As the most egregious infractions of the prior administration were disowned, Obama's lawyers claimed authority to continue war indefinitely across space and time, devising formal legal frameworks for targeted killings. The move appropriated righteous anger around inhumanity and torture in the prior years for the sake of something unknown in the annals.

The rise of armed drone strikes under Obama's watch was merely the symbol of the extension and expansion of endless war. Alongside his reliance on no-footprint drones as a new mode of cleaner and more humane killing, Obama simultaneously turned to the light-footprint U.S. Special Forces. In the beginning, the two options worked well together, with the evanescent footfalls of assets on the ground helping the drones overhead and their operators far away to do their work. But whatever its signature, Obama's pattern far transcended any method or technology. Not only was the price for the world of Obama's perfection of humane war high but also it ended in catastrophe at home.

"Lawyerliness suffused the Obama administration," observed Charlie Savage, the gifted *New York Times* reporter who broke many explosive national security stories during the Obama years. There was a lawyerly institutional process, compared with the Bush era, with more consultation within the executive branch than before. And that was not all. "Lawyerliness shaped Obama's governance as a matter of style and thought, not just process," Savage added, gesturing toward how legality in war mattered beyond checking boxes.

But Savage's own reporting—on a journalistic beat without earlier parallel, reflecting the rising profile of law in debate on U.S. foreign affairs—demonstrated that lawyerliness often served as an elaborate rationalization process. The president's men and women, Savage concludes, "were trying to fight al-Qaeda while adhering to what *they saw* as the rule of law." But what they saw as the rule of law meant little more than self-regulation, devising rules and enforcing them against themselves. It had about as much effect as a dieter's attempt at self-control, authorizing extension and expansion of endless war without limitation. Such dynamics were, however, offset by a commitment to humane standards of fighting war. While those standards were by no means perfect in legal theory or military practice, they had rhetorical power for some Americans and significant effects on the fighting itself. Even if the expansion and endurance of American war under Obama's watch had been legal, its humanization still helped sidestep moral and policy limits.

Obama continued a process begun in the later Bush years, but he more credibly advertised the country's uprightness as steward of the least brutal form of war possible. And he transformed the war itself. Expansion and humanization went together, branding Obama's wars with an ominous trademark. According to his lawyers themselves, American power recognized few if any limits on where its deployment could reach and how long it could last, as a series of permission slips for U.S. intervention stretching back decades continued to pile up. Whatever the validity of the permission slips, the war they authorized often came framed as legally virtuous in the manner of its fighting. The most remarkable thing, in short, was how the legerdemain with which going to war was treated worked in tandem with intense concern, both ethical and optical, for making war humane.

More fatefully still, his critics accepted this disparity in order to demand more humanity from Obama's fight, especially more faithful compliance with the law of humane war—conceding the war footing itself until it was too late. His election devastated a peace impulse, in part because he had allowed the perception that he was its standard-bearer. And then the president's audience accepted his invitation to think that its humanity made ongoing American war ethically salubrious or even uplifting. The sometimes real humanization of the war on terror helped entrench and legitimate its unaccountable extension in time and expansion in space.

Beyond its other shortcomings, the transformation of American war incurred a gargantuan risk that neither its defenders nor its opponents saw for the longest time. In November 2016, it blindsided them. "He has relentlessly questioned the efficacy of force," claimed the journalist Jeffrey Goldberg toward the end of Obama's two terms, "but he has also become the most successful terrorist-hunter in the history of the presidency, one who will hand to his successor a set of tools an accomplished assassin would envy." This outcome was scary, no matter how tightly controlled, humanely practiced, and judiciously governed—and that was before the true identity of Obama's successor became known only six months after Goldberg wrote.

The United States faced threats, and it was not as though Obama could have turned a blind eye to terrorism. He was a politician whose career depended on protecting the American people first and foremost. But not only did Obama design a far bigger and more encompassing form of war than necessary, and not only did he undermine America's earlier if partial commitments to a legal order consecrating peace to do so. His policies also helped create the conditions for a shocking and terrible finale.

No dove, Donald Trump nevertheless capitalized on the perception that mainstream politicians were committed to endless wars. And he won. The arc of the moral universe ran through the humanization of interminable conflict. But it bent toward an ogre. More and more humane forms of fighting abroad had now brought disaster at home, too. Then Trump went on to repeat the pirouette from antiwar candidate to endless war president that Obama had performed.

AFTER ITS CONVULSIVE EXPLOSION IN 2002–2003 AS THE IRAQ WAR loomed, a fledgling peace movement reappeared in Bush's second term as Afghanistan remained tumultuous and the Iraqi occupation unraveled. But a more humane form of war had taken hold in the interval, which would make it increasingly difficult for a peace politics to gain traction. While the antiwar cause shaped the results of presidential elections in 2008 and 2016, it never recrystallized as a prominent movement.

The leading peace activists of the later Bush years were closely associated with the military itself, reflecting growing exhaustion and the war's unpopularity among grieving families and wounded soldiers. The most famous protestor, Cindy Sheehan, set up a camp outside Bush's Texas ranch in summer 2005, memorializing her son who had perished in Iraq the year before. On the model of earlier Vietnamese protest among soldiers, Iraq Veterans Against the War was formed around the same time and grew in membership.

In the Vietnam era, disaffected military families and returning veterans helped to expand peace activism. When vets returned from Iraq, there was no massive or even medium-sized cause for them to join. The fiasco of the Iraq occupation in Bush's second term was so dire, however, that Obama definitely had an opening. He embraced it against his rival Hillary Clinton in the nominating contest and then against the Republican John McCain in the general election. It helped that both his rivals had backed Bush's military adventurism.

In *Dreams from My Father*, the superlative memoir he published more than a decade before his presidential campaign, Obama beautifully described the entangled identity that made him a perfect global icon for a cosmopolitan age that seemed to be dawning. With his African father and Indonesian childhood, Obama could bring the United States closer to becoming the racially egalitarian power at home and abroad of which its best seers, like Martin Luther King, Jr., had dreamed. In what turned out to be his most fortunate speech, delivered in the fall of 2002 while he was still an obscure Illinois state senator, Obama condemned the looming war in Iraq as "dumb." Even then, he made clear he was not against all wars, remembering the Civil War that destroyed slavery, and his maternal grandfather's military service in World War II. (He enlisted in the U.S. Army the day after Pearl Harbor and fought in General George Patton's European divisions.) And while Obama incarnated a post-racial world order in person, he was not opposed to a global hierarchy with the United States benevolently at the top.

In the more conventional campaign book that followed in 2006, *The Audacity of Hope*, Obama lionized America's commitment in 1945 to abjure the self-aggrandizement of empires past for a "willingness to exercise constraint in the exercise of its power." Not least to make its ascendancy legitimate, the United States should go to war only when allowed by the rules the country had helped to write. In the campaign, Obama certainly took advantage of the opprobrium around torture and other American transgressions to make his case. But he also capitalized politically on his growing reputation as an opponent of reckless war, while leaving vague how he would rethink the U.S. counterterrorist policy and global role if elected.

It was forgivable, therefore, that so many Americans inferred that

Obama might fight just wars when push came to shove but would pivot away from belligerency toward peace. "The Bush administration responded to the unconventional attacks of 9/11 with conventional thinking of the past, largely viewing problems as . . . principally amenable to military solutions," as Obama put it in July 2007, still trailing Clinton by ten points. He allowed many to conclude that believable change would never entrench militaristic thinking. Later that summer, having already introduced an Iraq De-escalation Bill in the U.S. Senate in January, Obama emphasized plans to undo America's Iraq mistake. While his remark that he would use force against terror when it posed a direct threat passed mostly unnoticed, he also made much of the need to "dry up" its sources, stressing foreign aid and public diplomacy. Years later, in his bestselling memoir in 2020, Obama reflected on what unfolded under his presidency and how it clashed with his intentions for young foreigners who turned to anti-Americanism and violence. "I wanted somehow to save them—send them to school, give them a trade, drain them of the hate that had been filling their heads. And yet the world they were a part of, and the machinery I commanded, more often had me killing them instead."

After the fact, it became popular to deny with a knowing air that Obama had authorized the most fantastic projections of his audience. For all Obama's public image as a man of peace, those ransacking his rhetoric from even before he won the nomination can find clues to his later stances. In his August 2007 speech, Obama envisioned a military "more stealthy, agile, and lethal." The next year he openly promised "more troops, more helicopters, more satellites, more Predator drones in the Afghan border region," even vowing to use them without the consent of Pakistan if necessary. All the same, he invited his audience to see what they wanted in him. The promise of American peace was crucial to Obama's support. World-weary commentators who purport never to have been surprised by his militarism routinely downplay or miss this fact, reducing the drama of his presidency and trivializing the verdict on its finale.

Obama went on to best Clinton partly on the strength of his

skepticism of the Iraq War. Clinton had endorsed the war consistently with her inveterate posture as a liberal hawk. During the campaign, she had attempted to alter the disastrous optics by pointing out that, as a U.S. senator, Obama had waited nearly two years to revive his then-unknown reservations about the Iraq War and had repeatedly voted to fund it. In the general election, Obama's rhetoric of peace continued much as before, as supporters projected on his candidacy great expectations. He did not act to contain those expectations, because their benefits were so valuable. And of course, rhetorical flights are normal in running for office. Clinton remarked at the time that you campaign in poetry, but you govern in prose. But Obama's lyrical peace candidacy was another matter. In the long run, the costs of disappointment racked up by the endless war he pursued all the same would prove to be enormous.

Obama's stance from the start involved a double reaction to Vietnam, one part old and one part new, and these reactions conditioned everything that followed under his administration. The old part was a fear ingrained deep in the psyche of Democrats since Vietnam of moving too far toward peace, even when they have come to power in the aftermath of failed wars. Obama certainly called for diplomatic engagement and increased foreign aid. But he followed the pattern of Democrats since George McGovern's catastrophic defeat in 1972 of avoiding at all costs any perception of weakness on national security. "Obama needed to cope with the legacies of two Georges," Bush and McGovern, as the foreign policy analyst James Mann incisively put it. The two predecessors defined the Scylla and Charybdis of Obama's thinking in the campaign, as well as in office. The new part was that Obama and his mostly young foreign policy staffers refused any obsession with a "Vietnam syndrome" that required balancing America's global military presence against the risks of blowback and quagmire. "There are things to learn from previous engagements," sagely observed Ben Rhodes, Obama's thirty-something foreign policy advisor and speechwriter, "but the touchstone isn't always going to be Vietnam."

The combination of the image he cultivated with the views he held meant that Obama enjoyed unique latitude from day one. He benefited from expectations that he would establish a fundamentally new policy. As a result, he could pursue a global struggle against terrorists wherever they went, with less objection and even scrutiny. That Obama's election itself dealt the antiwar movement its most grievous blow left him considerable flexibility to accommodate critics to his right. One reason for the evaporation of antiwar pressure was partisan: those who opposed Bush's conflicts only because they were led by a Republican dropped their concerns. But the main cause was faith that Obama would change America's ways. "This is our time," Obama promised in Chicago's Grant Park the night of his election, "to restore prosperity and promote the cause of peace." Overnight, Medea Benjamin's Code Pink hemorrhaged most of its support. "We find that though the core members of Code Pink are just as angry at Obama as we were at Bush," she acknowledged in one interview, "a lot of the people who supported Code Pink became quiet when Obama got elected."

But if one part of his progressive audience attributed to him a much greater commitment to revisiting the basic premises of the war on terror than any evidence justified, another embraced Obama as their leader for nearly opposite reasons. Beyond loyalty to candidate and party, they thought that it wasn't U.S. military interventions themselves that were beyond the pale, but only the inhumane versions of them. As events would prove, Obama reliably pursued their agenda. Abetting a process Bush had started, Obama could save American war-making by cleansing it of the diversionary intervention into Iraq and the contamination of outrageous brutality that had marred that intervention from the start.

AS JANUARY 20, 2009, APPROACHED, ENTHUSIASM FOR A BREATHTAKING pivot away from Bush's war on terror grew. Within two days of his inauguration, Obama signed executive orders to ban torture and rescind all Bush-era legal directives governing the treatment of prisoners. Immediately, he earned plaudits for following through on his promises. "Bush's 'War on Terror' Comes to a Sudden End," ran the headline of a *Washington Post* story on his third day in office. ("Obama says he has no plans to diminish counterterrorism operations abroad," the reporter clarified below the fold.) Few noticed Obama's own first drone strike, which took place that same third day of his administration.

It dawned agonizingly slowly on an expectant world that there were going to be profound continuities in wartime policies. Obama immediately set out to deal with Guantánamo and exit Iraq. But the truth was that, in his flashy act of humanizing detention and ending the heavy-footprint wars that created the need for it, Obama was pushing to a large extent on an opening door. Bush himself had drawn the conclusion that Iraq needed to be wound down, though he did so too late and too slowly to stave off the growing popular rage that helped doom Clinton and then McCain in turn. After the "surge" in U.S. troop commitments to Iraq in 2007–2008, they were already in decline when Obama took office. The same reversal was even more advanced at Guantánamo. By the time Bush left office, the prisoner population there had fallen from around 750 to around 250.

And by the time Obama took office, Bush's abusive interrogation policies had also been curbed. In 2005, the Republican-controlled Congress had limited the government's interrogation authority, against Bush's initial resistance. True, as late as 2007, Bush issued an executive order sticking to John Yoo's original position that the Geneva Conventions did not apply to terrorists, at least for Central Intelligence Agency purposes. It was only in the last days of Bush's second term that warnings issued five years before not to rely on Yoo's original torture memos evolved into official prohibitions. In the wake of the to-and-fro, Obama could capitalize on the impression of official barbarity and create a new optics of humanity on arrival.

Jane Mayer, the *New Yorker* journalist who had done the most to craft the liberal narrative of just struggle against the prior president, exulted in the deletion of Yoo's torture memos. "Obama consigned to history the worst excesses of the Bush administration's 'war on terror,'" she commented the first week of the new presidency. A "stunning political turnabout" had now occurred. It captured the sensibilities of many relieved by the restoration of a taboo after a bout of sacrilege. In retrospect, the euphoria appears more naïve and shortsighted, confirming as it did a selective injunction against only one kind of profane behavior, while opening a space for more of another.

In her glowing affirmation of the legal prohibition of inhumanity, Mayer did not mention, let alone protest, that the Obama administration failed to withdraw Bush-era permission slips around *going to war* in 2001 or 2003. In fact, the memos on the use of force that Yoo drafted after September 11 were as dubious, legally speaking, as the noxious ones concerning detention and treatment of terrorists that Bush officials discreetly and Obama showily shredded. But the memos authorizing war were treated very differently, remaining sources for future engagements. At the very start of his administration, Obama adopted a war framework that placed no limitations in space or time on the conduct of counterterrorism. This would matter much more than banning torture symbolically or fiddling with prisoner and trial rules.

As he navigated his first few months, Obama pivoted to governing and learned it would be difficult to shift all of Bush's policies even if he wanted to do so. A pitter-patter of revelations brought a knowledgeable few up short, even as Obama found his honeymoon period interrupted by the spectacle of Dick Cheney indicting him publicly for going soft. A few months after he suspended the use of military commissions to try detainees, Obama moved to reanimate them, accepting the need for special institutions given the secrecy of the evidence often involved. And the complexities of shuttering Guantánamo—thorny ones that not even Obama could master in eight years—were also already clear by spring. The bigger event by far, however, was surreptitious and mostly unremarked.

In February, Elena Kagan, Harvard Law School dean and future Supreme Court justice, testified before Congress after Obama nominated her to be solicitor general. She hinted that the administration endorsed a "global battlefield" concept of the war on terror that would allow capture anywhere without constraint, subject only to the humane controls of the laws of war. Building on that testimony, a landmark March 2009 legal brief publicly gave clear and jaw-dropping notice of Obama's version of the war paradigm, formalizing and globalizing it in a way that Bush had never done officially.

The work was organized by a Harvard law professor on leave named David Barron (a future federal judge), acting as head of the Office of Legal Counsel, after a two-hour meeting in which the president outlined his desired goal. The brief arrogated extraordinary authority to detain those already in Guantánamo indefinitely if necessary, offset by a promise to revisit policies for future captured terrorists—of which there would uncoincidentally be next to none. The brief applied no geographical limitations on where captured terrorists could come from. Though the memo cautiously restricted its arguments to detainees currently at Guantánamo, the framework was to prove most consequential for the targeted killing operations that had already begun. It was the initial rationale for what became a spree of humane killing on which the sun might never set in space or end in time.

Looking back on the spring of 2009, when Obama pivoted from being a kind of peace candidate by nondenial to becoming a permanent if humane war president, it is easy to understand why the most fateful developments were missed—even by those who were driving them. A few were taken aback—incensed about detention length and trial rules—without recognizing Obama's pivot from capturing anyone to the tactics of raining death from the sky and sending the Special Forces to visit and kill. Ironically, the fact that harsh treatment of detainees—though it was practically moribund—was still theoretically possible caused distraction during a momentous interval. Single-minded concern with American abuse of captives, and the specter of Guantánamo, where it was feared that abuse would continue taking place, once again masked the deeper horror of an escalating shadow war.

In May 2009, Obama went to the National Archives to speak in the presence of the Constitution, symbolic of his devotion to law and America's most sterling commitments. The day before, he met in the Oval Office with a group of civil libertarians and human rights advocates. "No one questions your values," began Anthony Romero, the American Civil Liberties Union head who had referred snarkily in *The New York Times* to the revival of military commissions as of a piece with a "Bush-Obama doctrine." "But when your substantive policies are not substantively different than your predecessor's, then the comparisons are fair."

Obama met him with a stony gaze, broken only by a surly glare. Didn't his critics understand? Obama wondered. He was on their side, but he had to govern all citizens, including those Cheney was rabble-rousing from the no-holds-barred right. And Obama's angling to reform America's health-care system in a unique moment of opportunity might require compromises on other fronts; politics is no place for purity. At the time, Obama was accelerating Bush's troop withdrawal from Iraq in anticipation of near total withdrawal by 2011. In Afghanistan, he raised troop levels for four years before drawing them down. There, Obama became embroiled in a revival of colonial-era counterinsurgency strategies that had been bruited regularly over the decades within Western militaries when failure loomed, and that now became associated with the rise and fall of General David Petraeus. With the right books by his bedside, Obama earnestly ruminated about whether it would have been possible for the United States to salvage its Vietnam mistake after 1968, not by killing even more fighting men but by winning the hearts and minds of local populations.

Neither approach was to work. But the deeper and enduring reality of Obama's first phase in office was that by making other moves, he was engineering an unprecedented new form of global engagement that would blur the line between war and policing. What had once been brutal, albeit with beginnings and conclusions, was becoming humane—but never-ending.

There is no doubt that, in the moment, Obama conscientiously struggled most with the hardest of the hard-core Guantánamo detainees. His policies were, like his predecessor's, consigning them to a permanent stay there—indeed, to this day. They could not be let go as innocent, nor punished after being tried by commission or in court (sometimes because of compromised evidence), nor transferred to other countries, no matter how sweet the deal. Obama hoped to see the Guantánamo remnant kept in detention under some legal framework and not at one man's whim. He thought that empowering the president to detain anyone at will forever was an enormous danger for the future. And he demanded a new legal regime with approval from Congress or the courts or both.

At the National Archives, in a speech drafted by the cherubic Rhodes, Obama laid out his hopes for his war as defined by applicable law, emphasizing prior mistakes that he would now correct. In the immediate aftermath of September 11, he acknowledged, "too many of us—Democrats and Republicans, politicians, journalists, and citizens—fell silent." International law was not mentioned in the speech. But he clearly meant that the basic values of humane fighting, not of making war itself, had been spurned. The message was that a return to American exceptionalism in the conduct of hostilities would put things right.

MOST AMERICANS WERE SLOW ON THE UPTAKE AS THE RECIPE FOR endless war was mixed in spring 2009. The government embraced the eternity of a conflict sweetened by the insistence that it proceed humanely—if not exactly in conformity with the limits international law imposes on how war is fought, then in the spirit of those limits. Obama was awarded the Nobel Peace Prize in October and gave his dazzling acceptance speech in December. By that time, none could deny that Obama's fate was one he had chosen as much as suffered. He would remain a wartime president, with the compensation of unprecedented care and control.

Since the shocking October morning of the news from Oslo, Obama himself had been self-conscious about the contradictions of his elevation into peace emissary. "Even as we strive to seek a world in which conflicts are resolved peacefully," he explained in the White House Rose Garden after thanking his rambunctious new dog and unimpressed children for helping keep perspective on his global stardom, "we have to confront the world as we know it today." No peace prize could absolve him, he observed, of the need to "confront a ruthless adversary that directly threatens the American people and our allies." Embarrassed by the situation, Obama flew to Norway in December—after polite inquiries first whether attendance was required.

Obama was a throwback of sorts to the prize's very first co-recipient, Henry Dunant, in 1901: an advocate of humanity in warfare with a highly uncertain relationship to the ideal of a peaceful world. But where the founder of the laws of war was a grizzled recluse when he won, Obama acknowledged that he was "at the beginning, and not the end, of my labors on the world stage," with "slight" accomplishments to his name so far. Dunant represented philanthropic Christianity and the use of personal mobilization to push states to be humane, whereas Obama—though directly concerned with the implications of his professed Christianity for the ethics of war and peace—stood at the pinnacle of an armed superpower. Above all, Dunant had been pressured by the peace movement at the turn of the twentieth century into agreeing that the imperative of humane war should never function to postpone the goal of peace that the prize honored. After the turn of another century, Obama had already conceded an indefinite postponement in the name of keeping Americans safe.

Onstage, Obama engaged in his trademark reflection, "with an acute sense of the costs of armed conflict," as he meditatively put it, "filled with difficult questions about the relationship between war and peace, and our effort to replace one with the other." The premise of his Nobel lecture was that terrorism, which he privately demoted as a boring regulatory quandary, was so new and threatening that it required thinking "in new ways about the notions of just war and the imperatives of a just peace." And for a president, at least of the United States, an antiwar stance in power was out of the question, no matter the illusions some had cultivated when Obama ran. All respect was due to his elected ancestor Martin Luther King's rejection of war when he won his own Nobel in 1964 with the message that "violence never brings permanent peace," and "solves no social problem: it merely creates new and more complicated ones." But neither King nor Mohandas Gandhi before him had led a great nation.

It was a brilliant self-defense, not only of the ethics of Obama's own role but also of American violence in a world where, he insisted, too many naïvely demand peace. "In many countries," Obama remarked, "there is a deep ambivalence about military action today, no matter what the cause. And at times, this is joined by a reflexive suspicion of America, the world's sole military superpower." As the *New York Times* editorialists pointed out in lauding Obama's rhetoric, "he directly challenged the widespread ambivalence and aversion" toward the Afghan war among Americans, too. Obama channeled his own Christian guru: not King with his commitment to brotherhood and peace but the American theologian Reinhold Niebuhr, who had converted from pacifism to Cold War apologetics in recognition of the depth of human sin. In doing so, Obama came close to affirming that endless war is a metaphysical necessity.

It would be hard to imagine an interpretation of Jesus Christ's message more foreign to the one that had motivated the earliest peace activists in the United States and beyond. War continues forever not because of any legal authority or any specific threat; rather, God's plan is for peace to be elusive. "We must begin by acknowledging the hard truth," Obama observed. "We will not eradicate violent conflict in our lifetimes." Evil was to be opposed with just war in a fallen and refractory world that ruled out durable peace. There were limits to the president's humility and skepticism, however. Obama did not mention Niebuhr's insistence that Americans themselves could sin, since all God's children blended light with darkness.

In his eloquent rationale for the uses of U.S. military power for a new age, the saving grace, perhaps, was that Obama insisted on humane constraints. It was hardly inappropriate to recall America's onetime contribution to a less war-torn globe, almost single-handedly "constructing an architecture to keep the peace" in 1945. And that contribution during and after the Cold War left the world a "legacy for which my own country is rightfully proud" given the overall betterment for humanity, though there may have been costs and mistakes along the way. But in the face of terror, what the American contribution required was not an end to war but precisely playing by the rules of humane warfare.

Obama's aide Samantha Power, a former journalist admired for her fervent calls for American humanitarian intervention, had accompanied him as a "stowaway" on the trip. She had prepared for her boss an earnest memo with "a history of humanitarianism, an account of the relationship between human rights and conflict, and thoughts on violence from Hume, Kant, Martin Luther King, Jr., Niebuhr, and Henry Dunant." And at her urgent suggestion, Obama's speech carved out the possibility of American war to stop atrocity, without explaining how it fit with standards that prohibited such uses of force.

But a commitment to global justice and international law, Obama insisted, primarily required attention to the manner of U.S. military activities. "I am convinced that adhering to standards, international standards, strengthens those who do, and isolates and weakens those who don't," he concluded. "We must also think clearly about how we fight." Invoking Dunant by name and the morality of Geneva Conventions, Obama was clear: "I believe the United States of America must remain a standard-bearer in the conduct of war."

OBAMA TURNED TO ARMED DRONES MORE TIMES IN HIS FIRST YEAR alone than Bush had in the entirety of his presidency. Almost from the start, Obama's policy called for engaging in targeted killing with gusto, not only by drone but also with the Special Forces or standoff missiles sent from long distances. And as Obama re-created a war less bounded in space and let it bleed in time, his lawyers formalized the system. Introduced in secret and then normalized in public, targeted killings transformed the war on terror so that it stretched across a widening arc of the earth. Soon it was to be advertised as a humane enterprise, conducted with concern for the innocent in harm's way.

By the end of Obama's time in office, no-footprint drones had struck almost ten times more than under his predecessor's watch, with many thousands dead. The air force now trained more drone operators than aircraft pilots, and the architecture of drone activity had been extended deep into the African continent, not merely across the Middle East and South Asia. The same trend line followed the deployment of the light-footprint Special Forces, which operated in or moved through 138 nations—or 70 percent of all countries in the world—in Obama's last year in office. Actual fighting took place in at least thirteen, and targeted killing in some of those.

There had been many incentives to draw Obama toward such policy. First and foremost was the need to get the war off America's front pages, and stop body bags from coming home, which had made Bush's popularity crater. The month after the Nobel speech, on Christmas Day, the near destruction of Northwest Flight 253 en route from Amsterdam to Detroit by the Nigerian terrorist Umar Farouk Abdulmutallab, "the underwear bomber," caused Obama enormous consternation. The near miss under his watch led the president to intensify in practice what he had defended in theory and his lawyers had blessed. An equally enormous incentive was the need to avoid the damaging attacks against revolting abuses that his predecessor had suffered for the treatment of captured prisoners at Abu Ghraib and Guantánamo, along with the CIA's black sites. If no one was captured, no one could be mistreated. But beyond these factors, Obama embraced humanity in warfare not merely as what the law required but as a morally legitimate and legitimating enterprise.

The intense focus of advocacy groups and administration lawyers alike on the legal niceties of humane detention and treatment contributed significantly to a perverse outcome. The brutal treatment of captives had tainted the legitimacy of a heavy-footprint war under the prior administration. Now a concern to remove that taint led the United States to kill by preference in the new one—though the country took steps to make its regime of death more compassionate. While advertising its alleged care, the emerging form of Obama's war negated the constraints on extending and expanding war itself that previous generations had prioritized. As the Obama administration continued, the abuses to the laws prohibiting force accumulated almost without counterexample.

Targeted killing had a history before Obama, but he owned it and reinvented the law of self-defense. The once-unpopular claim that it was legal had been concocted in the laboratory of Israel, stretching back to that country's beginnings. There, targeted killing—including by armed drone as early as 1984—was openly called assassination. Americans avoided that term, and not just out of the desire for euphemism: in response to the unholy revelations after Vietnam about the malfeasance of the intelligence community, U.S. law had explicitly banned assassination by name. What was legally problematic about targeted killings under international rules governing the resort to force was neither the death that resulted nor the means, drone technology or Special Forces, that dealt it. Rather, it was whether war could be fought against terrorists in the first place, especially when starting such a war broke the rules requiring an imminent threat of armed attack, along with the consent of states where they were located.

True, there was a single U.S. legal authorization for targeted killing—the attack on Osama bin Laden that President Bill Clinton had signed in secret in 1999. But that attempt ended up never taking place, and Clinton almost immediately withdrew any clear permission to kill. Bush officials had condemned Israeli practices as late as summer 2001. "Israel needs to understand that targeted killings of Palestinians don't end the violence but are only inflaming an already volatile situation and making it much harder to restore calm," a State Department spokesman commented two weeks before Al-Qaeda hit the United States, following up on multiple reprimands over the years, including by Bush himself on Valentine's Day the winter before. Americans had not deployed armed drones yet in any situation, in spite of CIA tinkering and war-gaming.

The basic moves to create a global battlefield were made in the days after September 11, as Bush unleashed the CIA to hunt terrorist masterminds anywhere, even as he planned one heavy-footprint war and then another in specific places for the Department of Defense to lead. Armed drones were first used by the CIA in the course of the Afghan intervention, shortly before the agency sent a Predator to hunt and kill the Al-Qaeda leader Qaed Salim Sinan al-Harethi in Yemen on November 3, 2002. But Bush waited almost eighteen months before undertaking another targeted killing by drone: the Taliban militant Nek Muhammad was killed in Pakistan's tribal areas on June 18, 2004. By the end of his time in office, fifty deployments of armed drones outside Afghanistan and Iraq had killed around five hundred people, but Bush and his lawyers neither justified nor normalized the practice.

Some in the Obama administration—most notably the chief counterterrorism advisor and later CIA director John Brennan in a 2011 speech—defended the expansion of targeted killings by offering assurances that they were restricted to "badlands" rather than allowed everywhere. The point was to distinguish Obama's expanded war from Bush's, but the risk was that it worked only by rehabilitating a version of old colonialist arguments that John Yoo had invoked in 2001 to lift otherwise binding legal constraints when it came to "failed states." Worse, the enlargement of the war on terror through targeted killings, and its extension in space or time, was not singled out for public scrutiny. Instead, there were debates around Obama's killing of one American, and later whether too many civilians were caught up in the fracas.

Anwar al-Awlaki was a U.S. citizen with constitutional and other protections that other terrorists did not enjoy. After a drone executed the radical cleric in Yemen on September 30, 2011, and another killed his teenage son two weeks later, scrutiny peaked—

not just on the left but on the libertarian right, thanks to the activism of Senator Rand Paul of Kentucky. Barron had written a memo authorizing the killing, which leaked shortly after al-Awlaki's death (with a longer revision disclosed in 2014), and there was a stir. What didn't occur was a debate around the circumvention of the international legal prohibition on the practice of targeted killing even when the targets were not American and even when no civilians died.

If "self-defense" against terrorists was legal at all before September 11, it was clear that the United Nations Charter at least required each act to respond to imminent or ongoing armed attack, as well as to meet standards of necessity and proportionality. In effect, however, Americans invoked and stretched international law for the sake of an end run around the domestic assassination ban, as one participant recalled: "Activities that before 9/11 we would have said were assassination—now we are simply exercising our sovereign right of self-defense." Back in Berkeley (where he still teaches) and under a cloud, Yoo gamely insisted that, since the war on terror was a war, killing enemies anywhere could not possibly count as assassination or murder. Not only Bush but Obama, too, adopted that argument to little pushback.

But the appearance of continuation of Bush's policies went even deeper, amusing those who had followed earlier disputes, except when they were appalled by the consequences. Debates always raged around what counted as an "imminent" attack, of course, but the world had reacted with horror when Bush's National Security Strategy in 2002 had forthrightly claimed the need to engage in preemptive self-defense without any imminent threat. It was a claim that also figured in Yoo's justification of the Iraq War, though the United States never cited it at the United Nations itself. In a parody of having their cake and eating it, too, Obama's lawyers invoked the "elongated imminence" of threats they said justified force, which skeptics regarded as a deadly if laughable oxymoron. Not only was targeted killing allowed in self-defense, but also Obama asserted the legality of doing it preemptively, avoiding the word only to embrace the thing.

Then there was the extraordinary stretch of the law to cover new terrorist groups, which went along with the expansion of Obama's war to new places. Domestic law posed little barrier to targeted killing itself, at least for non-Americans, because in its Authorization for the Use of Military Force, Congress had allowed armed force to be used against any "persons" connected to the September 11 attacks. But it became a burning question whether a morphing Al-Qaeda and new groups (including copycats that claimed its prestigious name) were close enough to those involved in September 11 to earn legalized death. The notion of "associated forces" of Al-Qaeda allowed wider strikes. It had obscure origins in the Bush era but came into its own in the Obama years, after his lawyers adopted it in the landmark March 2009 legal brief. It was applied to groups such as the Islamist al-Shabaab outfit in Somalia with few or no ties to Al-Qaeda and to individuals in virtue of their membership in this and other far-flung outfits.

But however well it worked to ensure the domestic legality of the war's expansion, the entire scheme was unknown to modern international law. Even if the United States could defend itself against terrorists, there was still the need to show that new players in the war on terror posed a big enough threat of force (an imminent one, moreover). Saying they were part of Al-Qaeda allowed Obama's lawyers to skip this step. "The United States takes the legal position that—in accordance with international law—we have the authority to take action against al-Qa'ida and its associated forces without doing a separate self-defense analysis each time," Brennan remarked in his 2011 speech, flashing an astonishing license to kill. In the spirit of the March 2009 brief, what began as a rationale for detention off hot battlefields became a justification for killing. Many of the individuals and groups in question had never struck at the United States, and the threat they posed was debatable. They died anyway.

Perhaps the most remarkable violation of the rules meant to

keep war from breaking out involved the Islamic State (ISIS), which exploded in prominence in 2014 amid the disorder of western Iraq and ultimately extended the territory it controlled deep into Syria. After its beheading of captives went viral on social media, Obama first downplayed ISIS as the "junior varsity" team, unworthy of fear or rage. Before long, he turned to pursue it intensively, in what evolved into a conventional war with a very hot battlefield. ISIS did not exist in 2001 when Congress authorized war. And Al-Qaeda and ISIS were foes by the time Obama moved against it. To satisfy themselves, Obama's lawyers deemed ISIS to be Osama bin Laden's "true inheritor" in order to avoid congressional sign-off on Operation Inherent Resolve, which started in 2014.

Even more troublingly, the United States began to bomb ISIS (as well as another Al-Qaeda offshoot called the Khorasan group) on Syrian territory that year. For crossing another border on the map in the name of self-defense, the administration required a rationale under international law—one it made up from scratch. In its required explanation to the Security Council, Samantha Power, now Obama's charismatic and passionate ambassador to the United Nations, invoked a debatable argument. Self-defense, she explained, allows for attacking nonstate actors even when the state from which they operate is not connected to or responsible for its activities, so long as it is "unwilling or unable" to control them.

There was little to support America's creative doctrine. Its defenders were not above citing radioactive precedents once thought to epitomize transgression, such as the U.S. incursion into Cambodia to reach Viet Cong "sanctuaries"—an incursion that nearly earned President Richard Nixon an impeachment article. The doctrine was later canonized in some ad hoc principles and given flimsy substantiation in an academic piece by a former government lawyer. But few lawyers outside the United States and its allies accepted the permissive argument. It did not appear to matter.

There were legal arguments for each of the steps Obama took, their credibility differing from case to case. Taken together, however, they blessed an expanding war with unpredictable consequences. Nor was the belligerent legerdemain confined to counterterrorism, in spite of Obama's opening to Cuba after decades of tension and deal with Iran in hopes of keeping it from becoming a nuclear power. In 2011, the United States commenced a United Nations–authorized humanitarian intervention in Libya but transformed it into an illegal regime change, with deplorable consequences for that country. The Libya operation depended on an essentially unlimited rationale for presidential war that the attorneys provided. After coming out as Nobel Peace Prize warrior on principle, by the end of his time in office Obama had been true to his word.

IF SO LITTLE OF THIS REGISTERED IN THE MAINSTREAM OF U.S. public debate, it was because the Obama administration responded to the bad optics of continuity with Bush and the questionable legality of wars it perpetuated or started by playing up the humanity of the fighting.

In the eyes of its critics, the administration's efforts to fight humanely were inadequate and quasi-legal at best. Still, it was clear that American policymakers—including in the military—cared about the humanity of their war. Their response affected how it was conceived and conducted, and also how it was legitimated.

The administration's March 2009 brief on detention once again set the framework, declaring that (for detainees, as later for drone strikes) the war was a "non-international armed conflict" under the Geneva Conventions scheme. For detainees, this reaffirmed the Supreme Court's decision in *Hamdan v. Rumsfeld* (2006) that at the very least the minimal standards of Common Article 3 of the treaty applied. The trouble was that Common Article 3 says nothing about targeting. The Geneva additional protocol of 1977 for non-international armed conflicts had never been controversial in U.S. politics (compared with its sister treaty on international armed conflict). But it had never been ratified either, creating a legal environment in which Americans could decide what parts of the law they liked. What rules would apply from the sky and in the Special Forces' work off battlefields would be whatever rules the government decided to impose.

In the early years of targeted killing, calls for transparency by activists coexisted with growing evidence of civilian death that contradicted assurances by the United States that no collateral damage was occurring. To their credit, early skeptics, such as the United Nations expert Philip Alston, did not confine their demands for information to the problem of excessive civilian death. They insisted as well on clarity about how the practice could overcome the hurdles of international law governing the use of force. Even then, the lion's share of the early critiques of targeted killing concerned how the humane standards of the laws of war applied. This focus anticipated the prime debate of the later Obama administration, which was whether too many innocent people were dying, not whether the interventions themselves were legal, where American force could go, and how long it could stay.

For the year starting in summer 2011, the drone program began to receive more intense scrutiny in the press. The Obama administration would lift secrecy partially and strategically over the period that followed. By doing so, it normalized targeted killing—not hard to do given the enthusiasm for the death of Osama bin Laden in Pakistan on May 2, 2011, in a dramatic commando raid. At the same time, it set out to demonstratively minimize collateral harm. What if the alternative to targeted killing was indiscriminate killing, and what if the alternative to the virtue of drones was the vice of much-less-humane wars like Iraq and Vietnam—or the whole history of warfare? It was a no-brainer.

Absurdly, early statements for public consumption claimed that *no* collateral damage was being inflicted, which outside reporting easily contradicted. "We're exceptionally precise and surgical," Brennan enthused in an appearance in June 2011, blessing a program that was not yet public. "We do not take such action that might put those innocent men, women, and children in danger. In fact, I can say [of] the types of operations that the U.S. has been involved in in the counterterrorism realm that nearly for the past year there hasn't been a single collateral death because of the exceptional proficiency and precision of the capabilities we've been able to develop."

That was far from the truth. Obama himself had been so upset by excesses in the new incursion he ordered into Yemen that he stopped the drone attacks there for a year before the al-Awlaki strike. Most embarrassing was word of the unsavory practice of "signature strikes." These targeted males of fighting age in a given area without certainty that they were individually terrorists, let alone threatening ones. It was a presumption reminiscent of the Vietnam-era practice of declaring "free-strike" zones in which anyone remaining was presumptively an enemy, though no comparable fiesta of killing resulted. As the war wore on, administration estimates of civilian casualties were raised, even as outside monitors reached much higher totals.

Obama clearly believed that, properly humanized and regulated, the game was worth the candle. He made some attempts to pry the drone war from the CIA, and the Department of Defense's Joint Special Operations Command took a bigger role. As he ran for reelection in 2012, aware that someone else could inherit his handiwork, Obama prompted a process to codify drone policy. He even told Jon Stewart on an episode of *The Daily Show* two weeks before winning that he wanted a "legal architecture" to make sure that "not only am I reined in but any president's reined in." And after winning, he gave his speech at the National Defense University at Fort McNair—the one Medea Benjamin so rudely interrupted in 2013—divulging that he had issued an Executive Order a year earlier clarifying the humane controls his administration placed on targeted killing.

This "Presidential Policy Guidance" was an essential document. Where the March 2009 legal brief signaled war without limits in time or space, the PPG (as it was known) belatedly promised that it was to be humanely conducted. Written in 2012, the document was only publicly released two years later, when it drew some criticism. It mixed its own brew of what the Harvard international lawyer Naz

Modirzadeh cuttingly called "legal-ish" standards. The guidance document promised that outside areas of active hostilities, and "absent extraordinary circumstances," no killing would occur unless capture was "infeasible" and there was a "near certainty" that no one other than the terrorists would suffer. And where Bush had given the CIA blanket authority to strike anywhere, Obama acted punctiliously. He met weekly to pore over "kill lists" that he personally vetted, and he formally committed to doing so in the guidance document.

The "near certainty" that an intervention would harm only terrorists imposed a standard higher than the law required, since in armed conflict the rules prohibit only disproportionate collateral damage and death. At the same time, it was less than what the human rights law of policing demanded: capturing and even inviting surrender of quarries, except when killing is the only choice. Leaving aside the worry that the medium standard the administration adopted wasn't binding law—and as "policy" could be ditched when a new president came in—Modirzadeh issued a worrisome complaint. The optics of near perfect humanity, she suggested, were "being used to give an international law-like gloss" to "an approach that most allies see as violating" other parts of international law, most of all the rules controlling force. "The authors knew that they were writing a policy for something they anticipated would be criticized for being unlawful," she added, "so they threw in a lot of nice concepts." The stylishness of a crime did not make it less of one, however, any more than it would make sense to praise a robber who straightened the picture on the wall after robbing the safe.

The lawyer Martin Lederman, a former Obama official who had co-authored Barron's memos, took umbrage. How could anyone, he wondered, have the effrontery to complain about the attempt to humanize the war? Brutal war was worse than humane war—right? Lederman did not confront whether humanization could work as a spoonful of sugar intended to help the medicine of endless war go down. To explain the involvement of less-partisan lawyers, Modirzadeh offered a credible reason for the dubious compromise: the point of making war humane was not so much to manage appearances as to massage the conscience. "The Obama administration lawyers needed to justify doing something that probably wasn't allowed under binding international law (not a new problem, but a troubling one for these particular lawyers)," she commented. While in fact committing to a globalized counterterror war that "reeked" of the stench of the prior administration's lawlessness, they "said they would only actually unleash the US's mighty lethal force under a very complex and opaque set of legal-sounding requirements." By undoing limits on continuing or expanding war while imposing them on fighting, they were the good guys.

Both sides in the exchange were right. What drove the elaboration of humane war under the Obama administration was a desire to be good and a desire to mask evil. But one of the insidious functions of the humanization of endless war was to prompt activists to demand *even more humane war* than the good guys were willing to offer. Some critics, especially non-Americans starting with Alston, brought international human rights standards to bear on the war, which could be seen as an ambitious or bold move. Obama offered something partway down a continuum between war and policing. Why not go all the way, these critics reasoned? If war was going to occur off battlefields and without time limit, so the impulse went, it really ought to resemble the permanent institution of policing with its far more stringent rules on killing, only now on a global scale.

The risk in this argument was considerable. In order to implore maximum humanization, it conceded that illegal war would be increasingly endless and everywhere. Still, it was remarkable that Obama's lawyers went as far as they did. By giving greater protection under their homemade set of rules than the law of war required (especially to any civilian nearby the target), they channeled the spirit of human rights law as cosmetic prettification. Noble in conception, the treatment of endless war as a permanent regime with rights accruing to civilians—and perhaps to combatants, too, in some distant millennium if their capture was ever deemed feasible—provided cover and legitimation. As Modirzadeh suggested, it also salved the conscience. For some insiders, the extension and expansion of intervention could receive ethical clearance through making it more humane. For outsiders, the question remained: Did the humanization of so nightmarish a practice as endless global war make it better or worse?

When the campaign against ISIS began in 2013, the administration clarified that the Presidential Policy Guidance didn't apply, and the less-stringent rules for civilian protection applicable to "areas of active hostilities" governed instead. Rather than requiring confidence that no civilians would die, U.S. forces worked in this phase of the war—as they had long done in Afghanistan and Iraq—within the military's evolving understanding of how much collateral harm was too much. In the new tradition of "operational law," military lawyers closely advised commanders and policymakers on targeting. And now the Pentagon applied innovative methodologies of estimating civilian death before strikes, and institutionalized a "non-combatant casualty cut-off value" that allowed only a certain number of people in harm's way to be predicted to die before strikes required higher authority. It was an attempt to manage optics and prevent blowback, as well as to steer clear of the illegally disproportionate collateral harm that international law forbids. Understandably, debate raged about whether such institutionalized metrics for controlled death were humane enough, or humane at all.

With rare exceptions—such as a lonely Michael Ratner of the Center for Constitutional Rights—activists in movements and nongovernmental organizations omitted the expanding war itself from their concerns. But Ratner himself heatedly condemned the drone war as illegal per se. "I do not expect miracles from one man on top of a huge national security establishment that is hard to buck," Ratner conceded. Unfortunately, Obama's presidency had proved far worse. "Disaster," in fact. "It's a continuation of the Bush policies, and in some cases, the deepening of those policies."

Mainstream advocates failed to join Ratner. There was little effort to use denunciations of inhumanity to advance an antiwar politics. It wasn't just Human Rights Watch, which continued to monitor Obama's wars for affronts to humanity without condemning the wars themselves. New groups teemed. In 2003, a young activist from Lakeport, California, Maria Ruzicka, founded the Center for Innocent Civilians in Conflict. She was tragically killed before her thirtieth birthday in a suicide car bombing near the Baghdad airport in 2005. The group continued her work as the war on terror became cleaner in conception and execution, insisting the results were still too dirty.

But as a Democrat, Obama more easily escaped opprobrium or even scrutiny. Lawyers for the cause saw too many suffering victims needing immediate help, and no recourse for systemic change. Elite professionals in the leading nongovernmental organizations such as Human Rights Watch, along with law school human rights clinics, assigned themselves the narrower remit of monitoring abuses of captives and civilians. Their work was necessary and stalwart. A torrent of critical journalism and human rights reports dramatized the hell and terror of living under the drones and identified a syndrome of Pentagon undercounting of those who died in conventional and unconventional wars.

There was only one problem with the activist emphasis: many of the forces in government that were prone to downplay harm shared the activists' goal of increasingly humane war. During the Obama years, with decades of self-humanization behind it, the military could boast that "Americans are proud that their armed forces fight with professionalism and humanity," with air power leading the way—though there was always room to improve and "chase success." Humanitarian and military lawyers bickered around how much wartime humanity was going to be enough. They tacitly agreed not to fight over the war. As the critics of the activist compromise had warned long ago, the campaign to seek more humane war did not challenge the enterprise. That compromise could even usher belligerency toward an outcome no one had anticipated: a new form of nonviolent control.

AS HIS EPIC ENCOUNTER WITH MEDEA BENJAMIN IN 2013 PROVED, Obama himself hoped to stand for humanizing the war from the top. Benjamin urged him to defend or relinquish that standing. What made the moment exceptional was the spectacle of the activist for peace demanding even more humane conflict from a leader certain he was bringing it about. He, in turn, willingly pondered more forthrightly than most activists the evil of the very endless war his policies crystallized and entrenched. For he knew that inhumanity wasn't its biggest drawback.

If Benjamin's strategy to end America's wars was to play up their inhumanity, it also gifted Obama pat responses. When she interrupted the president, she began by singling out the continuing horrors of Guantánamo, even as the United States strove to present the prison as a more and more humane site. "There are 102 people on a hunger strike," she noted correctly. "You're our commander-in-chief," she interrupted again, "you can close Guantánamo Bay." Only then, seconds before her removal, did Benjamin turn to drones, indicting signature strikes.

Benjamin intuited that drones without footprints were a sequel to the heavy-footprint wars of the Bush years. The technology was chosen for its difficulty to monitor but also its allegedly more humane precision. But she insisted that diplomacy was a better alternative to all forms of war: "I think it's time to really reflect on the paths not chosen and those paths not chosen include policing instead of a military focus," she remarked at one point. "And focusing on the muscle that has been so deteriorated in the last ten years and that's diplomacy."

Obama countered in his speech that Congress wouldn't let him close Guantánamo. And when it came to the hard-core terrorists who would require interdiction, it was essential that a regime of humanity had been achieved. The death of Osama bin Laden thanks to the Special Forces had come with modest collateral damage to noncombatants (one of his wives died alongside his twenty-three-year-old son and two others). It achieved superior outcomes compared with a quickly evolving if still imperfect technique of bombs from the sky. Yet the raid had required "meticulous planning" and "some luck," Obama observed, and that wasn't always possible. Drones served when the Special Forces could not and vice versa.

Benjamin explained in an interview that she was moved to scream during the solemn National Defense University address when Obama claimed that his administration killed America's enemies only when it could not capture them. "Despite our strong preference for the detention and prosecution of terrorists," Obama explained, "sometimes this approach is foreclosed." Benjamin knew that was false. The preference was weak to the point of nonexistence, and "sometimes" had come to mean "always": capture was never deemed "feasible" in practice because of the risk of American casualties. But Obama was sure that either armed drones or the Special Forces, or both in tandem, easily qualified as more ethical than the warfare of the past.

"Conventional airpower or missiles are far less precise than drones, and are likely to cause more civilian casualties and more local outrage," Obama argued. "And invasions of these territories lead us to be viewed as occupying armies, unleash a torrent of unintended consequences, are difficult to contain, result in large numbers of civilian casualties and ultimately empower those who thrive on violent conflict." It wasn't that he didn't care about collateral damage and especially civilian losses, deaths that "will haunt us as long as we live," Obama noted. But "doing nothing is not an option." There were fine points to debate about how to regulate humane war, and what existing international law required, but it was obvious that humane war itself was the only intelligent option. If it verged on globalized policing, then so much the better. For Obama, reservations about any residual inhumanity in effect demanded not the end of America's wars but that he push them further toward something he had long promised they were already becoming.

Yet there were signs at Fort McNair that Obama, reflective to his core, was dissatisfied with his own answers. After Benjamin's unceremonious removal by military police and the Secret Service, he dwelled on his misgivings. Given to observing that terrorism caused fewer American deaths than car accidents or falls in the bathtub, he occasionally had to be badgered by advisors into choices commensurate with popular fear. He worried, too, that counterterrorist priorities "swamped" his other foreign policy aspirations. With his trademark calm and intellectualism, Obama openly wondered whether the strides toward humane war he himself demanded could come at a price.

"The voice of that woman is worth paying attention to," Obama meditated off-script, surprising his audience. "Obviously I do not agree with much of what she said, and obviously she wasn't listening to me in much of what I said. But these are tough issues, and the suggestion that we can gloss over them is wrong." Obama affirmed clearly that his policies for targeting killings were legal, under domestic and international standards. Yet he intuited that endless war, however humane, could still be a mistake. The whole enterprise required a second look, in spite of its morality and success in his mind. "Neither I, nor any president, can promise the total defeat of terror," he ruminated. "For all the focus on the use of force," he added, "force alone cannot make us safe. We cannot use force everywhere that a radical ideology takes root; and in the absence of a strategy that reduces the wellspring of extremism, a perpetual war—through drones or Special Forces or troop deployments—will prove self-defeating, and alter our country in troubling ways." He even concluded that "this war, like all wars, must end."

Obama was his own best critic. It was hard to know whether he actually cared about the imperative of peace, as opposed to wanting part of his audience to think he did. "The Obama administration has never been able to embrace the framework of its liberal critics, except in certain vague terms that amount to statements of aspiration and values affinity," two conservative defenders of the policies put it. "This war, like all wars, must end, it agrees—even as it prosecutes the war further." It was extraordinary, all the same, that Obama voiced the fear of endless war as he did.

Authentic or not, Obama's statement reflected growing perceptions that a dreadful error had been made at the start of the war he inherited, or somewhere along the way on his own watch. A failure to undo it could lead to unanticipated results. "Since World War Two," the inveterate pragmatist explained to graduating West Point cadets the following spring, "some of our most costly mistakes came not from our restraint, but from our willingness to rush into military adventures without thinking through the consequences." Nor were the costs merely for victims far away.

Unfortunately, the brief moment in which the idea of ending war surfaced as a policy aspiration fit poorly with the main purpose of Obama's address, which was to launch and laud a durable framework for humane operations. And Obama's honorable appeal for a peace was almost immediately overtaken by the rise of ISIS, which liquidated caution for good. Someone very different—a rough beast slouching toward the presidency—would have to voice skepticism about endless war instead.

THE BALLAD OF HAROLD KOH, OBAMA'S LEAD INTERNATIONAL LAWYER in his decisive early years in power, was surely the most piercing and tragic song about the humanization of war. It was an increasingly discordant melody that began with the dulcet promise of a better world, even as its darker finale sounded the harsh tones of a still violent one.

Koh, born in the Boston area in 1954, was deeply loyal to the memory of his father, a South Korean textile merchant's son from Cheju Island off the southern tip of the peninsula. Koh's father connected his hopes for democracy at home to rules in the world, excelling in his studies and becoming a diplomat and international lawyer. The elder

Koh protested against his country's dictatorial U.S. client, Syngman Rhee, for allowing anticommunism to justify the trampling of domestic and foreign rules. The utopia of liberal democracy in a world under law appealed to the elder Koh, and the younger one considered his father "my first, last, and only teacher."

After finishing his education in the United States, the elder Koh worked for a year as the number two in South Korea's embassy in Washington, in a brief window of liberal democracy between Rhee's fall and a military coup in 1961. He watched many of his former colleagues serve a new autocratic regime. "Many people profess to care about the rule of law, but they're weak-willed and when push comes to shove, they don't live their commitments," the son remembered his father teaching him about the hard questions people face and the right answers they must always give. Equally if not more important, however, the elder Koh, who Americanized (while never seeking citizenship) and took the name Arnold, taught the "goodness" and "reach" of his adopted country's power.

Part of the reason was the opportunity it extended to his family. In exile, Koh and his wife became the first Asian Americans to teach at Yale Law School. Years later, his son, after college and law school at Harvard, led that school as dean before agreeing to work for Obama in summer 2009. It was plain to Koh—as it had been to his father—that the United States played a beneficent role in the world, not as another empire but instead as a "remarkable country," fostering "a reverence for international law and commitment to human rights within its newest immigrants."

Koh's earlier career had involved stints in the Departments of Justice and State. But he was best known for his liberal foreign affairs views. He insisted on Congress's role rather than presidential unilateralism—and wrote a brief for one of Ratner's failed suits to enforce the War Powers Resolution. Koh was also associated with the fledgling field of international human rights law. His student John Yoo took from the Korean War a different lesson: that U.S. presidents need to define the law by acting on their own. Yoo recalled that he challenged his teacher by arguing that his restrictive views would have forbidden intervention to save their ancestral nation. "How could this guy rather live in a Communist rice paddy?" Yoo remembered thinking. Koh shot back: "Well, that's the price of obeying the Constitution."

Koh's track record made him a controversial appointment by Obama, especially since Republicans were ready to cite his many public statements and writings that denounced the transgressions Yoo had insisted were legal. Koh had come out against military commissions right away and passionately inveighed against torture when it was revealed. And Koh had not only warned against the likely outcomes of going into Iraq in 2003 but also recommended that the United States get United Nations authorization if it did so, and he condemned the intervention as illegal after the fact. Mocking Bush's claim in his second inaugural address to fight an axis of evil, Koh derided him as "torturer-in-chief" and described the wayward country under him as part of an "axis of disobedience."

After his late nomination by Obama in March 2009, Koh had to wade through a grueling confirmation battle to become the State Department's legal advisor. But even in these early days, David Barron contacted him in the frantic midst of finalizing the foundational war-on-terror brief, and Koh appreciated that the arguments affirmed that the president could never transgress the humane standards of the international laws of war. It was already clear there would be no policy of torture under the new administration. But it was also clear that humane detention policies would compensate for extreme assertions about the conflict's possible length—and, worse, the underlying premise was that a far-flung war without fronts against terrorists was legal in the first place.

By turns jolly and pugnacious, with a slight limp due to a childhood bout of polio, Koh could turn into an aggressive bulldog when defending his deepest beliefs. And once in office, he was not above confrontation as he tried to roll back the decision that had already been made to hold the remnant of Guantánamo prisoners indefinitely without charge. In the early months, he also pushed back at the concept that there could be deterritorialized war off battlefields, cannily playing to the lawyerly Obama's own misgivings about signing on to Bush's endless war. "You never know who is going to be president four years from now," the president mused in one White House meeting. "I have to think about how Mitt Romney would use that power." "If your name is on it," Koh replied, "you'll own it."

Obama already owned it. The decisive moment came for Koh personally in September 2009. After a sleepless night rethinking a meeting where the terrorist Saleh Ali Saleh Nabhan was marked for death in Somalia, and eliminated before morning by U.S. Navy SEALs, Koh pondered the difficulties of distinguishing between lawful and unlawful targeted killings. He hadn't prepared in his career for marking young people for death but for teaching them law. "How did I go from being a law professor to someone involved in killing?" he wondered to himself. Yet counterterrorism raised novel legal questions old rules did not cover, and his client—Barack Obama—deserved good-faith answers to them, not moralistic carping from armchair critics outside government. Koh considered at least some eliminations valid, and the challenge was isolating them from doubtful cases. And he learned, through hours spent reading classified intelligence, just how dangerous the enemies plotting to kill Americans really were.

Even after moving to a more permissive stance than many in his former communities (and certainly his old ally Ratner) would tolerate, Koh tangled with his opposite number at the Pentagon, the more flexible Jeh Johnson, over limits. They disagreed especially over how much connection adversaries had to have to Al-Qaeda, and how high-ranking they had to be, to count as associated forces and therefore legally targetable. Koh congratulated Johnson for helping deny permission to the military to kill lower-ranking Somali terrorists, though

Johnson later reversed course under pressure. The program was becoming systemic, and Koh could not control forever who was killed under it.

It was Koh's moral commitment that led him to volunteer to articulate and defend the entire policy to the world, at first in nonspecific terms that would not reveal details of the targeted killings operations, still ostensibly secret. He evidently hoped his public explanation would provide an occasion for institutionalizing strict limits. In March 2010, in a heavily vetted speech, Koh ascended the dais at the meetings of the American Society of International Law in Washington, D.C., and assured the audience that America's self-defense was within legal bounds in its fighting. "Targeting practices, including legal operations conducted with the use of unmanned aerial vehicles, comply with all applicable law," he remarked, "including the laws of war."

In the conversation after the speech, the Notre Dame international law professor Mary Ellen O'Connell asked Koh how he could sign on to the concept of a global battlefield, with its degradation of the rules of using force, no matter the respect for the humanity of the fight. In reply, Koh denied that he had gone that far. In a miniature version of the president's encounter with Medea Benjamin the next year, Koh sidestepped one of the few American international lawyers who consistently kept her focus through the Bush and Obama years on when and whether states can fight, not merely how. "A global war on terror by any other name would smell as bad," O'Connell reflected to herself in the aftermath.

Presenting himself as the "conscience for the U.S. government with regard to international law," Koh insisted in his speech that his reputation as a human rights activist required that he uphold a public legal framework for counterterrorism that Bush had left unwritten. Citing an old professor, he explained: "There's nothing wrong with a lawyer holding the United States to its own best standards and principles." This claim masked the reality that Koh had openly embraced the new law of force in self-defense that Bush and Obama invented across these years: that across an arc of the earth and for an indefinite period, states could attack suspected terrorists without violating the United Nations Charter (or America's domestic assassination ban, for that matter). In compensation, Koh promised, such killing would take place humanely, targeting only combatants and avoiding civilian harm.

Given the source, there may have been no more graphic example of how expansion of force and its humanization worked in nefarious tandem. If Obama's normalization of endless war had been Nixon going to China, the human rights activist Koh's justification of targeted killing was seen similarly. People in the CIA and the military called him "Killer Koh" out of earshot, while remote operators reportedly toyed with making T-shirts reading: "Drones: If they're good enough for Harold Koh, they're good enough for me."

If Koh stuck to his stance, it might have been because he retained an intuition that in a world of despots, his country needed to reserve the right to do good *in spite* of apparent United Nations Charter rules. A longtime supporter of humanitarian intervention, Koh was deeply influenced by the notion that the United States could and should wield an altruistic "smart power." It was an approach pioneered by the Democratic Party innovator Richard Holbrooke after the McGovernite disaster, and also something like Hillary Clinton's official framework as secretary of state (as Koh noted in his Washington address). Though the United States had once organized the Nuremberg trials to stigmatize aggression, Koh opposed criminalizing it now for fear it would keep a benevolent power like the United States from stopping atrocity.

When the humanitarian intervention in Libya transitioned into regime change, Koh offered no public explanation of the propriety under international law. But he was accused of hypocrisy when he helped the Obama administration do an end run around the domestic War Powers Resolution. He testified before Congress that the "hostilities" requiring congressional sign-off after sixty days did not include bombing, especially at low-enough levels. After all, he said, the word "hostilities" was "an ambiguous term of art."

Koh worked on his own "legal-ish" standards for targeted killing and other things while in office, but he left before Obama gave his National Defense University speech and the Presidential Policy Guidance was set in stone. Still, anticipating Obama's own reflections on the dangers of endless war, Koh gave a talk at the Oxford Union just after his departure from government about the need to exit the era of belligerency, no matter how humane he had proposed to make it. "This conflict has come to feel like a Forever War: it has changed the nature of our foreign policy and consumed our new millennium," he forthrightly acknowledged. "It has made it hard to remember what the world was like before September 11."

Koh certainly didn't relinquish his sense that there were legal and moral justifications for Obama's version of the war on terror. He also argued that more transparency would prove how different Bush and his successor really were. As Obama would contend at the National Defense University, drones were humane if well governed. But Koh insisted that "it is still possible for President Obama to end the Forever War, piece by piece, during his second term." Now that Al-Qaeda was degraded, the end of the war was in sight, so long as the United States disengaged from Afghanistan and lawyers stopped agreeing that any new groups could count as part of the original foe. Alas, neither happened.

BEYOND THE COMPROMISES MADE BY ADVOCATES OUTSIDE GOVERNMENT and especially inside, the deepest blame for the perpetuation of endless war fell on Obama himself. He established a working relationship with a public that allowed itself to be convinced that his policies of endless and humane war, though not exactly what they had signed up for, were morally wholesome. This effect depended utterly on Obama's rhetorical genius. It worked through the first-person plural but also required the audience to accept that they shared in the compromises of humane war that politicians chose and lawyers crafted.

The exchange began by enveloping the listener in atonement for the moral transgression of inhumanity. Obama was often tasked for failing to hold perpetrators of torture under the prior regime accountable, in a decision he made in his earliest days in office. But to concentrate on this point misses his constant invitation to Americans to see that "we" had tortured and that "we" are not the kind of people who would ever do so again. "We did a whole lot of things that were right, but we tortured some folks," he said confessionally and disarmingly at a White House news conference in summer 2014. "We did some things that were contrary to our values," he continued, and "we have to, as a country, take responsibility for that."

Americans were children of darkness, too, when it came to inhumanity in the past. But they could still strive for the light, in the form of more humane war in the present and future. Over and over again, Obama's characteristic reaction to the inhumanity he was editing out of endless warfare became: "That's not us. That's not who we are." "The little clump of words about who we are as Americans pops out of the president's mouth so often it's easy to miss it," one observer noticed. That the formulation was negative rather than positive ruled out the occasional ditches into which Americans had fallen—out of character—and left the sense that it was their posture of upstanding virtue that really defined them. It was appropriate, Obama convinced his audience negatively, for counterterrorist engagements to continue or expand, once made consistent with America's exceptional humanity.

Torture was not us—but endless war is. Commenting on an obscure television program the day of the National Defense University speech, Ratner praised Medea Benjamin for her interruptions. Obama had referenced ending the war, Ratner acknowledged, but "he doesn't really give any way to end continuous warfare, because he never addresses the very reasons . . . as to why the U.S. is in continuous warfare. He doesn't talk about the fact that it's about U.S.

hegemony, domination, control." Ratner concluded: "Yes, that's who we are."

A few years later, however, it turned out that some of "us" were restive. Two days before the South Carolina Republican primary in February 2016, Donald Trump appeared with the CNN host Anderson Cooper onstage. Trump had lost in Iowa to Senator Ted Cruz of Texas but then won big in New Hampshire the day before he spoke. In this Bush-friendly, pro-military state, Trump did something almost unthinkable within the Republican mainstream of the time: he blasted the Iraq War as possibly the "worst decision" in U.S. history. "We have destabilized the Middle East," he went on, causing the rise of the Islamic State and conflicts in Libya and Syria.

He won South Carolina the next day by ten points and never looked back. In every presidential debate, Trump reiterated that he had opposed the Iraq War from the start—proof that voters could trust him as commander-in-chief and ignore the chorus of national security experts who deemed him unfit. "Strange as it may be to hear," reflected one Never Trump Republican, after his loathed enemy had ascended to the highest office in the land, "the current president of the United States—a hero of the Republican party and the conservative movement—has the same view of the Bush administration and the Iraq War as the hard Left. As Code Pink, for example."

In the general election campaign against Hillary Clinton in 2016, it was pointed out repeatedly that Trump had not, in fact, opposed the Iraq War—just as routinely as he insisted he had done so. And while Clinton acknowledged her error in voting to authorize the war, she brushed off the subject, as if the lesson to be learned was never again to let Bush invade Iraq in 2003. It fell to Trump to recognize the war as a disaster that warranted meaningful change in American national security. The hashtag #EndEndlessWar originated in 2014 from grassroots activism among progressives around the annual congressional ritual of renewing war funding. Two years later, the shock was that the mainstream of both parties, and Clinton not least, had left Trump an opening to convince millions of Americans that he was the candidate more worthy of the hashtag.

By the starkest of contrasts, he left no doubt about his opinion of humane war. Trump's statements involved worse than callous disregard for suffering in conflict; he actively praised brutality. In his most extraordinary defense of returning to the open racism of U.S. foreign policy of the past, he said that nonwhite people from "shithole countries" counted for less, an assumption many had assumed was publicly quarantined. In power, Trump continued to regard the taboo around torture that so many had spent so much energy constructing as if it simply didn't apply to him—like so many other "norms" his enemies treated as nonnegotiable even when they were, like this one, of recent date. On the campaign trail, Trump had scandalously reported that torture works. He did so again as president when Gina Haspel's nomination to lead the CIA was briefly in jeopardy, on account of her involvement with Bush-era tactics. In 2017, a draft executive order leaked, proposing to reopen black sites abroad, where it was feared torture would begin again.

But a funny thing happened on the way to the dismaying restoration of brutal war that Trump personally favored. The executive order was never issued, in part because Secretary of Defense James Mattis found torture unconscionable. And Trump's proposals were met by the howls of leading Republicans, such as Senate Majority Leader Mitch McConnell. The CIA itself pushed back, reflecting a period of institutional self-correction parallel to the one the military had undergone after Vietnam—even if neither held anyone accountable for past crime. During the election campaign, the former CIA director Michael Hayden commented that if Trump wanted to reinstate waterboarding, "he better bring his own bucket." He didn't have one.

Less aggravating to the liberal public was the prospect that Trump would embrace a less-sanitary targeting philosophy. In his first year in office, Trump deleted the Presidential Policy Guidance, replacing it with a more permissive "Principles, Standards, and Procedures" document. Once again, the bark proved worse than the bite: Trump retained the general requirement that the prediction of any civilian death at all takes a targeted strike off the table. Even as he proved willing to pardon some accused American war criminals (once again to outrage from within the military and not only outside), Trump, to a remarkable and surprising extent, was locked into the humanity of war, too.

Was the same to be true of its endlessness? Could and would Trump follow through on the antiwar candidacy that, like so many of Obama's supporters eight years before, millions of his supporters (including military veterans) had somehow found credible? In office, not only did Trump promise to "end the endless wars" in his most famous presidential antic, a tweet; he also made the promise in one of his rare moments of solemnity. When he read a prepared text as his State of the Union address before Congress in 2019, Trump sounded very much like his predecessor at the National Defense University: "Great nations do not fight endless wars." If anything, he was more consistent in expressing that message.

Elected to make his nation great again, Trump ushered it into a new stage of ongoing decline. As he did so, he strove mightily to discontinue aspects of endless war—the Afghan part most notably—even as he intensified the war overall. Sometimes his attempts to withdraw forces provoked howls of rage across the political spectrum—and among his own servants, especially when he abandoned Kurdish allies by beginning a pullout from Syria in 2019. To a more divided reception, Trump bombed the Syrian government in retaliation for chemical attacks, advancing the dubious legal rationale that Obama had crafted and left behind before halting his own intervention at the last minute. By comparison, Trump's augmentation of the military budget (which he constantly bragged about), his escalation of the use of the Special Forces even beyond the high-water mark Obama reached, and his expansion of the drone empire with ever more strikes, encountered little bipartisan complaint. After all, it was just the policy of the prior two presidents, only more so.

Whatever history's judgment of the intrinsic merits of the war on terror, and the consequences for the world and for itself, the results left the country with a paradox it had not yet faced and had therefore done nothing to overcome. Through three presidents, the shambolic last one included, the United States could take strides to keep its wars humane. But it did so while entrenching its globalized militarism, as one antiwar candidate then another became an endless-war president.

Epilogue

ON JANUARY 3, 2020, AN AIRBUS 320 CARRYING QASSIM SOLEIMANI landed in Iraq. A popular Iranian general, Soleimani was also the master of regional proxy war. He was there to meet high-ranking officials in what was becoming Iran's client state, as U.S. influence waned. The morning did not turn out the way Soleimani expected.

Iraq was not an exception to American success elsewhere. Direct U.S. involvement in Afghanistan since September 11 had fared no better, as the once-ousted Taliban reassumed power over large stretches of the country and made the mountainous redoubt the grave of one more empire. A few weeks before Soleimani landed, *The Washington Post* had run "The Afghanistan Papers," a shattering exposure for our own time that recalled the revelations about the bungling and failure in Vietnam that Americans had read a half century before. "We didn't have the foggiest notion of what we were undertaking," said Douglas Lute, the army three-star general who oversaw the conflict from the White House during the administrations of George W. Bush and Barack Obama. The self-study that Daniel Ellsberg had leaked all those decades before had led to national soul-searching after a Supreme Court battle. By contrast, the news that the military considered its task in Afghanistan unwinnable from the earliest days after September 11 caused no public debate.

Richard Nixon's ouster led Congress to reassert its role in foreign affairs as well as to institutionalize fundamental checks on intelligence, though both reforms were reduced to minimal significance in the decades after. In our own time, the impeachments staged around Donald Trump did not bear on the war on terror. The truth was that Trump did not shatter norms when it came to the war on terror. He mainly aimed to take the policies of his predecessors further than they had, finalizing troop pullouts in unwinnable heavy-footprint wars while increasing America's light- and no-footprint presence worldwide, and striking boldly when he deemed it necessary for the purposes of global control.

That Soleimani had long been seen as the second-most-powerful man in Iran didn't exempt him from becoming a target of Trump's. On that January morning just outside the Baghdad airport, Soleimani's two-car convoy was struck by a Reaper drone. A successor to the Predators widely used in the prior two presidential administrations, and with a price tag of $64 million apiece, this fancy hardware hovered above its prey for ten minutes before firing its Hellfire missiles. Its airborne capacity allows operators to identify the target with certainty, and even glimpse his clothing, before the body wearing it is burned to a crisp on impact.

Interestingly, Soleimani's death caused a brief legal stir. Indeed, in the United States, a much more aggressive and larger crew of international lawyers than at any time since Vietnam attempted to raise consciousness about the importance of rules prohibiting force abroad. It happened in part because the killing seemed for a long moment to risk a frightening escalation, or even the possibility of war between nations. The trouble was that critics had little to go on because so many precedents for expansive war had already been set: earlier presidents had bestowed a gift of permission slips for intervention practically anywhere, and the gift kept on giving, though no one ever imagined that Trump would turn out to be its beneficiary.

Soleimani was the kind of high state official who had remained immune from U.S. targeting. The nearest precedent since World War II was Ronald Reagan's strike on the home of the Libyan leader Moammar Qaddafi in 1986, which no one admitted was an attempt to target the dictator personally. But there was much more continuity than novelty in Soleimani's killing, and the consensus of national security lawyers was that the law allowed for it. "That is our system," the former government lawyer and Harvard professor Jack Goldsmith noted on Twitter, with a faint tone of regret. In war, although it is a matter of life and death, the United States had long since descended into a syndrome in which "one person decides." He might have added: and in which one country does.

Along the way, acts of one-off killing such as this had been normalized in U.S. policy and deemed legal and right. And even though the U.S. strike took place on the territory of a state that had not consented to Soleimani's killing, permissive doctrines had already been forged to cover that eventuality. Trump benefited from the fact that no civilians died in the attack, which had been given the green light only after verification—even under Trump—that the innocent and uninvolved were out of harm's way. And, by the time days later that Trump's lawyers issued their theory of the strike's legality, public attention had moved on.

Still, far beyond the minor grumbling of the late Obama years, the genuine national debate around Trump's aggressive move was revealing. It was striking that American security and its limits were debated in terms of international law. Learned interpretations of concepts such as "imminence" graced the news and op-ed pages of national publications, something that had never happened earlier during the war on terror when prior administrations reduced to meaninglessness the requirement that self-defense requires a looming threat. Similarly, invocation of the domestic law's prohibition of "assassination" stretched back to revelations of U.S. Cold War malfeasance. Such talk, too, had never really happened due to prior drone activity, except when a U.S. citizen had been terminated.

The debate was brief and evanescent. Yet it hinted that recovery from America's embrace of a growing syndrome might be possible. It mattered for the first time since Vietnam that the country's wars are lawless, even if they are now more humane. The aftermath of the Soleimani killing also proved, however, that when a country is caught in the depths of a syndrome, recovery can be very difficult to achieve. More bipartisan consensus crystallized than in previous decades that there actually were (or at least ought to be) limits in American war-making. In the aftermath, for the first time since Vietnam, the House and Senate passed a resolution limiting future interventions by the president, though not with enough votes to survive a veto. One reason for the resolution was that Trump's brazen act threatened major war. But it was hard not to conclude that the deepest reason for concern and denunciation this time was that the president who had ordered the hit was so far outside the mainstream.

The attack on the killing stigmatized the president, but only time will tell if it will lead to meaningful reform, especially now that Joe Biden's election victory has restored "normalcy." And it was equally significant that the debate over the legality and wisdom of the strike was nearly swamped by the horror and rage around Trump's dramatic talk and empty promise of bombing cultural sites in Iran in blatant violation of the 1954 and 1972 treaties protecting them. "We will follow the laws of armed conflict," Trump's defense secretary reassured an anxious world within days—without agreeing that the U.S. execution of Soleimani had broken the law forbidding use of force and risked another Middle Eastern quagmire.

FOR ALL ITS APPEAL AND IMPORTANCE, THE IDEA OF MORE HUMANE war can obscure the residual violence that it still involves. Around the world, brutal ground war is hardly a thing of the past. And even America's direct light- and no-footprint engagements today spill too much blood.

"War is represented as an unfortunate obligation thrust upon the exceptional nation, the United States, by a dysfunctional world which the United States has a salvationist responsibility to mend, albeit by force of arms," writes the anthropologist Hugh Gusterson, who has done extensive fieldwork in Waziristan, a poor, remote tribal region in Pakistan where U.S. drones have been deployed for more than a decade. Under current practices, elastic definitions of combatants combine with the undercounting of civilians killed by the explosions to sugarcoat the drone program's lethality and political volatility. The ways of life of those who survive, often traumatized, are rent to shreds in the process. Invocations of the care and precision of drone violence still abet or accompany too much violence, as the lure of "humanizing security" helps Americans to take the bait of war.

Horrified by any level of illicit death, Gusterson notes that the death toll in Waziristan has mounted into the thousands, even while the real evil faced by people there is the "living death" of "fear as a way of life." Increasingly, the fate of some foreign populations is not dying but living under drones or in fear that the Special Forces will stop by. Human rights activists have found that people who live in permanent fear are prey to the same sorts of responses caused by suffering from or witnessing outright violence, including classic symptoms of post-traumatic stress. After all, they live in a situation in which anyone can be targeted without notice and the constant risk of fatality or injury cannot be eliminated. What is most appalling, in this view, is a new "military humanism" that masks the same old death-dealing.

It is hard to argue with these conclusions, not merely in Afghanistan but across Syria, where in recent years the United States has complied with (its version of) the laws of armed conflict, razing a city in the midst of an internationalized civil war, as Americans debated whether they were too involved or uninvolved in the gory catastrophe. And this is not even to mention the charnel house of Yemen, in recent years the scene of a proxy war—led by Saudi Arabia, joined by Obama, and intensified by Trump—or the trade in U.S.-made arms that others use to kill and maim around the world.

The bitter truth, however, is that exposing America's illicit violence, and showing that humanity is just a cover for it, has not worked. The claim that the carnage is humane in form and legally contained by rules has provided it legitimacy. Ripping off the mask and revealing ongoing magnitude of violence by government actors has changed nothing. And without downplaying the residual violence of our wars, humane war is more than a mask: four thousand dead—on the high side of current civilian mortality estimates for Waziristan—is not four million or even four hundred or forty thousand. The degree of residual violence is lower than when Vietnamese rice growers faced America's intense bombardments in 1968, or when Algerian sheep herders got caught up in French counterinsurgency in 1958, or when Malayans suffered under similar treatment from the British in 1948, to say nothing of the genocidal brutality of centuries of earlier expansion and rule. European empires routinely touted the humanity of their ends, bringing "civilization" and "progress" to the world, while Americans—more regularly treating their country's global superintendence as glum necessity and unchosen evil—have transformed warfare by embracing the humanity of their means.

Our moral focus on the persistent violence of war, against civilians and detainees as well as even fighters in the field, surely still makes a great deal of sense. The same vigilance is required for domestic policing, as American events in 2020 proved again. The incidence of unacceptable American violence, abroad and at home, is too high to conclude otherwise. And yet the worst aspect of the coming of humane war may be this: the physical violence is not the most disturbing thing about it.

DURING THE YEARS OF ESCALATING DRONE WARFARE, THE PENTAGON began publishing "road maps" for an even newer approach to war. The final destination would be full automation, with less and less human involvement—except for the victims. Buzzing overhead but also self-driven on the ground, or skating the waves or patrolling underneath them, weapons that do not require human operators have become the fever dream of the future of war. And as the laws of war have struggled to keep up, the scary fact is that current principles augur a new stage of war: humane control with much less direct human control.

Decades ago, robotics specialists anticipated an "army of none," but it has become imaginable only with recent advances in computerization and miniaturization—and the pressure of America's war on terror. Autonomous weapons systems, after all, are the ultimate no-footprint weapon, promising to put military drone operators out of their jobs. And while experts in the technology have debated our algorithmic future in war, especially the stages of diminishing control, custodians of the laws of war have begun fighting over how the rules apply, and whether humanity needs new ones. "World War R" could exempt humans on both sides from combat—but somehow that does not seem likely, given the existence of great powers continuing to strive for more and more asymmetry and more and more immunity for their side, and more exposure and injury for the other.

In a very different tactic than what prevailed in the organization between the 1970s and the war on terror, Human Rights Watch has led the way in appealing for a ban on "killer robots." It has called for new law, not observance of old law, and demanded abolition, not palliation. In 2012, the group began a campaign that has drawn together a host of other nongovernmental organizations and (so far) thirty countries interested in stopping the new technology of war before it gets off the ground. Pakistan, where drones have flown the most missions and attacked with the most intensity, was the first to join, in 2013.

Along with other great powers, the United States has pushed back against the attempt—reminiscent of the earliest responses to the prospect of air war a century before—to regulate before the threat materializes. If our country doesn't act fast to explore the new weaponry and get in front, its representatives say, it will fall behind other states taking the low road—or a terrorist group doing so on its own. In 2017, a Group of Government Experts began meeting to develop standards for autonomous weapons systems. If properly designed, these systems will allow for more careful and caring war, such authorities insist. For sure, obedience to the requirement to avoid civilian harm can be programmed into robots; in future wars, they can gather on their own what human leadership needs to know before a strike is approved.

In spite of the possibility that machines will bring us even more humanity in war, the arguments of the new abolitionists are strong. The natural concern is that these new machines will become "slaughterbots." They will repeat the pattern of promising to be even more precise than clumsy prior tools of war, only to become even more grievously fatal than before, and to more innocent people. Either they will—like the airplane—kill on a more massive scale than before or they will—like the drone—allow discrimination of targets in some episodes but rain down more death through more operations. States spending billions in a new arms race for new technologies have rejected these concerns.

In time-honored fashion, great powers and other states in a position to benefit from the revolution in means of warfare have insisted that the alternative of banning robot war in advance is even less humane. Do humanitarians really want that outcome? Can they seriously argue for what may be more violence rather than less? And these states have agreed with alacrity that—while new law is not needed, and especially not a moratorium or prohibition—the existing "international humanitarian law" of war applies even when humans are no longer in the driver's seat or the drone operator's chair. For now, the talk in diplomatic circles is of norms of "appropriate standards of human judgment" or "meaningful human control" pending better understanding of what these autonomous machines can do—and how soon.

Just as with armed drones before, the short-term question on both sides of the debate is whether autonomous weapons systems will succeed or fail in bringing the utopia of humane war down to earth, advancing or retarding its likelihood. But the long-term question may well turn out to be the opposite—whether the dream is in fact a nightmare.

IN THE DAYS WHEN THEY WERE TAKING THEIR BIGGEST STEP ON THE path to humane war, Americans were apt to wonder if they were living in the best of times. Along all metrics, it was an ideal present, some said, with future progress as far as the eye could see, and looming threats more trivial than worrywarts believed. The *New York Times* columnist Nick Kristof ended every year by conceding that bad things had happened—but added that, beneath visible notice and beyond the distractions of bad headlines, the human condition improved with every collective trip around the sun. Steven Pinker, a psychologist from Canada teaching at Harvard University, argued that it was a new era of enlightenment and progress. He made the decline of war in particular and violence in general central to his case for prosecuting holdouts to optimism. But even before Trump's election led many toward despondency, and the recognition of enduring ills, it was clear that the best of times sometimes come together with the worst of times.

You can strive for peace, only to bring it through empire and endless war, a bitter lesson that Americans have had to learn in the last century. You can strive—after long decades of acceptable brutality—for more humane approaches to those wars but end up fighting more of them than you intended, even while believing or saying that their humanity makes them more tolerable. Blatant racism and massive death might no longer infect their conduct, even as the wars themselves presuppose an extraordinary ongoing hierarchy among nations. The importance of editing war crimes out of your wars should not excuse spurning your onetime commitment to peace—courting the risk that it will seem to have been delusional or rhetorical all along. The best incarnation of your nation's better angels, Barack Obama can calmly explain, as you nod with gratitude for the eloquence and reasonableness of the case he makes, why the trade-offs in expanding and extending a superpower's violence made sense once it was made more humane. But I worry that with better can also come worse, not because improvement is a lie but because there is no single arc to the moral universe that guarantees that progress comes without regress on other fronts. The one can even facilitate the other.

In your calculus, after all, you might have been wrong. The idea of humane war might have turned out to be less an ideal choice than an imperial excess and tragic mistake. Not only might you fail to reckon with its immediate legacy—all the war-making that occurs when your worse angels accede to the presidency. You also have not begun to come to grips with whether a global policing system burnished with your humane aspirations but under your nation's sole authority amounts to a humbling new form of permanent subjugation for others, as offensive to peace in its own way as your errant drones and sloppy Special Forces. Worst of all, as you daily set examples of more humane violence, is the possibility that others will visit on Americans themselves the same treatment, in the eternal process of the rise and fall of great powers. Improvement itself can be a recipe for new modes of abasing ourselves and dominating our fellow human beings—not diminishing inequality but reinventing its terms.

In his concern that advocates for more humane war could help make it endless for a public that tolerates it, Leo Tolstoy fixated on corporal wrongs and physical violence. Advocacy aimed at humane war, he contended, was no more ethically plausible than agitation for humane slavery, with daily episodes of torture replaced by everlasting—but kind and gentle—direction of labor and service. Audiences who accept endless war out of the belief that its humanity excuses them, the truculent moralist inveighed, were fooling themselves. They were no better than those who rest content with more humane techniques of animal slaughter, leaving them to carve their steaks and fricassee their chickens with eager gusto and in good conscience.

Tolstoy's arresting comparisons help explain how so much remaining violence is ignored by those who accept our wars and press for them to be free from civilian harm and captive mistreatment. But the analogies themselves risk ignoring the fact that sometimes domination and rule can take place nonviolently. In the current and future trajectory of humane conflict, it may turn out that the most ominous feature of America's evolving war is that it has begun to edit out physical violence—including the killing of combatants—to make war something new: a form of decreasingly violent policing.

Amazingly, what count as some of the most visionary proposals for regulating war actually pray for this outcome. With deterritorialized and endless war now the way of the world, indeed, perhaps the best reform is not to end it but to contain it, creating for abroad the kind of regulated security that's routine at home. In this spirit, it can sometimes seem the height of idealism to demand global policing: so humane a form of war that some might question whether it is even war anymore.

One group contends, for example, that the laws of war already accepted by states require the capture rather than killing of enemies when feasible (though, like most countries, the United States rejects this interpretation, insisting that soldiers are fair game for death now or later, from near or far, and without further ado). And a newfangled movement to defend the human right to life of soldiers themselves would mean that, as in lawful policing, combat could require not merely accepting but inviting surrender of foes. Soldiers' lives matter.

It is easy to imagine already how autonomous weapons systems might intersect with such calls to convert war into policing in the spirit of humane control. What if the new robots are not killers after all? What if, one day, they can algorithmically distinguish between the evil and the innocent, or even calculate mathematically how much collateral damage is too disproportionate to be legal? What if they can capture rather than kill adversaries? What if, after inviting surrender, these caring machines only terminate those who flee or resist, holding their quarry until spirited off for humane internment?

We are nowhere near that utopia of course. The brutal wars of the American past could return. But the main question is whether this utopia would be dystopian in a new fashion, since we have taken unprecedented steps with primitive tools to begin bringing it about. For all his interest in corporal violence, Tolstoy also knew that physical cruelty is not the worst thing we do, and pain is not the quintessence of war's evil. Suffering is a wrong, but a law and politics focused on eradicating or minimizing it could only take its rightful place in a broader project of challenging hierarchy in all its forms, including nonviolent ones. Though better than outrageous death and pain, humane policing is a depressing goal whether abroad or at home when it succeeds and not just when it fails—especially when conducted by the rich and powerful on the poor and weak.

You don't have to agree with Tolstoy that war is never for a good cause to conclude that it almost always is not. You certainly don't have to think, as he did, that state power can only take the form of violence or of an insidiously nonviolent form of subjugation, and is best abolished for that reason. The very freedom and justice that Tolstoy prized might even depend on such power or, in the direst straits, on war itself. Even if so, his worries about reforming violence certainly do pertain to the wars America has fought lately—and to the new version of military force it has, like no power in history, made imaginable for our common global future. A future of bloodless global discipline is a chilling thing, just as the alternative to killer police ought not to be the control and domination that leaves its victims alive and unscathed. You may conclude we need policing, not just locally but globally, but that commitment could never justify intensively policing some while immunizing others against any enforcers to stop their crimes.

At our stage in the coming of humane war, its advocates and audiences should reevaluate whether they have lost their way in helping to entrench continuing violence, which they could struggle to end instead. If the quest for more humane war could someday minimize not just collateral death and damage but even combatant killing and injury, the looming threat of something far more disquieting is also real. What if the elemental aim of endless war is not the death of enemy soldiers but rather the potentially nonviolent control of other peoples? Would that be tolerable?

With such concerns in mind, Tolstoy insisted that the deepest evil in politics in general and war in particular is moral subjugation. A decade before his death, the tireless preacher issued a hortatory pamphlet called *The Slavery of Our Times* (1901), ambitiously broadening the notion to encompass all forms of domination. And as he wrote in *Resurrection*, the didactic novel of his postconversion years, if it is best to call it "murder" when "commanders of armies pride themselves on their victories," then perhaps the best way to think about "violence" is metaphorically, occurring when "those in high places vaunt their power" even when they inflict no pain.

Brought to its logical conclusion, humane war may become increasingly safe for all concerned—which is also what makes it objectionable. Humane war is another version of the slavery of our times, and our task is to aim for a law that not only tolerates less pain but also promotes more freedom.

APPENDIX

Making American War Humane, 1863–

1863: President Abraham Lincoln issues Army **General Orders No. 100**, written by the Columbia University professor Francis Lieber. Sometimes called the "Lieber Code," it bans excesses such as torture and recommends (though does not require) giving quarter to opponents who lay down their arms. The goal of the code, however, is to make war not more humane but more intense, and it licenses no-holds-barred counterinsurgency.

1864: The first **Geneva Convention** codifies standards for treatment of the sick and wounded on the battlefield. European states negotiate the agreement and are the first to join, under the auspices of what becomes the International Committee for the Red Cross, founded by Swiss gentlemen. Though devised only to respond to the suffering of soldiers on the battlefield, it is the first act of the project to make war humane. The United States ratifies the treaty in 1882.

1874: European states gather (excluding nongovernmental groups) to propound the **Brussels Declaration**, codifying existing customs of war around land war and occupation regimes in response to the disorder and civilian uprisings of the Franco-Prussian War and the Paris Commune.

1899: The **Hague Conventions of 1899** are finalized at the end of a conference the Russian tsar had called for the sake of disarmament and peace. With U.S. participation, the fallback agreements include fuller-scale regulations on land war than before. Major innovations are made to regularize occupation of territory and safeguard prisoners of war by requiring humane treatment. Within combat, the new rules ban the use of soft-tipped ammunition and exclude hospitals and sites of cultural significance as targets. Aerial bombardment is prohibited for five years.

1907: A second peace conference leads to the **Hague Conventions of 1907**, with minor changes and updates to the earlier Hague treaty on land warfare. The temporary prohibition of aerial bombardment is extended in anticipation of a future conference that would finalize it—but that conference never takes place.

1923: **Rules of Air Warfare** are drafted by states, limiting aerial bombardment to "military objectives" and banning it where targets cannot be struck without "indiscriminate bombardment of the civilian population." No states ultimately ratify the agreement.

1925: The **Geneva Protocol** bans the wartime use of bacteriological and gas weapons.

1929: A new **Geneva Convention**, officially named the Convention Relative to the Treatment of Prisoners of War, is signed, which adds to the earlier Hague Convention rules protecting captured soldiers.

1945: The **United Nations Charter** is finalized, consecrating the peace American and Allied victory secures—and with no attempt to provide for more humane war. The treaty prohibits the threat or use of force in the international system, except when authorized by the United Nations Security Council, or in self-defense until the Security Council acts.

1945–46: The **International Military Tribunal**, also known as the Nuremberg trials, prioritizes trying Nazi leaders for aggressive war, while finding many guilty for crimes against humanity and the rules of war. A comparable inquest for crimes in East Asia takes place in Tokyo from 1946 to 1948, giving disruptions of the peace even more priority (compared with violations of rules of war) than Nuremberg did.

1948: The **Universal Declaration of Human Rights** is passed by the United Nations General Assembly, including an article prohibiting torture.

1949: The current and still-operative **Geneva Conventions** are finished. Updating the more minimal protections of the Hague Conventions, civilian safeguards are provided in a standalone instrument for the first time. Most of the rules are devised for "international armed conflict." But Common Article 3 governs "non-international" conflict, with minimal rules for prisoner treatment and trial. In the long run, these rules bind all states.

1950: As the Korean War breaks out, all parties agree to abide by the Geneva Conventions, especially for prisoner treatment.

1954: States conclude a **Hague Convention for the Protection of Cultural Property** that expands the list of off-limits targets in war and provides for the return of property after hostilities.

1955: The United States formally ratifies the Geneva Conventions. The Swiss gentleman Jean Pictet finishes a doctoral thesis rebranding the laws of war "international humanitarian law" (IHL), and as International Committee for the Red Cross leader in future decades sees the label accepted as the proper one for what legal regulation of war aspires to achieve.

1965: As the escalation of the Vietnam War begins, Secretary of State Dean Rusk publicly announces that the United States "has always abided by the humanitarian principles enunciated in the Geneva conventions and will continue to do so."

1968: At a Tehran Conference to celebrate the Universal Declaration of Human Rights, as well as in a United Nations General Assembly Resolution, it is proposed that human rights apply in situations of armed conflict, not simply the protections of the laws of war.

1977: Supplements to the Geneva Conventions called **Additional Protocols** formalize a ban on targeting civilians for the first time and impose a prohibition on "excessive" collateral harm, now interpreted to mean harm disproportionate to anticipated military advantage. While the first protocol updates long-standing rules on "international armed conflict," the second protocol goes far beyond the slim rules in Common Article 3 for "non-international armed conflict." The United States never ratifies the agreements, though it does signal that it accepts some of their content as unwritten law—leaving the country free to decide which parts.

1985: The United Nations **Convention Against Torture** prohibits torture and cruel, inhumane, and degrading treatment in all circumstances, both within and outside the territory of states that ratify. The United States does so in 1994.

1990–91: The first Gulf War, ordered by President George H. W. Bush to repel the Iraqi leader Saddam Hussein's aggression against Kuwait, becomes the first American war in which military lawyers assist in target selection, as well as the first international conflict that Human Rights Watch monitors for violations of the laws of war.

2001–2002: After attacks in Manhattan and Washington, D.C., the George W. Bush administration resolves—following memos by the lawyer John Choon Yoo—that Common Article 3 of the Geneva Conventions should not apply to Al-Qaeda terrorists. Yoo also proposes to exclude fighters for the Taliban altogether from coverage under the laws of war.

2004: The U.S. Supreme Court decides ***Rasul v. Bush***, which permits federal courts to entertain petitions for writs of habeas corpus from detainees at Guantánamo Bay, even as the Bush administration official Jack L. Goldsmith warns against reliance on some of Yoo's prior guidance.

2006: The U.S. Supreme Court decides ***Hamdan v. Rumsfeld***, which finds that Common Article 3 of the Geneva Conventions (if not a more stringent standard) applies to the war on terror, and rules that the Bush administration's military commissions were therefore inadequate to try detainees.

2009: President Barack Obama's new administration formally rescinds the Bush-era guidance on detention. It files a **Memorandum Regarding the Government's Detention Authority Relative to Detainees Held at Guantánamo Bay** that classifies the war on terror as a "non-international armed conflict," mentioning no boundaries in time and space. That choice, without saying so, provided a framework for killing operations already under way and left opaque whether and what standards did apply to a globalizing war.

2011: After long study, the Obama administration concludes that what *Hamdan v. Rumsfeld* set as a legal floor for the war on terror—Common Article 3 of the Geneva Conventions—was also its legal ceiling, meaning that any further constraints were those imposed as policy rather than obligation.

2013: The Obama administration finishes the **Presidential Policy Guidance** (PPG), an internal secret playbook for the conduct of targeted killings outside areas of active hostilities. Institutionalizing a clear process for strikes, the document prohibits them—in theory—when there is any risk of collateral injury whatsoever.

2016: The Presidential Policy Guidance is made public.

2017: After his election, President Donald Trump's administration rescinds the Presidential Policy Guidance and replaces it with a **Principles, Standards, and Procedures** framework. It weakens Obama's rules—in particular by not requiring presidential sign-off on killing—while still prohibiting strikes that threaten civilian life in any way.

2021: In the early months of his administration, President Joseph Biden promised to finalize troop withdrawal from Afghanistan by the twentieth anniversary of September 11, 2001, even as Congress debated whether to rescind its original authorizations for the war on terror. Biden also began reviews of drone and targeted killing policy and of military deployments worldwide. Even so, in the first weeks of his administration, he ordered missile attacks on militias operating in Syria as alleged Iranian proxies, in what was widely viewed as a blatant violation of international law governing the use of force. In spite of Biden's campaign rhetoric—like Trump's in 2015—to "end endless war," it was left very open what parts of the humane and stealthy American war invented over the prior decades would remain.

Notes

1. THE WARNING

18 *"You will see ghastly sights"*: Leo Tolstoy, "Sevastopol," in *Works*, 21 vols. (1928–37), 4: 96.

18 *"angel of death"*: Ibid., 108.

18 *"Yes, there are white flags"*: Ibid., 151.

18 *"Hundreds of men"*: Ibid., 247.

19 *"Thousands of people crowd together"*: Ibid., 152.

20 *"in the rising of the sun"*: Cited in Martin Ceadel, *The Origins of War Prevention: The British Peace Movement and International Relations, 1730–1854* (1996), 5.

20 *"All history is the decline of war"*: Ralph Waldo Emerson, "War," in *Complete Works*, 12 vols. (1903–1904), 11: 159.

21 *"war system of the commonwealth"*: David Donald, *Charles Sumner and the Coming of the Civil War* (1960), 105, and chap. 5.

21 *"allegiance to the war god"*: Cited in Merle Curti, "Non-Resistance in New England," *New England Quarterly* 2 (1929): 56; see also Thomas F. Curran, *Soldiers of Peace: Civil War Pacifism and the Postwar Radical Peace Movement* (2003).

21–22 *it took off after 1850*: Christina Phelps, *The Anglo-American Peace Movement in the Mid-Nineteenth Century* (1930).

22 *"A peace society which allowed"*: Merle Curti, *The American Peace Crusade, 1815–1860* (1929), 77.

23 *"We tremble even at the very thought"*: Friedrich Nietzsche, *Daybreak: Thoughts on the Prejudices of Morality*, trans. R. J. Hollingdale (1997), 46.

23 *Dorothea Dix made pilgrimage*: James Crossland, *War, Law and Humanity: The Campaign to Control Warfare, 1853–1914* (2018), chap. 2, is an excellent narrative; see also John F. Hutchinson's provocative *Champions of Charity: War and the Rise of the Red Cross* (1996).

24 *He then returned*: Corinne Chaponnière, *Henry Dunant: La Croix d'un homme* (2010).

24 *Dunant wrote a pamphlet*: Henry Dunant, *Un souvenir de Solférino* (1863), 12, 58, 76.

25 *"better, a thousand times better"*: Edmond de Goncourt and Jules de Goncourt, *Journal*, 9 vols. (1891–96), 2: 121.

26 *"advance God's reign on earth"*: Gustave Moynier, "La Convention de Genève au point de vue religieux," *Revue chrétienne* 46 (1899): 163.

26 *"We must leave to war"*: The doctor and Moynier are cited in Louis Appia and Gustave Moynier, *La Guerre et la charité: Traité théorique et pratique de philanthropie appliquée aux armées en campagne* (1867), 132, 134.

26 *"War without the spilling of blood"*: Gustave Moynier, *Essai sur les caractères généraux des lois de guerre* (1895), 45; see also François Bugnion, *Gustave Moynier, 1826–1910* (2011), and Yves Sandoz, "The Red Cross and Peace: Realities and Limits," *Journal of Peace Research* 24 (1987): 287–96.

27 *"One thing I would do"*: Leo Tolstoy, *War and Peace*, trans. Aylmer Maude and Louise Maude, in *Works*, 7: 486.

28 *"They talk to us of the rules of war"*: Ibid., 487.

28 *"the dominance of the destructive principle"*: Carl von Clausewitz, *On War*, rev. ed., trans. Michael Howard and Peter Paret (1984), 223.

28 *"Mistakes which come from kindness"*: Ibid., 75.

29 *"It would be futile"*: Ibid., 76.

29 *"The fact that slaughter"*: Ibid., 260.

29 *"How much are those to be pitied"*: Francis Lieber, *Manual of Political Ethics*, 2nd ed., 2 vols. (1890), 2: 430; see also John Fabian Witt, *Lincoln's Code: The Laws of War in American History* (2012), esp. 177–78.

29 *"blood" was the "vital juice"*: Cited in James Childress, "Francis Lieber's Interpretation of the Laws of War," *American Journal of Jurisprudence* 21 (1976): 44n.

29 *"Christ taught principles"*: Lieber, *Manual of Political Ethics*, 2: 435.

30 *horrendous acts such as . . . denying quarter*: Article 60 of Lieber's code forbade orders to deny quarter but permitted commanders to kill those who surrendered if they could not feasibly take prisoners. Aside from Witt, *Lincoln's Code*, see Richard Baxter, "The First Modern Codification of the Laws of War: Francis Lieber and General Orders No. 100," *International Review of the Red Cross* 3 (1963); Rotem Giladi, "A Different Sense of Humanity," *International Review of the Red Cross* 94 (2012): 81–116; and Aaron Sheehan-Dean, *The Calculus of Violence: How Americans Fought the Civil War* (2018), 182–97.

30 *"Battle exists for its own sake"*: Clausewitz, *On War*, 248, 596, 143.

30 *"If destruction of the enemy"*: Lieber, *Manual of Political Ethics*, 2: 451–52; compare Witt, "Two Conceptions of Suffering in War," in Austin Sarat et al., eds., *Knowing the Suffering of Others: Legal Perspectives on Pain and Its Meanings* (2014).

30 *Prussian theoretician*: Andreas Herberg-Rothe, "Tolstoy and Clausewitz: The Dialectics of War," in Rick McPeak and Donna Orwin, eds., *Tolstoy on War* (2012).

30 *"The only aim is to weaken"*: Tolstoy, *War and Peace*, 7: 485.

31 *"by itself would change"*: Ibid., 486–87.

31 *"intense wars are of short duration"*: Lieber, *Manual of Political Ethics*, 2: 451–52.

31 *"a slope where there is no stopping"*: Cited in Jean S. Pictet, "The Development of International Humanitarian Law," in C. Wilfred Jenks et al., *International Law in a Changing World* (1963), 117.

31 *"secret agents of pacification"*: Moynier, *Essai*, 101. One commentator suggests the Red Cross adopted peace as its "unspoken mission," but to say so is to elevate and generalize what was merely an occasional opportunistic claim to a fringe benefit, as if it had been a constant and direct goal. Nicholas Berry, *War and the Red Cross: The Unspoken Mission* (1997).

31 *"The humanization of war"*: Gustave Moynier, *Conférence sur la Convention de Genève* (1897), 29–31, translation slightly varied from the citation in Geoffrey Best, *Humanity in Warfare* (1980), 10.

32 *wars of the twentieth century*: Prince Andrei's devotion to intensification in the cause of peace, a twentieth-century philosopher wrote, anticipated Cold War "theories of 'massive deterrence'—especially by the threat of nuclear attack—theories which have not proved either strategically feasible or morally tolerable

in practice." W. B. Gallie, *Philosophers of Peace and War: Kant, Clausewitz, Marx, Engels, and Tolstoy* (1978), 119.

32 *"like the lightning"*: Tolstoy, *War and Peace*, 7: 562 (translator's note).

32 *"Get rid of falsehood"*: Ibid., 487.

32 *"a great idea, a stupendous idea"*: Leo Tolstoy, *Diaries*, ed. and trans. R. F. Christian, 2 vols. (1985), 1: 101.

33 *were only to become world-famous*: William B. Edgerton, "The Artist Turned Prophet: Leo Tolstoj After 1880," in William Harkins, ed., *American Contributions to the Sixth Annual Congress of Slavists* (1968).

33 *Tolstoy adopted a vision of nonresistance*: Colm McKeogh, *Tolstoy's Pacifism* (2009).

34 *"approval and acceptance of persecutions"*: Leo Tolstoy, *What I Believe*, in *Works*, 11: 313, 314–15.

34 *"the first to proclaim"*: Leo Tolstoy, introduction to V. Tchertkoff and F. Holah, *A Short Biography of William Lloyd Garrison* (1904), rpt. in *William Lloyd Garrison on Non-Resistance* (1924), 55.

34 *"as that of a close friend"*: Cited in Jayme Sokolow and Priscilla Roosevelt, *Leo Tolstoy's Christian Pacifism: The American Contribution* (1987), 20.

34 *"greatest of all American writers"*: Cited in ibid., 24.

35 *"no aspect of the question"*: Leo Tolstoy, *The Kingdom of God Is Within Us*, in *Works*, 20: 21.

35 *"thank them for the great help"*: Letter to *North American Review*, April 1901, in *The Complete Works of Count Tolstoy*, 24 vols. (1905), 23: 462.

35 *"To many people of our society"*: Letter to Ernest Howard Crosby, in Leo Tolstoy, *Last Steps: The Last Writings*, ed. Jay Parini (2009), 78.

35 *violence was never acceptable*: Cited in George Woodcock and Ivan Avakumovic, *The Doukhobors* (1968), 184.

35 *"only real giant"*: Count S. Stakelberg, "Tolstoi Holds Lincoln World's Greatest Hero," *New York World*, February 7, 1909.

36 *bands of "Tolstoyans"*: Charlotte Alston, *Tolstoy and His Disciples: The History of a Radical International Movement* (2014).

36 *a still existing Tolstoyan farm*: Jordan Michael Smith, "A Trip to Tolstoy Farm," *Longreads*, September 12, 2018.

36 *"It is the greatest misfortune"*: Cited in R. V. Sampson, *The Discovery of Peace* (1978), 108.

36 *"denouncer of obvious evils"*: A. N. Wilson, *Tolstoy: A Biography* (1988), 116, 101.

37 *Those arguments had revolved*: Though he gave up the intensification argument in war (and was a great critic of capital punishment), Tolstoy still registered its attractions when it came to criminal law reform in *Resurrection*, his last novel, where one character insists that blinding or killing convicts "would be cruel, but it would be effective" compared with making penalties and prisons more humane. Leo Tolstoy, *Resurrection*, trans. Louise Maude, in *Works*, 19: 333.

37 *"It's true that slavery"*: Cited in Anne Hruska, "Love and Slavery: Serfdom, Emancipation, and Family in Tolstoy's Fiction," *Russian Review* 66 (2007): 627.

37 *he helped administer the abolition*: Liza Knapp, "Tolstoy's *Sevastopol Tales:* Pathos, Sermon, Protest, and Stowe," in Elizabeth Cheresh Allen, ed., *Before They Were Titans: Essays on the Early Works of Dostoevsky and Tolstoy* (2015); John MacKay, *True Songs of Freedom: "Uncle Tom's Cabin" in Russian Culture and Society* (2013), chap. 2.

38 *"Where violence is legalized"*: Leo Tolstoy, *What Must We Then Do?*, in *Works*, 14: 164, 166.

38 *"The partisans of error"*: *New York Times*, January 17, 1897.

39 *legal codes constrained*: George Breathett, "Colonialism and the Code Noir," *Journal of Negro History* 73 (1988): 10.

39 *"with such humanity"*: Randy Browne, *Surviving Slavery in the British Caribbean* (2017), 49.

39 *the slaveholding class adopted*: Joyce Chaplin, "Slavery and the Principle of Humanity," *Journal of Social History* 24 (1990): 299–315.

40 *American slave codes*: Mark Tushnet, *The American Law of Slavery, 1810–1860: Considerations of Humanity and Interest* (1981).

40 *humane slavery*: Christa Dierksheide, *Amelioration and Empire: Progress and Slavery in the Plantation Americas* (2014), 159.

40 *"more tolerable for the slaveowner"*: Winthrop Jordan, *White Over Black: American Attitudes Toward the Negro, 1550–1812* (1968), 368.

41 *"a sense of urgency"*: David Brion Davis, "The Emergence of Immediatism in British and American Antislavery Thought," *Mississippi Valley Historical Review* 29 (1962): 225.

41 *the slaughter of animals*: Josephine Donovan, "Tolstoy's Animals," *Society and Animals* 17 (2009): 38–52.

41 *"man feels a sense of horror"*: Tolstoy, *War and Peace*, 8: 348.

42 *"already it is* fashionable*"*: James Turner, *Reckoning with the Beast: Animals, Pain, and Humanity in the Victorian Mind* (1980), 47.

42 *"the magnanimity and sensibility"*: Tolstoy, *War and Peace*, 7: 487.

42 *he convinced his new friend*: Aylmer Maude, *The Life of Tolstoy*, 2 vols. (1930), 2: 168–71.

43 *"As long as there are slaughterhouses"*: This citation, though widely attributed to Tolstoy, is possibly apocryphal and I haven't located it.

43 *"to see with my own eyes"*: Leo Tolstoy, "The First Step," in *Works*, 21: 124, 126, 128–29.

43–44 *"a kind, refined lady"*: Ibid., 124, 132–33.

45 *"It is no service"*: Michael Walzer, *Just and Unjust Wars: A Moral Argument with Historical Illustrations* (1977), 334.

45 *"All is vanity"*: Tolstoy, *War and Peace*, 6: 369.

2. BLESSED ARE THE PEACEMAKERS

47 *Suttner would win the Nobel*: Irwin Abrams, "Bertha von Suttner and the Nobel Peace Prize," *Journal of Central European Affairs* 22 (1962): 286–307.

47 *"a happy augury"*: Cited in Bertha von Suttner, *Memoirs: The Record of an Eventful Life*, 2 vols. (1910), 1: 343.

48 *Tolstoy kept abreast*: Leo Tolstoy, *The Kingdom of God Is Within Us*, in *Works*, 21 vols. (1928–37), 20: 146–249.

48 *"For the disappearance of war"*: Cited in Suttner, *Memoirs*, 2: 372.

48 *letters to sundry correspondents*: Leo Tolstoy, *Writings on Civil Disobedience and Non-Violence* (1967); Leo Tolstoy, "Letter to a Draftee," *The Atlantic*, February 1968.

48 *"If the policy of Tolstoy"*: "Tolstoy as a Peacemaker," *Advocate of Peace*, December 1910.

49 *an old peasant saying*: "Ein Tag bei Leon Tolstoi," *Neue Freie Presse*, May 29, 1896.

49 *"a high priest"*: Leo Tolstoy, "Nobel's Bequest," in *Writings on Civil Disobedience and Non-Violence* (1967); Bertha von Suttner, "Randglossen zur Zeitgeschichte," *Die Friedens-Warte* 12 (1910): 229.

49 *"The stroke of lightning"*: Cited in Brigitte Hamann, *Bertha von Suttner: A Life for Peace*, trans. Ann Dubsky (1996), 73.

50 *"really two masses of men"*: Bertha von Suttner, *Lay Down Your Arms: The Autobiography of Martha von Tilling*, trans. T. Holmes (1894), 22.
50 *"The mere mention"*: Ibid., 13, 36.
51 *"a jolly rattling war"*: Ibid., 96.
51 *"In these words"*: Ibid., 98–99.
51 *"the war god"*: Ibid., 244.
52 *"What is the flag"*: Anonymous [Bertha von Suttner], *Das Maschinenalter: Zukunftsvorlesungen über unsere Zeit* (1899), 285. Ironically, Suttner is somewhat more favorable to the Red Cross in *Lay Down Your Arms*, 220.
53 *more than a million members*: A.C.F. Beales, *A History of Peace: A Short Account of the Organized Movements for International Peace* (1931), is still worth consulting; the leading survey since is Sandi Cooper, *Patriotic Pacifism: Waging War on War in Europe, 1815–1914* (1991); on Britain, Martin Ceadel, *Semi-Detached Idealists: The British Peace Movement and International Relations, 1854–1945* (2000); on Germany, Roger Chickering, *Imperial Germany and a World Without War: The Peace Movement and German Society, 1892–1914* (1975); on France, Nadine-Josette Chaline, *Empêcher la guerre: Le pacifisme du début du XIXe siècle à la veille de la Seconde Guerre mondiale* (2015); on the United States, see below.
53 *"a comical sewing bee"*: Cited in Chickering, *Imperial Germany*, 93.
53 *"There is no reason"*: Bertha von Suttner, "Die Friedensbewegung und die Frauen," *Die Waffen nieder!* 4 (1895): 254.
53 *"Although it is self-evident"*: Bertha von Suttner, "Universal Peace: From a Woman's Standpoint," *North American Review* 169 (1899): 50–51; see also Hamann, *Bertha*, chap. 13.
54 *Selling millions of copies*: It was originally published as *Europe's Optical Illusion* (1909); Howard Weinroth, "Norman Angell and *The Great Illusion*," *Historical Journal* 17 (1974): 551–74; Martin Ceadel, *Living the Great Illusion: Sir Norman Angell, 1872–1967* (2009)
55 *bilateral treaties with partners*: William Jay, *War and Peace: The Evils of the First and a Plan for Preserving the Last* (1842). Arbitration in bilateral relations was commonly traced back to the treaty concluded by his father, John Jay, between the United Kingdom and the United States in 1795, or even to the Middle Ages or the Greeks. James Brown Scott, *The Hague Peace Conferences of 1899 and 1907*, 2 vols. (1909), chap. 5. See also Kristina Lovrić-Pernak, "Aim: Peace—Sanction: War: International Arbitration and the Problem of Enforcement," in Thomas Hippler and Miloš Vec, eds., *Paradoxes of Peace in Nineteenth Century Europe* (2015).
56 *"by the help of God"*: James Brown Scott, ed., *Texts of the Peace Conferences at the Hague, 1890 and 1907* (1908), 1–2.
56 *fodder for windy debate*: Dan L. Morrill, "Nicholas II and the Call for the First Hague Conference," *Journal of Modern History* 46 (1974): 296–313.
56 *"Holy Bertha!"*: Cited in Chickering, *Imperial Germany*, 231.
56 *Even a gruff Tolstoy*: "Äusserungen hervorrangender Persönlichkeiten über das Czarenmanifest," *Die Waffen nieder!* 7 (1898): 395–96.
56 *Nicholas's personal interactions*: Peter van den Dungen, "The Making of Peace: Jan de Bloch and the First Hague Conference," *Occasional Papers of the California State University Center for the Study of Armament and Disarmament* (1983).
57 *hundreds of thousands of signatures*: Cooper, *Patriotic Pacifism*, 98.
57 *flew a white flag*: Bertha von Suttner, *Die Haager Friedenskonferenz* (1900).

57 *lip service to the cause*: Jost Dülffer, *Regeln gegen den Krieg?: Die Haager Friedenskonferenzen* (1981); Arthur Eyffinger, *The 1899 Hague Peace Conference: The Parliament of Man, the Federation of the World* (1999); Maartje Abbenhuis, *The Hague Conferences and International Politics, 1898–1915* (2019).

57 *"hypocritical institutions"*: Leo Tolstoy, "Concerning the Conference of Peace," in *Complete Works*, 23: 439.

58 *with little to show*: Compare Randall Lesaffer, "Peace Through Law: The Hague Conferences and the Rise of *Ius Contra Bellum*," in Maartje Abbenhuis et al., eds., *War, Peace, and International Order? The Legacies of the Hague Conferences* (2017).

58 *"an epoch-making date"*: Suttner, *Memoirs*, 2: 228, 249.

58 *"No other brief for peace"*: "Bertha von Suttner," *The Nation*, June 25, 1914.

58 *"Law, the first daughter"*: Cited in Cecilie Reid, "Peace and Law: Peace Activism and International Arbitration, 1905–1907," *Peace and Change* 29 (2004): 531.

58 *"I wish to dwell"*: Bertha von Suttner, "Nobel Lecture," in Frederick Haberman, ed., *Nobel Lectures: Peace, 1901–1925* (1972), 89.

59 *"America's glory and grandeur"*: Suttner, *Memoirs*, 2: 416.

59 *"lead the lion"*: Bertha von Suttner, *Speech Addressed to Pacifists in San Francisco* (1912).

60 *"regarded it as a settled thing"*: William Barton, *The Life of Clara Barton: Founder of the American Red Cross*, 2 vols. (1922), 2: 146.

60 *"the Monroe Doctrine"*: Cited in ibid., 2: 150. On the origins of the American Red Cross for humanitarian relief abroad, and its mainstreaming among political elites in the decades straddling World War I, see Julia Irwin, *Making the World Safe: The American Red Cross and a Nation's Humanitarian Awakening* (2013).

60 *Nothing so far interfered*: Frederick W. Holls, "The Results of the Peace Conference in Their Relation to the Monroe Doctrine," *Review of Reviews* 20 (1899): 560–66.

61 *"one of the greatest events"*: Cited in David Patterson, *Toward a Warless World: The Travail of the American Peace Movement 1887–1914* (1976), 39.

61 *The new breed of practitioners*: Benjamin Coates, *Legalist Empire: International Law and American Foreign Relations in the Early Twentieth Century* (2016).

61 *Peace was a mainstream idea*: C. Roland Marchand, *The American Peace Movement and Social Reform, 1898–1918* (1972).

61 *"great apostle of arbitration"*: Cited in David Nasaw, *Andrew Carnegie* (2006), 653; see also David Patterson, "Andrew Carnegie's Quest for World Peace," *Proceedings of the American Philosophical Society* 114 (1970): 371–83.

62 *offered Suttner a pension*: Michael Lutzker, "The Formation of the Carnegie Endowment for International Peace," in Jerry Israel, ed., *Building the Organizational Society: Essays on Associational Activities in Modern America* (1972).

62 *He became a Tolstoy nut*: Merle Curti, "Bryan and World Peace," *Smith College Studies in History* 16 (1931), esp. 135–39; Kenneth Wenzer, "Tolstoy and Bryan," *Nebraska History* 77 (1996): 140–48.

62 *Bryan distributed as souvenirs*: "The Bryan Peace Treaties," *American Journal of International Law* 7 (1913): 823–29; Ernest May, "Bryan and the World War, 1914–15" (Ph.D. diss., University of California, Los Angeles, 1951); Merle Curti, *Peace or War: The American Struggle, 1636–1936* (1936), 226.

63 *"was at home"*: Carl Sandburg, "Letter of Appreciation," Carl Sandburg Papers, MSS 169, Special Collections and Archives, Henry M. Seymour Library, Galesburg, Illinois, also in *Philip Green Wright Memorial Booklet* (1934), Site Research Files, Carl Sandburg State Historic Site, Galesburg, Illinois. See also Carl Sandburg's entry on Philip Wright in *Dictionary of American Biography*, 21 vols. (1937), 20: 563–64.

63 *Wright helped the poet*: Quincy Wright, "The Lombard Years," *Journal of the Illinois State Historical Society* 45 (1952): 307.

63 *"United States of World Government"*: James Hamilton Lewis, "The Political New Day for America," *National Magazine* 46 (1917): 546.

63 *"exactly the thing called for"*: Quincy Wright to Philip Wright, July 14, 1917, Quincy Wright Papers, Box 1, Folder 15, Special Collections Research Center, University of Chicago Library.

64 *cited Alfred Lord Tennyson's*: Philip to Quincy Wright, July 4, 1917, in ibid.

64 *"technical discussions on questions"*: Quincy to Philip Wright, July 24, 1917, in ibid.

64–65 *sided nearly unanimously*: Sandi Cooper, "The Reinvention of the 'Just War' Among European Pacifists Before the First World War," in Harvey Dyck, ed., *The Pacifist Impulse in Historical Perspective* (1996). On socialists, see Georges Haupt, *Socialism and the Great War* (1972).

65 *socialists took Wilson's rationale*: Thomas J. Knock, *To End All Wars: Woodrow Wilson and the Quest for a New World Order* (1992).

65 *"the great war for peace"*: William Mulligan, *The Great War for Peace* (2014).

65 *war resistance became rife*: See Adam Hochschild, *To End All Wars: A Story of Loyalty and Rebellion, 1914–1918* (2011), for a popular account of the British scene.

65 *Women's International League*: Catia Confortini, *Intelligent Compassion: The Women's International League for Peace and Freedom and Feminist Peace* (2012).

66 *Woolf conceded by 1938*: Virginia Woolf, *Three Guineas* (1938, 1966), 3.

66 *"a great smattering of Tolstoy"*: F. Scott Fitzgerald, *This Side of Paradise* (1920), 161.

66 *glorification of the trench experience*: Daniel Todman, *The Great War: Myth and Memory* (2005).

67 *peace movement had altered*: Cecelia Lynch, *Beyond Appeasement: Interpreting Interwar Peace Movements in World Politics* (1999).

67 *delayed the country's entry*: Michael Kazin, *War Against War: The American Fight for Peace, 1914–1918* (2017).

67 *twelve million adherents*: Curti, *Peace or War*, 273.

67 *continued her activism*: Lucia Ames Mead, ed., *The Overthrow of the War System* (1915); Jane Addams et al., *Women at the Hague: The International Congress of Women and Its Results* (1916); Jane Addams, *Peace and Bread in Time of War* (1922).

67 *"man-selling"*: Lucia Ames Mead, *Swords into Plowshares: The Supplanting of the System of War by the System of Law*, pref. Bertha von Suttner (1912); Lucia Ames Mead, *Law or War* (1928), 1.

68 *Outright pacifists remained inveterate*: John Nelson, *The Peace Prophets: American Pacifist Thought, 1919–1941* (1967); Charles Chatfield, *For Peace and Justice: Pacifism in America, 1914–1941* (1972).

69 *hopes for peace became mainstream*: Quincy Wright, *The Role of International Law in the Elimination of War* (1961).

69 *"The fundamental problem"*: Christian L. Lange, "Histoire de la doctrine pacifique et de son influence sur le development du droit international," *Recueil des cours de l'Académie de droit international* 13 (1926): 422.

69 *"Many people will approve"*: Cited in Emily Hill Griggs, "A Realist Before 'Realism': Quincy Wright and the Study of International Politics Between Two World Wars," *Journal of Strategic Studies* 24 (2008): 87.

69 *hold Wilhelm II accountable*: Quincy Wright, "The Legal Liability of the Kaiser," *American Political Science Review* 13 (1919): 120–28. Twelve Germans were brought to trial at Leipzig for war crimes in 1921.

70 *"a growing feeling that war"*: Cited in Gary Jonathan Bass, *Stay the Hand of Vengeance: The Politics of War Crimes Tribunals*, new ed. (2002), 65, 74; my "From Aggression to Atrocity: Rethinking the History of International Criminal Law," in Kevin Jon Heller et al., eds., *Oxford Handbook of International Criminal Law* (2020), tracks the theme.

70 *The Kaiser fled*: William Schabas, *The Trial of the Kaiser* (2018).

70 *Even within the League*: Stephen Wertheim, "The League That Wasn't: American Designs for a Legalist-Sanctionist League of Nations and the Intellectual Origins of International Organization, 1914–1920," *Diplomatic History* 35 (2011): 797–836.

71 *Wright immediately volunteered*: Quincy Wright, *Limitation of Armament* (1921).

71 *Its promise continued for a decade*: See, e.g., Albert Einstein, "The Road to Peace," *New York Times Magazine*, November 22, 1931, and Otto Nathan and Heinz Norden, eds., *Einstein on Peace* (1960), for his multifarious activism over the decades; John Wheeler-Bennett, *The Pipe-Dream of Peace: The Story of the Collapse of Disarmament* (1935).

71 *the rest of his career*: Quincy Wright, *Significance to America of the Geneva Protocol* (1925).

72 *"Voluntary methods are doubtless"*: Quincy Wright, "The Outlawry of War," *American Journal of International Law* 19 (1925): 77–78.

72 *"There has apparently been"*: Quincy Wright, "Changes in the Conception of War," *American Journal of International Law* 18 (1924): 760.

73 *to make more explicit and formal*: Wright, "Outlawry," 89–91.

73 *"King Canute did not increase"*: Ibid., 103.

73 *"the hopelessness of outlawing war"*: Ibid., 97.

74 *"does not outlaw war"*: Carl Schmitt, *The Concept of the Political*, new ed. (2007), 50n (translation altered). That this was not a uniquely German position is indicated by its support by Edwin Borchard, a Yale law professor and neutralist, whom Schmitt cited: "The Kellogg Treaties Sanction War," *Zeitschift für ausländisches öffentliches Recht und Völkerrecht* 1 (1929): 126–31.

74 *responsibility of the United States*: I agree with my colleagues Oona Hathaway and Scott Shapiro, in *The Internationalists: How a Radical Plan to Outlaw War Remade the World* (2016), that war could be seen as illegal before World War II, but this book modifies their case by adding that (1) interwar rule-change domesticated pre-1914 and more radical ideas, (2) required the institutionalization of American hegemony for rule-change to become operative, and (3) came at a high price—not least for American war, however eventually humane in the long run.

74 *"The historical significance"*: William Rappard, *The Quest for Peace since the World War* (1940), 170.

74 *"any interests or rights"*: Cited in John Vinson, *William E. Borah and the Outlawry of War* (1957), 157.

74 *reserved his nation's right*: Gaynor Johnson, "Austen Chamberlain and the Negotiation of the Kellogg-Briand Pact, 1928," in Johnson, ed., *Locarno Revisited: European Diplomacy 1920–1929* (2004).

75 *William Borah*: Vinson, *William E. Borah*; Robert Maddox, "William E. Borah and the Crusade to War," *The Historian* 29 (1967): 200–220; Charles DeBenedetti, "Borah and the Kellogg-Briand Pact," *Pacific Northwest Quarterly* 63 (1972): 22–29; Christopher Nichols, *Promise and Peril: America at the Dawn of a Global Age* (2011), chaps. 6–7.

75 *"Wars of aggression"*: Quincy Wright, "Neutrality and Neutral Rights Following the Pact of Paris for the Renunciation of War," *Proceedings of the American Society*

of International Law 24 (1930): 81; after the revival of American commitment to neutrality in the following decade, see the more dyspeptic Quincy Wright, "The Present Status of Neutrality," *American Journal of International Law* 34 (1940): 391–415.

76 *"converted violence into legality"*: Quincy Wright, "The Stimson Note of January 7, 1932," *American Journal of International Law* 26 (1932): 342, 344; see also Quincy Wright, "The Manchurian Crisis," *American Political Science Review* 26 (1932): 53–76, and "The Legal Foundation of the Stimson Doctrine," *Pacific Affairs* 8 (1935): 439–46.

76 *"The collective system"*: Quincy Wright, "The Path to Peace," *World Unity* 13 (1933): 135.

77 *not a good idea*: John Bassett Moore, "An Appeal to Reason," *Foreign Affairs* 11 (1933): 547–88, esp. 586–87 for the biblical analogy. See also Edwin Borchard and William Potter Lage, *Neutrality for the United States* (1937), and Wright's hostile review, "American Neutrality," *Southern Review* 3 (1937): 747–61.

77 *"If it is practically certain"*: Quincy Wright, *The United States and Neutrality* (1935), 2.

3. LAWS OF INHUMANITY

79 *"In Nobel's will"*: Cited in Brigitte Hamann, *Bertha von Suttner: A Life for Peace*, trans. Ann Dubsky (1996), 204, with the term *Kriegserleichterer* and its cognates retranslated here and in subsequent quotations.

80 *"You do not humanize carnage"*: Cited in Bertha von Suttner, *Memoirs: The Record of an Eventful Life*, 2 vols. (1910), 1: 328n.

80 *"Men continue to kill"*: Henry Dunant, *Un souvenir de Solférino* (1863), 150–51.

80 *"a step along the path"*: Cited in Hamann, *Bertha*, 204–205.

80 *"Give me a few lines"*: Ibid.

81 *almost any form of military force*: John Fabian Witt, *Lincoln's Code: The Laws of War in American History* (2012), is undoubtedly right that war was legalized anew in the nineteenth century, but from the perspective of its victims such legalization lacked humanitarian content (notwithstanding the Clausewitzian "humanitarianism" of Francis Lieber's assumption that limitless force may include side benefits) and functioned principally to permit and legitimate violence, at the opposite pole from the current emergence of "humane war."

82 *libraries, and the main cathedral*: Rachel Chrastil, *The Siege of Strasbourg* (2014), 76–78.

83 *Swiss and other philanthropists*: Eyal Benvenisti and Doreen Lustig, "Monopolizing War: Codifying the Laws of War to Reassert Governmental Authority, 1856–1874," *European Journal of International Law* 31 (2020): 127–69, on which this paragraph is also based.

83 *"While the inert matter"*: Gustave Moynier, *Essai sur la caractère générale des lois de la guerre* (1895), 95–96.

84 *They rejected pacifism outright*: While Moynier sometimes spoke of how humane war would lead to the abolition of war, others gave no sign of that sequential hope and defended on principle the concession of the eternity of war-making to states in hopes of making their clashes more humane; for a good example, see the leading French figure Antoine Pillet's famous lectures, *Le Droit de la guerre*, 2 vols. (1892), First Lecture, attacking Helmuth von Moltke's glorification of war but ruefully accepting war as an enduring evil.

84 *"a general codification"*: Gustave Moynier, *Étude de la Convention de Genève* (1870), 31. Though he was horrified by the radical pacifists who had staged an 1867 conference

in his own city, Moynier joined Passy's more mainstream movement. André Durand, "Gustave Moynier and the Peace Societies," *International Review of the Red Cross* 36 (1996): 532–50.

85 *"Eternal peace is a dream"*: Though the comment was first published in 1881, I cite Helmuth von Moltke, *Gesammelte Schriften*, 8 vols. (1891–93), 5: 194.

85 *a proviso that the Prussians boasted about*: Compare Isabel V. Hull, *Absolute Destruction: Military Culture and the Practices of War in Imperial Germany* (2005), esp. 119–26. In general, Hull's brilliant work in this area ignores that legalization generally legitimates rather than restrains—quite apart from her excessive distinction of Germany from other powers, which interpreted permissive rules to conform to their practices, after better controlling the rulemaking process in the first place to exclude their own prospective conduct from limitation.

85 *"not only* as *humane"*: James Crossland, *War, Law, and Humanity: The Campaign to Control Warfare, 1853–1914* (2018), 118; Rolin-Jacquemyns is cited in Ernest Nys, "The Codification of International Law," *American Journal of International Law* 5 (1911): 896. Crossland now provides the best overall coverage of the topics in this section; for excellent detail far beyond the ostensible topic of the rise of international accountability, see Daniel Marc Segesser, *Recht staat Rache oder Rache durch Recht?: Die Ahndung von Kriegsverbrechen in der internationalen wissenschaftlichen Debatte, 1872–1945* (2010).

86 *they assured themselves*: Antoine Pillet, "Le Droit international public," *Revue générale de droit international public* 1 (1894): 1–32; Pablo Kalmanovitz, *The Laws of War in International Thought* (2020), chap. 5; see also Dietrich Schlindler, "J. C. Bluntschli's Contribution to the Law of War," in Marcelo Kohen, ed., *Promoting Justice, Human Rights, and Conflict Resolution Through International Law* (2007).

86 *"conferences for consolidating war"*: Cited in Hamann, *Bertha*, 164; on the conference, see Hans Wehberg, *La Contribution des Conférences de la paix de La Haye au progrès du droit international* (1932), and Arthur Eyffinger, "A Highly Critical Moment: Role and Record of the 1907 Hague Peace Conference," *Netherlands International Law Review* (2007): 197–228.

86 *"the humanizing of war"*: Suttner, *Memoirs*, 2: 228, 249.

86 *"trap that opens up"*: Cited in Hamann, *Bertha*, 145.

87 *"moderation in war"*: R. H. Bacon, *The Life of Lord Fisher of Kilverstone: Admiral of the Fleet*, 2 vols. (1929), 121–23.

87 *"the hands of the retrograde"*: Cited in André Durand, "L'évolution de l'idée de la paix dans la pensée d'Henry Dunant," in Roger Durand, ed., *De l'utopie à la réalité: Actes du Colloque Henry Dunant* (1988), 378–79.

87 *"We are too sensible"*: Cited in Hamann, *Bertha*, 144.

88 *"sending butchers"*: Cited in Crossland, *War, Law, and Humanity*, 181. Stengel and Suttner had feuded. Karl von Stengel, *Der ewige Krieg* (1899), and Bertha von Suttner, ed., *Herrn Dr. Carl Freiherrn von Stengels und andere Argumente für und wider den Krieg* (1899).

88 *"At least . . . no one can now say"*: Alfred Fried, "Kriegsgesetze," *Die Friedens-Warte* 1 (1899): 25.

88 *early civilian protection*: Jonathan Gumz, "International Law and the Transformation of War, 1899–1949: The Case of Military Occupation," *Journal of Modern History* 90 (2018): 621–60.

88 *"Why are a wound"*: Leo Tolstoy, "Concerning the Conference of Peace," in *Complete Works*, 23: 442; see also Elena Kempf, "Humanitarian Calculus: The Making

and Meaning of Weapons Prohibitions in International Law, 1868–1925" (Ph.D. diss., University of California, Berkeley, forthcoming).

88 *"splintered bones"*: Edward M. Spiers, "The Use of the Dum Dum Bullet in Colonial Warfare," *Journal of Imperial and Commonwealth History* 4 (1975): 3.

89 *such eloquent verbiage*: F. de Martens, *La Paix et la guerre* (1901), interprets the new treaties from his point of view; on the clause, see Rotem Giladi, "The Enactment of Irony: Reflections on the Origins of the Martens Clause," *European Journal of International Law* 25 (2014): 847–69.

90 *"a sacred horror"*: Cited in Durand, "L'évolution," 357.

90 *"Dunant has been honored"*: Cited in Hamann, *Bertha*, 204.

90 *"I believe there has been a feeling"*: Cited in Jean G. Lossier, "The Red Cross and Peace: Trends and Their Evolution," *Revue internationale de la Croix-Rouge*, Supplement, 4 (1951): 28–29, treated as a direct citation in the original French version.

90 *"an unnecessary evil"*: [Gustave Moynier,] "La Croix-Rouge et l'œuvre de la paix," *Bulletin international des Sociétiés de la Croix-Rouge* 126 (1901): 74.

91 *"If these laws"*: Gustave Moynier, "Die Härten des Krieges und das Völkerrecht," *Deutsche Revue* 17 (1892): 337–38.

91 *"global color line"*: Marilyn Lake and Henry Reynolds, *Drawing the Global Colour Line: White Men's Countries and the International Challenge of Racial Equality* (2008).

91 *"clearly as the ultimate destiny"*: Cited in Duncan Bell, *Dreamworlds of Race: Utopia: Empire and the Destiny of Anglo-America* (2020), 107.

91 *"I am as you are"*: Cited in ibid., 50.

92 *"murder of men by men"*: Cited in ibid., 334–35.

92 *Kellogg-Briand Pact*: See Daniel Gorman, *The Emergence of International Society in the 1920s* (2012), chap. 9.

92 *Colonial war*: Nasser Hussain, *The Jurisprudence of Emergency: Colonialism and the Rule of Law* (2003), and a vast successor literature.

92 *not within colonies*: Giovanni Mantilla, *Lawmaking Under Pressure: International Humanitarian Law and Internal Armed Conflict* (2020), 35–45.

93 *"guerrilla war"*: "The partisan of the Spanish Guerrilla War of 1808 was the first who dared to wage irregular war against the first regular modern army," one thinker noted. Carl Schmitt, *The Theory of the Partisan*, trans. A. C. Goodson (2004), 4.

93 *"War was being carried on"*: Leo Tolstoy, *War and Peace*, trans. Aylmer Maude and Louise Maude, in *Works*, 21 vols. (1928–37), 8: 287.

93 *counterinsurgent "small wars"*: C. E. Callwell, *Small Wars: Their Principles and Practice* (1896). For a jaundiced view of the actual record over two centuries of frequently rediscovered and highly touted theories of victory in unconventional conflicts, see Douglas Porch, *Counterinsurgency: Exposing the Myths of the New Way of War* (2013).

93 *Asymmetry, unlike counterinsurgency*: Compare Beatrice Heuser, *Rebellen, Partisanen, Guerilleros: Asymmetrische Kriege von der Antike bis Heute* (2013).

93 *the battle of Adwa*: Raymond Jonas, *The Battle of Adwa: African Victory in the Age of Empire* (2011).

94 *"the most signal triumph"*: Winston Churchill, *The River War: An Account of the Reconquest of the Sudan* (2000), 300.

94 *"Muslim peoples"*: Fedor de Martens, *Traité de droit international*, 3 vols., trans. Alfred Léo (1883–87), 1: 238–40.

95 *"selfish interest"*: Joseph Hornung, "Civilisés et barbares," *Revue de droit international et de législation comparée* 17 (1885): 17, and 18 (1886): 188; compare Andrew

Fitzmaurice, "Liberalism and Empire in Nineteenth-Century International Law," *American Historical Review* 117 (2012): 122–40.

95 *"The men of the white race"*: Gustave Moynier, *L'État indépendant du Congo au point de vue juridique* (1887), 3–4.

95 *Always omitted*: Albert Wirz, "Die humanitäre Schweiz im Spannungsfeld zwischen Philanthropie und Kolonialismus: Gustave Moynier, Afrika und das IKRK," *Traverse* 5 (1998): 95–111.

96 *"have not recognized"*: Hornung, "Civilisés" (1885), 7.

96 *clearly were different*: Compare Dierk Walter, *Colonial Violence: European Empire and the Use of Force*, trans. Peter Lewis (2017), esp. chap. 3, as well as Kim Wagner, "Savage Warfare: Violence and the Rule of Colonial Difference in Early British Counterinsurgency," *History Workshop Journal* 85 (2018): 217–37, and the controversy that follows in the same journal. For culture and difference, see Patrick Porter, *Military Orientalism: Eastern War Through Western Eyes* (2013).

96 *racial theory more and more*: Harald Kleinschmidt, *Diskriminierung durch Vertrag und Krieg* (2013), esp. part iv; Jennifer Pitts, *The Boundaries of the International: Law and Empire* (2018).

98 *"to wage it with humanity"*: A. Conan Doyle, preface to *The War in South Africa: Its Cause and Conduct* (1902).

98–99 *The world did not see*: The classic is S. B. Spies, *Methods of Barbarism?: Roberts and Kitchener and Civilians in the Boer Republics*, 2nd ed. (2001); for contemporary legal commentary, Frantz Despagnet, *La Guerre sud-africaine au point de vue du droit international* (1902).

99 *sententious paeans*: Bertha von Suttner, "Present Status and Prospects of the Peace Movement," *North American Review* 171 (1900): 653–63.

99 *"the mirror to the face"*: W. T. Stead, *"Methods of Barbarism": The Case for Intervention* (1901), 4.

99 *"The difference between"*: Ibid., 5.

99 *"methods of barbarism"*: On the pro-Boers, see Arthur Davey, *The British Pro-Boers, 1877–1902* (1978), and Stephen Koss, ed., *The Pro-Boers: The Anatomy of an Antiwar Movement* (1973).

100 *"When a nation adopts"*: Doyle, *War in South Africa*, 72.

101 *"His Majesty's government"*: Cited in Tony Lucking, "Some Thoughts on the Evolution of Boer War Concentration Camps," *Journal of Army Historical Research* 82 (2004): 160; see also Candice Millard, *Hero of Empire: The Boer War, a Daring Escape, and the Making of Winston Churchill* (2016), part iv.

101 *making them a model*: See Aidan Forth, *Barbed-Wire Imperialism: Britain's Empire of Camps, 1876–1903* (2017), and Andreas Stucki, "'Frequent Deaths': The Colonial Development of Concentration Camps Reconsidered, 1868–1974," *Journal of Genocide Research* 20 (2019): 305–326.

101 *Hermann Goering reportedly*: Nevile Henderson, *The Failure of a Mission: Berlin, 1937–39* (1940), 21.

101 *"It was the duty"*: Doyle, *War in South Africa*, 81, 85.

102 *referred the problem*: For details of the system, and on Hobhouse, see Spies, *Methods*, esp. 247–52, 288–92; Peter Warwick, *Black People and the South African War* (1983); and improved numbers from Stowell Kessler, "The Black and Coloured Concentration Camps of the Anglo-Boer War 1988–1902," *Historia* 4 (1999), and *The Black Concentration Camps of the Anglo-Boer War, 1899–1902* (2012).

103 *"Fighting desperate savages"*: Ibid., 81–82, 109–110.

103 *"The Indians' fight"*: John Underhill, "Newes from America," in Charles Orr, ed., *History of the Pequot War: Contemporary Accounts* (1897), 51.

103 *"It was the end"*: John Fiske, *The Beginnings of New England: Or, the Puritan Theocracy in Its Relations to Civil and Religious Liberty* (1899), 131–34, also for the "eccentric daredevil" comment.

104 *"in a savage state"*: James Kent, *Commentaries on American Law*, 4 vols. (1826), 1: 3, 45.

104 *"Will it not be"*: Cited in W. Fitzhugh Brundage, *Civilizing Torture: An American Tradition* (2018), 45.

105 *"The known rule"*: John Grenier's brilliant *The First Way of War: American War Making on the Frontier* (2005), 16–19.

105 *"They know what"*: Francis Lieber, *Guerrilla Parties Considered with Reference to the Laws and Usages of War, Written at the Request of Major-General Henry W. Halleck* (1862), 9, 20–21.

105 *rudimentary trials*: See Michael Fellman, *Inside War: The Guerrilla Conflict in Missouri During the American Civil War* (1989), 84–86.

106–107 *by President George W. Bush's lawyers*: John Yoo, "Military Interrogation of Alien Unlawful Combatants Held Outside the United States," March 14, 2003, as discussed in Jodi Byrd, *Transit of Empire: Indigenous Critiques of Colonialism* (2011), 226–28.

107 *"It is difficult"*: Geo. Williams, "The Modoc Indian Prisoners," in *Official Opinions of the Attorneys-General of the United States*, 43 vols. (1852–1996), 14: 250, 252–53.

107 *tried by commission*: James Speed, "Military Commissions," *Opinions*, 11: 316, 306–307.

107 *was a sham*: Doug Foster, "Imperfect Justice: The Modoc War Crimes Trials of 1873," *Oregon Historical Quarterly* 100 (1999): 247–87.

107 *Even when it was invoked*: Neither Speed nor Williams mentioned it, but the same applied during the Dakota wars of the 1860s, where native enemies were tried by military commission because direct (though still legal) killing proved difficult or impossible for logistical and strategic reasons. Maeve Glass, "Explaining the Sioux Military Commission of 1862," *Columbia Human Rights Law Review* 40 (2009): 743–98.

107 *"I want the world"*: The Modoc versions of the story were told by the onetime army colonel A. B. Meacham, on his own and after touring the country with Wi-ne-ma, Kintpuash's cousin who married a white settler from Kentucky and then served the Americans as a translator during the war, saving Meacham's life at the peace meeting after warning of a likely Indian plot to strike there; forty years later, Wi-ne-ma's son also told the "Indian history" of the war. The account that follows cites and synthesizes the versions in A. B. Meacham, *Wigwam and Warpath, or, the Royal Chief in Chains* (1875), chaps. 19–21; A. B. Meacham, *Wi-ne-ma (The Woman-Chief) and Her People* (1876), citation at 8; and Jeff C. Riddle, *The Indian History of the Modoc War* (1914). Of the many excellent secondary accounts, my views are closest to the recent unvarnished reconstructions by Benjamin Madley, "California and Oregon's Modoc Indians: How Indigenous Resistance Camouflages Genocide," in Alexander Hinton et al., eds., *Colonial Genocide in Indigenous North America* (2014); Benjamin Madley, *An American Genocide: The United States and the California Indian Catastrophe, 1846–1873* (2016), chap. 9; and Robert McNally, *The Modoc War: A Story of Genocide at the Dawn of America's Gilded Age* (2017). Also brilliant on how the war has been represented over time is Boyd Cothran, *Remembering the Modoc War: Redemptive Violence and the Making of American Innocence* (2014).

108 *"Had he slain"*: Meacham, *Wigwam*, 301.

108 *"I just as well"*: Riddle, *Indian History*, 38.
108 *"free from restraint"*: Meacham, *Wigwam*, 304.
108 *"How many times"*: Jean Pictet, *L'Épopée des Peaux-Rouges* (1988, 1994), 33.
109 *"utter extermination"*: Cited in Madley, "California," 114.
109 *"We feel confident"*: Letter of Lucretia Mott et al. to Ulysses S. Grant, July 12, 1873, in ibid., House of Representatives, 43rd Congress, *Executive Document No. 122* (1874): 310.
110 *"We have never considered"*: Cited in Carol Faulkner, *Lucretia Mott's Heresy: Abolition and Women's Rights in Nineteenth-Century America* (2011), 201.
111 *"Murder is almost"*: Cited in Xiangyun Xu, "The Crucible of Empire: The American Experience in the China Relief Expedition of 1900" (Ph.D. diss., Pennsylvania State University, 2019), 239.
111 *was a "race war"*: Paul Kramer, *The Blood of Government: Race, Empire, the United States, and the Philippines* (2006).
111 *"American soldiers"*: Cited in Andrei Mamolea, "The Myth of Legalism in US Foreign Relations" (Ph.D. diss., Graduate Institute-Geneva, 2018), 87. The defense journalist Max Boot has counseled to keep abuses "in proper perspective" since it was "a more brutal time." Max Boot, *The Savage Wars of Peace: Small Wars and the Rise of American Power* (2003), 126–27. See also Brian McAllister Linn, *The Philippine War, 1899–1902* (2000).
112 *"The war of 1898"*: "Our Savage War 'For the Cause of Humanity,'" *The Nation*, April 20, 1899.
112 *"methods which have proved"*: Cited in Mamolea, "Myth," 94.
113 *Doing so did not demand*: I am in dialogue with Will Smiley's excellent "Lawless Wars of Empire?: The International Law of War in the Philippines, 1898–1903," *Law and History Review* 36 (2018): 511–50, esp. 523–34, except in refusing to define a fight that excludes almost all enemies from any protection whatsoever, making forbearance a mere policy option, as either humanized (except on Francis Lieber's definition) or legalized. It was too early, I believe, for legitimation through humanizing international legality, though Smiley rightly identifies it as the scary eventuality.
113 *"Injun warfare"*: Stuart Creighton Miller, *"Benevolent Assimilation": The American Conquest of the Philippines, 1898–1903* (1982), chap. 11.
113 *"I want not prisoners"*: Cited in Moorfield Storey and Julian Codman, *Secretary Root's Record: "Marked Severities" in the Philippines* (1902), 33. As the best student of the Samar campaign comments, "Very few of Smith's orders were unprecedented in recent American practice, including official commands." Stuart White, "General Chaffee's Small Wars: Institutional Culture, Command Intention, and Restraint in American Expeditionary Wars, 1899–1902" (Ph.D. diss., University of Calgary, 2016), 397.
113 *"I want all persons killed"*: Smiley, "Lawless," 538, reads Smith to restrict killing only to fighters, which is not what "*capable of* bearing arms" means, whether or not an image-managing Root added the proviso "in actual hostilities."
113 *"ignorant of what constitutes"*: "Welcomed to the Capital," *New-York Tribune*, November 14, 1902.
114 *"humanity and kindness"*: "Peace and Amnesty Declared in the Philippines," *Boston Globe*, July 4, 1902.
114 *Philippine insurgents*: John Gates, "Philippine Guerillas, American Anti-Imperialists, and the Election of 1900," *Pacific Historical Review* 46 (1977): 51–64; as Miller stresses, anti-imperialism as much as imperialism frequently depended on white racialist assumptions: Miller, *"Benevolent Assimilation,"* chap. 7.

114 *"water cure"*: Frank Schumacher, "'Marked Severities': The Debate over Torture During America's Conquest of the Philippines, 1899–1902," *Amerikastudien* 51 (2006): 475–98; Paul Kramer, "The Water Cure," *The New Yorker*, February 25, 2008; Brundage, *Civilizing Torture*, chap. 5.

115 *Roosevelt's damage control*: See Louise Barnett, *Atrocity and American Military Justice in Southeast Asia: Trial by Army* (2010), as well as Mamolea, "Myth," chap. 2.

115 *"I believe in"*: W. E. Burghardt Du Bois, "Credo," *Independent*, October 6, 1904.

115 *"swept away"*: Giulio Douhet, *The Command of the Air* (1942), 181.

116 *"Idle ladies and gentlemen"*: Leo Tolstoy, *Christianity and Patriotism* (1894), in *Works*, 20: 489. When the Russo-Turkish War came in 1905, it roused Tolstoy's ire, too. Leo Tolstoy, "Bethink Yourselves!," in *Works*, 21: 204–271.

116 *"It was no coincidence"*: Jean-Paul Sartre, "On Genocide," in John Duffett, ed., *Against the Crime of Silence: Proceedings of the International War Crimes Tribunal* (1968, 1970), 613.

116 *Germany did violate the laws*: Alan Kramer, *Dynamic of Destruction: Culture and Mass Killing in the First World War* (2007), chap. 4.

116 *the British blockade*: Compare Isabel Hull, *A Scrap of Paper: Breaking and Making International Law During the Great War* (2014).

117 *the trench-ridden western front*: Stéphane Audoin-Rouzeau and Annette Becker, *14–18: Understanding the Great War* (2002), chap. 2.

117 *The category of "civilian"*: Amanda Alexander, "The Genesis of the Civilian," *Leiden Journal of International Law* 20 (2007): 359–76.

117 *"Not only is it more bloody and destructive"*: Sigmund Freud, "Thoughts for the Times on War and Death," in *Standard Edition of the Complete Psychological Works*, 24 vols., ed. James Strachey (1953–74), 14: 278–79.

117 *"It is more utopian"*: Heinrich Lammasch, *Das Völkerrecht nach dem Kriege* (1917), 4.

117 *"In four brief years"*: H. G. Wells et al., *The Idea of a League of Nations* (1919), 9, 25.

118 *"The failure of international law"*: "The League of Nations and the Law of War," *British Year Book of International Law* 1 (1920–21): 124. See J. L. Kunz, "Plus de lois de guerre?," *Revue générale de droit international public* 41 (1934): 22–57, responding to this premature obituary as well as even more generalized skepticism such as H. Erle Richards, *Does International Law Still Exist?* (1914), or Ernst Zitelmann, *Haben wir noch ein Völkerrecht?* (1914).

118 *"The war has"*: Quincy Wright, "The Effect of the War on International Law," *Minnesota Law Review* 5 (1920–21): 517.

4. AIR WAR AND AMERICA'S BRUTAL PEACE

120 *"I am a one hundred percent"*: William Manchester, *American Caesar: Douglas MacArthur, 1880–1964* (1978), 16.

120 *"not as a commander"*: Ibid., 547.

121 *"the* pax Britannica": Quincy Wright, "International Law and the World Order," in Walter Laves, ed., *The Foundations of a More Stable World Order* (1941), 124–25.

121 *"The excessively brutal"*: Quincy Wright, "The Path to Peace," *World Unity* 13 (1933): 136.

122 *As the great debate raged*: James Martin, *American Liberalism and World Politics, 1931–1941*, 2 vols. (1964), esp. chaps. 8, 16, 21–22, 25, 30; for the other side, see Manfred Jonas, *Isolationism in America, 1935–1941* (1966).

122 *remarkable opinion*: Edwin Borchard, "The Attorney-General's Opinion on the Exchange of Destroyers for Naval Bases," *American Journal of International Law* 34

(1940): 690–97, and Quincy Wright, "The Transfer of Destroyers to Great Britain," ibid., 680–89.

122 *he celebrated the Lend-Lease program*: Quincy Wright, "The Lend-Lease Bill and International Law," *American Journal of International Law* 35 (1941): 305–314.

123 *"localizing at important points"*: James Brown Scott, ed., *Proceedings of the Hague Peace Conferences* (1920), 354.

123 *drowned out*: See *Annuaire de l'Institut de droit international* 26 (1913): 533–34.

123 *more brutal than accepted conduct*: Sven Lindqvist, *A History of Bombing*, trans. Linda Haverty Rugg (2001), 31–32.

124 *"What aerial war will mean"*: W. Evans Darby, "The Peril of the Air," *Advocate of Peace* 74 (1912): 245.

124 *"There never yet"*: The memorial is reprinted in Darby, "Peril of the Air (Concluded)," *Advocate of Peace* 74 (1912): 264.

124 *"Barbarization of the Air"*: Bertha von Suttner, *Die Barbarisierung der Luft* (1912).

124 *"the present war"*: "Attacks by Airships Not Governed by Law," *New York Times*, October 19, 1914.

125 *"strategic bombing"*: For the theory, Thomas Hippler, *Bombing the People: Giulio Douhet and the Foundations of Air-Power Strategy* (2013).

125 *Somali insurgency easily terminated*: Thomas Hippler, *Governing from the Skies: A Global History of Aerial Bombing*, trans. David Fernbach (2014), chap. 4.

125 *"practically wiped out"*: Cited in Lindqvist, *History of Bombing*, 48.

125 *"the great humanity of bombing"*: Cited in Priya Satia, "The Defense of Inhumanity: Air Control and the British Idea of Arabia," *American Historical Review* 111 (2006): 36.

126 *"inflict various degrees"*: Cited in Charles Townshend, "Civilization and 'Frightfulness': Air Control in the Middle East Between the Wars," in Chris Wrigley, ed., *Warfare, Diplomacy, and Politics: Essays in Honour of A.J.P. Taylor* (1987), 148.

126 *"is capable of transforming"*: J. M. Spaight, *Air Power and War Rights* (1924), 2.

127 *interpret "military objectives" narrowly*: J. M. Spaight, *Air Power and the Cities* (1930), 201.

127 *"for the purpose of terrorizing"*: Hague Rules of Air Warfare (1923), Arts. 22, 24; see also Alex Meyer, *Völkerrechtlicher Schutz der friedlichen Personen und Sachen gegen Luftangriffe* (1935).

127 *"come of a white race"*: Walter Harris, *France, Spain, and the Rif* (1927), 36, vii.

128 *the sole real advance*: Anna Chotzen, "Beyond Bounds: Morocco's Rif War and the Limits of International Law," *Humanity* 5 (2014): 33–54; there was also a new Geneva Convention negotiated in 1929 to beef up the Hague treaty rules on prisoners of war and to update the original Geneva Convention's provisions for wounded soldiers.

128 *"essentially a Christian doctrine"*: Elbridge Colby, "How to Fight Savage Tribes," *American Journal of International Law* 21 (1927): 280–81, replying to Quincy Wright, "The Bombardment of Damascus," *American Journal of International Law* 20 (1926): 263–80.

129 *"a more modernized"*: Ibid., 283–84.

129 *"actually and geographically"*: Elbridge Colby, "Aërial Law and War Targets," *American Journal of International Law* 19 (1925): 704.

129 *"If a few 'non-combatants'"*: Colby, "How to Fight," 287.

129 *"There is a popular fallacy"*: Elbridge Colby, "The Progressive Character of War," *American Political Science Review* 18 (1924): 373, 366, the first a citation from the assistant secretary of war, Dwight Davis, speaking in St. Louis in 1923.

129 *"When airplanes destroy towns"*: Elbridge Colby, "War Crimes," *Michigan Law Review* 23 (1925): 509.

130 *first among equals*: Stephen Wertheim, *Tomorrow, the World: The Birth of U.S. Global Supremacy* (2020).

130 *still possible to create*: Quincy Wright, "International Law and the World Order," in Walter Laves, ed., *The Foundations of a More Stable World Order* (1941), 124–25.

130 *"A transition from a hegemonic"*: Quincy Wright, "The Present Status of Neutrality," *American Journal of International Law* 34 (1940): 414–15; see also Quincy Wright, *The Causes of War and the Conditions of Peace* (1935), esp. chap. 4.

131 *what Wright had intended*: See Daniel Gorman, "International Law and the International Thought of Quincy Wright, 1918–1945," *Diplomatic History* 41 (2017): 336–61, and Or Rosenboim, *The Emergence of Globalism: Visions of World Order in Britain and the United States, 1939–1950* (2017), chap. 6.

131 *"the ramparts to defend"*: Quincy Wright, "American Policy and the War," in William Allen White, ed., *Defense for America* (1940), 16.

131 *"Totalitarianism both in principle"*: Quincy Wright, "International Law and the Totalitarian States," *American Political Science Review* 35 (1941): 742.

132 *"The effect of bombing"*: U.S. Army Training Regulations, No. 15–70 (1922), para. 24; compare M. W. Royse, *Aerial Bombardment and the International Regulation of Warfare* (1928), and Paul Whitcomb Williams, "Legitimate Targets in Aerial Bombardment," *American Journal of International Law* 23 (1929): 570–81.

132 *"if a nation ambitious"*: Billy Mitchell, *Winged Defense: The Development and Possibilities of Modern Air Power* (1925), 14, 25–26.

132 *until the success over Japan*: Tami David Biddle, *Rhetoric and Reality in Air Warfare: The Evolution of British and American Ideas About Strategic Bombing, 1914–1945* (2002).

132 *"raging infernos"*: "The Bombing of Chungking: Mme. Chiang Kai-Shek's Account," *The Times* (London), June 14, 1939.

133 *"ruthless bombing from the air"*: "Start of Strife Brings Quick Action by President in Behalf of Noncombatants," *New York Times*, September 2, 1939; "Roosevelt Plea for Civilians," *New York Herald Tribune*, December 1, 1939. There had been a number of earlier Department of State condemnations of Japanese civilian bombing: *Foreign Relations of the United States: Japan, 1931–1941*, 2 vols. (1943), 1: 498–506 and 595–96.

133 *"absolutely convince the Germans"*: Cited in Mark Clodfelter, *Beneficial Bombing: The Progressive Foundations of American Air Power, 1917–1945* (2010), 179.

133–34 *"The Allies stand for something"*: George Bell, "Bombing Policy," in *House of Lords Speeches*, ed. Peter Raina (2009), 61–62.

134 *"in this matter"*: Arthur Harris, *Bomber Offensive* (1947), 177.

134 *"Attempts to humanize"*: "Massacre by Bombing," *New York Times*, March 1944, responding to Vera Brittain, "Massacre by Bombing: The Facts Behind the British-American Attack on Germany," *Fellowship* 10 (1944): 50–63; for the American stir it caused, see A. C. Grayling, *Among the Dead Cities: The History and Moral Legacy of the World War II Bombing of Civilians in Germany and Japan* (2006), chap. 5.

135 *"the prophets of calamity"*: J. M. Spaight, *Bombing Vindicated* (1944), 15, 50, 156; the articles of the late 1930s were "The Lawless Arm," *Army Quarterly* 31 (1935): 66–72, and "The Chaotic State of the International Law Concerning Bombardment," *Royal Air Force Quarterly* (January 1938).

135 *"the war was over"*: Richard Kohn and Joseph Harahan, eds., *Strategic Bombing: A Conversation* (1988), 69.

136 *"Emotions forgotten since"*: Cited in John Dower, *War Without Mercy: Race and Power in the Pacific War* (1986), 33.

137 *"Even a dead Jap"*: Ibid., 152–53, in the midst of a whole chapter on the common analogy of Japanese with Native Americans.

137 *"The use of atomic bombs"*: Cited in Tsuyoshi Hasegawa, *Racing the Enemy: Stalin, Truman, and the Surrender of Japan* (2005), 299. Alongside Art. 23 of the Hague treaty, Japan also referenced Art. 22: "The right of belligerents to adopt means of injuring the enemy is not unlimited."

137 *The organization's wholesale failure*: Christian Streit, *Keine Kamaraden: Die Wehrmacht und die sowjetischen Kriegsgefangenen 1941–1945* (1978).

137 *Carl Jacob Burckhardt*: See, e.g., Jean-Claude Favez, *The Red Cross and the Holocaust* (1999).

138 *"rules of moderation"*: L. Oppenheim, *International Law: A Treatise*, 5th ed., ed. Hersch Lauterpacht (1935), vii.

138 *"times in which international law"*: W. E. Hall cited in Wright, "International Law and the World Order," 121.

139 *"objectively pro-fascist"*: George Orwell is cited in (and this paragraph depends on) Devin Pendas, "Against War: Pacifism as Collaboration and Resistance," in Evan Mawdsley, ed., *Cambridge History of the Second World War*, 3 vols. (2015), 3: 477; Leilah Danielson, *American Gandhi: A. J. Muste and the History of Radicalism in the Twentieth Century* (2014).

139 *"peace force"*: Quincy Wright, "Peace and Political Organization," *International Conciliation* 369 (1941): 451–67; Wright, "Fundamental Problems of International Organization," ibid., 468–92; Wright, "An International Police Force," *New Europe*, March 1944; Quincy Wright et al., letter to the editor, *New York Times*, November 5, 1944, defending the constitutionality of international policing; Robert Hillmann, "Quincy Wright and the Commission to Study the Organization of Peace," *Global Governance* 4 (1998): 485–98.

140 *"We should . . . assume"*: Quincy Wright, letter to the editor, *Forum and Century* 103 (1940): 206, cited in Trygve Throntveit, "A Strange Fate: Quincy Wright and the Trans-War Trajectory of Wilsonian Internationalism," *White House Studies* 10 (2011): 367; see also Robert Divine, *Second Chance: The Triumph of Internationalism in America During World War II* (1971).

140 *"institutions to determine"*: Quincy Wright, "Peace Problems of Today and Yesterday," *American Political Science Review* 38 (1944): 517.

140 *"like a wild beast"*: Quincy Wright, *A Study of War* (1942), 1348.

141 *There was no legal barrier*: Quincy Wright, "War Criminals," *American Journal of International Law* 39 (1945): 257–85.

141 *"This inquest"*: *Trial of the Major War Criminals Before the International Military Tribunal*, 42 vols. (1947–49), 2: 98.

141 *"War is essentially"*: Ibid., 22: 426.

141 *The Soviets, insisting*: Francine Hirsch, *Soviet Judgment at Nuremberg: A New History of the International Military Tribunal After World War II* (2020).

141 *"main preoccupation"*: Judith N. Shklar, *Legalism* (1963), 174.

142 *"Once the evil of war"*: Herbert Wechsler, "The Issues of the Nuremberg Trial," *Political Science Quarterly* 62 (1947): 17. On the marginality of the Holocaust at Nuremberg, see Donald Bloxham, *Genocide on Trial: War Crimes Trials and the Formation of Holocaust History and Memory* (2001).

142 *"Sanctions to be effective"*: Quincy Wright, "The Law of the Nuremberg Trial," *American Journal of International Law* 41 (1947): 47.

143 *"The record on which"*: *Trial*, 2: 100.

143 *American internationalism mutated*: Stephen Wertheim, "Instrumental Internationalism: The American Origins of the United Nations, 1940–3," *Journal of Contemporary History* 54 (2019): 265–83.

143 *"International law has a secondary"*: Clyde Eagleton, "International Law and the Charter of the United Nations," *American Journal of International Law* 39 (October 1945): 752, and for a more general presentation, my *The Last Utopia: Human Rights in History* (2010), chap. 5.

144 *"We have retained"*: Cited in Gaddis Smith, *The Last Years of the Monroe Doctrine, 1945–1993* (1994), 55.

144 *"unlikely that sanctions"*: Quincy Wright, "The U.N. Charter and the Prevention of War," *Bulletin of Atomic Scientists* 3 (1947): 58.

144 *But the hypothetical*: Quincy Wright, "Why Are We Faced with Two Worlds?," *Christian Register*, August 1947, rpt. in *Man, God, and the Soviets: 52 Religious Liberals Speak Up* (1952).

145 *After all the wretched things*: Josef Kunz, "The Chaotic Status of the Laws of War," *American Journal of International Law* 45 (1951): 37–61.

146 *The ICRC emerged*: Gerald Steinacher, *Humanitarians at War: The Red Cross in the Shadow of the Holocaust* (2017).

146 *It was especially revolutionary*: Throughout I follow Boyd van Dijk, *Preparing for War: The Making of the Geneva Conventions* (2021). See also Boyd van Dijk, "'The Great Humanitarian': The Soviet Union, the International Committee for the Red Cross, and the Geneva Conventions of 1949," *Law and History Review* 37 (2019): 209–235.

146 *shaped the U.S. negotiation posture*: Olivier Barsalou, "Preparing for War: The USA and the Making of the 1949 Geneva Conventions on the Laws of War," *Journal of Conflict and Security Law* 23 (2017): 49–73.

147 *"humane blockade"*: See Geneva Conventions (1949) IV, Art. 23, and Nicolas Mulder and Boyd van Dijk, "Why Did Starvation Not Become the Paradigmatic War Crime in International Law?," in Kevin Jon Heller and Ingo Venzke, eds., *Contingency in the History of International Law* (2021).

148 *a rather awkward alliance*: Along with van Dijk's account, see Giovanni Mantilla, "International Law at the Edge of Sovereignty: The Political Origins of Common Article 3 to the 1949 Geneva Conventions" (forthcoming), and "The Protagonism of the USSR and Socialist States in the Revision of International Humanitarian Law," *Journal of the History of International Law* 21 (2019): 181–211, who also highlights the interests of small states in more constraint.

148 *the intent at the time*: Pictet's 1952 commentary makes this entirely clear: Jean Pictet, ed., *The Geneva Conventions of 12 August 1949: Commentary*, 4 vols. (1952–60), 1: 28–37 (repeated for subsequent conventions).

148 *"In times of war"*: Jean Pictet, "The New Geneva Conventions for the Protection of War Victims," *American Journal of International Law* 45 (1951): 470.

148 *"the humanitarian Conventions"*: J. M. Spaight, "Weapons of Mass Destruction," *Journal of the Royal United Service Institution* 99 (1954): 61.

149 *There would not have been*: Attention to negotiation of the Geneva Conventions and state legal commitment to them scants the equally if not more important topic of anticipated and evolving state legal compliance—and my point in this book is to propose a chronological framework for the American case.

149 *hay of counterinsurgent violence*: In a fascinating emerging literature on the law of war in later empire, see Fabian Klose, "The Colonial Testing Ground: The International

Committee of the Red Cross and the Violent End of Empire," *Humanity* 2 (2011): 107–126, Boyd van Dijk, "Internationalizing Colonial War: On the Unintended Consequences of the Interventions of the International Committee of the Red Cross in South-east Asia, 1945–1949," *Past & Present* 250 (2021): 243–83, and other works.

149 *"a peace offensive"*: Timothy Johnston, "Peace or Pacifism?: The Soviet 'Struggle for Peace in All the World,' 1948–1954," *Slavonic and East European Review* 86 (2008): 259–82.

149 *"Peace propaganda"*: Cited in Petra Goedde, *The Politics of Peace: A Global Cold War History* (2019), 1, which these paragraphs follow.

150 *"these advantages are trifling"*: Albert Schweitzer, *The Problem of Peace in the World Today* (1954), 11.

151 *MacArthur's choice meant*: Paul Thomas Chamberlin, *The Cold War's Killing Fields: Rethinking the Long Peace* (2018).

151 *the day the Security Council*: Speculation still swirls around the reason for Malik's absence; see William Stueck, "The United Nations, the Security Council, and the Korean War," in Adam Roberts et al., eds., *The United Nations Security Council and War* (2008).

151 *"under the guise of aid"*: *Foreign Relations of the United* States *1950*, 7 vols. (1976), 7: 158.

152 *"imaginary line"*: A. M. Rosenthal, "U.N. Action Urged," *New York Times*, October 1, 1950.

152 *"uniting for peace"*: See UN Gen. Ass. Res. 376(V), "The Problem of the Independence of Korea," and 377(V), "Uniting for Peace" (November 1950). As one observer has delicately commented, "With US General MacArthur in charge of the military campaign, there is little doubt that the US-led forces would have ventured into North Korea without Resolution 376." Nigel White, "The Korean War, 1950–53," in Tom Ruys and Olivier Corten, eds., *The Use of Force in International Law: A Case-Based Approach* (2018), 25.

152 *The United States would do so*: The United States committed to train in light of new rules earlier, and its main World War II army rules manual appeared in 1956. See William Downey, Jr., "Training in the Geneva Conventions of 1949," *American Journal of International Law* 46 (1952): 143–44; Josef Kunz, "The New U.S. Army Field Manual on the Law of Land Warfare," *American Journal of International Law* 51 (1957): 388–96.

152 *"present instructions"*: "M'Arthur Warns Reds on Captives," *New York Times*, July 5, 1950.

152 *But racial egalitarianism*: Compare Inderjeet Parmar, "Racial and Imperial Thinking in International Theory and Politics: Truman, Attlee, and the Korean War," *British Journal of Politics and International Relations* 18 (2016): 351–69.

153 *"the onerous task"*: Cited in Manchester, *American Caesar*, 34, 639.

153 *"reversion to old-style fighting"*: Cited in Bruce Cumings, *The Korean War: A History* (2010), 252n6, 168–69.

153 *"Our Red foe scorns all the rules"*: Cited in ibid., 252n6.

153 *the experience took Americans back*: See ibid., 168–69.

153 *as many may have died*: See ibid., 132–33.

153–54 *at No Gun Ri*: Charles Hanley et al., *The Bridge at Nogun Ri: A Hidden Nightmare from the Korean War* (2002).

154 *"reprisals against the forces"*: "United States Courses of Action with Respect to Korea," National Security Council Report 81/1 (September 9, 1950), para. 24.

154 *turn prisoners over*: Cited in Cumings, *Korean War*, 196; compare Geneva Conventions (1949) III, Art. 12.

154 *participation in atrocities*: Taewoo Kim, "Limited War, Unlimited Targets: U.S. Air Force Bombing of North Korea During the Korean War, 1950–1953," *Critical Asian Studies* 44 (2012): 467–92. Compare the apologetic interpretation of the air war and the entire conflict in Sahr Conway Lanz, *Collateral Damage: Americans, Noncombatant Immunity, and Atrocity After World War II* (2006), chap. 2, and "The Struggle to Fight a Humane War: The United States, the Korean War, and the 1949 Geneva Convention," in Matthew Evangelista and Nina Tannenwald, eds., *Do the Geneva Conventions Matter?* (2017).

155 *"The city I'd seen before"*: Cited in Kim, "Limited War," 488.

155 *"To antiwar protestors"*: Harry Summers, Jr., foreword to Mark Moyar, *Phoenix and the Birds of Prey: Counterinsurgency and Counterterrorism in Vietnam*, new ed. (2007), xi.

156 *Wright showed no reason*: Waqar Zaidi, "Stages of War, Stages of Man: Quincy Wright and the Liberal Internationalist Study of War," *International History Review* 40 (2018): 416–35.

156 *Wright was still hopeful*: Quincy Wright, "Collective Security in Light of the Korean Experience," *Proceedings of the American Society of International Law* 45 (1951): 165–82.

157 *"the* moral *basis"*: Quincy Wright, "Empires and World Governments," *Current History* (1960): 66.

157 *he pinned everything*: Quincy Wright, "The Escalation of International Conflicts," *Journal of Conflict Resolution* 9 (1965): 434–49; Quincy Wright, "Legal Aspects of the Vietnam War," in Jung-Gun Kim, ed., *Essays on the Vietnam War* (1968), 51, for American illegality.

5. THE VIETNAMESE PIVOT

161 *a* New Yorker *article*: Jonathan Schell, "Quang Ngai and Quang Tin 1 and 2," *The New Yorker*, March 9 and 16, 1968; *The Military Half: An Account of Destruction in Quang Ngai and Quang Tin* (1968), and the exchange with Marjorie Schell, January 1970, in Telford Taylor Papers, Arthur W. Diamond Law Library, Columbia University Law School (hereinafter Taylor papers), Series 14, Subseries 6, Box 193.

164 *European powers waging*: For international law in the major postwar counterinsurgencies by Britain and France, see Brian Drohan, *Brutality in the Age of Human Rights: Activism and Counterinsurgency at the End of the British Empire* (2018), and Fabian Klose, *Human Rights in the Shadow of Colonial Violence: The Wars of Independence in Kenya and Algeria*, trans. Dona Geyer (2013).

164 *argument made no sense*: Adlai Stevenson, then United Nations ambassador, offered the self-defense theory that ultimately became the U.S. government's central rationale under international law for all its uses of force. For his statements, see Department of State, *Digest of United States Practice in International Law* (1983), 1751. Much more powerful would have been a claim against the United States that its response to North Vietnam was disproportionate to the armed attacks made on the southern regime, but critics of the war rarely offered this theory and it was not central to debate.

165 *"has always abided"*: [Dean Rusk,] "U.S. Continues to Abide by Geneva Conventions of 1949 in Viet-Nam," *Department of State Bulletin*, September 13, 1965.

165 *directed his forces*: U.S. Military Assistance Command Directive 190–3.

166 *surprising amount of information*: Eric Norden, "American Atrocities in Vietnam," *Liberation* 10 (1966): 14–27.

166 *"may be likened to water"*: Mao Zedong, *On Guerrilla Warfare* (1961), 93.

167 *"every effort"*: United States Military Assistance Command, Vietnam, Directive 525–13 (May 1971).

167 *pioneered by the British*: David French, *The British Way in Counter-Insurgency 1945–1967* (2011).

168 *There was just no interest*: Bernd Greiner, *War Without Fronts: The U.S.A. in Vietnam*, trans. Anne Wyburd and Victoria Fern (2009), including 95–103 on rules of engagement; Daniel Lang, "Casualties of War," *The New Yorker*, October 18, 1969, and *Casualties of War* (1969).

168 *"tends to become universal"*: Cited in Simeon Man, *Soldiering Through Empire: Race and the Making of the Decolonizing Pacific* (2018), 9; Daniel Lucks, "African American Soldiers and the Vietnam War: No More Vietnams," *The Sixties* 10 (2017): 196–220.

168 *"mere gook rule"*: Philip Shabecoff, "Murder Verdict Eased in Vietnam," *New York Times*, March 31, 1970.

168 *"Would we have pursued"*: James Thomson, Jr., "How Could Vietnam Happen?," *The Atlantic*, April 1968.

168 *"I think it is uncontestable"*: Hans Morgenthau in Erwin Knoll and Judith Nies McFadden, eds., *War Crimes and the American Conscience* (1970), 136.

169 *"do what you want"*: James S. Olson and Randy Roberts, *My Lai: A Brief History with Documents* (1998), 42.

169 *after the My Lai cover-up*: Greiner, *War Without Fronts*; based on similar sources, but including perpetrator recollection, see Deborah Nelson, *The War Behind Me: Vietnam Veterans Confront the Truth About U.S War Crimes* (2008). Compare Guenter Lewy, *America in Vietnam: Myth, Illusion, and Reality* (1980), chaps. 7–10. On the JAG corps and military justice, see George S. Prugh, *Law at War: Vietnam, 1964–1973* (1975), and William Thomas Allison, *Military Justice in Vietnam: The Rule of Law in an American War* (2007).

169 *the U.S. use of napalm*: William F. Pepper, "The Children of Vietnam," *Ramparts* 5 (1967): 59; Denise Chong, *The Girl in the Picture: The Story of Kim Phuc, the Photograph, and the Vietnam War* (2000); Robert M. Neer, Jr., *Napalm: An American Biography* (2013). Activism began in the late 1960s leading to the Convention on Certain Conventional Weapons in 1980, which attempts to narrow recourse to some of the most offensive tools of the preceding era, such as land mines and napalm.

170 *"to bomb them back"*: Curtis LeMay, *Mission with Le May: My Story* (1965), 565.

170 *His reporting challenged*: These *New York Times* pieces were immediately gathered as Harrison E. Salisbury, *Behind the Lines: Hanoi, December 23, 1966–January 7, 1967* (1967).

170 *the initial impact of his reporting*: Phil Goulding, *Confirm or Deny: Informing the People on National Security* (1970).

170 *had occurred to no one*: It has been claimed without evidence that when the Joint Chiefs of Staff rejected the 94-target list composed for Rolling Thunder, McNamara informally checked it with Defense Department counsel; but even this account concludes of Johnson's target picking: "With the exception of the General Counsel's approval of the JCS 94-target list, the record is rather clear that Secretary McNamara and the White House never sought advice with regard to

U.S. responsibilities and rights under the law of war with respect to the conduct of Rolling Thunder"—or, one can add, other aerial campaigns through 1973. Legal compliance in air war still occurred "very little, and then more by coincidence than choice." W. Hays Parks, "Rolling Thunder and the Laws of War," *Air University Review* 33 (1982): 15–16, 14.

170 *distressing evidence accumulated*: The major sources were Frank Harvey, *Air War—Vietnam* (1967); John Gerassi, *North Vietnam: A Documentary* (1968); and Cornell Air War Study Group, *The Air War in Indochina* (1972). The best reflection on the legality of the air war at the time, given such revelations, was a student paper, Lawrence C. Petrowski, "Law and the Conduct of the Vietnam War," in Richard Falk, ed., *The Vietnam War and International Law*, 4 vols. (Princeton: Princeton University Press, 1968–76), 2: 439–515, esp. 487–500.

170 *handed over all captured enemies*: The Geneva Conventions (III, Art. 12) allow such transfers only if the capturing power ensures the detaining power follows the treaty's requirements; but it's clear that the South Vietnamese shortcomings in this regard were rather serious.

171 *"interrogation specialists"*: Anthony B. Herbert, *Soldier* (1973).

171 *"Charging a man with murder"*: *Apocalypse Now*, dir. Francis Ford Coppola (1979).

172 *"You Are Old, Father Bertrand"*: Cited in Yoojin Chae, "'May This Tribunal Prevent the Crime of Silence': The Russell Tribunal on War Crimes in Vietnam" (B.A. thesis, Dartmouth College, 2018), 8.

172 *"The only relevant figure"*: "Everyone but Kafka," *New York Herald Tribune*, August 4, 1966.

172 *the Russell tribunal faithfully reflected*: See Bertrand Russell, *War Crimes in Vietnam* (1967); John Duffett, ed., *Against the Crime of Silence: Proceedings of the Russell International War Crimes Tribunal* (1968); Jean-Paul Sartre, *On Genocide* (1968).

173 *The two central figures*: See "William L. Standard, 78, a Lawyer for Seafarers and Writer on War, Dies," *New York Times*, May 7, 1978; "Joseph Crown; Questioned Vietnam Policy," *New York Times*, October 22, 2002.

173 *worked especially closely*: See Randall B. Woods, ed., *Vietnam and the American Political Tradition: The Politics of Dissent* (2003).

173 *The lawyers' main weapon*: I have followed these activities based on a bequest of papers Joseph Crown left to Columbia University, which are available as Lawyers Committee on American Policy Towards Vietnam Records, 1962–1979, Rare Books and Manuscript Library, Columbia University (hereinafter Lawyers Committee papers).

173 *Dean Rusk's public justification*: Dean Rusk, "The Control of Force in International Relations," *Department of State Bulletin*, May 10, 1965; summing up the terms of rebuttal in a title, Standard eventually published *Aggression: Our Asian Disaster*, pref. Morse (1971).

174 *only 700 signatures*: "American Policy vis-à-vis Vietnam," *Congressional Record*, 89th Cong., 1st Sess. (September 23, 1965), 111: 24903–910; "700 Lawyers Submit Anti-Viet War Brief," *New York World-Telegram and Sun*, Friday, November 12, 1965.

174 *"no State has the right"*: United Nations General Assembly Resolution 2131 (XX), Declaration on the Inadmissibility of Intervention in the Domestic Affairs of States and the Protection of Their Independence and Sovereignty (1965).

174 *not truly a state*: This paragraph follows Kevin Jon Heller and Samuel Moyn, "The Vietnam War and International Law," in Pierre Asselin et al., eds., *Cambridge History of the Vietnam War* (forthcoming), and our future book on the same topic.

175 *a fuller response*: The first result was a short letter from McDougal and others, which appears in *Congressional Record*, 89th Cong., 2nd Sess. (February 23, 1966): 112: 3843; the second result was John Norton Moore and James L. Underwood with McDougal, "The Lawfulness of United States Assistance to the Republic of Viet Nam," May 1966, distributed by the American Bar Association to all congressmen, the full text of which is in *Congressional Record*, 89th Cong., 2nd Sess. (July 13, 1966), 112: 15519–67; a shorter version is Moore, "The Lawfulness of Military Assistance to the Republic of Viet-Nam," *American Journal of International Law* 61 (1967): 1–34. Compare William Conrad Gibbons, *The U.S. Government and the Vietnam War: Executive and Legislative Roles and Relationships*, 4 vols. (1986–92), 4: 246n.

175 *American Bar Association resolution*: Austin A. Wehrwein, "Bar Group Finds U.S. Policy Legal Under U.N.," *New York Times*, February 22, 1966; "A.B.A. Under Attack for Vietnam Stand," *New York Times*, March 15, 1966; letter of Standard and Crown to Edward W. Kuhn, ABA president, March 15, 1966, Lawyers Committee papers, Box 10; compare Eberhard P. Deutsch, "The Legality of the United States Position in Vietnam," *ABA Journal*, May 1966, and Standard, "United States Intervention in Vietnam Is Not Legal," *ABA Journal*, July 1966.

175 *finally made public*: Meeker had previously treated this as sufficiently unimportant as to pass on a memo prepared by a subordinate, "Legal Basis for United States Actions Against North Vietnam," March 1965, which a congressional staffer who saw it called "the sloppiest piece of legal work I have ever seen." Cited in Gibbons, *The U.S. Government and the Vietnam War*, 3: 79n.

175 *Meeker lived*: Peter Vankevich, "Leonard Meeker, 1916–2014: An Extraordinary Life," *Ocracoke Observer*, December 5, 2014.

175 *His landmark memo*: [Leonard C. Meeker,] "The Legality of United States Participation in the Defense of Viet Nam" (March 4, 1966), *Department of State Bulletin*, March 28, 1966.

175 *a book-length memo*: A draft, "The Military Involvement of the United States in Vietnam: A Legal Analysis, October 1, 1966," can be found in Lawyers Committee papers, Box 11. The book is Lawyers Committee, *The Vietnam War and International Law* (1967). Leonard Meeker, "Viet-Nam and the International Law of Self-Defense," *Department of State Bulletin*, January 9, 1967; Hedrick Smith, "U.S. Aide Says Law Justifies Vietnam Bombing," *New York Times*, December 14, 1966.

176 *"demonstrations of military might"*: Letter to the editor, *New York Times*, July 6, 1966.

176 *urged the International Court*: "Lawyers' Group Urges Ruling by World Court on Vietnam," *New York Times*, December 9, 1966.

176 *The Lawyers Committee also*: See esp. Consultative Council member Lawrence R. Velvel's "The War in Vietnam: Unconstitutional, Justiciable, and Jurisdictionally Attackable," *Kansas Law Review* 16 (1968): 449–503, and *Undeclared War and Civil Disobedience: The American System in Crisis*, pref. Richard Falk (1970).

176 *a five-point peace program*: "Lawyers Group Asks Congress to End 'Disastrous' Vietnam Policy," *New York Times*, April 1, 1969.

176 *"the turn of the tide"*: Letter of Crown to Morse, October 23, 1969, Lawyers Committee papers, Box 11.

177 *confirmation hearings of William Rehnquist*: "Lawyers' Anti-Viet Group Weighs Presidential Bill of Impeachment," *New York Law Journal*, January 19, 1968; for Nixon, see Lawyers Committee, Boxes 20–21, and Richard Falk, "Why Impeachment?," *The New Republic*, May 1, 1971; William Standard and Joseph Crown, "Rehnquist's Achilles Heel" (letter to the editor), *New York Times*, November 14, 1971.

177 *more emphasis fell on war crimes*: "Toronto Declaration on Vietnam, Laos, and Cambodia: A Realistic Program to End the War," jointly issued by Canadian Lawyers Committee on Vietnam and Lawyers Committee on American Policy Towards Vietnam, Lawyers Committee papers, Box 7; Ross H. Munro, "Lawyers Call for Unconditional Withdrawal of All U.S. Forces from Indo-China Theatre," *Globe and Mail*, May 25, 1970.

177 *Crown visited Hanoi for a week*: "Report of Delegation to Hanoi October 14–21 [1971] of Lawyers Committee on American Policy Towards Vietnam," Lawyers Committee papers, Box 3. In one of its last acts, the committee sent a letter to congressmen in protest of the Christmas bombings, January 16, 1973, Box 22. "[Nixon's] employment of B-52 carpet bombing against densely populated civilian cities as Hanoi and Haiphong—unprecedented in military history—to force North Vietnam to capitulate to his terms constitutes a war crime under the Nuremberg principles," it noted.

177 *he had become a critic*: As Falk explained to a correspondent in fall 1967, "I have grown doubtful myself about [the] affirmation of an American role to thwart Communist-led aggression." Richard A. Falk Papers, Syracuse University Library (hereinafter Falk papers), Letter to Eugene Maier, Box 7, Corres. M II.

178 *"unchallengeable preeminence"*: Leonard B. Boudin, "War Crimes and Vietnam: The Mote in Whose Eye?," *Harvard Law Review* 84 (1971): 1940.

178 *Falk signed on with alacrity*: Letter of Richard Falk to William Standard, November 1, 1965, Lawyers Committee files, Box 9.

178 *classic* Yale Law Journal *article*: Richard Falk, "International Law and the United States Role in the Viet Nam War," *Yale Law Journal* 75 (1966), 1122–60; in the immediate aftermath, see John Norton Moore, "International Law and the United States Role in Viet Nam: A Reply," *Yale Law Journal* 76 (1967): 1051–94, and Richard Falk, "International Law and the United States Role in Viet Nam: A Response to Professor Moore," *Yale Law Journal* 76 (1967): 1095–1158.

178 *"not the view"*: R. R. Baxter, "Legality of the American Action: The War in Vietnam," *The Times*, September 5, 1967, and Falk's reply, *The Times*, October 9, 1967

178 *memorandum justifying U.S. engagement*: See letter of Louis B. Sohn to William Standard, November 2, 1965, Lawyers Committee papers, Box 9, enclosing memo disputing the lawyers' brief and invoking the right of self-defense as rationale for American intervention.

179 *"Needless to say"*: Letter of Richard Falk to Nicholas deB. Katzenbach, September 22, 1966, Falk papers, Box 7, Folder Corres. K.

179 *"an appeal to legal reason"*: Letter of Richard Falk to Burns Weston, July 13, 1967, Falk papers, Box 7, Folder Corres. Lawyers Committee on American Policy Towards Vietnam.

179 *"less a fig-leaf"*: Richard Falk, "Law, Lawyers, and the Conduct of Foreign Affairs," *Yale Law Journal* 78 (1969): 922.

179 *Falk visited Hanoi*: "Two U.S. Law Professors Meet with Hanoi Premier," *New York Times*, July 3, 1968.

180 *"a very sharp shift"*: "Address of Richard Falk, Delegate of the United States, World Congress of Lawyers for Vietnam," Lawyers Committee papers, Box 2.

180 *their book-length compilation*: Clergy and Laymen Concerned About Vietnam, *In the Name of America: The Conduct of the War in Vietnam by the Armed Forces of the United States as Shown by Published Reports* (self-published, 1968). Like the Russell tribunal allegations and the Lawyers Committee experts' brief discussed below, it was published marginally and ignored for a long time; compare Ed-

ward B. Fiske, "Clerics Accuse U.S. of War Crimes," *New York Times*, February 4, 1968.

180 *"not to encourage legal debate"*: Richard Falk, "International Law and the Conduct of the Vietnam War," in Concerned Clergy, *In the Name of America*, 27.

180 *"brutal solidarity burning"*: Martin Luther King, Jr., "Beyond Vietnam," in King, *"In a Single Garment of Destiny": A Global Vision of Justice* (2012), 166–68, 177–78.

182 *"The Circle of Responsibility"*: Richard Falk, "The Circle of Responsibility," *The Nation*, January 26, 1970.

182 *"juridical farce"*: Falk, "International Law and the United States Role in the Vietnam War: A Response to Professor Moore," 1095.

182 *"The Nuremberg principles suggest"*: Falk, "Circle of Responsibility"; see also Richard Falk, "War Crimes and Individual Responsibility," *Church and Society* 61 (1971): 23–32 and 61–62; and Richard Falk, "Son My: War Crimes and Individual Responsibility," *Toledo Law Review* 3 (1971): 21–41.

182 *war correspondent Neil Sheehan*: Neil Sheehan, "Should We Have War Crimes Trials?," *New York Times*, March 28, 1971; compare the letters in response praising the paper for the bold step of commissioning the review at all, *New York Times*, April 25, 1971; see also Mark Sacharoff, "War Crimes: Made in the U.S.A.," *The Nation*, January 25, 1971.

183 *Winter Soldier investigation*: Vietnam Veterans Against the War, *The Winter Soldier Investigation: An Inquiry into American War Crimes* (1971). Among academics, the Committee of Concerned Asian Scholars mobilized prominently; see *The Indochina Story: A Fully Documented Account* (1970), much of which deals with war crimes.

183 *"war criminals"*: Richard Falk, "In Defense of the Movement," *New York Times*, November 28, 1971.

183 *Citizens Commission of Inquiry*: See Falk papers, Box 15, Folder AFSC-War Crimes. The Citizens Commission held events around the country and in April 1971 collaborated with Rep. Ron Dellums to hold war crimes hearings; see Citizens Commission of Inquiry, *The Dellums Committee Hearings on War Crimes in Vietnam* (1972). An international group also rendered judgment: Frank Browning and Dorothy Forman, eds., *The Wasted Nations: Report of the International Commission of Enquiry into United States Crimes in Indochina, June 20–25, 1971*, pref. Richard Falk (1972).

183 Crimes of War: Richard Falk, Gabriel Kolko, and Robert Jay Lifton, eds., *Crimes of War: A Legal, Political-Documentary, and Psychological Inquiry into the Responsibility of Leaders, Citizens, and Soldiers for Criminal Acts in Wars* (1971). For a high-profile reception, see Anthony Lewis, "Law and War," *New York Times*, April 26, 1971. Richard Falk, Irene Gendzier, and Lifton, eds., *Crimes of War: Iraq* (2004).

183 *"Song My [Lai] is merely"*: Gabriel Kolko, "War Crimes and the Nature of the Vietnam War," Congressional Conference on War and Individual Responsibility, February 20–21, 1970, in Falk papers, Box 19, Folder "War and National Responsibility."

183 *"illegal, immoral and criminal"*: "Ex-Senator Aids Bomber's Defense," *New York Times*, October 20, 1973; compare Richard Falk, "The Claim of Violent Resistance and the Nuremberg Obligation," *Contact* 4 (1973), and "The Nuremberg Defense in the Pentagon Papers Case," *Columbia Journal of Transnational Law* 13 (1974): 208–238, esp. 210–11.

183 *"with Jean-Paul Sartre"*: Falk et al., eds., *Crimes of War*, xi.

184 *Nuremberg trial veteran Telford Taylor*: He first commented in Telford Taylor, "Judgment on Mylai," *New York Times*, January 10, 1970, then wrote *Nuremberg and Vietnam: An American Tragedy* (1970, 1971), excerpted as "Nuremberg in Son

My," *New York Times*, November 20, 1970, as well as "Nuremberg to Vietnam: Crime and Punishment," *War/Peace*, November 1970.

184 *"Professor Falk makes up"*: "War Crimes, Just and Unjust Wars, and Comparisons Between Nuremberg and Vietnam," *Columbia Journal of Law and Social Problems* 8 (1971): 129.

184 *Sheehan had attacked*: Neil Sheehan, "Conversations with Americans," *New York Times*, December 27, 1970; compare the letters of Edward Herman and Ralph Schoenman, and Sheehan's response to them, *New York Times*, January 24, 1971.

185 New York Times Book Review *essay*: Sheehan, "Should We Have War Crimes Trials?"

185 *A former supporter*: See Jonathan Bush, "Soldiers Find Wars: A Life of Telford Taylor," *Columbia Journal of Transnational Law* 37 (1999): 675–92.

185 *"the only person alive"*: Falk comments in a Columbia University symposium, "War Crimes, Just and Unjust Wars," 113–14; Falk also participated with Noam Chomsky in the *Yale Law Journal* symposium on the book: Richard Falk, "Nuremberg: Past, Present, and Future," *Yale Law Journal* 80 (1971): 1501–528.

185 *Taylor was moved to intervene*: Geoffrey Cowan and Judith Coburn, "The War Criminals Hedge Their Bets," *Village Voice*, December 4, 1969, to which the former undersecretary of the air force Townsend Hoopes, then famous for his anatomy of escalation, replied. See Townsend Hoopes, "The Nuremberg Suggestion," *Washington Monthly*, January 1970, with replies by the journalists in the February issue. In 1967, Taylor had attended a conference organized by Columbia law students on the possible relevance of Nuremberg to Vietnam; see Taylor papers, Series 9, Subseries 1, Box 1, Folder 11.

185 *"Those to whom"*: Erwin Knoll and Judith Nies McFadden, eds., *War Crimes and the American Conscience* (1970), 8. The conference, sponsored by several Democrats, involved the ubiquitous Falk as well as Hannah Arendt, Daniel Ellsberg, Hans Morgenthau, Jonathan Schell, and others.

186 *Taylor protested*: Letter of Telford Taylor to Jean Highland, April 23, 1971, Taylor papers, Series 8, Subseries 2, Box 16, Folder 152.

186 *"fallen victim to a mistaken attitude"*: Telford Taylor to Allen Ginsberg, March 9, 1970, Taylor papers, Series 14, Subseries 6, Box 193.

187 *"was a long time ago"*: Knoll and McFadden, eds., *War Crimes*, 32–33.

187 *Falk was wrong*: Taylor, *Nuremberg and Vietnam*, chap. 5.

187 *Rejecting Falk's arguments*: Ibid., 118–21; on this point, see already Nuremberg prosecutor Benjamin Ferencz's "War Crimes Law and the Vietnam War," *American University Law Review* 17 (1968): 403–423.

187 *actions he felt were unquestionably criminal*: For instance, Taylor deemed the gang rape and murder reported by Daniel Lang "apparently" not a war crime because he was not sure South Vietnamese civilians were protected persons under the Geneva Conventions and because the victim seemed to have been taken from "friendly" territory. Ibid., 134.

187 *For there were a lot*: Such a move could also serve to minimize culpability, as in the case of Richard Baxter's post–My Lai criticisms of Falk; when he attacked Falk's charge of aggression early in the war, Vietnam was for Baxter an international conflict; later it turned out to be a civil war, with, alas, few laws governing its conduct. See Baxter, "Comments," in Peter D. Trooboff, ed., *Law and Responsibility in Warfare: The Vietnam Experience* (1975).

188 *"impeccable"*: See "Vietnam and the Nuremberg Principles: A Colloquy on War Crimes," *Rutgers-Camden Law Journal* 5 (1973): 7 for the "impeccable" comment.

188 *"no urban holocausts"*: Taylor, *Nuremberg and Vietnam*, 144.

188 *no one had been punished*: Compare Hamilton DeSaussure, "The Laws of Air Warfare: Are There Any?" *International Lawyer* 5 (1971), 527–48.

188 *"legally, I was of no use"*: Joan Baez, *And a Voice to Sing With: My Story* (1987), 199. In a similar spirit, see her undated note in Taylor papers, Series 8, Subseries 1, Box 4, Folder 93.

188 *"We might not have seen"*: Deirdre Carmody, "4 Who Visited Hanoi Tell of Destruction," *New York Times*, January 2, 1973; Telford Taylor, "Hanoi Under the Bombing: Sirens, Shelters, Rubble, and Death," *New York Times*, January 7, 1973; see also Telford Taylor, "North Vietnam," *The Atlantic*, May 1973.

189 *violated an emerging understanding*: Telford Taylor, "Defining War Crimes," *New York Times*, January 11, 1973. After reading Drew Middleton, "Hanoi Films Show No 'Carpet Bombing,'" *New York Times*, May 2, 1973, Taylor sent him an angry letter acknowledging that the city (unlike Dresden and Nagasaki) had survived but insisting on the fact that indiscriminate bombing had indeed taken place. Taylor papers, Series 8, Subseries 1, Box 4, Folder 93.

189 *"It is hardly a tribute"*: Boudin, "War Crimes in Vietnam," 1940.

189 *"a* minimalist indictment*"*: Richard Falk, "Nuremberg and Vietnam," *New York Times*, December 27, 1970; see similar reviews by John Fried, calling the work one of a "tormented conservative," *American Political Science Review* 65 (1971): 1257–58, and by Richard Wasserstrom, "Criminal Behavior," *New York Review of Books*, June 3, 1971.

190 *Taylor stated clearly*: Taylor cited *In re. Yamashita*, 327 U.S. 1 (1946). Neil Sheehan, "Taylor Says by Yamashita Ruling Westmoreland May Be Guilty," *New York Times*, January 9, 1971; William Westmoreland, *A Soldier Reports* (1976), 379.

190 *the two barnstormed around*: See Falk's memorial essay, "Telford Taylor and the Legacy of Nuremberg," *Columbia Journal of Transnational Law* 37 (1999): 693–723, esp. 698–99.

190 *"To say judges should not"*: Taylor, *Nuremberg and Vietnam*, 184.

190 *"of small moment"*: Taylor, "Defining War Crimes."

190 *"Whatever peace-keeping"*: Taylor, *Nuremberg and Vietnam*, 188; similarly, see his letter to the editor with Wolfgang Friedmann and Walter Gellhorn on Laos, which considered the relevant incursion "not so much [a matter] of international law as of moral and political responsibility." "What Is to Be Done in Indochina?," *New York Times*, February 21, 1971.

191 *he balanced*: Telford Taylor, "Judging Calley Is Not Enough," *Life*, April 9, 1971; Taylor, "The Course of Military Justice," *New York Times*, February 2, 1972; Taylor, foreword to Leon Friedman, ed., *The Law of War: A Documentary History* (1972).

191 *"It is a humbling realization"*: Richard Falk, review (of Frances FitzGerald, *Fire in the Lake: The Vietnamese and the Americans in Vietnam* [1972]), *Texas Law Review* 51 (1973): 618.

192 *From the ashes of Hanoi*: Compare Richard Drinnon, *Facing West: The Metaphysics of Indian Hating and Empire Building* (1980), part 5.

6. "CRUELTY IS THE WORST THING WE DO"

193 *"The helpless, the sufferers"*: Samuel J. Hynes, *The Soldier's Tale: Bearing Witness to Modern War* (1997), 221.

194 *"In an air war"*: Samuel Hynes, *Flights of Passage: Reflections of a World War II Aviator* (1988), 186, 216, 241.

194 *"the helpless and the innocent"*: Hynes, *Soldier's Tale*, 227.

195 *"have radically altered"*: Ibid., 221.

196 *second-oldest great Genevan family*: Alexis Favre, "La Dynastie Pictet, une marque imposée," *Le Temps*, December 30, 2016.

196 *"fight war by endeavoring"*: Jean S. Pictet, "The Development of International Humanitarian Law," in C. Wilfred Jenks et al., *International Law in a Changing World* (1963), 124.

196 *the statement was "anodyne"*: Jean Pictet, transcript of interview with Claude Lanzmann, United States Holocaust Memorial Museum, Record Group 60.5054, 19.

197 *"You know those people"*: "The Man Who Wrote the Rules of War," *The Guardian*, August 11, 1999.

197 *the Christian premise*: Max Huber, *Le Bon Samaritan* (1943), in English as *The Good Samaritan: Reflections on the Gospel and Work in the Red Cross* (1945).

197 *"It is even open"*: Jean S. Pictet, "La Croix-Rouge et les Conventions de Genève," *Recueil des cours de l'Académie de Droit International* 76 (1950): 113–14.

198 *relabeled the whole field*: Jean Pictet, "Le Droit international humanitaire" (Ph.D. diss., University of Geneva, 1955).

198 *Attacks once justified*: International Committee of the Red Cross, Draft Rules for the Limitation of the Dangers Incurred by the Civilian Population in Time of War (1956). See the treatment of this idea as an experimental proposal of the 1950s in Pictet, "The Development of International Humanitarian Law," 124.

198 *He hoped to overcome*: Jean Pictet, *Les Principes de la Croix-Rouge* (1955).

198 *reconceiving the state*: James Sheehan, *Where Have All the Soldiers Gone?: The Transformation of Modern Europe* (2008).

198 *"Young people"*: Jean Pictet, "La Doctrine de la Croix-Rouge," *Revue internationale de la Croix-Rouge* (1962): 270.

199 *Pictet had initially dreamed*: Jean-S. Pictet, "La Défense de la personne humaine dans le droit futur," *Revue internationale de la Croix-Rouge* 29 (1947): 104–125; Pictet, "La Croix-Rouge," 1–117; compare Pictet's master's similar views, Max Huber, "Le Droit des gens et l'humanité," *Revue internationale de la Croix-Rouge* 34 (1952): 646–69, as well as the post-Christian metaphysics of his fellow committee member and poet Jean-G. Lossier, in *La Solidarité: Signification morale de la Croix-Rouge* (1948) and *Les Civilisations et le service du prochain* (1958).

199 *This came to naught*: Boyd van Dijk, "Human Rights in War: On the Entangled Foundations of the 1949 Geneva Conventions," *American Journal of International Law* 112 (2018): 553–82.

199 *until after September 11, 2001*: "Human Rights in Armed Conflicts," International Conference on Human Rights, Tehran, Resolution 23, UN Doc. A/Conf.32/41 (1968), "Respect for Human Rights in Armed Conflicts," U.N. Gen. Ass. Res. 2444 (XXIII) (1968); compare Warren Hewitt, "Respect for Human Rights in Armed Conflicts," *New York University Journal of International Law and Politics* 4 (1971): 41–65. For a skeptic, see the British colonel G.I.A.D. Draper's papers on the theme in the 1970s, rpt. in G.I.A.D. Draper, *Reflections on Law and Armed Conflicts: Selected Works*, ed. Michael Meyer and Hilaire McCoubrey (1998).

199 *"international humanitarian law"*: This chapter is informed throughout by the hypotheses of Amanda Alexander, "A Short History of International Humanitarian Law," *European Journal of International Law* 26 (2015): 109–138, and Page Wilson, "The Myth of International Humanitarian Law," *International Affairs* 91 (2017): 563–79. The best archivally rooted account is now Giovanni Mantilla, *Lawmaking Under Pressure: International Humanitarian Law and Internal Armed Conflict* (2020), chaps. 4–5.

199 *"massacres, torture"*: Jean Pictet, "The Need to Restore the Laws and Customs Relating to Armed Conflicts," *International Review of the Red Cross* 9 (1969): 477.

199 *"struck a shrewd first blow"*: Jean S. Pictet, "The Red Cross and Peace: Is the Work of the Red Cross Prejudicial to the Movement to Outlaw War?," *Revue internationale de la Croix-Rouge*, Supplement, 4 (1951): 129, 134; see also Lossier's series "The Red Cross and Peace," *Revue internationale de la Croix-Rouge*, Supplement, 4 (1951): 26–36, 143–54, and 213–22.

200 *But he forthrightly prioritized*: Jean Pictet, "La Croix-Rouge, facteur de paix dans le monde," *Revue internationale de la Croix-Rouge* 49 (1967): 489–96.

200 *"Revision of the law"*: Pictet, "Need to Restore," 477.

201 *The biggest controversy*: For the best study, see Amanda Alexander, "International Humanitarian Law, Postcolonialism and the 1977 Geneva Protocol I," *Melbourne International Law Journal* 17 (2016): 15–50; see also Eleanor Davey, "Decolonizing the Geneva Conventions: National Liberation and the Development of Humanitarian Law," in A. Dirk Moses et al., eds., *Decolonization, Self-Determination, and the Rise of Global Human Rights Politics* (2020), and, on the intersection of postcolonialism and calls for humane war, Helen Kinsella, "Superfluous Injury and Unnecessary Suffering: National Liberation and the Laws of War," *Political Power and Social Theory* 32 (2017): 205–231. It should be noted that postcolonial states often had an interest in making internal armed conflict less regulated, in order to leave them carte blanche to deal with their own domestic opponents.

201 *They all put the most effort*: Tarak Barkawi, "From Law to History: The Politics of War and Empire," *Global Constitutionalism* 7 (2018): 315–29.

204 *"most significant innovation"*: Aryeh Neier, *The International Human Rights Movement: A History* (2012), 211.

204 *"violations of the laws"*: Americas Watch, *Violations of the Laws of War by Both Sides in Nicaragua, 1981–1985* (1985); David Weissbrodt, "Humanitarian Law in Armed Conflict: The Role of International Nongovernmental Organizations," *Journal of Peace Research* 24 (1987): 297–306.

205 *"We weren't against war"*: Kenneth Roth, "The Human Rights Movement and International Humanitarian Law," in Carrie Booth Walling and Susan Waltz, eds., *Human Rights: From Practice to Policy* (2010), 27.

205 *"By far the largest"*: Human Rights Watch, *World Report 1992* (1992).

205 *"We think we are"*: Aryeh Neier to Margo Picken, March 7, 1991, following Margo Picken to Aryeh Neier, February 28, 1991, both Ford Foundation Grants, Reel R6362, Rockefeller Archives Center (RAC).

206 *Ford commissioned a study*: Picken to Neier, August 11, 1992, Reel R6362, RAC.

206 *its main objection*: I am grateful to Kenneth Roth for sharing the draft Sebastian Brett paper with me.

206 *"accelerate the human rights"*: Neier to Picken, Reel R6362, RAC.

206 *The U.S. bombings*: Human Rights Watch, *Needless Deaths in the Gulf War: Civilian Casualties During the Air Campaign and Violations of the Laws of War* (1991). For the Pentagon visit, see W. Hays Parks, "The Gulf War: A Practitioner's View," *Dickinson Journal of International Law* 10 (1991): 419.

206 *"Until the time"*: Roth, "Human Rights Movement," 31.

207 *"quell the restless students"*: Peter Barnes, "All-Volunteer Army?," *The New Republic*, May 9, 1970. See also Amy Rutenberg, *Rough Draft: Cold War Military Manpower Policy and the Origins of Vietnam-Era Draft Resistance* (2019).

207 *"shift of the cost"*: Galbraith cited in Walter Oi, "All-Volunteer Military Was a Highlight of Nixon's Presidency," *New York Times*, May 1, 1994.

208 *"Ending the draft"*: Mike Gravel, letter to the editor, *New York Times*, June 22, 1971.

208 *"It could make it too cheap"*: Joseph Califano, Jr., "The Case Against an All-Volunteer Army," *Washington Post*, February 21, 1971; Califano, "Doubts About an All-Volunteer Army," *The New Republic*, March 3, 1973.

208 *immunized the well-off*: Jennifer Mittelstadt, *The Rise of the Military Welfare State* (2015).

209 *"overdependence on upper-middle-class"*: Sam Brown, "The Defeat of the Antiwar Movement," in Anthony Lake, ed., *The Legacy of Vietnam: The War, American Society, and the Future of American Foreign Policy* (1976), 124.

209 *Judge Advocate General lawyers*: Frederic Borch, *Judge Advocates in Combat: Army Lawyers in Military Operations from Vietnam to Haiti* (2001).

210 *"law of war program"*: John Rawcliffe, "Changes to the Department of Defense Law of War Program," *Army Lawyer*, August 2006.

210 *Prugh, a Virginian*: George Smawley, "The Past as Prologue: Major General George S. Prugh, Jr. (Ret.) (1942–1975)," *Military Law Review* 187 (2006): 96–173.

210 *"Every evening for years"*: George Aldrich, "Some Reflections on the Origins of the 1977 Geneva Protocols," in Christophe Swinarski, ed., *Etudes et essais sur le droit international humanitaire et sur les principes de la Croix-Rouge* (1984), 132.

211 *"became sensitive to charges"*: Ibid.; for one military study of the damaging role of the news coverage in Vietnam, see William Hammond, *Public Affairs: The Military and the Media, 1968–1973* (1996).

211 *"We want, of course"*: George Prugh, "Current Initiatives to Reaffirm and Develop International Humanitarian Law Applicable in Armed Conflict," *International Lawyer* 8 (1974): 262.

211 *after Vietnam was on board*: See, e.g., Walter Reed, "Laws of War: The Developing Law of Armed Conflict," *Case Western Reserve Journal of International Law* 9 (1977): 18.

212 *"a pro-terrorist treaty"*: Douglas Feith, "Law in the Service of Terror: The Strange Case of the Additional Protocol," *National Interest* 1 (1985): 47; see also Guy Roberts, "The New Rules for Waging War: The Case Against Ratification of Additional Protocol I," *Virginia Journal of International Law* 26 (1985): 109–170, and George Aldrich, "Progressive Developments of the Laws of War: A Reply to Criticisms of the 1977 Geneva Protocol I," *Virginia Journal of International Law* 26 (1986): 693–720, deeming Feith's work "curious, passionate, but underinformed" (700n32).

212 *"would undermine"*: Douglas Feith, *War and Decision: Inside the Pentagon at the Dawn of the War on Terrorism* (2008), 39.

212 *"undermine humanitarian law"*: Ronald Reagan, "Message to the Senate Transmitting a Protocol to the 1949 Geneva Conventions," January 29, 1987.

212 *"protection for prisoners"*: "Denied: A Shield for Terrorists," *New York Times*, February 17, 1981.

212 *Feith later bragged*: Feith, *War and Decision*, 40–41.

212 *In the long run*: Ironically, it would turn out that the war on terror after 2001 would count as a "non-international armed conflict" covered not by the radioactive first protocol but by the second—rules that Feith had deemed harmless because he understandably assumed they dealt with civil wars that would not constrain and therefore concern the United States.

212–13 *the United States began accepting*: Michael J. Matheson, "The United States Position on the Relation of Customary International Law to the 1977 Protocols Addition to the 1949 Geneva Conventions," *American University Journal of Inter-*

national Law and Policy 2 (1987): 419–36, esp. 426 on Art. 51 proportionality; later see, e.g., Theodore Richard, *Unofficial United States Guide to the First Additional Protocol* (2019).

213 *position became dominant*: Alexander, "A Short History," is especially brilliant on this point.

214 *the only fair response*: Compare David Luban, "Military Necessity and the Cultures of Military Law," *Leiden Journal of International Law* 26 (2013): 315–49. Craig Jones, *The War Lawyers* (2020), appeared too late to integrate in my parallel account.

214 *"ensure that legal advisers"*: On the consequences of Additional Protocol I, Art. 82, see W. Hays Parks, "The Law of War Adviser," *JAG Journal* 31 (1980): 1–52.

215 *"operational law"*: David Graham, "Operational Law: A Concept Comes of Age," *Army Lawyer*, July 1987.

215 *"War looks messy"*: Vanessa Blum, "JAG Goes to War," *Legal Times*, November 12, 2001; see also Laura Dickinson, "Military Lawyers on the Battlefield: An Empirical Account of International Law Compliance," *American Journal of International Law* 104 (2010): 1–28.

215 *had begun training*: Terrie Gent, "The Role of Judge Advocates in a Joint Air Operations Center," *Airpower Journal* 13 (1999): 45.

216 *the Gulf War gave them*: John Embry Parkerson, Jr., "United States Compliance with Humanitarian Law Respecting Civilians During Operation Just Cause," *Military Law Review* 133 (1991): 31–140.

216 *they became fixtures*: Stephen Myrow, "Waging War on the Advice of Counsel: The Role of Operational Law in the Gulf War," *United States Air Force Academy Journal of Legal Studies* 7 (1996–97): 131–58; Charles Dunlap, Jr., "Law and Military Interventions: Preserving Humanitarian Values in 21st Century Conflicts," paper for Harvard University conference "Humanitarian Challenges in Military Intervention," November 29, 2001; Michael Lewis, "The Law of Aerial Bombardment in the 1991 Gulf War," *American Journal of International Law* 97 (2003): 481–509; for the most sophisticated study, Janina Dill, *Legitimate Targets?: Social Construction, International Law, and US Bombing* (2015), chap. 5.

216 *"Desert Storm was the most"*: Parks, "Gulf War," 393.

216 *"absolutely indispensable"*: Steven Keeva, "Lawyers in the War Room," *ABA Journal* 77 (1991): 59, 55.

216 *"My Lai must never"*: Jeffrey Addicott and William Hudson, Jr., "The Twenty-Fifth Anniversary of My Lai: Time to Inculcate the Lessons," *Military Law Review* 139 (1993): 153–54.

216 *"savvy American commanders"*: Dunlap, "Law and Military Interventions," 6; see also Michael Lohr and Steve Gallotta, "Legal Support in War: The Role of Military Lawyers," *Chicago Journal of International Law* 4 (2003): 465–78.

217 *the Powell doctrine*: See Colin Powell, "Why Generals Get Nervous," *New York Times*, October 8, 1992, and the narrative in Andrew Bacevich, *The New American Militarism: How Americans Are Seduced by War* (2005), chap. 2.

217 *a few observers*: Chris af Jochnick and Roger Normand, "The Legitimation of Violence: A Critical History of the Laws of War," *Harvard International Law Journal* 35 (1994): 49–95, which the Gulf War prompted.

217 *would protest so loudly*: Graham was particularly incensed in, for example, David Graham, "The Law of Armed Conflict and the War on Terrorism," *International Law Studies* 80 (2006): 331–36. See also Richard Jackson, "Stick to the High Ground," *Army Lawyer*, July 2005.

218 *"were simply incomprehensible"*: Malcolm Gladwell, "Getting Over It," *The New Yorker*, November 1, 2004.

220 *"the worst thing we do"*: Judith N. Shklar, *Ordinary Vices* (1986), 44.

220 *not abhorrent but normal*: W. Fitzhugh Brundage, *Civilizing Torture: An American Tradition* (2018).

220 *a cause for new alarm*: Marnia Lazreg, *Torture and the Twilight of Empire: From Algiers to Baghdad* (2008).

221 *an article prohibiting torture*: Tobias Kelly, *This Side of Silence: Torture, Human Rights, and the Recognition of Cruelty* (2012).

221 *Association for the Prevention of Torture*: Barbara Keys, *Broken Dreams: Global Human Rights and the Struggle to End Torture* (forthcoming).

221 *not until decades later*: Jayne Huckerby and Nigel Rodley, "Outlawing Torture: The Story of Amnesty International's Efforts to Shape the U.N. Convention Against Torture," in Deena Hurwitz et al., eds., *Human Rights Advocacy Stories* (2009).

222 *It touched off a wave*: "The Tiger Cages," *Life*, July 17, 1970; later see, e.g., Sylvan Fox, "4 South Vietnamese Describe Torture in Prison 'Tiger Cage,'" *New York Times*, March 3, 1973. For the relation of South Vietnamese torture stories and the human rights revolution, see Barbara Keys, "The End of the Vietnam War and the Rise of Human Rights," in A. Dirk Moses et al, eds., *Decolonization, Self-Determination, and the Birth of Global Human Rights Politics* (2020).

222 *"There may be no"*: Elaine Scarry, *The Body in Pain: The Making and Unmaking of the World* (1985), 61.

222 *another 2000 law*: Patrick Hagopian, *American Immunity: War Crimes and the Limits of International Law* (2013).

222 *"We have come"*: David Graham, "My Lai and Beyond: The Evolution of Operational Law," in John Norton Moore and Robert Turner, eds., *The Real Lessons of the Vietnam War: Reflections Twenty-Five Years After the Fall of Saigon* (2002), 377.

223 *"the nation's interventionist"*: Mark Lempke, *My Brother's Keeper: George McGovern and Progressive Christianity* (2007), 85.

224 *schooled neoconservatives*: Justin Vaïsse, *Neoconservatism: The Biography of a Movement* (2010), chap. 4.

224 *"The roll call of policies"*: Richard Holbrooke, "A Sense of Drift, a Time for Calm," *Foreign Policy* 23 (1976): 97–112.

225 *"the specter of Vietnam"*: George H. W. Bush, "Radio Address to United States Armed Forces," March 2, 1991.

225 *"Whereas the end"*: Robert W. Tucker and David Hendrickson, *The Imperial Temptation: The New World Order and America's Purpose* (1992), 6–7.

226 *more than 80 percent*: Congressional Research Service, *Instances of Use of United States Armed Force Abroad, 1798–2020* (2020).

227 *Security Council had approved*: United Nations Security Council Res. 688 (1991), though some worried that the interdiction regimes at the 32nd and 36th parallels had never been mentioned in the resolution. See Tarcisio Gazzini, "Intervention in Iraq's Kurdish Region and the Creation of the No-Fly Zones in Northern and Southern Iraq, 1991–2003," in Tom Ruys and Olivier Corten, eds., *The Use of Force in International Law* (2018).

227 *cited self-defense*: "Excerpts from UN Speech: The Case for Clinton's Strike," *New York Times*, June 28, 1993.

227 *the United States treated "self-defense"*: Dino Kritsiotis, "The Legality of the 1993 US Missile Strike on Iraq and the Right of Self-Defence in International Law," *International and Comparative Law Quarterly* 45 (1996): 162–77; compare W. Mi-

chael Reisman, "The Raid on Baghdad: Some Reflections on Its Lawfulness and Implications," *European Journal of International Law* 5 (1994): 120–33.

228 *presidential unilateralism*: Walter Dellinger, "Deployment of U.S. Forces into Haiti," September 27, 1994, in *Opinions of the Office of Legal Counsel* (1980–), 18: 173–79.

228 *"For the purpose"*: Leon Wieseltier, "Force Without Force," *The New Republic*, April 26, 1999.

228 *"When it comes to the use"*: John Yoo, "War Powers: Where Have All the Liberals Gone?," *Wall Street Journal*, March 15, 1999.

229 *Not merely imminent threat*: Abraham Sofaer, "U.S. Acted Legally in Foreign Raids," *Newsday*, October 19, 1998, adding for good measure that the United Nations Charter ought to be interpreted not to require an "armed attack" in the first place to justify self-defense, whatever its text might say.

229 *the most extraordinary*: Jules Lobel, "The Use of Force to Respond to Terrorist Attacks: The Bombing of Sudan and Afghanistan," *Yale Journal of International Law* 24 (1999): 537–57.

229 *"just and necessary war"*: William Jefferson Clinton, "A Just and Necessary War," *New York Times*, May 23, 1999. I should mention that I was a lowly intern at the National Security Council at the time of the events, and recall pinning this piece with pride to the wall of my cubicle.

229 *some American international lawyers*: Louis Henkin, "Kosovo and the Law of 'Humanitarian Intervention,'" *American Journal of International Law* 93 (1999): 824–28.

230 *on Kosovo*: However, see Kenneth Roth, "U.S. Hesitates on Kosovo," *New York Times*, September 21, 1998, faulting Clinton for being "reluctant to respond forcefully." "We will remember 1999 as the year in which sovereignty gave way in places where crimes against humanity were being committed," Roth commented after the intervention. Craig Whitney, "Hands Off: The No Man's Land in the Fight for Human Rights," *New York Times*, December 12, 1999.

230 *Human Rights Watch assessed*: See Human Rights Watch, *Under Orders: War Crimes in Kosovo* (2001), and *The Crisis in Kosovo* (2000).

230 *those carping from outside government*: Center for Law and Military Operations, *Law and Military Operations in Kosovo, 1999–2001: Lessons Learned for Judge Advocates* (2001), 48–51, esp. 50.

231 *"Frankly, it is puzzling"*: Charles Dunlap, Jr., "Kosovo, Casualty Aversion, and the American Military Ethos: A Perspective," *United States Air Force Academy Journal of Legal Studies* 10 (1999–2000): 98, 103.

231 *"The law of war"*: Theodor Meron, "The Humanization of Humanitarian Law," *American Journal of International Law* 94 (2000): 239, 278. This article sums up what I was taught, by Meron himself, when I took a Harvard Law School class on the then-backwater topic of the laws of war in 2000.

231–32 *"the law of September 10"*: Benjamin Wittes, *Law and the Long War: The Future of Justice in the Age of Terror* (2008), chap. 1.

232 *"To us their descendants"*: Leo Tolstoy, *War and Peace*, trans. Aylmer Maude and Louise Maude, in *Works*, 21 vols. (1928–37), 7: 256.

7. THE ROAD TO HUMANITY AFTER SEPTEMBER 11

233 *Alberto Gonzales explained*: Alberto Gonzales, "Martial Justice, Full and Fair," *New York Times*, November 30, 2001.

234 *"We should call"*: Joseph Margulies, "My Friend Michael," *Verdict*, May 16, 2016.

234 *"the death knell for democracy"*: Michael Ratner, "From Magna Carta to Abu Ghraib" (2005), unpublished (which, like other materials noted below as unpublished, is available at michaelratner.com).

234 *scandalous photos*: In an interview, Margulies referred to the Abu Ghraib photos as "the best amicus brief we could have gotten." Interview of Joseph Margulies by Anna Wherry, October 26, 2019, audio in my possession.

234 *"state of exception"*: The most famous expression of this view was Giorgio Agamben, *State of Exception* (2005); see later Mark Danner, *Spiral: Trapped in the Forever War* (2015), which the present book argues got the later war on terror wrong precisely because it was a humanized affair under law, which helps account for its endlessness. Compare earlier Ian Lustick, *Trapped in the War on Terror* (2006).

236 *debates around interventions*: Rebecca Sanders brilliantly argues that the United States after September 11 elaborated a culture of "legal rationalization" that she calls "plausible legality." Law is a field of contending interpretations, some of which enough people accept; and I mean to add that, after September 11, contention occurred and more constraint was imposed mainly when it came to how wars were fought rather than whether or for how long. Rebecca Sanders, *Plausible Legality: Legal Culture and Political Imperative in the Global War on Terror* (2018); for exhaustive factual compilation of the events in the next two chapters, but with the resort to force left out entirely and revealingly, see Richard Abel, *Law's Wars: The Fate of the Rule of Law in the US "War on Terror"* (2018).

237 *"act of war"*: George W. Bush, "Address to a Joint Session of Congress and the American People," September 20, 2001.

237 *Americans watched*: John Bodnar, *Divided by Terror: American Patriotism After 9/11* (2021).

238 *Goldsmith's background*: For biography, see Jack Goldsmith, *In Hoffa's Shadow: A Stepfather, a Disappearance in Detroit, and My Search for the Truth* (2019), and "Jack Goldsmith," Canale Funeral Directors, www.canalefuneraldirectors.com/obituaries/Jack-Goldsmith-33378/#!/Obituary.

239 *Yoo co-authored an article*: Harold Hongju Koh and John Choon Yoo, "Dollar Diplomacy/Dollar Defense: The Fabric of Economics and National Security Law," *International Law* 26 (1992): 715–62.

239 *a 1999 co-authored piece*: Jack Goldsmith and John Yoo, "Seattle and Sovereignty," *Wall Street Journal*, December 7, 1999. They also co-authored "Missile Defense Defense," *American Lawyer*, April 2001, and "Missiles Away," *Legal Times*, May 7, 2001.

239 *"new sovereigntists"*: Peter Spiro, "The New Sovereigntists: American Exceptionalism and Its False Prophets," *Foreign Affairs* 79 (2000): 9–15; Curtis Bradley and Jack Goldsmith, "My Prerogative," *Foreign Affairs* 80 (2001): 188; compare Jens David Ohlin, *The Assault on International Law* (2015).

240 *"saw Vietnam through the lens"*: John Richardson, "Is John Yoo a Monster?," *Esquire*, August 24, 2009.

241 *The day after September 11*: United Nations Security Council Resolutions 1368 (September 12, 2001) and 1373 (September 28, 2001).

241 *Nor did it say*: Christian Tams, "The Use of Force Against Terrorists," *European Journal of International Law* 20 (2009): 359–97.

241 *"effective control"*: International Court of Justice, *Nicaragua v. United States* (1986), paras. 109, 115.

242 *The world looked on*: The U.S. ambassador to the United Nations John Negroponte did send a letter to the organization's Security Council on October 7, citing a self-

defense rationale under international law, and while there were a few references by officials to Afghanistan as a "harboring" state, most U.S. statements referred to the collaborative relationship between Al-Qaeda and the Taliban as making strict association or what lawyers call "attribution" unnecessary; for more, see Michael Byers, "The Intervention in Afghanistan, 2001–," in Tom Ruys and Olivier Corten, eds., *The Use of Force in International Law* (2018).

242 *no criticism stirred*: For an isolated protest in real time, see Olivier Corten and François Dubuisson, "Opération 'liberté immuable': une extension abusive du concept de légitime défense," *Revue générale de droit international public* 106 (2002): 51–77.

243 *"undermine U.S. military culture"*: This objection is in Gonzales's words in his Memorandum for the President, January 25, 2002, rpt. in Karen Greenberg and Joshua Dratel, eds., *The Torture Papers: The Road to Abu Ghraib* (2005), 120.

244 *"enhanced interrogation techniques"*: Jay S. Bybee, Memorandum to Alberto Gonzales, August 1, 2002, rpt. in ibid.

244 *While there was little concern*: For some early counterexamples proving the rule, see Michael Byers, "Preemptive Self-Defense: Hegemony, Equality and Strategies of Legal Change," *Journal of Political Philosophy* 11 (2003): 171–90, or Sean Murphy, "Assessing the Legality of Invading Iraq," *Georgetown Law Journal* 92 (2004): 173–257.

244 *a government investigation*: Office of Professional Responsibility, Department of Justice, Investigation into the Office of Legal Counsel's Memoranda Concerning Issues Relating to the Central Intelligence Agency's Use of "Enhanced Interrogation Techniques" on Suspected Terrorists, July 29, 2009.

245 *"simply ridiculous"*: John Yoo, *War by Other Means: An Insider's Account of the War on Terror* (2006), 21.

245 *"Why are the pacifists"*: Lynn Chu and John Yoo, "Why Are the Pacifists So Passive?," *New York Times*, February 12, 2007.

245 *"effort to inject"*: John Yoo, "The High Court's Hamdan Power Grab," *Los Angeles Times*, July 7, 2006; see also John Yoo, "What Rights for Terrorists?," *San Diego Union-Tribune*, August 6, 2006.

245 *Yoo could gloat*: John Yoo, "How the Presidency Regained Its Balance," *New York Times*, September 17, 2006.

246 *Ratner's Jewish parents*: The best biographical information is in a series of seven interviews with Paul Jay on the Real News Network, entitled "Reality Asserts Itself," posted at therealnews.com/series/reality-asserts-itself-michael-ratner.

247 *unwavering throughout his life*: Sam Roberts, "Michael Ratner, Lawyer Who Won Rights for Guantánamo Prisoners, Dies at 72," *New York Times*, May 11, 2016.

247 *He idolized Che Guevara*: Michael Ratner, "Che: The Heroic Guerrilla," in Michael Ratner and Michael Steven Smith, eds., *Che Guevara and the FBI: U.S. Political Police Dossier on the Latin American Revolutionary* (1997).

247 *"acts of aggression"*: David Deutschmann and Michael Ratner, eds., *Washington on Trial: The People of Cuba v. the U.S. Government* (1999).

247 *Interviewed on September 12*: Ronald J. Grele, "The Reminiscences of Michael Ratner," Rule of Law Oral History Project, Columbia Center for Oral History, September 12, 2013.

247 *He sued perpetrators*: Michael Ratner, "Perspectives on *Filartiga*: The Vindication of International Human Rights in United States Courts," *Harvard Human Rights Journal* 5 (1992): 235–45; Michael Ratner and Beth Stephens, *International Human Rights Litigation in U.S. Courts* (1996).

247 *Goldsmith ultimately helped*: Jack Goldsmith (with Curtis Bradley), "The Current

Illegitimacy of International Human Rights Litigation," *Fordham Law Review* 66 (1997): 319–69; Jack Goldsmith, Amicus Curiae Briefs for Chevron Corporation et al., *Kiobel v. Royal Dutch Petroleum*, United States Supreme Court, February 3 and August 8, 2012.

247 *"radical leftist"*: Harold Koh, "Michael Ratner: The Leading Progressive Lawyer of a Generation," *Just Security*, May 12, 2016.

247 *the cause of Haitian migrants*: Michael Ratner, "How We Closed the Guantanamo HIV Camp: The Intersection of Politics and Litigation," *Harvard Human Rights Journal* 11 (1998): 187–220. See the narratives in Brandt Goldstein, *Storming the Court: How a Band of Law Students Sued the President—and Won* (2005), and Jeffrey Kahn, *Islands of Sovereignty: Haitian Migration and the Borders of Empire* (2019).

248 *"military advisers"*: *Crockett v. Reagan*, 558 F.Supp. 893 (1982).

248 *they did not give up*: See Michael Ratner and David Cole, "The Force of Law: Judicial Enforcement of the War Powers Resolution," *Loyola of Los Angeles Law Review* 17 (1984): 715–66, and successor cases to litigate illegal aid to the Contras in Nicaragua and the 1983 Grenada intervention, *Sanchez-Espinoza v. Reagan*, 770 F.2d 202 (1985), and *Conyers v. Reagan*, 765 F.2d 1124 (1985).

248 *He helped another group*: *Dellums v. Bush*, 752 F.Supp. 1141 (D.D.C. 1990); see also Michael Ratner, "War Powers Clock" (letter to the editor), *New York Times*, September 26, 1990.

248 *persisted with such litigation*: *Campbell v. Clinton*, 203 F.3d 19 (D.C. Cir. 2000), which the Supreme Court refused to rehear, and H. Lee Halterman, Michael Ratner, et al., "The Fog of War [Powers]," *Stanford Journal of International Law* 37 (2001): 197–204.

248 *followed the priorities*: Michael Ratner, "International Law and War Crimes," in Ramsey Clark et al., *War Crimes: A Report on United States War Crimes Against Iraq* (1992).

249 *"tendency to bypass"*: Jules Lobel and Michael Ratner, "Bypassing the Security Council: Ambiguous Authorizations to Use Force, Cease Fires, and the Iraqi Inspection Regime," *American Journal of International Law* 93 (1999): 125, 154.

249 *"Where Have All"*: John Yoo, "War Powers: Where Have All the Liberals Gone?," *Wall Street Journal*, March 15, 1999.

249 *"intervene militarily"*: Jules Lobel and Michael Ratner, "Humanitarian Intervention in Kosovo: A Highly Suspect Pretext for War," *CovertAction Quarterly* 67 (1999): 5; see also Jules Lobel and Michael Ratner, "Humanitarian Military Intervention," *Foreign Policy in Focus* 5 (2000): 1–3; Jules Lobel and Michael Ratner, letter to Congressman Dennis Kucinich (1999), unpublished; and Michael Ratner, "Lawless War: The War Against Yugoslavia as a Harbinger of an Insecure Future for the Peoples of the World" (1999), unpublished.

249 *"at least the U.S."*: "Democracy Now" with Amy Goodman, April 27, 1999.

250 *a "crime of aggression"*: "Democracy Now," March 25, 1999.

250 *"What can you say"*: "Democracy Now," April 27, 1999.

250 *"of obviously wanting"*: David Cole and Michael Ratner "Less Secure and Less Free: Civil Liberties and the War on Terrorism," *Fathom*, October 2, 2001; see also Ratner's speech to the National Lawyers Guild, "Crime Against Humanity and Not War: Making Us Safer at Home and Stopping a Human Carnage Abroad," October 3, 2001, unpublished.

251 *"the similarity to the open-endedness"*: "Authorizing Use of United States Armed Forces Against Those Responsible for Recent Attacks Against the United States,"

Congressional Record, September 14, 2001; for the best reporting on the origins of the text, see Gregory Johnsen, "60 Words and a War Without End: The Untold Story of the Most Dangerous Sentence in U.S. History," *Buzzfeed*, January 16, 2014.

251 *"spin out of control"*: "Authorizing Use."

251 *"rhetoric" of "revenge"*: "Democracy Now," September 17, 2001; see also Michael Ratner, "The Danger of Responding with Force," *Columbia Law Report*, Fall 2001.

251 *"war on terror"*: Richard Falk, "Defining a Just War," *The Nation*, October 11, 2001; Michael Ratner and Jules Lobel, "Is This Really a Just War?," *The Nation*, November 8, 2001; Falk and Ratner debated in person on "Democracy Now," November 1, 2001.

251 *He suggested it would*: "No Time for Cowboy Politics," *Center for Constitutional Rights Newsletter*, September 17, 2001.

251 *"We just gave up"*: Michael Ratner, interview with Jack Goldsmith, November 17, 2010, audio and transcript in my possession. Ratner added: "Not that we didn't think the wars were still illegal, like the second Iraq war, but Jules [Lobel] and I, we didn't see anywhere to go then where you had any chance of even getting a toehold."

252 *"None whatsoever"*: David Cole, "Michael Ratner, 1943–2016," *The Nation*, May 11, 2016.

252 *"Gitmo Bar"*: See, e.g., Michael Ratner and Ellen Ray, *Guantanamo: What the World Should Know* (2004).

253 *"prohibition on aggression"*: Michael Ratner and Jules Lobel, letter to the editor, *New York Times*, October 3, 2002, unpublished; Michael Ratner et al., *Against War with Iraq: An Anti-war Primer* (2003).

253 *"the largest antiwar movement"*: Barbara Epstein, "Notes on the Antiwar Movement," *Monthly Review*, July 2003.

253 *"the response of the political classes"*: Andrew Bacevich, *The New American Militarism: How Americans Are Seduced by War* (2005), 25.

254 *had reported on rumors*: Barton Gellman and Dana Priest, "U.S. Decries Abuse but Defends Interrogations," *Washington Post*, December 6, 2002.

254 *"This country has"*: Jane Mayer, *The Dark Side: How the War on Terror Turned into a War on American Ideals* (2008), 9.

255 *"should be the absolute leader"*: "The Torture Question," *Frontline*, August 4, 2005.

255 *In defense of it*: Authority of the President Under Domestic and International Law to Use Military Force Against Iraq, October 23, 2002. Under Bybee's signature, this memo also mounts an anticipatory self-defense rationale even more broadly rejected than its interpretations of Security Council resolutions. Alongside then State Legal Adviser Will Taft, Yoo contributed in his personal capacity to a forum in summer 2003 on the topic that was widely taken to represent the administration's views. See William Howard Taft IV and Todd Buchwald, "Preemption, Iraq, and International Law," which endorses "preemption" within a Security Council mandate, and John Yoo, "International Law and the War in Iraq," *American Journal of International Law* 97 (2003): 557–76, which does so independently. See later Marko Milanovic, "The OLC Memoranda on Iraq: Revisiting the Case for War," *EJIL: Talk*, January 10, 2009.

256 *"We're at war"*: Susan Sontag, "Regarding the Torture of Others," *New York Times Magazine*, May 23, 2004.

257 *"Torture may cause Jack Bauer"*: Jane Mayer, "Whatever It Takes," *The New Yorker*, February 12, 2007.

257 *emerging criticism*: Jodi Wilgoren and Elisabeth Bumiller, "In Harshest Critique Yet, Kerry Attacks Bush over War in Iraq," *New York Times*, September 21, 2004.

258 *coming out for using*: Jack Goldsmith and Bernard Meltzer, "Swift Justice for Bin Laden," *Financial Times*, November 7, 2001; see also Jack Goldsmith (with Curtis Bradley), "The Constitutional Validity of Military Commissions," *Green Bag* 5 (2002): 249–58, and (with Cass Sunstein), "Military Tribunals and Legal Culture: What a Difference Sixty Years Makes," *Constitutional Commentary* 19 (2002): 261–89.

258 *"The blood of the hundred thousand"*: Jack Goldsmith, *The Terror Presidency: Law and Judgment in the Bush Administration* (2005, 2007), 78.

259 *found it reasonable*: See Bradley and Goldsmith, "Constitutional Validity," 258.

259 *told his superiors*: Goldsmith, *Terror Presidency*, 39, 41–42.

259 *he insisted that the full spectrum*: Ibid., 119.

259 *But Goldsmith only formally*: For Goldsmith's account, see ibid., chap. 5.

259 *Yoo shot back*: Yoo, *War by Other Means*, 182–83.

260 *"Why don't we just"*: Goldsmith, *Terror Presidency*, 124.

260 *"War itself was encumbered"*: Ibid., 130, 69.

260 *His points of comparison*: To the extent Goldsmith had a theory of what prompted the change, he mentioned Watergate more than war: ibid., 68, 65–66, 81, 86, 183.

261 *"law and the long war"*: Benjamin Wittes, *Law and the Long War: The Future of Justice in the Age of Terror* (2008).

261 *Initially blackballed*: Marcella Bombardieri, "Harvard Hire's Detainee Memo Stirs Debate," *Boston Globe*, December 9, 2004.

262 *Goldsmith signed off*: Jack Goldsmith III, Draft Memorandum for Alberto Gonzales on Permissibility of Relocating Certain "Protected Persons" from Occupied Iraq, March 19, 2004, rpt. in Greenberg and Dratel, eds., *Torture Papers*.

262 *he did not forbid*: Jack Goldsmith III to Scott Muller, General Counsel, Central Intelligence Agency, May 27, 2004.

262 *Goldsmith expressed enthusiasm*: See Jack L. Goldsmith and Adrian Vermeule, "How We Can Bring Peace," *New York Times*, September 10, 2006.

263 *Goldsmith edged closer*: Jack Goldsmith, "The Accountable Presidency," *The New Republic*, February 1, 2010; easily Goldsmith's favorite reference for the ideal of a restrained presidency, however, has been Arthur Schlesinger, Jr.—that is, after Schlesinger recovered from his support for the Vietnam War and criticized the imperial presidency: see Goldsmith, *Terror Presidency*, 177–216, 236, and other writings.

263 *his own later acknowledgment*: Jack Goldsmith, *Power and Constraint: The Accountable Presidency After 9/11* (2012), esp. 182.

263 *"about the king"*: Ratner, "From Magna Carta."

263 *Ratner agitated*: Michael Ratner and Jules Lobel, "An Alternative to War," *Rethinking Schools*, December 2001, posted at www.rethinkingschools.org.

263 *"war paradigm"*: Ratner, interview with Goldsmith, 2010; as his colleague, the lawyer Jonathan Hafetz, later observed, the "strategy was to not challenge the concept of the war on terror directly in post-9/11 cases, but to challenge claims about habeas jurisdiction and the rights of individuals to be detained arbitrarily and not to be mistreated." Interview with Anna Wherry, November 25, 2019, audio in my possession.

264 *"such an action"*: Michael Ratner, "Should the U.S. Intervene in Libya?" (letter to the editor), *New York Times*, March 11, 2011.

264 *"the first time"*: Grele, "Reminiscences of Michael Rather," Columbia Oral History Project.

264 *And he returned*: See Center for Constitutional Rights, "Restore, Protect, Expand: Amend the War Powers Resolution" (2009).

264 *"Athens expanding its empire"*: Ratner, "From Magna Carta."

8. THE ARC OF THE MORAL UNIVERSE

267 *"heckler"*: Aaron Blake, "Code Pink Founder Heckles Obama Repeatedly," *Washington Post*, May 23, 2013; see also Rachel Weiner, "How Medea Benjamin Got to Heckle Obama," *Washington Post*, May 24, 2013.

267 *She liked how the name*: Baynard Woods, "Raising Hell in the Halls of Power," *Baltimore Sun*, July 25, 2017.

268 *"Unless we shine a light"*: Jacob Silverman, "Code Pink's Next Battle," *Tablet*, May 8, 2012.

268 *"to push the arc"*: Medea Benjamin, "Pushing Obama's Arc Towards Peace," *Truthout*, November 18, 2012.

269 *"Lawyerliness suffused"*: Charlie Savage, *Power Wars: Inside Obama's Post-9/11 Presidency* (2015), 63, 65.

269 *"were trying to fight"*: Ibid., 54 (emphasis added). Savage himself argues for a disparity between the "rule of law" and civil liberties, one respected and one not under Obama's approach. I argue, in contrast, for a more illuminating alternative distinction between resort to force and conduct of hostilities in light of applicable standards.

270 *helped entrench and legitimate*: Many critical views, especially outside the United States, were more totalistic and undifferentiated, but my argument is that humane war in law became legitimating for Americans and had real effects, however inadequate; see, e.g., Catherine Connolly, "'Necessity Knows No Law': The Resurrection of Kriegsraison Through the US Targeted Killing Programme," *Journal of Conflict and Security Law* 22 (2017): 463–96. But compare Markus Gunneflo, "Drones and the Decolonization of International Law," *MEI Insight* 191 (2018): 1–7.

270 *"He has relentlessly questioned"*: Jeffrey Goldberg, "The Obama Doctrine," *The Atlantic*, April 2016.

272 *Obama could bring*: Aziz Rana, "Decolonizing Obama," *n+1*, Winter 2017; for broader perspective, see Howard Winant, *The New Politics of Race: Globalism, Difference, Justice* (2004), and Nikhil Pal Singh, *Race and America's Long War* (2019).

272 *"willingness to exercise constraint"*: Barack Obama, *The Audacity of Hope: Thoughts on Reclaiming the American Dream* (2006), 285.

273 *"The Bush administration"*: Barack Obama, "Renewing American Leadership," *Foreign Affairs*, July/August 2007.

273 *"I wanted somehow"*: Barack Obama, *A Promised Land* (2020), 353.

273 *"more stealthy, agile"*: Barack Obama, "The War We Need to Win," Woodrow Wilson Center, Washington, D.C., August 1, 2007, and the campaign fact sheet that accompanied it.

273 *"more troops, more helicopters"*: "Obama's Remarks on Afghanistan and Iraq," *New York Times*, July 15, 2008.

274 *she had attempted*: David Welna, "Clinton Charges That Obama Erratic on War in Iraq," *Morning Edition*, National Public Radio, January 15, 2008; see also Michael Crowley, "Cinderella Story," *The New Republic*, February 27, 2008.

274 *"There are things to learn"*: James Mann, *The Obamians: The Struggle Inside the White House to Redefine American Power* (2012), xvii, 14.

275 *One reason for the evaporation*: Michael Heaney and Fabio Rojas, "The Partisan Dynamics of Contention: Demobilization of the Antiwar Movement in the United States, 2007–2009," *Mobilization* 16 (2011): 45–64.

275 *"We find that"*: Silverman, "Code Pink's Next Battle."

276 *"Obama says he has no"*: Dana Priest, "Bush's 'War on Terror' Comes to a Sudden End," *Washington Post*, January 23, 2009.

276 *Bush's initial resistance*: In 2004, Attorney General John Ashcroft reauthorized the Central Intelligence Agency to engage in the wide range of "enhanced" interrogation techniques used before. But Congress acted the next year to impose its limits. And even as his administration moved away from extraordinary renditions of captives, Bush's lawyers continued to narrow the recourse to harsh treatment. Charlie Savage, "The One-Paragraph Torture Memo," *New York Times*, December 9, 2014.

276 *Bush issued an executive order*: George W. Bush, Executive Order 13440: Interpretation of the Geneva Conventions Common Article 3 as Applied to a Program of Detention and Interrogation Operated by the Central Intelligence Agency, July 20, 2007.

276 *evolved into official prohibitions*: Steven Bradbury, General Memorandum for the Files Re: Status of Certain OLC Opinions Issued in the Aftermath of the Terrorist Attacks of September 11, 2001, January 15, 2009.

277–78 *"Obama consigned to history"*: Jane Mayer, "Behind the Executive Orders," *The New Yorker*, January 25, 2009. Some welcomed the dawning realities of cosmetically enhanced continuity with the Bush era. Writing in *The New Republic* in March 2009, Goldsmith described it as "an attempt to make the core Bush approach to terrorism politically and legally more palatable, and thus sustainable." Jack Goldsmith, "The Cheney Fallacy," *The New Republic*, May 18, 2009.

278 *"global battlefield"*: Charlie Savage, "Obama's War on Terror May Resemble Bush's in Some Areas," *New York Times*, February 17, 2009.

278 *The brief arrogated*: Brief for Respondents, In Re: Guantanamo Bay Detainee Litigation, D.C. District Court, March 13, 2009.

279 *"No one questions"*: William Glaberson, "Obama to Keep Tribunals, Stance Angers Some Backers," *New York Times*, May 15, 2009; the meeting is recounted in Daniel Klaidman, *Kill or Capture: The War on Terror and the Soul of the Obama Presidency* (2012), chap. 5.

279 *With the right books*: In a big literature, see John Nagl, *Counterinsurgency Lessons from Malaya and Vietnam: Learning to Eat Soup with a Knife* (2002); U.S. Army and Marine Corps, *Counterinsurgency Field Manual 3–24* (2006); David Kilcullen, *The Accidental Guerrilla: Fighting Small Wars in the Midst of a Big One* (2009); George Packer, "What Obama and the Generals Are Reading," *The New Yorker*, October 8, 2009; Moritz Feichtinger and Stephan Malinowski, "Transformative Invasions: Western Post-9/11 Counterinsurgency and the Lessons of Colonialism," *Humanity* 3 (2012): 35–63.

281 *"we have to confront"*: Barack Obama, "Remarks on Winning the Nobel Peace Prize," October 9, 2009.

281 *"with an acute sense"*: Barack Obama, "Nobel Lecture," December 10, 2009.

282 *"he directly challenged"*: "President Obama in Oslo," *New York Times*, December 10, 2009.

282 *Obama did not mention*: Compare, six years later, Barack Obama, "Remarks at National Prayer Breakfast," February 5, 2015.

283 *"a history of humanitarianism"*: Samantha Power, *The Education of an Idealist: A Memoir* (2019), 263. See also the account in Ben Rhodes, *The World as It Is: A Memoir of the Obama White House* (2018), chap. 7.

284 *the architecture of drone activity*: See, e.g., Eric Schmitt, "A Shadowy War's Newest Front," *New York Times*, April 22, 2018.

284 *moved through 138 nations*: Nick Turse, "The Year of the Commando," *TomDispatch*, January 7, 2017; Letter from the President to the Speaker of the House of Representatives and the President Pro Tempore of the Senate, June 13, 2016.

285 *had been concocted*: Ronen Bergman, *Rise and Kill First: The Secret History of Israel's Targeted Assassinations* (2018).

285 *single U.S. legal authorization*: See Barton Gellman, "CIA Weighs 'Targeted Killing' Missions," *Washington Post*, October 28, 2001, and the discussion in National Commission on Terrorist Attacks in the United States, *The 9/11 Commission Report* (2004), 131–33; further back, there had been a much more guarded discussion around killing Moammar Qaddafi collaterally in 1986. See Michael Schmitt, "State-Sponsored Assassination in International and Domestic Law," *Yale Journal of International Law* 17 (1992): 665–69.

285 *"Israel needs to understand"*: Jane Perlez, "U.S. Says Killings by Israel Inflame Mideast Conflict," *New York Times*, August 28, 2001. For Bush, see "Remarks on the Situation in the Middle East," February 14, 2001, in *Public Papers of the Presidents of the United States: George W. Bush 2001*, 2 vols. (2003), 1: 81.

286 *Americans had not deployed*: Christopher Fuller, *See It/Shoot It: The Secret History of the CIA's Legal Drone Program* (2017).

286 *Armed drones were first used*: For these events, including Pakistan's initial claim of responsibility in a deal with the CIA, see Mark Mazzetti, *The Way of the Knife: The CIA, a Secret Army, and a War at the Ends of the Earth* (2013), chap. 6.

286 *restricted to "badlands"*: John O. Brennan, "Strengthening Our Security by Adhering to Our Values and Laws," Harvard Law School, September 16, 2011.

286 *scrutiny peaked*: Scott Shane, *Objective Troy: A Terrorist, a President, and the Rise of the Drone* (2015).

287 *Barron had written a memo*: Charlie Savage, "Secret U.S. Memo Made Legal Case to Kill a Citizen," *New York Times*, October 8, 2011; Rand Paul, "Show Us the Drone Memos," *New York Times*, May 11, 2014; Savage, "Court Releases Large Parts of Memo Approving Killing of American in Yemen," *New York Times*, June 23, 2014.

287 *"Activities that before 9/11"*: Cited in Andris Banka and Adam Quinn, "Killing Norms Softly: US Targeted Killing, Quasi-Secrecy, and the Assassination Ban," *Security Studies* 27 (2018): 687. Obama officials defended their approach even after Trump won; see Ryan Goodman, "Why the Laws of War Apply to Drone Strikes Outside 'Areas of Active Hostilities' (A Memo to the Human Rights Community)," *Just Security*, October 4, 2017.

287 *Yoo gamely insisted*: John Yoo, "Assassination or War?," *San Francisco Chronicle*, September 18, 2005. Already in *The Audacity of Hope*, one year later, Obama signaled that he had no problem with unilateral self-defense in response to terror. Obama, *Audacity*, 308.

288 *unknown to modern international law*: For all this, including the influential analogy (due to Goldsmith after leaving government and relied on heavily by Obama's lawyers) between the concept of associated forces and doctrines in the premodern

international law of neutrality, see Rebecca Ingber, "Co-belligerency," *Yale Journal of International Law* 42 (2016): 67–120.

289 *"junior varsity"*: Steve Contorno, "What Obama Said About Islamic State as a 'JV' Team," *Politifact*, September 7, 2014.

289 *"true inheritor"*: Marty Lederman, "The Legal Theory Behind the President's New Military Initiative Against ISIL," *Just Security*, September 10, 2014.

289 *"unwilling or unable"*: On the "West Point process," from which the argument emerged, see John Bellinger III, "The Bush (43rd) Administration (2005–9)," in Michael P. Scharf and Paul R. Williams, eds., *Shaping Foreign Policy in Times of Crisis: The Role of International Law and the State Department Legal Adviser* (2010), esp. 143–45; on the doctrine, see Daniel Bethlehem, "Self-Defense Against an Imminent or Actual Armed Attack by Nonstate Actors," *American Journal of International Law* 106 (2012): 770–77, and Ashley Deeks, "'Unwilling or Unable': Toward a Normative Framework for Extraterritorial Self-Defense," *Virginia Journal of International Law* 52 (2012): 483–550.

290 *essentially unlimited rationale*: In domestic law terms, the presidentialist memo by Office of Legal Counsel head Caroline Krass in 2011 can be read to give the president carte blanche authority under the Constitution to go to war anywhere and for any reason, redefining "national interest" without limitation. Caroline Krass, "Authority to Use Military Force in Libya," Office of Legal Counsel, April 1, 2011.

290 *at the very least*: It took the Obama administration until 2011 to conclude a long study to treat the legal floor for detainee treatment in the treaty's Common Article 3 as its legal ceiling when it came to terrorists. (As Bush had for the Taliban, the government could always do more as a policy matter.) It masked this fact, in a confusing moment, by announcing that it considered more rules applicable to detainees under *international* armed conflict, which did not count Guantánamo detainees under non-international armed conflict, or terrorists outside zones of active hostilities. "Fact Sheet: New Actions on Guantánamo and Detainee Policies," White House, March 7, 2011; Julian Barnes, "Geneva Protections for al Qaeda Suspects?: Read the Fine Print," *Wall Street Journal*, March 14, 2011.

290 *says nothing about targeting*: Simultaneously in 2011, Obama resubmitted the treaty revisions of 1977 to the Geneva Conventions that provide more information about the rules for "non-international armed conflict" to the Senate, but it was another showy gesture masking the administration's decision to craft its own law for humane war.

291 *did not confine their demands*: Philip Alston, "Report of the Special Rapporteur on Extrajudicial, Summary, or Arbitrary Executions," UN Doc. A/HRC/14/24/Add.6, May 28, 2010.

291 *scrutiny in the press*: Tara McKelvey, "Media Coverage of the Drone Program," Joan Shorenstein Program Center on the Press, Politics, and Public Policy Discussion Paper D77 (2013).

291 *the virtue of drones*: Compare Caroline Kennedy and James Rogers, "Virtuous Drones," *International Journal of Human Rights* 19 (2015): 211–27.

291 *"We're exceptionally precise"*: John Brennan, "Obama Administration Counterterrorism Strategy," John Hopkins-SAIS, June 29, 2011, posted at www.c-span.org/video/?c4745055/user-clip-past-year-hasnt-single-collateral-death.

292 *Obama himself*: Shane, *Objective Troy*, 228.

292 *"signature strikes"*: See Kevin Jon Heller, "'One Hell of a Killing Machine': Signature

Strikes and International Law," *Journal of International Criminal Justice* 11 (2013): 89–119.

292 *estimates of civilian casualties*: Compare Scott Shane, "CIA Is Disputed on Civilian Toll in Drone Strikes," *New York Times*, August 11, 2011, with Scott Shane, "Drone Strike Statistics Answer Few Questions, and Raise Many," *New York Times*, July 3, 2016.

292 *"legal architecture"*: Scott Shane, "Election Spurred a Move to Codify U.S. Drone Policy," *New York Times*, November 24, 2012.

293 *"legal-ish" standards*: All the citations in this and the next paragraphs, including the term "legal-ish," are from Naz Modirzadeh, "A Reply to Marty Lederman," *Lawfare*, October 3, 2014; the article is Naz Modirzadeh, "Folk International Law: 9/11 Lawyering and the Transformation of the Law of Armed Conflict to Human Rights Policy and Human Rights Law to War," *Harvard National Security Journal* 5 (2014): 225–304.

293 *"absent extraordinary circumstances"*: "Procedures for Approving Direct Action Against Terrorist Targets Located Outside the United States and Areas of Active Hostilities," May 22, 2013.

293 *"kill lists"*: David Johnston and David Sanger, "Hunt for Suspects: Fatal Strike in Yemen Was Based on Rules Set Out by Bush," *New York Times*, November 6, 2002.

293 *took umbrage*: See, e.g., Marty Lederman, "Of So-Called 'Folk International Law' and Not-So-Grey Zones," *Just Security*, October 2, 2014.

294 *cosmetic prettification*: The Obama administration later acknowledged that aspects of the Convention Against Torture bound the United States beyond its own borders—but the main international human rights treaty, with its right to life, did not. The interpretation of international human rights law required no alteration of practices. United States Department of State, Fourth Periodic Report to the United Nations Human Rights Committee, December 30, 2011, paras. 502–505.

295 *"I do not expect miracles"*: Michael Ratner, "If We Don't Speak Up, Who Will?," *Socialist Worker*, December 14, 2009; "A New Stage in the War on Dissent: An Interview with Michael Ratner," *Socialist Worker*, October 19, 2010; see also "Obama's National Security State: Michael Ratner Interviewed," *International Socialist Review*, November 2010.

296 *Maria Ruzicka*: Jennifer Abrahamson, *Sweet Relief: The Maria Ruzicka Story* (2006).

296 *A torrent of critical journalism*: Stanford Human Rights Clinic, "Living Under Drones: Death, Injury, and Trauma from US Drone Practices in Pakistan" (2012); Azmat Khan and Anand Gopal, "The Uncounted," *New York Times Magazine*, November 16, 2017; Nick McDonell, *The Bodies in Person: An Account of Civilian Casualties in American Wars* (2018); Columbia Law School Human Rights Institute and Center for Civilians in Conflict, "In Search of Answers: U.S. Military Investigations and Civilian Harm" (2019).

296 *"chase success"*: Sarah B. Sewall, *Chasing Success: Air Force Efforts to Reduce Civilian Harm* (2015), chap. 7.

297 *strove to present the prison*: Rebecca Adelman, "'Safe, Humane, Legal, Transparent': State Visions of Guantánamo Bay," *Reconstruction* 12 (2013).

297 *"I think it's time"*: Allegra Funsten, "An Interview with Medea Benjamin," *Los Angeles Review of Books*, December 5, 2013.

298 *Benjamin explained*: Medea Benjamin, "Why I Spoke Out at Obama's Foreign Policy Speech," *Common Dreams*, May 24, 2013.

298 *"Despite our strong preference"*: Barack Obama, "Remarks at the National Defense University," Fort McNair, May 23, 2013.

299 *He worried . . . that counterterrorist priorities*: Goldberg, "Obama Doctrine."

299 *"The Obama administration has never"*: Kenneth Anderson and Benjamin Wittes, *Speaking the Law: The Obama Administration's Addresses on International Law* (2013), 228.

300 *"Since World War Two"*: Cited in David Milne, *Worldmaking: The Art and Science of American Diplomacy* (2015), 513.

300 *Someone very different*: Compare, after Trump's election, Obama's valedictory address on counterterrorism, where he does not reflect on the endlessness of war with remotely the same insight as three years before: Barack Obama, "Remarks on the Administration's Approach to Counterterrorism," MacDill Air Force Base, December 6, 2016, along with his foreword to "Report on the Legal and Policy Frameworks Guiding the United States' Use of Military Force and Related National Security Operations," December 2016.

300–301 *The elder Koh protested*: Kwang Lim Koh, "For a World Under Law," *Bostonia*, Summer 1959; Harold Hongju Koh, "Dad at Sixty," in Howard Kyongju Koh, ed., *Koh Kwang Lim: Essays in Honor of His Hwegap* (1982), 102.

301 *taught the "goodness" and "reach"*: Lesley Dingle and Daniel Bates, "A Conversation with Professor Harold Hongju Koh," May 28, 2019, Squire Law Library, University of Cambridge, www.squire.law.cam.ac.uk/eminent-scholars-archiveprofessor-harold-hongju-koh/conversation-professor-harold-hongju-koh.

301 *"remarkable country"*: Harold Hongju Koh, "A World Without Torture," *Columbia Journal of Transnational Law* 43 (2005): 642.

301 *insisted on Congress's role*: Harold Hongju Koh, *The National Security Constitution: Sharing Power After the Iran-Contra Affair* (1990), Harold Hongju Koh, "Presidential War and Congressional Consent: The Law Professors' Memorandum in *Dellums v. Bush*," *Stanford Journal of International Law* 27 (1991): 247–56.

302 *"How could this guy"*: Interview with John Yoo, February 24, 2011, George W. Bush Oral History Project, Miller Center, University of Virginia.

302 *Koh had not only warned*: Before the Iraq intervention, see his appearance on the *Charlie Rose* show, December 13, 2002, www.youtube.com/watch?v=g1FXGJ6g1WY&t=1030s, and, for its illegality, Harold Hongju Koh, "On American Exceptionalism," *Stanford Law Review* 55 (2003): 1523.

302 *"torturer-in-chief"*: Harold Hongju Koh, "Can the President Be Torturer in Chief?" *Indiana Law Review* 81 (2006): 1145–67, and "Transnational Legal Process after 9/11," *Berkeley International Law Journal* 22 (2002): 337. On commissions, see Harold Hongju Koh, "The U.S. Can't Allow Justice to Be Another War Casualty," *Los Angeles Times*, December 17, 2001; "We Have the Right Courts for Bin Laden," *New York Times*, November 23, 2002; "The Case Against Military Commissions," *American Journal of International Law* 96 (2002): 337–44; and "Against Military Tribunals," *Dissent*, Fall 2002; on torture, see Koh, "A World Without Torture" and "No Torture, No Exceptions," *Washington Monthly*, January 2008.

302 *Koh appreciated*: Savage, *Power Wars*, 120, where it is reported that Koh "blessed" the counterterrorism framework.

303 *"You never know who"*: Klaidman, *Kill or Capture*, 142–43.

303 *"How did I go"*: Ibid., 201–204.

303 *They disagreed especially*: Ibid., 207–209.

303 *Koh congratulated Johnson*: Savage, *Power Wars*, 276–79.

304 *"Targeting practices, including legal operations"*: Harold Hongju Koh, "The Obama Administration and International Law," American Society of International Law, March 25, 2010.

304 *"A global war on terror"*: Ari Shapiro, "U.S. Drone Strikes Are Justified, Legal Adviser Says," NPR, March 26, 2010.

304 *"conscience for the U.S. government"*: He also insisted in the speech that detention authority was limited by the laws of war, in effect alluding to the March 2009 Barron brief.

305 *the human rights activist Koh's justification*: Klaidman, *Kill or Capture*, 214, including for the Nixon to China analogy.

305 in spite *of apparent*: See later Harold Hongju Koh, "The War Powers and Humanitarian Intervention," *Houston Law Review* 53 (2016): 971–1033.

305 *Koh opposed criminalizing it*: Harold Hongju Koh and Todd Buchwald, "The Crime of Aggression: The United States Perspective," *American Journal of International Law* 109 (2015): 257–95.

306 *"an ambiguous term of art"*: Libya and War Powers: Hearings Before the Senate Committee on Foreign Relations, June 28, 2011; for ensuing debate, see Eric Posner, "Stop Complaining About Harold Koh's Interpretation of the War Powers Act," *The New Republic*, July 1, 2011; John Glaser, "John Yoo Is to Guantanamo What Harold Koh Is to Libya," *Antiwar Blog*, June 29, 2011; other views include Bruce Ackerman, "Legal Acrobatics, Illegal War," *New York Times*, June 20, 2011, and Dawn Johnsen, "Different Kinds of Wrong," *Slate*, July 5, 2011. For Ackerman's original hopes that Koh could restore balance after decades of wayward presidents, see Bruce Ackerman, "The Demonization of Harold Koh," *Daily Beast*, April 7, 2009.

306 *Koh worked on his own*: Klaidman, *Kill or Capture*, 218–20.

306 *"This conflict has come"*: Harold Hongju Koh, "How to End the Forever War?," Oxford Union, May 7, 2013.

307 *"We did a whole lot"*: Barack Obama, Press Conference, the White House, August 1, 2014.

307 *"The little clump of words"*: Andrew Ferguson, "Obama Negativa," *Weekly Standard*, December 16, 2016.

307 *"he doesn't really give"*: "Yes, Mr. President, This Is Who We Are," *The Real News*, May 23, 2013.

308 *"worst decision"*: CNN Republican Town Hall, February 18, 2016.

308 *"Strange as it may be"*: Jay Nordlinger, "'A Filthy, Disgusting Word,'" *National Review*, September 12, 2019.

308 *#EndEndlessWar*: Stephen Miles, "How the Grassroots Pushed Washington to #EndEndlessWar," *Responsible Statecraft*, December 9, 2019.

309 *a draft executive order leaked*: Mark Mazzetti and Charlie Savage, "Leaked Draft of Executive Order Could Revive CIA Prisons," *New York Times*, January 25, 2017.

309 *the howls of leading Republicans*: Tim Mak, "Paul Ryan, Mitch McConnell Rebuke Trump on Torture," *Daily Beast*, April 11, 2017.

309 *"he better bring"*: Nick Gass, "Former CIA Chief: Trump Will Have to Bring His Own Bucket to Waterboard," *Politico*, June 30, 2016.

309 *He didn't have one*: Elizabeth Grimm Arsenault, "With (or Without) Gina Haspel at CIA, Could Trump Revive the Torture Program?," *Washington Post*, May 8, 2018.

309 *deleted the Presidential Policy Guidance*: Charlie Savage and Eric Schmitt, "Trump Poised to Drop Some Limits on Drone Strikes and Commando Raids," *New York Times*, September 21, 2017; Luke Hartig, "Trump's New Drone Strike Policy," *Just Security*, September 21, 2017.

310 *"Great nations do not fight"*: Donald J. Trump, State of the Union Address, February 5, 2019.

310 *the dubious legal rationale*: See Jack Goldsmith, "What Happened to the Rule of Law?," *New York Times*, August 21, 2013, and later writings. At a press conference in Sweden, a few days after deciding not to strike without congressional authorization, Obama explained that illegal but legitimate acts under international law were defensible: "Under international law, Security Council resolution or self-defense or defense of an ally provides a clear basis for action. But increasingly, what we're going to be confronted with are situations like Syria, like Kosovo, like Rwanda, in which we may not always have a Security Council that can act—it may be paralyzed for a whole host of reasons—and yet we've got all these international norms that we're interested in upholding. We may not be directly, imminently threatened by what's taking place in a Kosovo or a Syria or a Rwanda in the short term, but our long-term national security will be impacted in a profound way, and our humanity is impacted in a profound way." Barack Obama, "Remarks in Joint Press Conference with Prime Minister Reinfeldt of Sweden," September 4, 2013.

310 *Trump's augmentation*: Peter Harris, "Why Trump's Drone Empire Shows He Wants Global Military Supremacy," *National Interest*, November 29, 2019. For casualties, see Neta C. Crawford, "Afghanistan's Rising Civilian Death Toll Due to Airstrikes, 2017–2020," *Costs of War*, watson.brown.edu/costsofwar/papers/2020/AirstrikesAfghanistan.

EPILOGUE

313 *"We didn't have the foggiest"*: Craig Whitlock, "At War with the Truth," *Washington Post*, December 9, 2019.

314 *Its airborne capacity allows*: Anthony Capaccio, "U.S. Reaper Drone Left Soleimani with Little Chance," *Bloomberg*, January 6, 2020.

315 *"That is our system"*: Jack Goldsmith, "The Soleimani Strike: One Person Decides," *Lawfare*, January 3, 2020.

315 *Trump's lawyers issued*: "Notice on the Legal and Policy Frameworks Guiding the United States's Use of Military Force and Related National Security Operations," February 14, 2020.

315 *Learned interpretations*: See, e.g., Oona Hathaway, "The Soleimani Strike Defied the U.S. Constitution," *The Atlantic*, January 4, 2020; Rebecca Ingber, "If There Was No 'Imminent' Attack from Iran, Killing Soleimani Was Illegal," *Washington Post*, January 15, 2020.

315 *prohibition of "assassination"*: See, e.g., Max Fisher and Amanda Taub, "A One-Word Accusation Swirls Around Trump's Deadly Strike," *New York Times*, January 7, 2020.

316 *passed a resolution*: Catie Edmondson, "In Bipartisan Bid to Restrain Trump, Senate Passes Iran War Powers Resolution," *New York Times*, February 13, 2020.

316 *"We will follow the laws"*: Peter Baker and Maggie Haberman, "Pentagon Rules Out Striking Iranian Cultural Sites, Contradicting Trump," *New York Times*, January 6, 2020.

316 *residual violence*: Compare David Kennedy, *Of War and Law* (2006), which this book shows offers some plausible arguments that date back to the very inception of the international legalization of war, supplementing the case with the additional worry that the results are foreseeably less legitimated violence than nonviolent control.

316 *brutal ground war*: Patrick Cockburn, *War in the Age of Trump* (2020).

316 *"War is represented"*: Hugh Gusterson, "Drone Warfare in Waziristan and the New Military Humanism," *Current Anthropology* 60 (2019): 577.

317 *"humanizing security"*: For the phrase, see Harold Hongju Koh, "State of Play and the Road Ahead: Humanizing Security," in Dapo Akande et al., eds., *Human Rights and 21st Century Challenges* (2020).

317 *Human rights activists have found*: Stanford Human Rights Clinic, *Living Under Drones: Death, Injury, and Trauma from US Drone Practices in Pakistan* (2012).

317 *razing a city*: See, e.g., Anand Gopal, "America's War on Syrian Civilians," *The New Yorker*, December 21, 2020; compare Luke Mogelson, "America's Abandonment of Syria," *The New Yorker*, April 27, 2020.

317 *trade in U.S.-made arms*: See, e.g., William Hartung, "We're Number One: U.S. Dominates Global Arms Trade—Again," *Forbes*, March 12, 2020.

317 *The claim that the carnage*: Eliav Lieblich, "The Facilitative Function of *Jus in Bello*," *European Journal of International Law* 30 (2019): 321–40; for legitimation effects among target populations, see Janina Dill, "Distinction, Necessity, and Proportionality: Afghan Civilians' Attitudes Towards Wartime Harm," *Ethics and International Affairs* 33 (2019): 315–42.

319 *experts in the technology*: For an early guide, P. W. Singer, *Wired for War: The Robotics Revolution and Conflict in the 21st Century* (2009); more recently, see Paul Scharre, *Army of None: Autonomous Weapons and the Future of War* (2018), and Frank Pasquale, *New Laws of Robotics: Defending Human Expertise in the Age of AI* (2020), chap. 6.

319 *the group began a campaign*: For the information clearinghouse, see stopkiller robots.org.

320 *states have agreed with alacrity*: See Group of Government Experts on Emerging Technologies in the Area of Lethal Autonomous Weapons Systems, Report of the 2019 Session, UN Doc. CCW/GGE.1/2019/3, September 25, 2019, with its new guiding principle on the applicability of international humanitarian law; for some rumination, see Nehal Bhuta et al., eds., *Autonomous Weapons Systems: Law, Ethics, Policy* (2016).

321 *Steven Pinker*: Steven Pinker, *Enlightenment Now: The Case for Reason, Science, Humanism, and Progress* (2018).

322 *decreasingly violent policing*: Contemporary policing is hardly nonviolent, of course, and owes some debts to historic counterinsurgency, but the norms governing it are different: compare United Nations Congress on the Prevention of Crime, "Basic Principles on the Use of Force and Firearms" (1990), and Stuart Schrader, *Badges Without Borders: How Global Counterinsurgency Transformed American Policing* (2020).

323 *One group contends*: Ryan Goodman, "The Power to Kill or Capture Enemy Combatants," *European Journal of International Law* 24 (2013): 819–53; Alexander K. A. Greenawalt, "Targeted Capture," *Harvard International Law Journal* 59 (Winter 2018): 1–58.

323 *a newfangled movement*: See, e.g., Jens David Ohlin, ed., *Theoretical Boundaries of Armed Conflict and Human Rights* (2016).

325 *"those in high places"*: Leo Tolstoy, *Resurrection*, trans. Louise Maude, in *Works*, 21 vols. (1928–37), 19: 154.

Acknowledgments

Ever since my children could get upset at themselves for drawing outside the lines, I have been telling them the story of the American artist James Whistler. In a warning to all reviewers, Whistler filed suit in response to the English critic John Ruskin's remark that the painter seemed to have done little more than hurl a pot of color at the canvas—and called the results fine art. But as Whistler later explained in *The Gentle Art of Making Enemies*, if there were laws for painting, they deserved suspicion. And Whistler understood not merely the search for a higher order than such rules allow, but also that a quick execution can conceal years of premeditation. When Ruskin's skeptical attorney inquired at trial how long it could possibly have taken him to achieve the work in question, Whistler offered the immortal reply: "All my life."

An example of what can happen when a lit major accidentally becomes a law professor, I can't say that I intend in this book to challenge rules—or make enemies—in precisely the same spirit as Whistler. But I have definitely incurred obligations going back as long as I can remember, and it is a pleasure to record them, while insisting on complete responsibility for the results.

One of my greatest debts is to John Fabian Witt, who in 2007 co-taught a course on the history of the laws of war with me at our then-common institution, Columbia University. Back then, John was devising his classic study of a topic it has taken me a little more time to ponder. That also meant I got to see more of the war on terror, and how—far from ending—it was transfigured under law. An interloper in American history (for that matter, in legal history), I learned a great deal from John from the first. And in the year or so more than a decade later when I finally wrote up my account, now as his Yale Law School colleague, I turned to him repeatedly.

This is the first book I have written on the faculty at Yale, and I had a lot of other help there. Along with John, my colleagues Oona Hathaway and Scott Shapiro looked over writing (in Oona's case, all of it) that both presupposed and tweaked their own exemplary scholarship. Martin Hägglund generously organized a manuscript workshop with several contacts and friends, including (aside from John and Oona) Beverly Gage, Bryan Garsten, John Mackay, Isaac Nakhimovsky, and Arne Westad. It was a privilege to audit Edyta Bojanowska's class on *War and Peace* to determine what I had gotten wrong in my drafting. Other Yalies who weighed in on this or that point include Bruce Ackerman, Owen Fiss, Anthony Kronman, Daniel Markovits, and Claire Priest. As for Paul Kahn, he went beyond his trademark wisdom, which I often persisted in rejecting, to let me use his house in Snug Harbor, Rhode Island, to draft the last chapter.

Heather Gerken, my dean at Yale Law, released me from teaching in 2019–20 to write the book, and I had extraordinary assistance from the Yale librarians Julian Aiken, Alison Burke, and especially Maryellen Larkin, as well as Rosanna Gonsiewski's daily help. One part of the research, on America's earlier intervention in Vietnam, stretches back further than that year, and though I may have forgotten some relevant debts, I recall clearly how much Kristen Loveland contributed then. More recent research assistance has been provided by the Yale students Sam Aber, Leanne Gale, Sam Hull, Matthew Linsley, Ann Manov, Hong Tran, and especially the absolutely indispensable Henry Jacob and Anna Wherry, without whom I could never have completed my work.

Many colleagues outside Yale commented during my intense period of attempting to make my premeditated agenda at least somewhat more credible, either at conferences or by correspondence, or at lectures organized at Brooklyn Law School, the annual *Constellations* conference, Cornell University (where the School of Criticism and Theory takes place), McGill University, the Middle Eastern Legal Studies Seminar, the University of Oxford Institute for Ethics, Law, and Armed Conflict (in a lecture in Henry Shue's honor), Rutgers University–Camden, Tel Aviv Law School, Washington University, and Whitman College. Those who provided comments of various kinds include Amanda Alexander, William Alford, Aslı Bâli, Maggie Blackhawk, Gabriella Blum, Duncan Bell, Benjamin Coates, Harlan Cohen, Talia Dan-Cohen, Mary Dudziak, Maeve Glass, Pablo Kalmanovitz, Adam Keiper, Barbara Keys, Aden Knaap, Adam Lebovitz, Andrei Mamolea, Karuna Mantena, Giovanni Mantilla, Thomas Meaney, Naz Modirzadeh, Aziz Rana, Tim Shenk, Boyd van Dijk, Matthew Waxman, Stephen Wertheim, and Adnan Zulfiqar—many of them with superlative contributions on the history and meaning of the laws of war or international affairs to their name themselves. Kevin Jon Heller (who definitely falls in that category) read the whole thing with his admirable expertise.

For the book chapters that approach our own era, I also turned to some participants, intentional or not, in the coming of humane war. Todd Buchwald, Kenneth Roth, and William H. Taft IV answered a few questions, while two colleagues whom I made into protagonists in this book, Jack Goldsmith and Harold Hongju Koh, consented to check over the materials concerning them, though they do not necessarily endorse my narrative. Jack has my deepest thanks for helping me most as a sounding board in figuring out what I wanted to say in this book, and in saying it more plausibly.

I owe Amelia Atlas, my agent, for her advice and guidance, and not least for arranging with Alex Star at Farrar, Straus and Giroux to edit this book. Working with Alex is a dream for any author but especially for an aging dog learning the new trick of a trade book, with no academic crutches allowed—and human characters required. If not from premeditation then from conception on, and through the last edits, Alex has been an ideal advocate and counselor. In the late stages, John Palattella, my old editor at *The Nation*, stepped in to fine-tune. At the publisher, Thomas Colligan, Janet Evans-Scanlon, Carrie Hsieh, John McGhee, Peter Richardson, Ian Van Wye, and Steve Weil also contributed to making the book possible.

Alisa Berger, my life partner, deserves more thanks than I can give her—including for rules I almost always follow. But I would like to dedicate this book to my daughters with love. All their lives the repository of my hopes for a better future, Lily and Madeleine have long since begun to teach me the meaning of creativity (and justice), and especially by disregarding lines every day.

Index

A NOTE ABOUT THE AUTHOR

Samuel Moyn is the Henry R. Luce Professor of Jurisprudence at Yale Law School and a professor of history at Yale University. He is a frequent contributor to *The New York Times, The Washington Post*, and other publications, and his books include *The Last Utopia* and *Not Enough: Human Rights in an Unequal World*.